Acclaim for Peter Ackroyd's

Thames

"*Thames* smells authentically of the water, of an author who has walked the towpath and knows not only the impressive statistics . . . but also the Turner watercolours of the Thames itself. . . . It is not just the subject that sets this book apart but also the compelling new perspectives that [Ackroyd] brings."
                                                                    —*The Times* (London)

"The pages glint with scintillating nuggets recovered from the river. . . . You might well think that the garlanded biographer of Dickens and Turner was born to write this extraordinary book."
                                                                    —*The Observer* (London)

"Mesmerising. . . . As soon as you open this account of the Thames, you will want to immerse yourself in it. . . . No one is better than Ackroyd at evoking the texture and atmosphere of the distant past."
                                                                    —*The Daily Telegraph* (London)

"An unmissable performance."   —*The Guardian* (London)

"[A book of] substance and unflaggingly interesting detail. . . . A very enjoyable and highly idiosyncratic account of the subject." —*The Spectator*

"[Ackroyd's] exhaustive reclaiming of the Thames inks in colorful new detail."   —*Time*

"A rich offering by a masterly writer."
                                          —*The Times Literary Supplement* (London)

"[Ackroyd] presents his material as a cornucopia of treats and insights delivered from all directions."   —*The Independent* (London)

Peter Ackroyd

Thames

Peter Ackroyd is the author of *London: The Biography*, *Albion: The Origins of the English Imagination*, and *Shakespeare: The Biography*; acclaimed biographies of T. S. Eliot, Dickens, Blake, and Sir Thomas More; thirteen novels; and the series Ackroyd's Brief Lives. He has won the Whitbread Book Award for Biography, the Royal Society of Literature's William Heinemann Award, the James Tait Black Memorial Prize, the Guardian Fiction Prize, the Somerset Maugham Award, and the South Bank Award for Literature. He lives in London.

Also by Peter Ackroyd

❧

FICTION

The Great Fire of London

The Last Testament of Oscar Wilde

Hawksmoor

Chatterton

First Light

English Music

The House of Doctor Dee

Dan Leno and the Limehouse Golem

Milton in America

The Plato Papers

The Clerkenwell Tales

The Lambs of London

The Fall of Troy

NONFICTION

Dressing Up: Transvestism and Drag: The History of an Obsession

London: The Biography

Albion: The Origins of the English Imagination

BIOGRAPHY

Ezra Pound and His World

T. S. Eliot

Dickens

Blake

The Life of Thomas More

Shakespeare: The Biography

Thames
THE BIOGRAPHY

Peter Ackroyd

ANCHOR BOOKS

A Division of Random House, Inc.

New York

The Library of Congress has cataloged the Nan A. Talese edition as follows:
Ackroyd, Peter, 1949–
Thames: the biography / Peter Ackroyd.—1st ed. in the U.S. of America.
p. cm.
Includes bibliographical references and index.
1. Thames River (England)—History.   2. London (England)—History.   I. Title.
DA670.T2A316 2008
942.2—dc22 2008002864

Anchor ISBN: 978-0-307-38984-8

Author photograph © Charles Hopkinson—BBC Worldwide
Book design by Ellen Cipriano
Maps by Reginald Piggott
Picture research by Lily Richards

www.anchorbooks.com

For Penelope Hoare

Contents

List of Illustrations

SECTION ONE

The source of the Thames at Trewsbury Mead.

Objects found in the Thames:

    the tooth of a mammoth;

    dagger and scabbard, 550–450 BC

    bronze bust of the Emperor Hadrian, *c*.AD 122.

Medieval pilgrim badges thrown in the Thames.

Ducking a Scold, 1812, etching by Thomas Rowlandson (1756–1827).

Angler on the riverbank, woodcut of 1663.

The Oarsman's and Angler's Map, 1893.

Radcot Bridge, the oldest bridge across the Thames, photographed in the 1900s.

Nets for catching eels near London, photographed in the 1890s.

An old fisherman and weir-keeper called Harper, Oxfordshire. Photographed by Henry Taunt, 1900.

Mapledurham mill, photographed in the 1900s.

A traveller waiting to be ferried across the Thames, woodcut of 1684.

A ferryman taking two men and a boy across the Thames at Cliveden. Photographed by Henry Taunt, 1885.

List of Maps

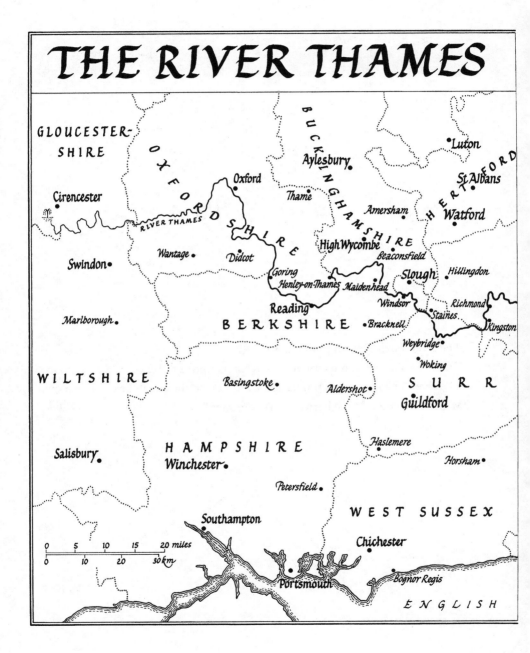

THE RIVER THAMES

FROM SOURCE TO SEA

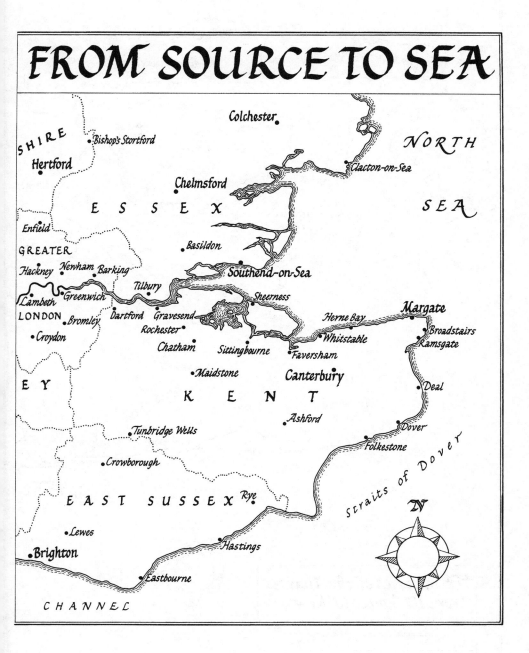

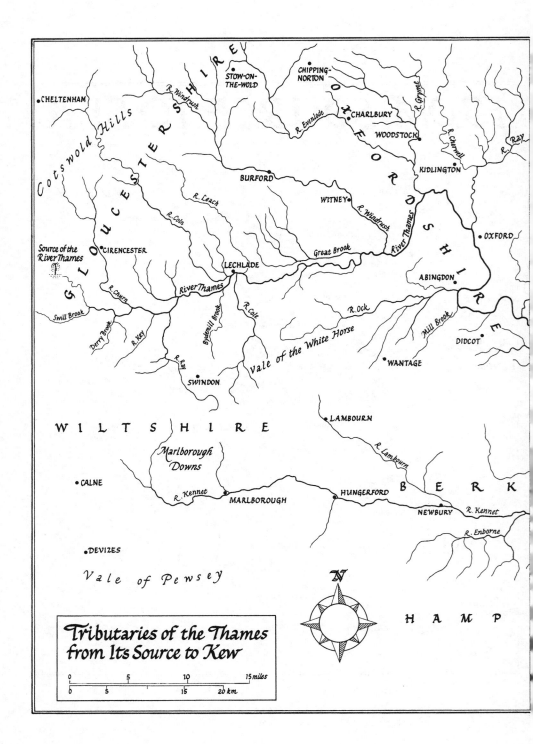

Tributaries of the Thames from Its Source to Kew

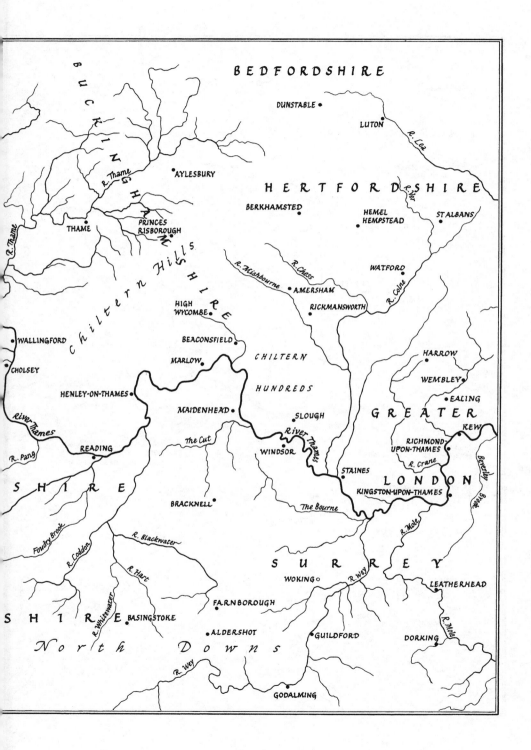

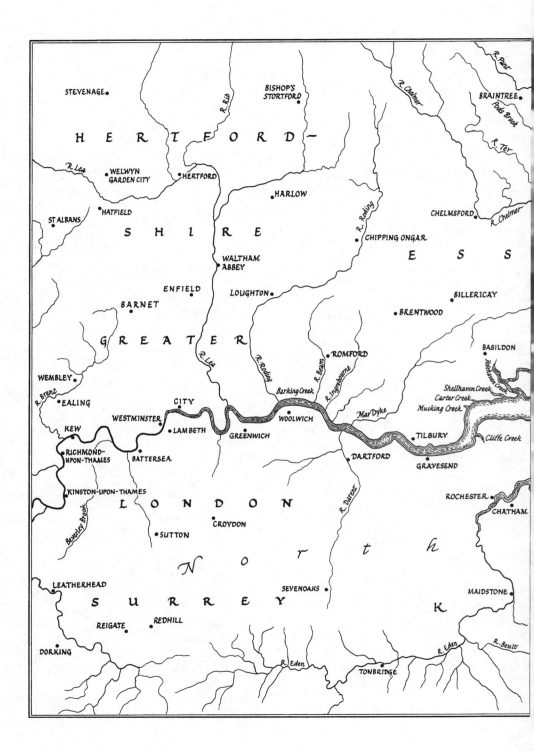

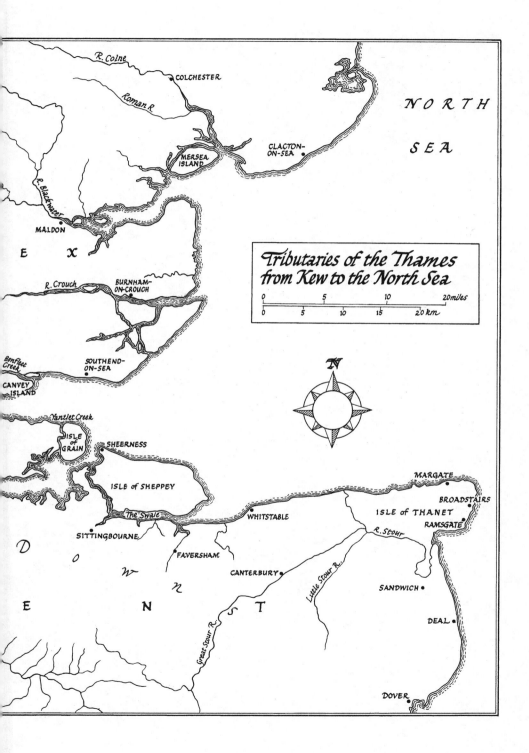

R. Colne

COLCHESTER

Roman R.

NORTH

SEA

MERSEA
ISLAND

CLACTON-
ON-SEA

R. Blackwater

MALDON

E X

R. Crouch

BURNHAM-
ON-CROUCH

Tributaries of the Thames
from Kew to the North Sea

0   5   10   20 miles
0   5   10   15   20 km

Benfleet
Creek

SOUTHEND-
ON-SEA

CANVEY
ISLAND

N

Yantlet Creek

ISLE
of
GRAIN

SHEERNESS

MARGATE

ISLE of SHEPPEY

BROADSTAIRS

The Swale

WHITSTABLE

ISLE of THANET

RAMSGATE

SITTINGBOURNE

R. Stour

D

FAVERSHAM

o

w

CANTERBURY

n

SANDWICH

E

N

Little Stour R.

T

DEAL

Great Stour R.

DOVER

PART I

The Mirror of History

The old Lord Mayor's Barge

CHAPTER I

The River as Fact

t has a length of 215 miles, and is navigable for 191 miles. It is the longest river in England but not in Britain, where the Severn is longer by approximately 5 miles. Nevertheless it must be the shortest river in the world to acquire such a famous history. The Amazon and the Mississippi cover almost 4,000 miles, and the Yangtze almost 3,500 miles; but none of them has arrested the attention of the world in the manner of the Thames.

It runs along the borders of nine English counties, thus reaffirming its identity as a boundary and as a defence. It divides Wiltshire from Gloucestershire, and Oxfordshire from Berkshire; as it pursues its way it divides Surrey from Middlesex (or Greater London as it is inelegantly known) and Kent from Essex. It is also a border of Buckinghamshire. It guarded these once tribal lands in the distant past, and will preserve them into the imaginable future.

There are 134 bridges along the length of the Thames, and forty-four locks above Teddington. There are approximately twenty major tributaries still flowing into the main river, while others such as the Fleet have now disappeared under the ground. Its "basin," the area from which it derives its water from rain and other natural forces, covers an area of some 5,264 square miles. And then there are the springs, many of them in the woods or close to the streams beside the Thames. There is one in the wood below Sinodun Hills in Oxfordshire, for example, which has been described as an "everlasting spring" always fresh and always renewed.

The average flow of the river at Teddington, chosen because it marks the place where the tidal and non-tidal waters touch, has been calculated at 1,145 millions of gallons (5,205 millions of litres) each day or approximately 2,000 cubic feet (56.6 cubic metres) per second. The current moves at a velocity between ½ and 2¾ miles per hour. The main thrust of the river flow is known to hydrologists as the "thalweg"; it does not move in a straight and forward line but, mingling with the inner flow and the variegated flow of the surface and bottom waters, takes the form of a spiral or helix. More than 95 per cent of the river's energy is lost in turbulence and friction.

The direction of the flow of the Thames is therefore quixotic. It might be assumed that it would move eastwards, but it defies any simple prediction. It flows north-west above Henley and at Teddington, west above Abingdon, south from Cookham and north above Marlow and Kingston. This has to do with the variegated curves of the river. It does not meander like the Euphrates, where according to Herodotus the voyager came upon the same village three times on three separate days, but it is circuitous. It specialises in loops. It will take the riparian traveller two or three times as long to cover the same distance as a companion on the high road. So the Thames teaches you to take time, and to view the world from a different vantage.

The average "fall" or decline of the river from its beginning to its end is approximately 17 to 21 inches (432 to 533 mm) per mile. It follows gravity, and seeks out perpetually the simplest way to the sea. It falls some 600 feet (183 m) from source to sea, with a relatively precipitous decline of 300 feet (91.5 m) in the first 9 miles; it falls 100 (30.4 m) more in the next 11 miles, with a lower average for the rest of its course. Yet averages may not be so important. They mask the changeability and idiosyncrasy of the Thames. The mean width of the river is given as 1,000 feet (305 m), and a mean depth of 30 feet (9 m); but the width varies from 1 or 2 feet (0.3 to 0.6 m) at Trewsbury to 5½ miles at the Nore.

The tide, in the words of Tennyson, is that which "moving seems asleep, too full for sound and foam." On its flood inward it can promise benefit or danger; on its ebb seaward it suggests separation or adventure. It is one general movement but it comprises a thousand different streams and eddies; there are opposing streams, and high water is not necessarily the same thing as high tide. The water will sometimes begin to fall before the tide is over. The average speed of the tide lies between 1 and 3 knots (1.15 and 3.45 miles per hour), but at times of very high flow it can reach 7 knots (8 miles per hour). At London Bridge the flood tide runs for almost six hours, while the ebb tide endures for six hours and thirty minutes. The tides are much higher now than at other times in the history of the Thames. There can now be a difference of some 24 feet (7.3 m) between high and low tides, although the average rise in the area of London Bridge is between 15 and 22 feet (4.5 and 6.7 m). In the period of the Roman occupation, it was a little over 3 feet (0.9 m). The high tide, in other words, has risen greatly over a period of two thousand years.

The reason is simple. The south-east of England is sinking slowly into the water at the rate of approximately 12 inches (305 mm) per century. In 4000 BC the land beside the Thames was 46 feet (14 m) higher than it is now, and in 3000 BC it was some 31 feet (9.4 m) higher. When this is combined with the water issuing from the dissolution of the polar ice-caps, the tides moving up the lower reaches of the Thames are increasing at a rate of 2 feet (0.6 m) per century. That is why the recently erected Thames Barrier will not provide protection enough, and another barrier is being proposed.

The tide of course changes in relation to the alignment of earth, moon and sun. Every two weeks the high "spring" tides reach their maximum two days after a full moon, while the low "neap" tides occur at the time of the half-moon. The highest tides occur at the times of equinox; this is the period of maximum danger for those who live and work by the river. The spring tides of late autumn and early spring are also hazardous. It is no wonder that the earliest people by the Thames venerated and propitiated the river.

The general riverscape of the Thames is varied without being in any sense spectacular, the paraphernalia of life ancient and modern clustering around its banks. It is in large part now a domesticated river, having been tamed and controlled by many generations. It is in that sense a piece of artifice, with some of its landscape deliberately planned to blend with the course of the water. It would be possible to write the history of the Thames as a history of a work of art.

It is a work still in slow progress. The Thames has taken the same course for ten thousand years, after it had been nudged southward by the glaciation of the last ice age. The British and Roman earthworks by the

Sinodun Hills still border the river, as they did two thousand years before. Given the destructive power of the moving waters, this is a remarkable fact. Its level has varied over the millennia—there is a sudden and unexpected rise at the time of the Anglo-Saxon settlement, for example—and the discovery of submerged forests testifies to incidents of overwhelming flood. Its appearance has of course also altered, having only recently taken the form of a relatively deep and narrow channel, but its persistence and identity through time are an aspect of its power.

Yet of course every stretch has its own character and atmosphere, and every zone has its own history. Out of oppositions comes energy, out of contrasts beauty. There is the overwhelming difference of water within it, varying from the pure freshwater of the source through the brackish zone of estuarial water to the salty water in proximity to the sea. Given the eddies of the current, in fact, there is rather more salt by the Essex shore than by the Kentish shore. There are manifest differences between the riverine landscapes of Lechlade and of Battersea, of Henley and of Gravesend; the upriver calm is in marked contrast to the turbulence of the long stretches known as River of London and then London River. After New Bridge the river becomes wider and deeper, in anticipation of its change.

The rural landscape itself changes from flat to wooded in rapid succession, and there is a great alteration in the nature of the river from the cultivated fields of Dorchester to the thick woods of Cliveden. From Godstow the river becomes a place of recreation, breezy and jaunty with the skiffs and the punts, the sports in Port Meadow and the picnic parties on the banks by Binsey. But then by some change of light it becomes dark green, surrounded by vegetation like a jungle river; and then the traveller begins to see the dwellings of Oxford, and the river changes again. Oxford is a pivotal point. From there you can look upward and consider the quiet source; or you can look downstream and contemplate the coming immensity of London.

In the reaches before Lechlade the water makes its way through isolated pastures; at Wapping and Rotherhithe the dwellings seem to drop into it, as if overwhelmed by numbers. The elements of rusticity and urbanity are nourished equally by the Thames. That is why parts of the river induce calm and forgetfulness, and others provoke anxiety and despair. It is the river of dreams, but it is also the river of suicide. It has been called liquid history because within itself it dissolves and carries all epochs and generations. They ebb and flow like water.

CHAPTER 2

The River as Metaphor

*T*he *river runs* through the language, and we speak of its influence in every conceivable context. It is employed to characterise life and death, time and destiny; it is used as a metaphor for continuity and dissolution, for intimacy and transitoriness, for art and history, for poetry itself. In *The Principles of Psychology* (1890) William James first coined the phrase "stream of consciousness" in which "every definite image of the mind is steeped . . . in the free water that flows around it." Thus "it flows" like the river itself. Yet the river is also a token of the unconscious, with its suggestion of depth and invisible life.

The river is a symbol of eternity, in its unending cycle of movement and change. It is one of the few such symbols that can readily be understood, or appreciated, and in the continuing stream the mind or soul can begin to contemplate its own possible immortality.

In the poetry of John Denham's "Cooper's Hill" (1642), the Thames is a metaphor for human life. How slight its beginning, how confident its continuing course, how ineluctable its destination within the great ocean:

> Hasting to pay his tribute to the sea,
> Like mortal life to meet eternity.

The poetry of the Thames has always emphasised its affiliations with human purpose and with human realities. So the personality of the river changes in the course of its journey from the purity of its origins to the broad reaches of the commercial world. The river in its infancy is undefiled, innocent and clear. By the time it is closely pent in by the city, it has become dank and foul, defiled by greed and speculation. In this regress it is the paradigm of human life and of human history. Yet the river has one great advantage over its metaphoric companions. It returns to its source, and its corruption can be reversed. That is why baptism was once instinctively associated with the river. The Thames has been an emblem of redemption and of renewal, of the hope of escaping from time itself.

When Wordsworth observed the river at low tide, with the vista of the "mighty heart" of London "lying still," he used the imagery of human circulation. It is the image of the river as blood, pulsing through the veins and arteries of its terrain, without which the life of London would seize up. Sir Walter Raleigh, contemplating the Thames from the walk by his cell in the Tower, remarked that the "blood which disperseth itself by the branches or veins through all the body, may be resembled to these waters which are carried by brooks and rivers overall the earth." He wrote his *History of the World* (1610) from his prison cell, and was deeply imbued with the current of the Thames as a model of human destiny. It has been used as the symbol for the unfolding of events in time, and carries the burden of past events upon its back. For Raleigh the freight of time grew ever more complex and wearisome as it proceeded from its source; human life had become darker and deeper, less pure and more susceptible to the tides of affairs. There was one difference Raleigh noticed in his history, when he declared that "for this tide of man's life, after it once turneth and declineth, ever runneth with a perpetual ebb and falling stream, *but never floweth again.*"

The Thames has also been understood as a mirror of morality. The bending rushes and the yielding willows afford lessons in humility and forbearance; the humble weeds along its banks have been praised for their lowliness and absence of ostentation. And who has ventured upon the river without learning the value of patience, of endurance, and of vigilance? John Denham makes the Thames the subject of native discourse in a further sense:

Though deep, yet clear; though gentle, yet not dull;
Strong without rage; without o'erflowing, full.

This suggests that the river represents an English measure, an aesthetic harmony to be sought or wished for, but in the same breath Denham seems to be adverting to some emblem of Englishness itself. The Thames is a metaphor for the country through which it runs. It is modest and moderate, calm and resourceful; it is powerful without being fierce. It is not flamboyantly impressive. It is large without being too vast. It eschews extremes. It weaves its own course without artificial diversions or interventions. It is useful for all manner of purposes. It is a practical river.

When Robert Menzies, an erstwhile Australian prime minister, was taken to Runnymede he was moved to comment upon the "secret springs" of the "slow English character." This identification of the land with the people, the characteristics of the earth and water with the temperament of their inhabitants, remains a poignant one. There is an inward and intimate association between the river and those who live beside it, even if that association cannot readily be understood.

In some sense, then, the Thames becomes the image of the nation, mollifying land and water in one capacious embrace, affording coherence and unity to disparate regions. It permits the growth and spread of a common culture. It creates harmony out of apparent discord, and in that capacity alone it has done more to establish the idea of Englishness than any other national feature.

The idealised images of English life, with their thatched cottages and village greens, their duckponds and hedged fields, derive from the landscape of the Thames. The river is the source of these day-dreams of Englishness. The traveller need only journey to Cookham, or to Pangbourne, or to Streatley, or to a hundred other villages and small towns along the Thames, to recognise the enduring importance of the river in the characterisation of national life.

The Thames has been a highway, a frontier and an attack route; it has been a playground and a sewer, a source of water and a source of power. It has been what the Romans called a "public" river, but it has also been a scene of deep private contentment. It has a personal, and an historical, force. John Keill, in *An Examination of the Reflections on the Theory of the Earth* (1699), remarked of rivers that "without them there could be no great Towns, nor any converse with far inland Countries, since without them it is almost impossible to supply a vast multitude of People with things necessary for life." The Thames has created civilisation here. It fashioned London.

That is why it has been described as a museum of Englishness itself. It embodies the history of the nation, from Greenwich to Windsor, from Eton to Oxford, from the Tower to the Abbey, from the City to the Court, from the Port of London to Runnymede. It is in that sense a great unifier. It suggests the community of struggling human beings who have always lived beside it. It represents the idealised and harmonious landscape of the country, too, particularly in those territories that border the Upper Thames. It has inspired the poetry of the English. It is heterogeneous and various, thus perfectly satisfactory to the national taste:

> The sundry varying soyles, the pleasures infinite
> (Where heate kills not the cold, nor cold expells the heate . . .
> The Summer not too short, the Winter not too long).

Thus Michael Drayton apostrophises the Thames in his *Polyolbion* (1612). Yet it remains relatively unspoiled. It has not greatly changed in the last two thousand years of human time.

For much of its course the river remains secluded and remote. It is still possible to walk along the path beside it, and see no one for many miles. In the upper areas near the source, and in the estuarial areas, there is the same isolation. It represents an escape from the world, "by the margin, willow-veiled." That is why it has a reputation for being placid, for being free from turmoil. Matthew Arnold said of the river at Staines that it "has yet a great charm from its entire loneliness." Canvey Island, in the estuary, was once described as "the loneliest place in the Home Counties."

CHAPTER 3

The Time of the River

꧁

*I*t is *history*, the river of history, along which most of the significant English events of the last two thousand years have taken place; but it is also the river *as* history.

The closer the Thames advances towards London, the more historical it becomes. That is its underlying nature. It has reflected the moving pageant of the ages. Its history is of course that of England or, rather, of the Britons and the Romans, the Saxons and the Danes and the Normans and the other migrating groups who decided to settle somewhere along its banks. Art and civilisation have flourished alongside it. Each generation has a different understanding of it, so that it has accumulated meaning over the centuries. In that process it has become a token of national character. The destiny of England is intimately linked with the destiny of the river. In mythic accounts it gives the island energy. It gives it fertility.

No one would deny the central importance of the Thames to London. It brought its trade, and in so doing lent beauty, squalor, wealth, misery and dignity to the city. London could never have existed without the Thames. That is why the river has always been central to English life, and can fairly claim to be the most historic (and certainly the most eventful) river in the world. You can learn more about the human condition in a voyage along the Thames than on any long journey over the oceans of the world. But water reflects. It has no form of its own. It has no meaning. So we may say that the Thames is in essence a reflection of circumstances—a reflection of geology, or of economics.

Yet there are continuities that suggest some deep inspiring life. There have been settlements of one kind or another in almost every spot. It has been the focus of human life ever since the first humans entered the region. So from the river we acquire an idea of human community. That is one of its most salutary features, so deeply imbued that we scarcely notice it. Along its banks the same methods of farming were used from the Bronze Age to the middle of the nineteenth century. The meadows were cut by long-handled scythes, and the heavy soil was ploughed; the wheat was sown and harvested, with the labourers cutting the corn with short sickles. The rushes were cut down in August, to be used for thatching; turf and brushwood were collected for the winter fire. These were ancient and persistent activities, helping to mould the landscape of the Thames while at the same time being moulded by it. Land divisions and field boundaries are a direct inheritance from our prehistoric forebears. The technique of building dry-stone walls has been preserved for some six thousand years. The river offers a deep sense of settlement and of belonging.

Time has a curious presence upon the river. The Thames does not live in human time. It lives in geological time. The figures in the earliest photographs, smudged and faint, are its human votaries already fading into invisibility. In *The Historic Thames* (1914) Hilaire Belloc writes that "you might put a man of the fifteenth century on the water below St. John's Lock, and, until he came to Buscot Lock, he would hardly know that he had passed into a time other than his own." John Betjeman described the whole river above Oxford as "medieval," and there is a sense in which it remains a perpetual remembrance of time past. There was an old rhyme:

> Ring out the bell from every steeple,
> It makes no difference to boating people.

The people of the river are suspended in the river's time, which has some deep affinity with a world that existed before the concept of time itself. Perhaps we will come to describe it as timeless. It runs in an eternal present that, according to philosophers, is the one part of time that does not really exist. But if it were to be stilled, it would lose its identity.

Yet, curiously enough, water has also been employed as a measurement of human time. The water clock or *clepsydra* was in use many thousands of years ago, and the first of these devices was a simple jar with a hole drilled through its bottom. But the Thames itself makes some claim to being "the place where time begins" since on its banks, at Greenwich, is the site of the prime meridian. A large red "time ball," constructed in 1833, rises up a pole on the turret of the Observatory and falls at precisely 1 p.m. as the signal of Greenwich Mean Time. The great clocks of London are by the river. Big Ben was preceded, at Westminster, by a "tall pointed tower" in Old Palace Yard by the Thames; this was, according to Stow, "a tower of stone containing a clock which striketh every hour on a great bell . . . the same clock, in a calm, will be heard into the city of London." There is the great clock on Shell Mex House. So the eternal river enters the human world.

The flow of the Thames has inspired another form of measurement. The Bridgettine convent at Syon and the Charterhouse at Sheen faced each other on opposite banks, and Henry VI declared that "immediately upon the cessation of the service at one convent it should commence at the other, and so should continue until the end of time." These perpetually flowing orisons are a spiritual image of the water running between them. The Thames can become an emblem both of time and of eternity, the Janus-faced aspects of the river like the sculptured heads on Henley Bridge looking both upriver and downriver. In his book, *The Stripling Thames* (1909), Fred Thacker pronounced it thus:

> Ancient river, changing never,
> Symbol of eternity,
> Gliding water, lapsing ever,
> Mirror of inconstancy.

It is the perpetual paradox.

One stretch, in itself inconsiderable, can act as a microcosm of the national life. There is a spot at Brentford, from which the Brentford ferry once ran. It is just downriver from a patch of land on the north bank of the Thames that for several centuries was known simply as "Old England"; it is now known on the maps as "Old Brentford." Close by this spot that marks the old ferry, the Cassivellauni fought against the invading force of Caesar in 54 BC. In the same place, 834 years later, Offa held a Council of the Church with his bishops. In the same place, in AD 1016, Edmund Ironside drove Cnut and his defeated Danes across the Thames. This was also the place, in 1642, where part of the battle of Brentford was fought between the forces of Charles I and the Parliamentary army. If there are riverine locations imbued with the spirits of the past, then this is surely one of them.

That may be the reason why the course of the river has been employed as a clue to the course of history itself. The Thames summons up the ideals of the past, as they flow into the present and advance towards the future. When Turner sailed down the Thames, with his sketchbook upon his lap, he was moved to create images of Dido and Aeneas, of Pompey and Cornelia, all the symbols of the mythological and classical past congregating by the banks. It would not be too wonderful to see the mother of Moses, or the daughter of a Pharaoh, suddenly appear among the rushes on the banks of the Upper Thames. The water here shares the same antiquity.

In some of Turner's sketches there is the sudden flourish of inspiration, the spontaneous improvisation of the moment when all the force of the riverine world breaks upon the paper; the paper is sometimes spattered with raindrops to emphasise his natural immersion in the scene before him. But then in some of the finished canvases Turner creates a vision of the Thames that can only be described as "timeless," with figures out of pastoral mythology decorating what seems to be a classically inspired landscape. But it is still recognisably the Thames, near Richmond or near Windsor.

The Thames contains all times. At the beginning of William Morris's *News from Nowhere* (1890), the narrator swims in the Thames; but the river transports him into a distant future where he exclaims, "How clear the water is this morning!" Even in that comic sketch of river life, Jerome K. Jerome's *Three Men in a Boat* (1889), the diurnal life of the late nineteenth century "had been drawn aside" for a moment and the narrator enters the world of the early thirteenth century. There is hardly one novel or study of the river that does not create a dream-fugue of the past. It is a backward and melancholy presence even in London itself where, on a dark night by the banks of the Thames, it is possible to re-create the shapes of the older city looming beside the water. The river is the oldest thing in London, and it changes not at all.

One peer of the realm, and adorer of the river, Francis Noel Buxton decided to brave its waters on 25 March 1952. He wished to test his theory that the Romans had crossed or forded the river by what is now the Westminster embankment. He decided to cross the water on foot, with the hope or expectation that there would still be some kind of path below the swirling and muddy waters. He went at low tide, which he estimated at 5 feet 3 inches (1.5 m), while his own height was 6 feet 3 inches (1.9 m). But the river did not accord with his calculations. He went down after reaching the second pier of Westminster, and was compelled to swim the remaining distance. It was deeper and darker than he had imagined but Lord Noel Buxton described himself as a "poetical archaeologist" concerned to invoke the underlying terrain of the river around us. He had seen the marsh that lay beneath the edifices of Westminster, and enumerated the plants that had once grown there; he glimpsed in imagination the palace of Cnut and the little Saxon monastery that had once stood on the site of the great abbey. This is a form of poetic field-walking, to use another archaeological term, in which the traces of the past are there for those who have eyes to see.

That is why there is a technique of divination known as hydromancy or the "reading" of water. The thoughts of anyone, standing by the river, seem of necessity to go both forwards and backwards; they may be guided by the flow of the water itself but there is also some quality of the river that encourages such contrary motion. There is an old and continually used expression attached to the river. It is the sense of being "suspended in time," a notion that suggests the slight sway backwards and forwards. It is the almost imperceivable motion of expectation and remembrance, poised between two worlds. And of course there are occasions when, if you gaze at one spot long enough, so that it seems to detach itself from the flow, then time stops. Is this the quality of timelessness? Or is it merely an absence, a gap, to which can be attributed no characteristic at all? It is a perplexity that presents itself on observing Turner's *The Thames at Eton*, exhibited in 1808, where the dark masses of water gather light into themselves and present a darker world than any natural reflection.

It is worth considering that, when you set out upon the river, you become in some way detached from the mundane world. That world becomes more remote, as if in passing from land to water you had crossed some other boundary. The feeling is akin once more to that of being "suspended." It may be that you have passed into a different time, or at least a different sense of time. For some, of course, the joy of entering the river is the sensation of "escaping" from time altogether. By general consent those who dwell by the Thames tend to be fatalistic, resigned to the wayward nature of the river and its sudden or occasional irruption into their lives. They, too, have become habituated to another level of time and transience.

Yet time twists. The river winds and meanders. The spirals within the current are a token of temporal turbulence, reaching from the surface to the deep water of the river-bed. The river elongates time. Those who wander by the tow-path live in a different time from those who pass in a car or train across the bridge. The river informs us that there are many zones of time. By winding so crookedly, northward and westward, it is in peril of losing itself in the labyrinth of its own making. At Penton Hook, between Chertsey and Staines, the river takes half a mile to travel a total distance of 20 yards (18 m). The watch or clock is useless here. By Blackwall the Thames crosses the meridian three times, an apt token of its waywardness.

The river is ever flowing but of course it is not eternal. It will cease, at that moment when the world itself ceases. But to human perception it is the closest imaginable approximation to everlasting process. In "The Brook" (1853) by Tennyson it is invoked in terms of eternity:

> For men may come and men may go,
>   But I go on for ever.

But this sentiment may provoke unease. The river ran before the creation of humankind, which has been endlessly contending with it from the earliest times—fording it, bridging it, riding it, harnessing it, damming it, diverting it, with the unspoken knowledge that the river will in the end persevere against any and every obstacle. It will always run.

The fourth Duke of Queensbury, known as "Old Q," grew tired of watching the Thames from his house at Richmond. "What is there to make so much of in the Thames?" he asked. "I am quite weary of it, there it goes, flow, flow, flow, always the same." Longfellow wrote that on the broad river "the slow years sailed by and ceased to be." Those who know the Thames well adopt a leisurely pace. The years are often said to "roll by" in implicit deference to the river. There are stretches where the water seems to move reluctantly. The Industrial Revolution passed by the Thames, and industry did not arrive upon its banks until after the First World War. There are still traces of archaic village life in the settlements beside the Upper Thames. Some villages—Lechlade and Cricklade, for example—seem to be preserved in their old age as if they were in implicit communion with the river that has always served them. Kenneth Grahame, the creator of Thames mythology in *The Wind in the Willows* (1908), remarked of one river village that it possessed a "holy calm" and a "natural life of somnolency"; the wanderer by the river-bank is in turn a "loafer" and "through golden spaces of imagination his soul is winging her untrammelled flight." That is for many the natural occupation of the river-wanderer, set free from the world of days and hours in order to soar among dreams. Those who dream by the river may dream of the future as well as of the past.

Yet it is hard to determine, in the life of the Thames, what is the beginning and what is the end. The concept of the hydrologic cycle, from sea to river, and from river to sea, poses a problem for those who exist in linear time. Can the Thames ever be said to really end? And, if so, where does this "ending" take place? Its end, theoretically, is the point at which it begins again. While it is continually going forward, it is also going backward. Isaac Rosenberg said of Stanley Spencer, who painted the Thames at Cookham on many occasions, that "his pictures have that sense of everlastingness, of no beginning and no end, that we get in all masterpieces." It may be that Spencer was imbued with this quality of "everlastingness" by his life near the river. Spencer painted the images of biblical antiquity in the setting of the twentieth century. And the endless life of the Thames suggests that the nature of all things is inherently cyclical.

That is why the future of the river was often described in terms of its primordial beginning. Shelley once prophesied that "the piers of Waterloo Bridge shall become the nuclei of islets of reeds and osiers, and cast the jagged shadows of their broken arches on the solitary stream." In Richard Jefferies's dystopic fiction, *After London* (1885), the future Thames is depicted as "a vast stagnant swamp." In dreams of the future the Thames is often depicted as reverting to some primitive state, with the supposition that somehow it has always remained primitive. The river contains its beginning within its end. The historian, Thomas Babington Macaulay, conjured up the spectre of a fallen world with "some traveller from New Zealand . . . in the midst of a vast solitude, taking his stand on a broken arch of London Bridge to sketch the ruins of St. Paul's." Here the river is a setting for some antique, almost primaeval, world of fallen stone.

If it seems to challenge the concept of time, it seems also to pose questions about the relation of time and space. Is the contingent space—the bank, the source—an aspect of the river's flow? Can the river be said to have a spatial context at all since it is in continual free flow? Would it be possible, for example, to make a transparent sculpture of the river as it is at this precise nano-second? It would be a thing impossible. So what is its body? How do you recognise and determine its volume?

William Morris owned two houses by the river. One was called Kelmscott Hall, in Hammersmith, and its garden ran down to the Thames. The other was in the village of Kelmscot (the true spelling), near Lechlade, where the land ran down to the same river. Morris enjoyed contemplating the fact that the water which ran under his window at Hammersmith had already passed the meadows and the grey gables of his country house. Space here itself seems to become fluid, infinitely impressionable. For Morris the two spaces, more than 100 miles apart, partake of the same enchantment. That may be why the writers and dreamers on the river, such as Lewis Carroll, always have a curiously malleable attitude towards spaces and places. They make them infinitely small or infinitely large.

But was Morris really correct in believing that it was the "same" water at Hammersmith and at Lechlade? There is a case for saying that the water of the river is everlastingly new, fresh and ever renewed. There are some curious physical facts to bolster the metaphysical argument. The Thames from Lechlade to Teddington, what can be called the non-tidal Thames, contains approximately 4,500 million gallons (20,450 million litres). The amount of rainfall in that region has been calculated as 4,360 million gallons (19,820 million litres). It is new water, perpetually circulated, perpetually purified, perpetually replenished. But another curious statistical fact will cast a strange light on this "newness." One drop of water, fallen in the Cotswolds, will have been drunk by eight different people before it reaches the sea. It is taken out, purified, and then reintroduced to the river. It can never be quite the same as it was yesterday, or last month, or a hundred million years ago. Or can it? It is the secret of its eternal renewal.

The true measure of the river may be found in the emotions that it summons up. For some who gaze upon it or wander beside it, it conjures images of their destiny, while for others it invokes the past. There are few people who do not enter some form of reverie when they sit by the flowing water, even if it lies only in the recognition of perpetual change. That is why, in books concerning the Thames, there is a continual lament about the encroachments of the present on the glories of the past. The Thames itself summons up this mood of regret.

Thomas Gray set the tone for river melancholy in his poem, "Ode on a Distant Prospect of Eton College" (1742). Once more the recognition of endless change induces sadness. Turner's paintings of the Thames are often concerned with embarkation, separation and withdrawal. In Dickens's novels the Thames is often the scene of meetings and partings. Water is the melancholy element. Everything is dissolved within it. There are people who come to the banks of the river in order to experience forgetfulness. The sight of the river can obliterate thought, and kill observation. It can even erase memory. It absorbs everything. It can induce sleep and oblivion, as well as contemplation. The river Lethe still exists within the river Thames.

Yet the idea of the cycle, and of perpetual rebirth, may also be the cause for celebration. Even now it can provoke feelings of escape and of adventure. There is always something waiting to be explored around the next turn of the river. When the Thames rushes out towards the sea it seems to be filled with new life and energy.

PART II

Father Thames

CHAPTER 4

Baptism

❧

hames is an old name. With the exception of Kent it is perhaps the most ancient name recorded in England. It is assumed to be of the same origin as that of the rivers Tamar, Teme and Taff; they may all be derived from Celtic *tam*, meaning smooth or wide-spreading. *Isa* or *esa* are both versions of a Celtic root word meaning running water, as in the present Ouse and Exe (Oxford is a corruption of Ousenford or Osenford). So we may construct a provisional translation for the Thames as running ooze. But this is merely informed supposition. The word may have another origin altogether. There is a river Temes in Hungary that flows into the Danube. There is a river Tamese in Italy, and the principal town of the Brutii in southern Italy was called Temesa.

There is also a tributary of the Ganges, known in Sanskrit as Tamasa. It derives from Sanskrit *tamasa*, or "dark." In the second book of the Hindu text *Ramayana* there is a chapter on "The Tamasa." So the name could be pre-Celtic. It may spring from the primordial tribes of the Mesolithic or Neolithic periods who, during their wanderings over the earth, shared a common language. The syllable *teme* may indeed indicate darkness, in the sense of holy or sacred fearfulness. It may be very ancient indeed, going back to the first naming of the world. It is a matter of interest, then, that in

the nineteenth and early twentieth centuries the Thames was often described as the "dark river" in unwitting echo of its first description.

Perhaps it was not renamed, by the Celts or the Romans or the Saxons,
because it was considered to be a numinous word. The river was known to
the Celts as Tamesa or Tamesis. The Romans, in the shape of the conqueror Julius Caesar, translated it as Thamesis. This was also the name
known to Tacitus and Dion Cassius. For the settling Saxons it became more
simply Temes or Temese. The fact that it retained its final "s," a rare oc-
currence in Anglo-Saxon, suggests very strongly that the Saxons knew the
word already before its Celtic or Roman vesture. They had heard of the
Thames as a great river over the seas. In a manuscript of 699 it is called
"Thamise." For Nennius, in his chronicles of the eighth and early ninth
centuries, it is "Tamisia." The name has no less than twenty-one variants
in its Latin and Saxon forms, with a further nine in Middle English. But
without exception they include *tame* or *teme*. This is the sacred element—
this putative word for darkness.

It soon enters chronicle history, within the ancient charters of the
Anglo-Saxons. In the first of them extant, from the seventh century, there
are references to land belonging to Abbot Aldhelm "*cujus vocabulum Temis
juxta vadum qui appelatur Somerford.*" Somerford Keynes still exists beside
the Thames, no more than 2 or 3 miles from the source; it has a church built
by Aldhelm himself (with a Viking carving) and the vestiges of Saxon
watermills.

The baptism of a river requires the figure of a guardian or deity. Ludd, Celtic
divinity of the Londoners, a mysterious and insubstantial god, may be related to Nudd or Nodens, who is the presiding deity of the Severn, but on
these curious matters no certainty can be found. There is a more rotund figure in the form of Old Father Thames, a water divinity of unknown origin
who bears a striking resemblance to the tutelary gods of the Nile and the
Tiber. His flowing beard and hair call up the strange association between
hair and water. The Ganges was supposed to flow through the matted hair
of Shiva; in Leonardo's notebooks there are drawings of hair and water that
have been closely aligned, as if in the swirls and ripples of the water there
was an echo of human organism. A Graeco-Roman sculpture of the Tiber,
with flowing beard and hair, is dated from the first century BC; it is to be
found at the base of the staircase of the Capitoline Hill in Rome. In the same
setting reclines the god of the Nile, with similar appearance and pose.

In the myths of Greece and Rome Achelous, the god of all rivers, is also the fount or source of all knowledge. He mourned the loss of one of his horns in combat with Hercules. That became the "horn of plenty" which in turn was transformed into the urn held by Father Thames; this can be construed as an expression of the fact that the river, once tamed, becomes fruitful. Yet the images also suggest other attributes. Achelous is a strong god, who can be tempted to fierceness and anger. He is ancient but he has the gift of perpetual self-renewal so that he holds within himself the secret of eternal youth. That is the origin of the "fountain of youth."

His avatar, Old Father Thames, is commemorated in a statue, once at Thames Head but now removed to Lechlade, the site of the first lock upon the water. He is here surrounded by barrels and bales of goods, in homage to the Thames as a river of commerce as well as sacred power. He also carries a spade, as an emblem of the industry required to create the locks that have in part tamed the water. There is another sculpture in the grounds of Ham House, beside the river, where it is known simply as "the river god"; this is from the mid-eighteenth century, a hundred years older than the image at Lechlade, and the god holds an urn in homage to a more ancient sense of sacredness. Other copies have been lost.

There is a sculpture of Father Thames in Trinity Square, where it acts as *genius loci* for the erstwhile headquarters of the Port of London Authority; the god carries a trident and, with his other hand, points eastwards towards the open sea. Once more his beard and hair are carefully detailed. He surmounts the emblems of Produce and Exportation, Commerce and Navigation. There is a bronze figure of Father Thames in the courtyard of Somerset House, and on the Strand front of that building there is a keystone carved in his image. There are great sculpted heads of Father Thames at the river entrance of Hammersmith Town Hall, and upon Vauxhall Bridge there is a bas-relief of the god in combat with the creatures of the deep. There is an image upon Kew Bridge, and another upon the bridge at Henley where his hair and beard are surrounded by bulrushes and fish. So he has not altogether been forgotten. He is still the deity revered by one of the great celebrants of the Thames, Alexander Pope, who described his

> . . . tresses drop'd with dews, and o'er the stream
> His shining horns diffus'd a golden gleam:
> Grav'd on his urn appear'd the moon, that guides
> His swelling waters, and alternate tides.

The poetry of John Denham in "Cooper's Hill" was once considered to be the purest in the language, as smooth and as mellifluous as the river that he invoked. He also paid homage to its deity as "Thames, the most loved of all the Ocean's sons." It would seem, then, that he comes from an old and distinguished family. He has a companion, however, who may claim even greater age and distinction.

The god of the Egyptians, Isis, has been generally associated with the Thames. The river itself has indeed been compared with the Nile, perhaps because of its fertility and its central place in the kingdom through which it flows. Sacrificial victims were thrown into the Nile to appease its deities; we will find the same rituals beside the banks of the Thames. There are reaches of the Thames that effortlessly summon up memories of the Nile. A stretch of the river just before Cricklade contains rushes and quicksands; a dreamy and melancholy passage of water at Chelsea has been compared to the Egyptian river. More importantly, however, the Nile and the tidal Thames contain intimations of death and rebirth, and of perpetual resurgence. They are both considered to be dark rivers.

One of the most famous monuments by the river must surely be that known as Cleopatra's Needle, although the obelisk has only a slender connection with the famous queen. But it does, however, have some association with the Nile. It was created by the pharaoh Thutmose III, and for fifteen hundred years it stood at Heliopolis beside the east bank of the Nile. It was transported to the Thames in 1878 and set upon the bank by means of hydraulic power. Its pink granite, quarried at Syene, has been blackened by the fogs and smoke of London. It is now the same colour as the river itself, a hallowed token of the turbid and mysterious Thames.

The connection between the Thames and the Nile is first made in the *Polychronicon*, or "Universal History," of Ranulphus Higden, monk of Chester, who lived in the first half of the fourteenth century. In that compilation of medieval learning Higden writes that "*Tamisia videtur componi a nominibus duorum fluminium, quae sunt Thama et Ysa aut Usa.*" Thus in translation: "Thamesis seems to be composed from the names of two rivers, that are the Thama and the Ysa or Usa." It is more than probable that the Ysa and Usa of Higden's account are in fact from the Celtic *isa* or *esa*. In the fourteenth century, then, the people along the banks of the river knew it from its Celtic term. Perhaps it was always known as the Ysa.

But then the historical record works its own recondite miracle. It was easy enough for Ysa to become the resplendent Isis. The error was prom-

ulgated by John Leland in his *Itinerary* (1546) where he announced that
"Isis riseth at 3 myles from Cirincestre." William Camden, in his *Britannia*
(1586), uses the same name in a record of "*Isis vulgo Ouse*" or "Isis, commonly known as the Ouse." It was without evidence or corroboration but
it proved remarkably suggestive. The same explanation was followed by
Holinshed and Stow. Such was Leland's prestige, in fact, that no one cared
to dispute it. In the late seventeenth century, for example, the Welsh
scholar, Edward Lhwyd, followed Leland as one "against whom I dare not
contend." So in *Parochialia* (1695) he writes of Dorchester as the place
"neere where the Thames dischargeth himself into Isis, from whence the
name Tamesis, the Thames, proceeds." By some strange process of misat-
tribution and misunderstanding, Thamesis was then considered to be the
conflation of Thames and Isis.

A theory was then proposed to explain the phenomenon: the "Isis"
emerged at the source and continued to Dorchester, while the element of
"Thames" came from the river Thame that entered at Dorchester. A glance
at the Anglo-Saxon records, where it was always known as the Thames,
would alone render the supposition worthless. Nevertheless it has persisted
for centuries. The parliamentary Acts from 1750 to 1842 refer to the
"Rivers Thames and Isis," as does the Thames Conservancy Act of 1894.
Even the maps of the Ordnance Survey still refer to its course from
Thames Head to Dorchester as that of the "River Thames or Isis." The
naming of rivers is a difficult matter.

But if it is a confusion, it is a fruitful one. The persistence of the fallacy of Thame and Isis suggests that it has some inner resonance, some essential rightness in defiance of the laws of etymology. Isis, after all, is
charged with general human memory. She is the Mother Goddess, the
benefactress of rivers. She is the womb of regeneration. She is the goddess
of fertility, the Lady of Abundance, the sister and consort of Osiris, who
rules the underworld. The fertile Thames emerges from unknown depths.
She is the female soul of the world, the anima, who may appear in a thousand different incarnations. Three Roman effigies of the son of Isis, Horus,
have been found in the waters by London Bridge. The image is that of the
mother giving birth to the son on a tidal river, representing one of the most
powerful of all myths of regeneration.

The cult of Isis was maintained throughout the Roman empire, and at
the temple of Isis in Pompeii water was sprinkled upon the heads of her adherents as blessing and benediction. The Thames itself was used for ritual

inundation and Christian baptism. Isis was the winged goddess, hailed as
"the oldest of the old," who was the protectress of agriculture and of the
arts of healing, of law and of justice. She was the "provider of sweetness
in assemblies." All of these activities, including the making of laws and the
dispensing of justice, have for many centuries, and perhaps for many thousands of years, taken place beside the banks of the Thames. We may think
of Runnymede. The Thames was the home of the Neolithic cursus. It is the
home of the present Parliament.

Thus in the poetry of rivers she has become pre-eminent. In the verses
of Spenser she is wreathed in ancientness like some primaeval god. At the
marriage feast in *The Faerie Queene*, the Thames is preceded by:

> His auncient parents, namely, th'auncient Thame;
> But much more aged was his wife than he,
> The Ouze, whom men doe Isis rightly name,
> Full weak and crooked creature seemed shee,
> And almost blind through Eld, that scarce her way could see.

In Drayton's *Polyolbion* there is a younger incarnation of the goddess:

> That *Isis, Cotswolds* heire, long woo'd was lastly wonne,
> And instantly should wed with *Tame*, old *Chiltern's* sonne.

And thus also in Warton:

> Beauteous Isis, and her husband Thame,
> With mingled waves for ever flow the same.

The poetry celebrates the sense of place, and creates in myth what has only
a perilous and ambiguous foundation in fact. It is the story of the human
race.

Isis is herself the progenetrix of all the river nymphs and river goddesses who decorate the streams and springs of the world. They are known
as water fays, water shapes, water nixies, water wreaths, water elfs and
water fairies. Virgil names fifty of them in the *Aeneid*. The Severn is named
after the British goddess Habrina or Sabrina. The Clyde comes under the
protection of Clota. The Dee belongs to Deva. Curiously enough the
Thames has been associated with no tutelary goddess—except, of course,

Isis herself. The absence of a known female deity may well have prompted Leland into making the connection with the Egyptian goddess in the first place. It was a way of affirming ancient beliefs about the power of the waters. That is why in 1806 Turner exhibited a painting of an idealised Thames, supposedly depicted at Weybridge, which he entitled *Isis*. It is a visionary conception of the river, with the darkening water flowing between great trees and with what seems to be the fragment of a ruined temple in the foreground.

When confronted with Father Thames and with Isis as the assumed deities of the Thames, it is perhaps not surprising that there has been some debate concerning the gender of the river. In the whole of the British Isles, however, only the Derwent is known unequivocally as "he." The Thames itself seems to switch identity. In its upper reaches it is presumed to be feminine, and was known to William Morris as "this far off, lonely mother of the Thames," yet as the river approaches London it is deemed to be masculine. When the river is fierce or strong, it is also regarded as masculine. So sexual stereotypes prevail in the understanding of nature itself. In the battle of the sexes, the tributaries of the Thames are generally regarded as feminine.

Isis represents the water as feminine. It is the water as the female principle, circling like amniotic fluid. In the images of Isis the water is also seen to be milk, the nutritive fluid. The water is feminine because, in mingling with clay, it creates shape and form. There are a host of associations and affiliations here that defy rational enquiry precisely because they go back to the earliest periods of human consciousness. So the Thames can enter mythic history alongside the Styx and the Acheron, Lethe and Phlegethon, a river that takes its traveller beyond the ordinary world and into another world of dream and spirit.

The legends of its sexuality are a recognition of the evident fact that the river is a living thing. The Thames has its own presence. It has its own organic laws of growth and change, charged with what Bernard Shaw described as a "life force." The surface of the water has so complex a wave structure that it seems to function as the membrane of a living organism, like the ear; its capillary structure, stirred by movement, communicates its changes to the whole. It has been so intimately concerned with human destiny, replete with desires and fears, that it has acquired a human personality.

Over many centuries it has been venerated and propitiated. In *The

Historic Thames Hilaire Belloc wrote that "I cannot get away from it, that the Thames may be alive." Some travellers have confessed to the sensation, along certain stretches of the river, of being watched. The great historian of the Thames, F. S. Thacker, has commented in *The Thames Highway* (1914) that "Thames is one living spirit, whole and indivisible, from the loneliness at Trewsbury Mead to his final loneliness seaward of the Nore." For many devotees there is indeed some spirit, some atmosphere, some brooding life that persists through time.

When the river is described it always assumes a human dimension. It is patient, making its way through every obstacle. It is ruthless, wearing down the hardest rocks. It is unpredictable, especially when its current is interrupted or diverted. Its course from source to sea has been categorised as one of youth, maturity and old age. Its character changes within each terrain. It becomes terrible and vindictive. It becomes sportive. It becomes treacherous. It becomes imperial. It becomes industrious. It gives human characteristics to its topography.

CHAPTER 5

The River of Stone

❧

The basin of the Thames is largely enclosed by hills, with the Cotswold Hills to the extreme west; at their northern end the Cotswolds sweep round towards Edge Hill, and then the hill wall moves across the Central Tableland until it reaches the long stretch of the East Anglian Heights that proceed eastward. On the south side of the river the hills, forming the rim of the basin, curve round by way of the Marlborough Downs and then the North Downs that proceed to the coast of Kent. The area of the basin itself rarely rises more than 200 feet (61 m) above sea level, and can be described as gently rippling, except for the great ridge of chalk that makes up the Chilterns. Over millennia the Thames has made its way through the chalk, but the Chilterns remain as a token of ancient cataclysm.

The geology of the Thames is in fact exceedingly complex, at least to those who are not professional geologists, but it is not without relevance to those who are interested in the distant ages of the earth. Above the area known as Goring Gap—where the river has forced its way through the ridge of chalk of which the Chilterns are a part—the topography consists of soft clay valleys and ridges formed out of sandstone or limestone. Below the Goring Gap the river flows across the "London Basin" comprised of chalk, sand, gravel and clay. The limestone of the Cotswolds to the west gives way to the area known as the Oxford Clay Vale which is succeeded by the chalk of the Chilterns and the Berkshire Downs; then, to the south of the Chilterns, lies the clay which is in turn succeeded by sandstone, sand and gravel.

Of course there are always local variations and differences, dependent upon the flow of ancient oceans and the tumults of the primaeval earth. There are areas of gravel and boulder clay, for example, that have been moved by the phenomenon of the ice ages known as "glacial drift." The river, too, has deposited various layers of gravel and loam along its course. The levels of clay and stone are tokens of patterns and processes that persisted for hundreds of millions of years, the emblems of a longevity inconceivable to humankind. They are ribbons in the hair of Gaia. As God asked Job, "Where wast thou when I laid the foundations of the earth? Declare, if thou hast understanding." In the late seventeenth century Bishop Burnet wrote a book entitled *A Sacred Theory of the Earth*; such a book could still be written about the river.

The area known as the London Basin provides an example of the variousness of the topography. It is made up of chalk overlaid with gravel and with clay, but the depth of the chalk varies at different locations; at Lambeth it lies 250 feet (76 m) beneath the surface while further downriver, at Rotherhithe, it is at a depth of 46 feet (14 m). The Saxon word for chalk is *chilt*, thus naming the Chilterns themselves. Above the chalk lie layers of red mottled clay and permeable sand, then the London clay laid down some sixty million years ago, and above that gravel and brick-earth.

These ancient stones still play an essential role in the life of the river; towns such as Greenwich and Greenhithe, Woolwich and Gravesend, are built upon outcrops of chalk. Just at the point where the Thames curves to the south, immediately before the entrance of the Cherwell, there is a stretch of ancient gravel. This is the site of Oxford. The stones are the foundations of present life. The brick-earth has, in addition, furnished the fabric of London dwellings. It has often been observed that the buildings of the Thames towns and villages seem to "fit" their surroundings, from the glowing Cotswold stone of a farmhouse to the flint walling and chalk plaster of a barn or dovecot. In every case the stone is part of the *genius loci*.

There was once the mystery of "dene-holes" by the river, large and interconnected subterranean tunnels clustered around the banks of the Thames like large vase-shaped structures with narrow necks; they consist of a vertical shaft with a bell-like chamber beneath, connected to other similarly shaped chambers. They have been variously interpreted as ancient observatories or grain pits, sepulchral chambers or refuges from invaders. It seems most likely, however, that they were constructed by the Saxons for some form of chalk-mining. But the evidence is unclear.

There is also the phenomenon of the terraces, formed when there has been a fall in sea-level. When the sea falls, the river cuts deeper through its previous floodplain, leaving it marked out as a terrace above the new floodplain. The Boyn Hill terrace lies 100 feet (30 m) above the present course of the river, for example, and was laid down some 375,000 years ago. This was succeeded by the Taplow terrace, some 50 feet (15 m) lower. The most recent is known more simply as the Flood Plain terrace. There are other gradations and variations of terraces, with other names. The alluvial floodplain of the Upper Thames is a relatively new development, dating no further back than the second millennium BC, but the terraces themselves are perhaps more obvious in London where they must be surmounted by human ingenuity. The steep climb from the Embankment to the Strand, by Charing Cross underground station, is the indication of a rift that took place over aeons of time. The rise between the middle and upper terraces of the Thames can in turn be seen beside the National Gallery to the north of Trafalgar Square. We are treading upon prehistory.

Those who trust the spirit of place must take account of these geological gradations and alterations. There is no reason to doubt that human consciousness is changed by the experience of living above clay, rather than above chalk, even though the nature of that change is not understood. It is a matter of speculation whether the oolite of the Cotswolds has a resonance different from the sandstone rock of Clifton Hampden. How does the fossiliferous clay of Woolwich compare to the sandy pebble of Blackheath? Does it make any difference that the inhabitants of the estuary walk above preserved primaeval forests? Does the vast marsh, beneath the surface of the Vale of the White Horse, exert its own influence?

The earliest inhabitants of the Thames Valley believed that there was an intrinsic power in stone, and the builders of the great monuments of Britain were concerned to use precisely the right kind of stone for their enterprise. Certain types of stone, from different geographical locations, had different powers and associations. The ancient tribes were perhaps more attuned to the natural world, and sensed what the twenty-first-century inhabitants of the Thames Valley ignore or reject.

There is, for example, reason to believe that the inhabitants north of the Thames once differed from those who lived to the south of the river. This may have to do in large part with tribal identity, county identity and general lack of contact; but topography and geology, the earth itself, may also play a part. Certainly the difference between north and south was once more marked. One historian of the Thames region, in the early twentieth century, spent much of his life examining the songs and the customs of the Thames people. In *Folk Songs of the Upper Thames* (1923) Alfred Williams notes that in Wiltshire and Buckinghamshire, the counties immediately south of the Thames, the people "are rather more boisterous and spontaneous, more hearty, hardy, strong, blunt, and vigorous, and a little less musical"; the inhabitants of Gloucestershire and Oxfordshire, north of the Thames, are "gentler, easier, softer in manner, but weaker, more pliable, and less sturdy than the others." The northerners are more refined and more artistic than the southerners but "they have not quite the same tenacity and independence of spirit."

Other observers noted similar tendencies. In the nineteenth century the principal entertainment of the northern counties was that of morris-dancing, while in the southern counties it was wrestling and sword-play. There is no record of morris-dancing in any of the counties south of the Thames. The stone of the north is mellow Cotswold stone; the stone of the south is flint and brick. There seems also to have been a human continuity, since the same differences in temperament and character can be identified between the Angles north of the Thames and the Saxons south of the river. There may also be some connection with the provenance of the law, with the contrast between Danish and Saxon legislation on either side of the Thames leading to differences in behaviour.

It is certainly true that, until relatively recent times, the same stock seems to have persisted in identifiable areas. In the mid-nineteenth century the inhabitants of the area by the Chiltern Hills were "more uncultivated" than their neighbours, the land known at the time as "wild country" with local names such as "Hell Hole" and "Gallows Common" not to be found on any maps. But in a history of the Thames, James Thorne's *Rambles by Rivers* (1847), it is stated that "this roughness does not cross the Thames" and that "the Berkshire men are civiller" with the same "vigour of mind" that Alfred Williams noticed half a century later.

The most obvious and characteristic difference was to be found in London itself, where the divisive presence of the Thames once fashioned two very different areas of human activity and human personality. It was forcibly expressed in the nineteenth century by Charles Mackay in *The Thames and Its Tributaries* (1840) where he asserted of the southern people that "the progress of civilisation does nothing for them . . . a thousand years effect nothing more than to change the wigwam into a hovel, and at the latter point they stop." He noted that on the northern side "railways are constructed" and other amenities are built while the inhabitants of the other bank "experience no improvement." This may be construed as an accident of topography, with the bogs and marshes of the southern stretch now largely removed by the unerring march of civilisation, but it was really no accident at all. It had to do with the nature of the place, and of the river that helped to create it. It is interesting that in the ninth century King Alfred declared that when he ascended the throne there were very few, if any, scholars "south of the Thames." The inhabitants on both sides of the Thames estuary still have very little awareness of each other.

The language is also different. To the south of the Thames the water crowfoot is known as the water lily, while to the north it is called rait. The ox-eye daisy was known in Wiltshire as dog daisy or horse daisy, while over the water in Oxfordshire it was known as moon daisy. The river has always been a frontier.

CHAPTER 6

Birth

The source is the place of enchantment, where the boundary between the visible and invisible realms is to be found. It is commonly deemed to be a sanctuary, guarded or protected by the spirits of the young water. The water issuing from the dark earth can also be seen as an image of human existence emerging from the unknown. We trace the stream from darkness, from the very place of origin in its blind cavern, until it issues to the light and open day. It is a metaphor of birth and death, of beginning and ending. Water itself represents the beginning of every living thing. The journey towards the source is the journey backwards, away from human history. Force and purity come from the source. Youthfulness derives from the source. So springs the myth of the fountain of youth. It is the *fons et origo*. It is the Well of Life or, in the Norse phrase, the Well of Wyrd.

In *Naturales Quaestiones* Seneca declared that "when you have come to understand the true origin of rivers, you will realise that you have no further questions." The source has always been considered to be the origin of power and of good fortune. When Shalmaneser III of Assyria found the source of the Tigris, "I took victims to sacrifice to my gods, I held a joyful feast." Caesar told the high priest of Egypt that he would give up his wars if he could find the source of the Nile. Nero sent an expedition to find that same source, without success. In the mythology of Egypt the river was created at the beginning of the world—of the universe—and its origin would remain for ever undisclosed. The source of the Yellow River, or Huang He, a vital presence in China for many thousands of years and the genuine nurse of its culture, was not discovered until 1952.

For many scholars the journey to the origin of rivers was in a literal sense a return to Paradise. It was believed that the waters of the primal Eden circulated in the subterranean regions of the earth, and emerged from the mouths of caverns and abysses to irrigate the upper lands. The source was the place where the mysteries of eternal life might be vouchsafed. In the sermons of Bernard of Clairvaux there is a prayer that "the rivers of grace circle back to their fountain-head that they may run their course anew" nourishing the trinity of the spring, the wellhead and the stream. In this context the closest thing to the soul is the primal spring. Thus Chaucer, living on the Thames at Greenwich, addressed a friend upriver:

> Scogan, that knelest at the stremes heed
> Of grace, of alle honour and worthinesse,
> In th'end of which streme I am dul as deed,
> Forgete in solitarie wildernesse . . .

It is appropriate that the source of the Thames represents in part a mystery. The Elizabethan antiquarian and topographer, William Harrison, complained that people "make as much adoo" about the origin of the river as was once made "in times past of the true head of Nilus which . . . was never found." He was referring to the fact that the Thames has two possible origins, one of them known as Seven Springs and the other more pertinently as Thames Head.

Geographically the palm might be awarded to Seven Springs in the parish of Coberley, or Cubberley, north of Cirencester; it is further from the sea than Thames Head by some 12 miles and, at 700 feet (213 m), more than 300 feet (91 m) higher above sea level. There is an ancient stone bulwark, with seven springs issuing from seven small openings in its wall. On the stone has been fixed a plaque with the words *Hic Tuus O Tamesine Pater Septemgeminus Fons*—"Here, O Father Thames, is your seven-sourced fountain." There is, however, one large impediment to this claim. The stream that issues from the seven springs has always been known as the

Churn, which eventually enters the Thames at Cricklade. No one doubts that it is ancient—its name derives from the Celtic word *chwern* or "swift"—only whether it is the source of the Thames.

The historical records are, on this matter, in agreement about the claims of Thames Head. In the early sixteenth century John Leland stated that the "Isis," by which name he called the Thames, rose "not far from a village cawlled Kemble, within half a mile of the Fosseway"; in the same century John Stow recorded that "the most excellent and goodly river beginneth in Cotswold, about a mile from Titbury, and as much from the hie way called Fosse," and William Camden reported that "it riseth not far from Tarlton, hard by the famous Foss-way." The authorities could be multiplied, but the inference is clear. The Fosse-Way has now been transfigured into the A 433, but the source of the Thames is to be found in its immediate vicinity.

It rises in a field known as Trewsbury Mead, and lies beside a Roman camp which is now a mound still called Trewsbury Castle. The camp was no doubt located here because of its proximity to the spring, and it is likely that peoples more ancient than the Romans had a settlement here. The name of the neighbouring village of Ewen is derived from the Saxon word for a spring or source. So from earliest times this place has been celebrated, or sanctified, because of its flowing waters. Over the centuries the locale acquires its identity. Thomas Love Peacock expressed this process in his paean to the river, *The Genius of the Thames* (1810):

> Let fancy lead, from Trewsbury Mead,
>   With hazel fringed, and copsewood deep,
> Where scarcely seen, through brilliant green,
>   Thy infant waters softly creep,
> To where the wide-expanding Nore
>   Beholds thee, with tumultuous roar . . .

As late as the eighteenth century there was a well at Trewsbury Mead, protected by a circular wall some 8 feet (2.4 m) in height. Then the wall was demolished or eroded, the well eventually filled in. All that remains as the mark of origin is a small group of stones like some basin or ring in the ground, in a hollow beneath a tree; in some respects these oolite stones, known as stone-brash or corn-grate, resemble a cairn or memorial of ancient worship.

The mythical properties converge at this place known as Thames Head. The tree protecting the source is an ash that has stood here for approximately two centuries. It once had "T.H." carved upon its bark—some still see the letters, and some do not. But the emblem is not important. It is in any case a highly significant tree. In the mythology of the Norse people the roots of the ash-tree went down into the lower world. It connected the three circles of existence, and was known to be the path of spirits. The giant ash was known as the World Tree or Yggdrasil. In that mythology there was always a spring or pool beside it. In that mythology, too, a river ran from the tree of life. What could be more appropriate than that it should guard the source of the Thames? But there are other significant associations. The ash-tree is sacred to Poseidon, and is the tree dedicated to the power of water.

At the source of many rivers are to be found temples, or stones carved with the figures of divinity. Often wooden carvings were placed at the source as votive offerings. A hoar stone was erected at Thames Head as a memorial. The same stone is mentioned in a grant of lands given by King Athelstan in the year 931, when it was used as a boundary. Or it may have marked a place of sepulture, where some principal person was buried beside the origin of waters. It was later used as a horse-block or "upping stock" where traveller and horse could pause to refresh themselves with the clear water. It was replaced in the last century by a marble plinth upon which is carved "The Conservation of the River Thames 1857–1974. This Stone Was Placed Here to Mark the Source of the River Thames."

Yet there was one problem for the thirsty horse and traveller during certain seasons of the year. Leland states that "in a great somer drought there appereth very little or no water, yet is the stream servid with many springes resorting to one bottom." In the late eighteenth century John Boydell remarked in his *History of the River Thames* (1796) that "I do not think you will ever find any water in summertime." The absence of water is still remarked two hundred years later. It is one of the mysteries of the Thames. There seems to be no nourishment at the source. For most of the year it remains dry ground. The line of the infant Thames can only be followed by a gentle declivity in the surrounding ground, so that it is possible to walk in the middle of the river without becoming wet.

There is of course water beneath the surface. A latter-day water diviner has calculated that there is running water at a depth of 5 or 6 feet (1.5 or 1.8 m), with a channel some 10 inches (254 mm) in width. At times of heavy rain the spring floods upward. There are photographs, taken in 1960 and 2000, of pools where there had been a well. In the photographs of 1960 small boys are to be seen in canoes beneath the ash-tree. There has been a diminution of water, however, and one early-twentieth-century oral historian recorded a local inhabitant as saying that "the springs be wakened in thaay owl 'ills, an ther yent so much water comes down as 'twas when I was a bwoy." The clearance of woods and forests in the region has meant less condensation but, in addition, human artifice has played its part. A steam engine was placed beside the well to pump water for the Thames and Severn Canal, which ran on higher ground close by, and in 1878 a pumping station was erected for the Great Western Railway works at Swindon.

Yet the lines and buried streams are still here. The path of the infant river in the declivity is marked by a straggling line of ancient thorns. Along that path there is a group of scattered stones that look very much like the ruins of a stone bridge; about half a mile further down is a large pool or basin, much more likely to be filled with water than Thames Head itself. It is known as Lyd Well or, in translation from Old English, "loud" spring. Yet Lyd may have a different connotation. It may be related to Ludd, the divinity of early London. There is an argument that Ludd is also the ancient god of the river. Lyd Well is the beginning of our pilgrimage beside the Thames.

PART III

Issuing Forth

The junction of the Cherwell and the Thames

CHAPTER 7

The Tributes

The Thames has many tributaries. There is good reason to honour
them. The gods were meant to dance at the confluence of waters.
The mingling of the tributary and the main river was deemed to
be sacred. The site of entry was a holy place, guarded by the three seated
goddesses who have been given the name of Matres. There is a significant
clustering of cursus sites, of presumed Neolithic date, around the conflu-
ences on the Upper Thames. So the meeting of the rivers is an occasion for
spiritual ritual.

There is one especial god for this purpose. The Celtic god Condatis—
who is in some late Roman inscriptions associated with Mars, no doubt in
his capacity as a healing power—takes his name from the Gallic epithet
"watersmeet." He is literally the god of the two streams, the *confluens*, and
was worshipped as such. It is true that his cult is especially associated with
northern Britain, and in particular with the area of the Tyne and the Tees,
but there is good reason to believe that such an important deity travelled
through the island.

The principal tributaries of the Thames are the Churn, the Thame, the
Colne, the Leach, the Windrush, the Evenlode, the Cherwell, the Kennet,
the Ver, the Wey, the Mole, the Medway, the Lea and the Roding. There are

smaller rivers and streams that refresh and replenish the river—the Ampney Brook, the Gatwick Stream, the Ray, the Cole, the Blackwater, the Ock, the Lambourn, the Pang, the Loddon, the Wye, the Bourne, the Hogsmill and the Ember. There are also waters that stream into the tidal river, among them the Brent, Stamford Brook, Beverley Brook, the Wandle, Chelsea Creek, the Hole Bourne, the Fleet, the Walbrook, Deptford Creek, Barking Creek, the Beam, Rainham Creek, the Mar Dyke, Dartford Creek, Bill Meroy Creek, Cliffe Creek, Mucking Creek, Shell Haven Creek, Hole Haven Creek, Cliffe Fleet, Salt Fleet and the Yantlet Fleet.

Many are now buried; many are forgotten; many are today unhonoured and unsung. There are London rivers, for example, that have long been forced beneath the ground where they remain as conduits or as sewers. Some of these buried waters may have found their own courses and become "shadow rivers" without a name, silently running within the earth. Yet these ancient rivers still exert an influence upon the world above them. They can make their presence known in odours and in creeping dampness; the buried Fleet, for example, can still flood basements along its course. The lost rivers were once deemed to be responsible for ague and fever, and their valleys (now carved between the streets and buildings of the city) were peculiarly susceptible to mist and fog. In more recent times the presence of the underground waters has been blamed for the prevalence of allergies in their vicinity.

Spenser honoured the meeting of the Thames with the Medway and with the Lea as a token of cosmic as well as of natural order. In the vast poetical topography of *Polyolbion* (1622) Drayton invokes the "clear *Colne* and the lively *Leech*," and "the bright *Elnlode*." Drummond of Hawthornden in *An Hymn of the Fairest Faire* (1623) writes of the stream and of the river as:

> . . . but one self-same essence, nor in ought
> Doe differ, save in order.

So the river can become a metaphor for spiritual grace. In painting, too, Turner was ever alert to the mythical powers of the tributary. One of his most celebrated paintings is entitled *Union of the Thames and Isis*. The setting is Dorchester Mead, just below the ancient hills of Sinodun, and at this place the Thame and the Thames converge. Yet Alexander Pope must carry the palm as the poet of confluence, and in *Windsor Forest* (1713) he becomes the hierophant chanting holy names:

> First the fam'd authors of his ancient name,
> The winding *Isis* and the fruitful THAME;
> The *Kennet* swift, for silver eels renowned,
> The *Loddon* slow, with verdant alders crown'd;
> *Cole,* whose dark streams his flow'ry island lave,
> And chalky *Wey,* that rolls a milky wave;
> The blue transparent *Vandalis* appears,
> The gulphy *Lee,* his sedgy tresses rears;
> The sullen *Mole,* that hides his diving flood,
> And silent *Darent,* stained with Danish blood!

And we in turn can call them out from their modest retreats. The Windrush, extravagantly named, rises among the hills of the Cotswolds, and passes through Bourton and Witney before joining the bosom of its parent. Was it so named because it winds among the rushes, or rushes like the wind? By meditating upon its name Drayton declared that it "scowres" the riverine landscape and "hies her fast / Through the Oxfordian fields"; but this was an exaggeration. It is pretty and it is peaceful, except at those points where it surges between the cottages of Bourton-on-the-Water. It is certainly true, however, that the Thames becomes wider and deeper immediately downstream from its confluence with the Windrush.

The Kennet mingles with the Thames at Reading. In *Polyolbion* Michael Drayton celebrated their confluence:

> At Reading once arrived, clear Kennet overtakes
> Her Lord the stately Tames, which that great Flood again
> With many signs of joy doth kindly entertain.

It is, in other words, a holy marriage or sacred union testifying to the life principle of the world. It is an emblem of fertility. One of the early variants of Kennet is Cunetio, so there may be some vestigial reference to the generative organ of the earth goddess. The bridge here is known as the Horseshoe Bridge, the horseshoe being an ancient symbol of fortune. At the mouth of the Kennet there is an ancient burial ground, now known as

Broken Bow, which may be a version of Broken Barrow. Objects of metal and of pottery have been dredged up at this confluence of waters, suggesting that offerings were made here. It is also clear from the archaeological evidence, with the finding of an extremely rare hut or shelter beside the river, that the area around the mouth of the Kennet and the Thames harboured a trading station in the mesolithic period. So this confluence was a commercial, as well as a sacred, site. The bridge itself is now covered with graffiti; among them "Christ Is Coming."

The Ock, down the river from Abingdon, is the sole outlet for the surplus waters of the Vale of the White Horse; it was once the cause of so many floods that it rivalled the Thames. On its banks have been discovered the remains of an Iron Age religious centre as well as a temple of Romano-Celtic provenance. There was also here a *mansio* or lodging house for pilgrims, and a structure that may either be an amphitheatre or a walled sacred pool. The propinquity of the river suggests the latter. There was also a cemetery sited here. Some of the Roman bodies contained coins in their mouths, so that they might pay the ferryman.

The "sullen Mole" falls into the river just below Hampton Bridge; it is not particularly sullen, if water can in any case be supposed to suffer from that mood, and its name seems suspiciously like poetic association with the habits of the subterranean animal. Pope in fact borrowed the phrase from Milton who has "the Sullen Mole that runneth underneath." Milton in turn took the description from Spenser who wrote that

> Mole that like a Mousling mole doth make
> His way still underground, till the Thames he overtake.

It is an impressive litany of poetic votaries for a small river, and the reference to the "underground" and to the mole are by no means fanciful. In the neighbourhood of Box Hill and Norbury Park, it disappears and then revives. At times of drought the stream is dry at this point, but then is restored near Leatherhead. The antiquary, William Camden, believed that the Mole ran down into a dark cavern beneath the earth from which it was lifted by the power of nature. Defoe noted the same phenomenon and believed that the cause lay in little channels known as "swallows." "Swallow holes" are in fact known to be a property of limestone rocks, which abound in this area. The Mole really does disappear and rise again, entering the Thames itself at Molesworth.

The river Churn begins its course among the headsprings at Seven Springs, which some believe to be the Thames itself, and in the space of 14 miles falls 400 feet (120 m) until it meets its quietus in the river. It was described by Michael Drayton as the "nimble-footed Churn"; an accurate description, at least by the standards of poetical topography. It is, or was, a dancing little trout stream until the clear water of the tributary mingles with the turbulent brown river at Cricklade.

Just below Shiplake Lock the Lodden runs into the Thames. Pope describes it as the "slow Loddon," but in truth it is not slow at all. It has a swift current, which in previous years supported many watermills. It also has a curious effect of its own. Swimmers of long experience have testified that anyone who swims *against* its current is invariably affected by sickness and nausea; there is no obvious explanation for this strange phenomenon, but nonetheless it is present. It leads inevitably to speculation that there are some parts of the river that create or harbour distinct properties that are not susceptible to rational analysis.

The Wandle discharges itself into the Thames by Battersea, and has one of the strongest currents among all the tributaries of the river. It is the stream from which Wandsworth derives its name. This is the "blue transparent *Vandalis*" of Pope's poem, the poet no doubt considering the English name and location to be in need of some Latinate uplift. In fact the name derives from the Saxon Wendleswurth or "Wendel's settlement." It also has another poem to its credit, although not one that would be allowed into Pope's polite company:

Sweet little witch of the Wandle!
Come to my bosom and fondle;
  I love thee sincerely,
  I'll cherish thee dearly,
Sweet little witch of the Wandle.

The name of the Ravensbourne has an exotic origin. It is said that Caesar, while camping with his army near Blackheath, noticed that a raven frequently alighted a short distance away. He conjectured that it came to this place to drink and, after further observation, a small clear spring was found in that place. The spring became known as the Raven's Well, and the tributary emerged as the Ravensbourne. There is a poem, of doubtful merit, devoted to its progress from "a crystal rillet" to a "flood." The "flood" itself, being of so deep a nature, later gave its name to Deptford or Deep-Ford. But it does have a certain historical importance. Its waters refreshed the rebellious followers of Wat Tyler and, at a later date, the rebels under Jack Cade. Perkin Warbeck, the pretender to the English throne, met his adherents by the banks of the Ravensbourne; it was here also that in 1497 the Cornish rebels under the command of Lord Audley were hewn to pieces by the captains of Henry VII. No other tributary of the Thames has such a history of insurrection and bloodshed.

The Lea river has been memorialised by Spenser as "the wanton Lea that oft doth lose his way," and indeed its course is of a wandering nature. It rises near Luton, in Bedfordshire, and then makes its way to Hertford and to Ware; it then passes close by Amwell, where the New River once also flowed, and touches upon Hoddesdon, Cheshunt, Waltham Abbey, Enfield, Edmonton, Tottenham, Stratford, Walthamstow and Bow until eventually it finds its surcease at Bow Creek close to Blackwall. It was once celebrated as a fishing stream, and the fisherman, or "Piscator," of Isaac Walton's *The Compleat Angler* frequents the river Lea and stays at the inns close to its banks. But the Lea is now pre-eminently the river of London's eastern suburbs, and of the industrial parks that have taken the place of the "stink industries" upon its banks. Leyton is "the town upon the Lea." Yet the river has a significant history. The invading Danes sailed up the Lea from Blackwall, and erected a fort at Ware. The bridge over the Lea, at Stratford or Stratford-le-Bow, enjoyed the distinction of being the oldest stone bridge in England, pre-dating London Bridge by a hundred years. Waltham Abbey is the last resting place of the last Saxon king of England, buried under the simple inscription of *"Harold infelix."*

The tributary of the Cherwell rises in the ironstone hills of Hellidon, and then flows through Northamptonshire and Oxfordshire for 40 miles before reaching the Thames. It is sometimes considered to be a minor stream but in fact it augments the volume of the Thames by approximately a third, as the river moves towards Iffley.

The river Effra is named from the Celtic word *yfrid*, or torrent, and in its pristine state it rose near the area now known as Crystal Palace. It flows through Norwood Cemetery, Dulwich, Herne Hill, Brixton and Kennington before entering the Thames at Vauxhall Bridge. There is a curious token of its past significance to be found in the remains of a wooden structure, tentatively dated to the middle Bronze Age, located on the south bank where the Effra joins the river. The remains of the wooden posts can still be seen at low tide, but of the Effra itself there is little sign. It has become what is known as a "subterranean river," long since buried by housing and other developments; parts of the river have been used as sewers since the seventeenth century, and it has been largely diverted into a storm relief sewer. It can only be entered through the sewers of Effra Road in Brixton. Its powers have departed.

The greatest of all the forgotten tributaries, however, must be the Fleet, which still flows into the Thames beneath Blackfriars Bridge; if you travel by boat beneath that bridge, you will see a circular opening through which its waters pour. It is the only visible sign of a buried power. Its name is most likely to derive from the Anglo-Saxon term for a tidal estuary, as in North-fleet. But it is possible that it comes from the fleetness, or swiftness, of its waters that gathered first among the wells and springs to the north of the city. They came together in the vicinity of Clerkenwell, and the then substantial river ran down Turnmill Street (the etymology of which is clear enough) before widening at Holborn (literally "old bourne" or old brook) where a bridge across it was erected. It then entered the valley down to the Thames, the contours of which are still apparent in the canyon of Farringdon Street that descends from Fleet Street to Bridewell.

In the medieval period it was in extensive use, most particularly by colliers coming from the north-east of England. One of the streets leading off Farringdon Street is still known as Sea-Coal Lane. In his survey of London John Stow writes that "in times past the course of the water running at London under Old-bourne Bridge into the Thames had been of such breadth and depth that ten or twelve ships at once, with merchandise, were wont to come to the aforesaid bridge of the Fleet, and some of them to Old-bourne Bridge." More unhappily it had also been a common depository for the refuse and sewage of Londoners ever since the city was built around it, and it was periodically cleansed. In 1502, for example, there was a grand cleaning "so that fish and fewel were rowed to the Fleet Bridge" but by the end of the sixteenth century it had become in parts an open sewer, obstructed by refuse of all descriptions, and had acquired a reputation as a noisome or even dangerous place. The inmates of the Fleet Prison, largely a gaol for debtors, petitioned against the disease and mortality that the vapours of the tributary seemed to harbour. In 1732 it was bricked in from Holborn Bridge to Fleet Street, and a market placed on the site. Thirty-three years later it was covered from Fleet Street to its outlet in the Thames.

It has the distinction, however, of being celebrated both by Ben Jonson and by Alexander Pope in what might be loosely described as an anti-pastoral tradition. In the poetry of the seventeenth and eighteenth centuries the Thames invokes images of purity and of clarity, but the Fleet was deemed to be its dark shadow. Ben Jonson, in a poem entitled "The Voyage Itself" (1610), invokes "the filth, stench, noise" of the tributary as an essential and elemental part of the city's life. Where the confluence of two rivers was once the occasion for celebration to the gods, the only deities dancing upon these waters are "Gorgonian scolds and harpies":

> . . . here several ghosts did flit
> About the shore, of farts but late departed,
> White, black, blue, green, and in more forms out-started.

It is a torrent of "steams" and "grease," of "laxative lettuce" and of "merd-urinous load," a wholly rank and miasmal river which has taken on the more unhappy characteristics "of Styx, of Acheron, / Cocytus, Phlegethon." The epic qualities of the river are here reversed. By the early eighteenth century the Fleet had become a symbol or epitome of London itself. As a poem in the *Tatler* of 1710 put it:

> Filth of all hues and odours seem to tell
> What street they sailed from, by their sight and smell.

In the *Dunciad* (1728) Pope widens and intensifies Jonson's excremental vision with his own description of the impure locale:

> To where Fleet-ditch with disemboguing streams
> Rolls the large tribute of dead dogs to Thames,
> The King of dykes! than whom no sluice of mud
> With deeper sable blots the silver flood.

It is the metaphorical space for "filth" and "love of dirt," the excremental centre of London's polluted life. In Pope's cloacal vision all of the cheap versifiers and pamphleteers dive into "the quaking mud" of the tributary as

if they were entering their natural element. The silver Thames has its ret-
inue of nymphs and goddesses, but the Fleet has its "Mud-nymphs," "Ni-
grina black, and Merdamente brown," who "suck in" their votaries with
their foul embrace. These are the real "nut-brown maids" who have migrated from the woods to the sewers, and taken on the hue and savour of
their ordurous surroundings. The national myth of the silver Thames rose
above these local inconveniences, so that all the mire and filth were pro-
jected upon the river or "ditch" of the Fleet. It was another service that the
tributaries paid to their superior.

PART IV

Beginnings

Cookham, where the historic and the prehistoric are
found in close association

CHAPTER 8

In the Beginning

❧

The history of the Thames is as deep and as dark as that of any sea. It was first merely a ripple in the moving surface of the earth. The stone matrix of the river was first created some 170 million years ago when the great oceans of the Jurassic period carried the seeds of the limestone and the clay that later became the substrata of the Thames; in this period pleiosaurs, and fish with beaks and teeth, swam above the bed which would eventually become the Thames.

The Cretaceous, the next period of the earth's history after the Jurassic, means "of the nature of chalk"; over the next 77 million years the fossils of the oceans laid down the chalk beds of southern England. They are the bases of the riverine landscape. In this period too the great continent of Pangaea ("All the World") began to break apart, creating the land-masses of America and Europe. A vast floodplain lay where southern England now exists. Above London swam elasmosaurs and mosasaurs, the giants of the deep, until they were destroyed in a global cataclysm marked by what is known as the "K-T Boundary."

The river first emerges as an observable entity some 30 million years ago, midway through the Cenozoic era in which we still live. The British Isles were connected to the European mainland by a bridge of land, where

now the North Sea runs, and the Thames was then a tributary of a much
larger river that flowed across Europe. The longest stretch of it is now
called the Rhine.

From the evidence of fossil remains it is possible in part to reconstruct
the landscape of the earliest Thames; there were palm-trees and laurels,
vines and citrus trees, as well as oaks and beeches. There were water-lilies
on the surface of the river, as well as long weeds that drifted through the
warm water. There was also a new form of plant; grass began to grow. In
certain respects it would have been a recognisable, tropical scene. Termites
and ants, beetles and spiders, flourished in the humid atmosphere; there
were also turtles, and crocodiles, in the Thames as well as lizards that resembled modern iguanas. In the river, too, swam eels and ancestors of the
perch and other bony fishes.

The Thames then ran on a much higher course than in its present incarnation. It stretched from Wales and the Bristol Channel across England
until it reached the Vale of Aylesbury; it flowed through St. Albans and
Chelmsford before passing through Romford and issuing into a great lake
somewhere south of Harwich. When the railway line from Romford to
Upminster was being built, in the 1890s, the ancient and forgotten channel
of the old river was discovered, like the fossil of a once living creature.
This lake close to Harwich, and close to the northern end of the land-mass
linking Europe and the British Isles, eventually spilled over the watershed
that divided the present North Sea from the English Channel.

It was a great and fast-flowing river, a tropical river, a jungle river, to
which the ancestors of the horse and the bison, the rhinoceros and the
lemur, came to drink. Then the climate began to grow colder. The jungle
habitat gave way to temperate forests, to grass plains and prairies. The
Thames flowed through all these changes. They represent inconceivable
passages of time, far beyond the time of human origin. It is impossible to
contemplate the ancientness of the river, only incidentally an aspect of the
human world. It still contains shells, sedges and rushes that belong to
prehistory.

The climate of the world grew ever colder and at the time of the First
Northern Glaciation, some 2.8 million years ago, a north polar ice sheet began to creep southward. The earth was now on the threshold of the human.
Hominids, or "ape-men" as they were once known, drank from the river
and slept in the trees beside its banks before moving onwards. But the

spread of the glaciers had a profound and permanent effect upon the Thames. It was pushed southward, closer and closer to its present course.

The ice eventually halted just north of the Chiltern-Berkshire ridge, and about one quarter of a million years ago the Thames created what is now known as the Thames Valley. The river had also entered the age of humankind. The first dwellers by the Thames came by land from the areas now known as central and western Europe. They are considered to be denizens of the Old Stone Age or Palaeolithic era, but this neutral category covers the longest period of human survival in the history of the world—some three times longer than the entire life of *Homo sapiens* on the planet, and a hundred times longer than the existence of the British Isles as an island. And, even then, the Thames was an ancient river.

The first inhabitants survived for half a million years, having arrived at some point between 500,000 BC and 450,000 BC but much is unknown. Of the people themselves, and of their relation to the river, we understand next to nothing. They are what in German are called *geschichtlos*, "people without history." But that is not to say that they were without traditions, stories, songs, ingenuity and enterprise. It is inconceivable, for example, that, over thousands of centuries, they did not learn how to build rafts or coracles—if only to reach the small islands in the middle of the river. The fact that no such boats have survived is meaningless; it is mere good fortune that anything at all from those remote times has been found.

The last major glaciation came to an end approximately twelve thousand years ago, after an ice-bound age of a thousand years. The more temperate climate attracted new settlers, as well as the elk and reindeer for which they hunted. This was the age in which hippos wallowed in Trafalgar Square, and elephants roamed down the Strand. In fact it represents a significant period in the history of the Thames, since from the arrival of Mesolithic settlers in 10,000 BC there has been an unbroken process of occupation and settlement in the Thames Valley.

The new arrivals first crossed by land, before the floods united the North Sea and the Channel. There were many different groups, and tribes of various identities, but the preponderant element beside the Thames was that of the fair-haired Maglemosians or "marsh people" first discovered in north-western Europe. They survived in small settlements perched on the gravel banks of the river, living predominantly by hunting and fishing.

They manufactured fish-hooks, and bark "floats" for their nets. But their signature lay in the manufacture of stone microliths, or small flints used as blades or points for spears. They cut back the birch and the pine to make large clearings, and they domesticated dogs for hunting or defence; the bones of fish and beavers, of pigs and wild-cats, of birds and badgers, have been found in profusion. They had spears and axes made of bone or antler; they were adept in the carving of wood and the stretching of leather. They made their dwellings, for example, by placing animal hide over a wooden cage of birch saplings. The hearth was in the centre of the hut. It is the pattern of the first houses by the Thames.

And they constructed boats, which benefited from advances in the technology of stone tools. The earliest boats of which archaeologists have knowledge were crafted in the Mesolithic period. They were canoes dug out of single tree-trunks; the trunks would have been cut and burnt to the requisite size and depth. One found in the river at Shepperton was some 18 feet (5.4 m) in length, and might have carried three or four people. The adze marks, where the wood had been shaped and fashioned, are still just discernible. Other boats, found on the river-bed of the Thames at Bourne End, were more than 25 feet (7.6 m) in length with a beam of almost 3½ feet (1.05 m). Seats had been carved out of the solid wood. The people may also have constructed coracles, with animal hide stretched over a frame of young willow branches, that were lighter and more manoeuvrable in the shallows. We may assume, then, that the Thames had become a navigable river. It was the beginning of a great change. Once the tribes had realised that the wind could carry them further and faster than their own unaided efforts, they could see further than the limits of their own physical labour. They had begun the slow rise to freedom. We can be sure, also, that the Thames had a powerful symbolic potential. It was an emblem of life and movement. It may be that the whole history of reverence and celebration associated with the river, from the baptisms of the twelfth century to the regattas of the twentieth century, is an atavistic remembrance of these earliest times of occupation.

That spirit of river worship was more carefully formalised by the time of the next settlers, who arrived in the region of the Thames in approximately 3,500 BC. Their age has become known as that of the Neolithic, and covered almost two thousand years of human history. In this relatively short period, however, human beings left an enduring presence upon the landscape of the Thames Valley. They came to areas that had already been extensively settled before them, and seem to have taken up a pattern of farming and woodland clearance. It was the beginning of the farming life that endured, relatively unchanged, until the middle of the nineteenth century. In fact the Neolithic field-patterns of Maidenhead were not finally erased until the 1960s.

The earliest phase of Neolithic occupation in the Thames Valley is marked by steadily changing modes of work and activity. In place of the microlith and the pointed spear are found sickles, polished stone axes and querns. Pottery appears for the first time. Bows were fashioned from the wood of the yew; the arrows were of wood, and tipped with flint. It was the same type of longbow, some 5 feet (1.5 m) in height, that was used by the archers at Agincourt. Its survival over thousands of years is another sign of continuity and sheer force of habit as the prime factors in human existence. We should not assume any sudden emergence of new artefacts but, rather, a slow evolution that would not even have been noticeable at the time of change.

There have been discovered more than eighty Neolithic settlements in the course of the Middle Thames alone, and we can assume that the banks of the river were occupied at various advantageous sites from source to sea. The people lived in huts and congregated in small, perhaps temporary, villages from which the wisps of smoke would have been seen for miles around. They grew crops but, more importantly, they reared stock; they grazed pigs in the woodland, oxen and sheep on the grassland, both of which types of land were plentiful by the river. There is very little evidence of Neolithic dwellings themselves, however, only the remains of postholes or ditches as the tokens of human habitation. There are deposits of flint, of course, and the traces of wheat, barley and beans.

In recent years the piles of a wooden structure have been found beside the river, where Runnymede Bridge now stands, and they have been deciphered as the remnants of a Neolithic wharf on both sides of the bank which was later superseded by a Bronze Age construction. If the interpretation is correct, then the Thames in the Neolithic and in the Bronze Ages was an important highway for transport and commerce. It is significant, too, that the course of the river was approximately that which survives still.

CHAPTER 9

The Sacred Lines

❧

*I*t is difficult to convey the mystery, the otherness, of early humankind. We do not know the purpose of the cursus monuments and causeway enclosures of the Neolithic period, and can only guess at the ritual significance embodied within their shape. The fact that they were placed beside the Thames offers another possible range of meanings. All we can say with any certainty is that these early tribes had a belief in the efficacy of special places, in the enclosure of ground, and in visibility. So they were led ineluctably to the river.

Aerial photography has over the past decades produced ghost images of ancient enclosures close to the Thames, shadow lands of lines and rectangles and circles scarcely visible within the modern terrain. Yet they are there, the sleeping faces of our ancestors still part of the land. Like the giant carvings of the Nazca they are now best seen from the air; but in the beginning they lent power and sacredness to the area in which they had been constructed.

The causewayed enclosures of the Thames region follow a general pattern; they consist of ditches arranged in the broad form of concentric ovals, with spaces or "entrances" between each segment of ditch and with causeways leading in or out of the ceremonial space. Some have only one

ovoid ditch, with an internal bank, but others have several concentric cir-
cuits. The presumption must be that they were altered, and developed, over
the passage of centuries. The ditches contained animal bones, pottery, and
flint in large quantities. More significantly, they also contained human
bones. The dead were buried here.

They may have been the site of regional or tribal gatherings, and may
in some sense have marked out the space or territory claimed by that group.
It is also very likely that they possessed other ritualistic or ceremonial func-
tions. They were not used for permanent human settlement, but for occasional or seasonal purposes. They were not defensive fortifications, like the
hill forts of the Iron Age, but more open and exposed. They could best be
seen by approach from a certain vantage, and so they play their part in the
endless celebration and recognition of the earth itself. The river itself acted
as a boundary, of course, and that limit may have needed to be periodically
and ceremonially confirmed. There are traces of buildings, and of pits
arranged in formal groupings, within certain sites. It is possible that some
of them marked out the temporary residences of an "elite" group of priests
or rulers. But there seems to be no one single meaning to these enclosures;
over the centuries they may have been employed for a variety of purposes.

Of the five aligned by the Thames, the enclosure at Abingdon is perhaps the most important. It employs the river as one of its boundaries, and
is thus in communion with its natural force. If it were periodically flooded,
as is likely, this would increase its sacredness in the eyes of those who visited it. The outer circle of Abingdon shows signs of human activity, while
the inner area seems to have been used for specific rites or ceremonies. At
the core was worship. The defined space might also offer a special form of
protection, blessed by the river. The connection between their ancestors
and the Thames must have been well known through folk myth and oral
memory. The river may even have played some part in the myths of human
origin itself. What could be more natural than for an enclosure to be raised
in close proximity to the ever-running Thames?

By the causewayed enclosure at Abingdon can be found a number of
long oval barrows. These burial mounds were covered in soil and chalk.
They would have gleamed white in the landscape. They have been placed
in alignment with the causewayed enclosure, and also in alignment with the
river itself. In much later generations the metaphor would still be clear, but
we cannot impose the patterns of the modern imagination upon remote ancestors. We can say only that the bodies of the dead were placed in formal

arrangements or positions, which may have been chosen in relation to the current and direction of the river.

There are in fact some twenty-five barrows, of varying types, in close proximity to the river. Their position seems to have been chosen for that particular vantage, and no other, close to the waters. They are generally on the site of previous Mesolithic activity, too, which suggests that the same riverine locations had been in employment for many thousands of years. They may have been the graves of chieftains or of priests, if the distinction existed. Some of them were built in different sections, and at different periods. One of the barrows by Abingdon was built in five stages. From the beginning of the enclosure to the end of the burials, the period of development and change lasts some two thousand years. They were related to the ancestral history of the Thames. The presence of the buried dead, at Abingdon and elsewhere, suggests another possibility. If the dead were crossing between worlds, then they might be associated with the flowing water; the river has special access to the underworld, through myriad passages. In various mythologies the dead travel to their new kingdom by way of a river. We come from, and return to, the water.

The long barrows contained mortuary rooms of stone and wood, and in many cases they were decorated with stone floors and portals; from the medieval period they have been called "sarcen" stones, reputed to have magical qualities. One of the most impressive of them, known to later Saxon settlers as Wayland's Smithy, is in the region of the Upper Thames. But there are others in closer proximity to the river, at Dorchester and at Stanton Harcourt, at Drayton and at Benson. They were ancestral places, where ties of kinship and continuity could be celebrated. The river itself, like stone, withstood time. This is not just a matter of ancient history. It is of cardinal importance in understanding the power of the river in human memory. If we do not understand its past associations, we will not understand the nature of its presence in the contemporary world.

At a slightly later stage of the Neolithic, approximately the period 3,600 to 3,000 BC, other great monuments were erected beside the Thames. The most extraordinary of them has become known as the cursus. It is essentially a human intervention in the landscape, whereby two parallel ditches with internal banks are carved across the earth. Their ends were sometimes enclosed, and sometimes left open; their length varied from 50 feet (15 m) to over 5 miles. The valley of the Thames is the most important setting for the construction of the cursus. There are clusters of them at North Stoke and South Stoke and at Drayton; there are cursus monuments at Stadhampton and at Sonning, at Stanwell and at Goring. All of them are close beside the river. None of them is found on the downs or the Cotswolds. They are, in other words, directly related to the Thames.

There is, for example, a very important cursus complex near the source of the river, at Lechlade and at Buscot Wick; there is also a series of cursus monuments, barrows, long barrows and long enclosures in the area of the river spanned by Abingdon and Dorchester. In both of these areas the archaeologists and palaeo-historians have surmised intense ritual activity over a period of almost two thousand years. The Drayton cursus, aligned close beside the Thames, was first constructed in 3600 BC and was employed for Early Bronze Age barrows around 2000 and 1800 BC. This is a long period of human history, in which the Thames was the centre of ritual or ceremonial observance.

The cursi were constructed on early gravel terraces, or on woodland that had been cleared especially for the purpose. They may have been used for processions, or ritual assemblies, or for races. Deposits of pottery and flint, as well as animal bone, have been discovered in the ditches along the lines of the cursus. But their form is as significant as their purpose. They were built in alignment with the river, which in stretches along the cursus route flowed north to south as well as west to east. The cursus imitates its flow. Between Drayton and Abingdon the cursus is aligned with the main channel of the river, except where the river itself bends around a ridge of sandstone and flows eastward. Its flow and direction are then adopted or imitated by a long barrow that faces eastward and connects with the end of the cursus itself. It is a form of sacred geometry. The sites of the cursi all seem to be connected, one with another, so that the long barrow at Drayton points towards the cursus monuments downriver at Dorchester.

The symbolic destination of the cursus is also related to the confluence of tributary and main river. Some monuments are in fact built beside a tributary, such as the Thame by Dorchester, and seem to "point" towards the mingling of the waters. There are cursus complexes that congregate around the confluence of the river Ock and the river Thames, as well as the rivers Leach and Cole with the Thames. There is also a linear ditch at Lechlade that marks out the confluence of two rivers. People worshipped at the confluence of rivers. It was a place of votive offering.

It seems likely, therefore, that the movement of people or of a few chosen members of the tribe was deliberately fashioned after the movement of the river, so that the participants were identifying themselves with the water or the sources of life. The cursus embodied linear flow. It may indeed have been a representation of the river, a symbol or even drawing of the Thames within the landscape. Just as the ritualised drawings of animals were a way of ensuring a plentiful supply of food, so the cursus may have been considered to be a way of controlling the river. It was in part a performance across the landscape, a form of ritual imitation that could also have been a form of initiation. It was a way of controlling the understanding of the landscape through which it moved. The cursus may also have included some notion of ritual cleansing or purification, so important in later uses of the river.

In one pit within the cursus at Drayton South were found ten human skulls; in another were found the crouched forms of a woman, a child and a baby. The Dorchester cursus itself crosses a mortuary enclosure. The ritual evidence goes very deep. It may be surmised that the riparian landscape was also a funerary or mortuary landscape, and that the river was very closely associated with death. The meaning of *tamasa*—"dark river"—is then clarified for later generations.

So the living and the dead are not necessarily or wholly separated. There is every reason to believe that these ancient people inhabited and used the areas of land in the immediate vicinity of the cursus, and there is evidence of domestic life close beside the banks of the river. There were no doubt also pathways and trackways, for people and for cattle, that run alongside the sacred markings. It is possible that towns (and eventually cities) grew beside the cemeteries of the dead, and that the origin of large-scale human settlement is to be found in the cults of ancestor worship. We may then have some explanation for the earliest towns and settlements by the Thames itself.

In the area of the cursus, at a later date still, were placed what have become known as henge monuments. These were essentially earthworks enclosed by ditches. On first inspection they resemble mortuary enclosures, but the henges simply mark out an area of the terrain generally located between the cursus and the river. This area might then at a later date be characterised by wooden or stone constructions, Stonehenge being of course the most celebrated example. There is a celebrated henge monument at

Stanton Harcourt in the Upper Thames Valley, known as "the Devil's Quoits." The fact that henges exist in the same riverine landscape as the causewayed enclosure and the cursus serves to illustrate one salient point: for many thousands of years the Thames remained a sacred and highly charged area.

CHAPTER 10

The Battle of the Thames

❧

hen Julius Caesar first arrived at the Thames, during his second invasion of 54 BC, he found the forces of the British tribes drawn up along the northern bank. It is the first instance in recorded history of the Thames being used as a defence. Caesar added that "the bank moreover was planted with sharp stakes, and others of the same kind were fixed in the bend of the river, beneath the water." Yet the Roman army prevailed and crossed the Thames. According to one account Caesar sent an elephant across the river to frighten the natives. If true, this was the first appearance of an elephant on the Thames since the Pleistocene era.

Caesar had formidable enemies. By the close of the Bronze Age the land about the Thames was marked out and controlled by specific tribes, united under one leader or family of leaders. These had become the "chiefdoms" of the Iron Age, a name that is taken to span a period of approximately five hundred years from 600 BC to 100 BC. The people of the Iron Age sailed upon the Thames in coracles made out of stretched hide over a frame of young willow branches. These were lighter, and more manoeuvrable in the shallows of the river, and a Roman writer from the sixth century BC, Avienus, described them thus: "they have no art of building ships

with pine and maple, or the tall fir, as is the custom of most men. Instead
they curve the frame—and this is the wonder of it—and with sewn skins
they fit the craft and sail the high seas in a shell of hide." His reference to
the "high seas," if it is not hyperbole, suggests that these early travellers
ventured from the mouth of the Thames into the open water on their way
to the European continent.

The picture is strengthened by the fact that a number of small kingdoms congregated on and about the Thames. We may imagine a group of
military aristocrats who held themselves responsible both for an area of
territory and for the people settled upon it. The British leaders also had
some allegiance or association with the tribal leaders of Gaul. It is even
possible that some of the tribes had come across the Channel. The Catuvellauni settled to the north of the Thames, their land stretching to the
Cherwell in the west; its capital was at Verlamion or (in Latin) Verulamium
near modern St. Albans. Under the leadership of Catuvellaunus this tribe
or group, which may have been no more than a band of warriors under a
chief, was also responsible for the defeat of the Trinovantes who occupied
the area north of the estuary. To the west, beyond the Cherwell, the Catuvellauni were faced by the Dobunni. They had a capital named Bagendon,
near Cirencester. To the south of the Thames were the Atrebates, whose
capital was called Calleva and is now the site of Silchester. Bagendon and
Calleva were linked by a road that crossed the Thames at Cricklade. The
evidence of coinage suggests that chieftains, on both sides of the river, contested relatively small spheres of influence. The evident fact that the river
still acted as a boundary and frontier between the tribes, separating, for example, the Atrebates and the Catuvellauni, could only have augmented its
importance in social and political rituals.

The site of Caesar's first battle of the Thames has been endlessly disputed. It was originally believed to have been close to Shepperton, at a
place known as Coway Stakes; here there were some wooden posts which,
according to the Venerable Bede, writing seven hundred years later, "at this
time remaining, were as big as a man's thigh." The stakes are no longer to
be found, but one of them was deposited in the British Museum with the
description that

> this stake was on 16 October 1777 drawn out of the bottom of the river
> Thames, in which at least five-sixths of its length was embedded; it
> stood with several others which (the water being uncommonly low)

were then easily to be seen. About one third of the river's breadth from
its south bank, a quarter of a mile above Walton Bridge.

It was surmised that these were the original stakes planted by the British
tribe of the Catuvellauni to prevent Caesar and his army from crossing
over to the other shore. There is some evidence in favour of this supposition. A Roman encampment was established just south of the river, by what
is now Walton-upon-Thames, and other Roman objects have been found in
the neighbouring parish of Oatlands. But the evidence of the wooden
stakes may be more prosaic. It has been suggested that they were the piers
of a bridge built by an early abbot of Westminster or the lines of a "swimming way" for cattle.

Other locales along the Thames have also been selected to bear the
privilege, or burden, of expediting Caesar's progress. They have included
Chertsey, Wallingford and Kingston. Brentford has been named, where a
column was placed by the bank to mark the supposed crossing. Chelsea is
another favoured spot. When in the 1850s a bridge was being constructed
there, connecting the Battersea shore with the Chelsea shore, many British
and Roman weapons were found together with human bones. So many
skulls were retrieved that the location became known as "our Celtic
Golgotha."

But the most likely crossing point was at Westminster. The first of the
Roman roads, Watling Street, makes its way from the coast of Kent to
Verulamium some 30 miles north of London; its point of intersection, between north and south, is at Westminster. The tide then stopped at Westminster and the river, flowing south to north along this stretch, spread out
across its own floodplain. There were a number of islands or eyots rising
from the water. The banks were low.

The river was approximately twice the width of that now running
through London and 14 feet (4.2 m) shallower. The river-bank at Southwark, for example, was some 300 feet (91 m) further back than it is now.
The Thames wove in coils, its broad curves moving through a marshy
riverine landscape; on the south side the grass and osier beds were interrupted by creeks and swamps, while on the north side the banks were covered with scrub. The river was replenished by many tributary streams and
rivers that have long since disappeared or vanished underground. At low
tide it moved slowly through banks of clean gravel and sand. Downriver
from Westminster, dotted among the waters, there were numerous islands

that were submerged at high tide. It seems likely that, at times of more favourable climate, the typical round-house dwellings of the Britons were built upon these islands. There were also fluctuations in the river level that can be measured in historical time; throughout the Roman period, for example, the level of the river fell, only to be restored in subsequent centuries. Much of the Roman waterfront is thus irrecoverably lost within the rising waters.

Caesar himself has left a significant account of the raids and fighting during his invasion. The Britons engaged with his forces in sporadic raiding parties, so that "one squadron relieved another and our men, who had been contending against those who were exhausted, suddenly found themselves engaged with a fresh body who had taken their place." He also remarks that his native enemies were "clad with skins: all the Britons stain themselves with woad, which gives a blue colour, and imparts a ferocious aspect in battle." Quantities of woad, or *Isatis tinctoria*, can still be found growing near the Thames.

Some ten years later, in AD 43, another invasion force of the Romans made use of the river. According to the classical historian, Dio Cassius, the British forces were defeated by the Roman legions somewhere along the course of the Medway. After this conflict the remnant of the British forces retreated to a point "where the Thames empties into the ocean and at flood-time forms a lake." The area of "the lake" is now deeply obscured, the Thames having risen approximately 15 feet (4.5 m) since the events here related, but the most likely site seems to be that of Lower Hope Point in the present estuary. The terrain of one of the most important battles in English history is irrecoverable.

Yet the stage was now set for the arrival of the emperor Claudius. He joined the legions that were waiting for him by the Thames and, crossing the river, defeated the British tribes on the northern shore before marching upon the enemy capital of Colchester. He remained in Britain for just sixteen days, but his mastery of the Thames ensured his mastery of the region itself. It was a signal victory that emphasises the central importance of the river in British history. At a later date there seems to have been more resistance further upriver, and there are reports of battles at Cricklade and at Thames Head; but the evidence is meagre. It is true, however, that the progress of Romanisation was always less evident in the upper reaches of the Thames.

So Caesar's invasions were followed by the more settled occupation of

Claudian legions, and within a hundred years there emerged a group of Romano-British farmers living close to the Thames and its tributaries. There were settlements along the river from source to sea—from Cricklade to Tilbury—and there were many villas and extensive estates to the north of the Thames near the Roman towns of Cirencester and Dorchester. It has been estimated that along the length of the Thames there were approximately six hundred villas that may have been owned by Roman veterans, or by prosperous Romanised natives; whatever the forms of ownership and tenure, it was a period of general affluence for the Thames region.

On the muddy foreshore of the Thames by East Tilbury have been discovered the relics of four large Romano-British huts, with walls of wattle and conical tiled roofs; in the immediate vicinity were large quantities of pottery and, since no kiln was found, it has been concluded that this was some kind of warehouse or storage centre for native ware. The huts were also beside a path which seemed once to lead down to a ferry, so this was also a crossing-point. When these basic huts are compared to the villas beside the Thames, complete with bath-houses and underfloor heating, it is possible to imagine a Thames valley society of landowners and serfs. It was a society that would persist, in one form or another, for many hundreds of years. The site of the huts, and the ferry, has now disappeared beneath the mud of the tidal Thames.

And then of course it is assumed that the Romans created London. It is much more likely, however, that there was already some form of British settlement here; one of the possible derivations of London is *Llyn-Din*, the British for "the hill by the pool." But by general agreement the Romans were the first people fully to exploit the natural resources of the area. The original slow and sluggish crossing-point at Westminster was not at all suitable as a port, and so the Romans chose a stretch along the river that was adequately defended, which could provide a harbour, and which was well served by the tides. Romans had a very different vision of the river. It was a line of power, both military and commercial, part of the linear consciousness of the empire. The river had not lost its power of association with the gods—hence the number of Roman relics found within its waters—but it had lost its primaeval sacredness. It was often the case, for example, that Roman roads would run straight through circular barrows and henges as a way of erasing their mythic power. The Romans built the first timber bridge across the Thames in approximately AD 52, with a permanent bridge being constructed at the turn of the first century. In the fourth century London's walls were extended to defend the riverside itself. The nature of the Thames had changed. It needed to be tamed and protected.

The river served its primary commercial function very well since London was described by the Roman historian Tacitus, just eighteen years after the Claudian invasion, as "though undistinguished by the name of a colony, much frequented by a number of merchants and trading vessels." From this early date the fortunes of the city were irretrievably tied to the presence of the tidal river. Like all great cities of ancient lineage, London was the creation of a river. And so a bustling port emerged along what had before been gravel banks and marshy inlets. The area of Southwark was also used for quays and warehouses; as the level of the river dropped, so the Romans were forced to build out further in order to maintain all the facilities of a port.

Some relics of this commerce have been found in the Thames. A flat-bottomed barge was discovered by Blackfriars Bridge in 1962; part of its cargo was a consignment of ragstone to be employed in the building of the Roman city. In 1918 the remains of a Roman cargo ship were found in some excavations by the bank of the river near Westminster Bridge. Such was the excitement that the timbers were carried on an especially built wagon in procession to the Museum of London.

The working life of the ancient city has also been recovered from the Thames, with numerous finds of nails and needles and knives, hairpins and oil-lamps and assorted pottery. From Roman times, too, we can date the beginning of the unhealthiness of the Thames. Wooden sewage pipes running down into the water have been found from a Roman edifice by the bank, at Cannon Street. In the history of the river there is a continuous association between the progress of commerce and the progressive fouling of the waters. Yet of course the Thames was still a major source of food. A manufactory of fish-sauce, or *garum,* in Roman London has provided evidence of the herring, sprat and sand-eel that were taken from the river.

When the Roman legions withdrew from Britain in the early fifth century, there was no sudden collapse of the civilisation that they had helped to create. The natives and the settlers were now, after 350 years, part of the same land. Their families had grown up beside the Thames. And that land was still productive, allowing for self-sufficient agriculture. It is significant that many of the Thames villages still in existence at the beginning of the twenty-first century were first settled before AD 500. These villages are often to be found beside Roman tracks or crossings, and within the vicinity of Romano-British buildings. There was no crisis of survival, and no gap in the historical record. It has been suggested by archaeologists that the larger villas were slowly falling into decay during the course of the fifth century, but the inhabitants of the region would have been more interested in the villas' fields than the villas themselves.

One section of the Thames estuary has always been known as the "Saxon shore." It was once generally believed that it was named after fortifications against Saxon invaders, but it is much more likely to have been called the "Saxon" shore because the Saxons were settled here. The first Saxons from the North Sea coast of Germany may have come to the region peaceably as traders, merchants and eventually as settlers. By the sixth century, one hundred years after the departure of the Romans, the East Saxons had colonised the territory north of the Thames in approximately the area now called Essex. The Middle Saxons inhabited Middlesex while, south of the river, the West Saxons and South Saxons were eventually united in the kingdom of Wessex. Before Wessex was formed there was a loose alliance of tribes or kinship groups in the area of the Upper Thames; they were known as the Gewisse or "the Trusty Ones." These sound very much like military bands or mercenaries, perhaps asserting their lordship over the weaker British settlements in the region.

The river remained an important source of power and of sovereignty. There was a seventh-century palace at Old Windsor, and Kingston was the site for the coronation of no less than seven Saxon kings; the chapel of St. Mary in that town was once considered to be the place of coronation and the seventeenth-century antiquarian, John Aubrey, noticed there portraits of Athelstan, Edred, Edwy, Edward the Martyr and Ethelred. There was another palace of the seventh century close to the river at Sutton Courtenay, and no doubt other great residences remain to be discovered. Religious and military power were not necessarily incompatible, and in 635 the first Bishop of Wessex was granted a Roman fort at Dorchester-on-Thames as the headquarters of his see.

There were Saxon settlements along the entire length of the Thames that survive still. Place names such as Sonning, Reading, Barking and Goring are Anglo-Saxon in origin. Teddington is derived from the name of a tribal leader known as Tudda. Petersham and Twickenham denote the Saxon presence of "hamms," or enclosures that lie in the bend of the river.

The Thames rises in a field known as Trewsbury Mead. It is guarded by an ash tree.
For many centuries this has been a sacred place.

The tooth of a mammoth.

Prehistoric dagger
and scabbard.

The river has always been a treasure
house of objects. Some were lost, some
were deposited for votive purposes, and
others just drifted. Thereby the Thames
has become a vast compendium of history.

Bronze head of the Emperor Hadrian.

St. Christopher and other medieval badges.

The Thames was considered to be sacred, the home of powerful gods to be propitiated. So pilgrim badges were thrown into its depths. And the sacred river was also used as an instrument of condign punishment.

Ducking a scold.

The Royal Recreation of Jovial Anglers

Proving that all men are *Intanglers*,
And all *Professions* are turn'd *Anglers*.

To THE TUNE OF, *Amarillis*. [1663. See vol. vi. p. 113.]

Fishermen have always loved the Thames. They have stood, or sat, upon its banks
for hundreds of thousands of years. For many thousands of years,
too, they have used a rod and line.

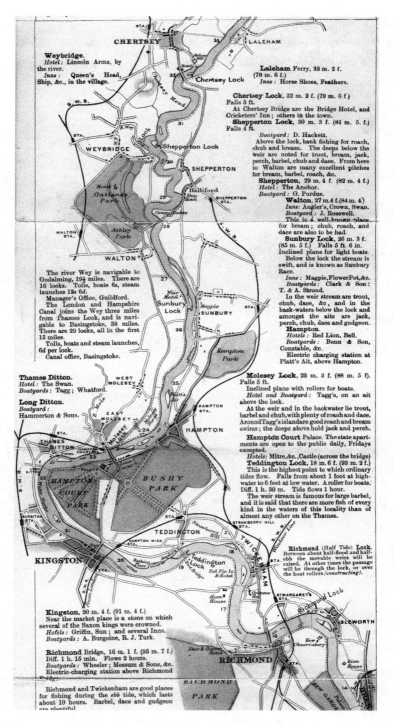

The Oarsman's and Angler's Map of 1893,
with hotels and inns along the route.

Radcot Bridge is the oldest bridge upon the Thames: there is a Saxon charter of
AD 958 referring to its existence. Today it is relegated to a side-channel.

Mills and weirs have always been a significant feature of the Thames world. They have been on the river for so long that there was a medieval saying, "as weary as the water of a weir." Millers and weir-keepers, however, were not always loved by the boatmen: they stopped the flow, and charged for the passage across their waters. Bottom left: eel nets outside London; above: Oxfordshire weir-keeper; below: Mapledurham mill.

London ferry, 1684.

The ferry is the oldest means of passage across the Thames. The ferry from Tilbury to the opposite shore, for example, was in use in prehistoric times. The ferryman himself became a figure of myth.

Cliveden ferry, 1885.

There are Saxon names on the estuary such as Fobbing, Mucking and Thurrock. Kemble is the modern version of the Saxon Camele. Terms such as "weir" and "eyot," still in use, are derived from the Anglo-Saxon. The Saxons seem thoroughly to have appropriated the river, to the extent that it still bears a Saxon identity. The Upper Thames cottages of the late eighteenth century bear a strong resemblance to their Saxon predecessors.

The river also acted as a boundary between Wessex and Mercia, contested and violated for many centuries. The monastery at Cookham, on the bank of the river, changed hands several times. Wessex is known in the *Anglo-Saxon Chronicle* as the kingdom south of the Thames—"*suthan Temese.*" It had been agreed, according to the account in the *Chronicle*, "that henceforth the river should divide their kingdoms, Mercia from Wessex, and that their kinsmen of all generations to come should keep it so." But the continuing if sporadic battles between Wessex and Mercia meant that by 755 "the river was still a trouble and not a joy as lesser rivers are; also are greater rivers a joy sometimes." At a later date a great battle between the two kingdoms was fought at Benson, on the Thames, in which Wessex was forced to withdraw to its old area south of the river.

The river also became an important trade route from the south-eastern part of the country to the central and southern regions. It was a means of communication for otherwise disparate communities. The principal market was of course London itself. In the seventh century the Saxons created Lundenwic, a little to the west of the Roman city, which quickly became an important port with vital trade links to continental Europe. It was primarily a settlement of East Saxons, who maintained a commercial connection with the valleys of the Elbe and the Rhine; the river brought in imports of timber and resin, and took out corn and wool. By the tenth century there are records of the tolls charged at Billingsgate, with vessels paying fourpence for lying at the wharf. Other quays, or hithes, were constructed along the river-bank, most of them in the protection of the wall that had been built to shield London from the invaders of the river.

Then in 893 a great Danish army landed at the estuary, and began a course of plunder towards London. They came with their women and children, and were intending to stay. It was truly an invasion of the Thames. The Danes concentrated on the Thames because they understood that control of the river would result in control of the surrounding country. It also offered a convenient means of access to various enemies scattered in adjacent territories. The Danes could attack both Mercia and Wessex from their river haven. But the river also left them open to counter-attack and in 895, according to the *Chronicle*, "the men of London fetched the Danish ships, and all they could not lead away they broke up, and all that were worthy of capture they brought into the Port of London." There were many attacks in succeeding decades that used the river as their point of entry. In 1010 Thorkell the Tall sailed up the Thames and put Oxford to the flame. Four years later Olaf, king of Norway, sailed up the river and laid cables around the piles of London Bridge; he attached the cables to his ships and, sailing away, pulled the bridge down. It is this incident that lies behind the children's rhyme "London Bridge is falling down."

The Danish king Cnut, or Canute, became the undisputed king of England from 1016 to 1035 precisely because he had gained control of the Thames. But he was aware of the limits of his power. According to a Norman poem he illustrated his inability to control the tides, as a lesson to his courtiers on the futility of earthly rule, not on the Sussex coast but sitting on his throne by the Thames. It was the tidal river at Westminster that provided the salutary example, since it was here that Canute erected his royal palace. "There is but one King," he is supposed to have said. "He whom heaven and earth and sea obey . . ." The Thames had become a great lesson in divine power.

Throughout these centuries of conquest and assimilation, the river played a formative role. According to the monastic chronicler of the sixth century, Gildas, the Thames was always the guardian river or the river of boundaries. It represented border country, the liminal area between two jurisdictions, and so became a significant site for meetings and conferences and negotiations between different parties. It was also employed for religious synods. The same places, such as Kingston and Dorney, would be used intermittently over a number of years and perhaps over a number of centuries. The most famous encounter at Runnymede, when Magna Carta was agreed, may only have been one of many such conferences that employed this sacred or at least elected place.

As a dividing line the river was guarded by spirits—nymphs, goddesses, gods, fairies and demons have all been invoked at different times as its protectors. If you trespassed across a boundary, you were offending the water spirits more than the owner of the adjoining land. But then the Thames has also become the home of saints.

PART V

The Sacred River

Lechlade. The spire can be seen by the Thames traveller for miles

CHAPTER II

Holy River

Thames villager of the 1770s left a confession of murder, after his own death, in which he claimed that "the purifying waters" of the river at Buscot "must slake me of my crime." In one of the Vedic *Puranas* it is declared that "all the rivers are sacred, all flow towards the sea; all are like mothers to the world, all purge away sin." The Thames itself has always been considered holy, an aspect of the peace that passes all understanding.

From the earliest stages of human life rivers themselves have been deemed to be sacred. The ancient Persians considered it blasphemous to pollute them. The Ganges has been treated as a god. Hindus have seen in the icicles of the Himalayan cavern, where the Ganges rises, the flowing hair of the god Shiva. The Abyssinians worshipped the Nile as a divinity. The Egyptians venerated the annual rise of the Nile with burnt offerings, sacrifices and rituals of fire; they saw the river in the form of the god Hapi. The twin rivers of Mesopotamia, the Tigris and the Euphrates, were venerated as the home of dragons; it was a recognition of the fact that the waters could be destructive as well as fruitful. In the cultures of Mesopotamia and the Nile Valley magicians and soothsayers would practise their arts by the rivers. In the Aboriginal cultures of Australasia the "dreamtime tracks" of the ceremonies followed the courses of the rivers. In "The Visions of Zosimos" (1937), Jung declares that "water and spirit are often identical."

The Thessalians worshipped the Peneus river on account of its beauty, the Scythians revered the Danube for its magnitude, the Aetolians venerated the Achelous for its ancientness. It is conjectured that in England the Druids worshipped the rivers that flowed from west to east, one of which is of course the Thames itself. That is why the sixth-century historian of England, Gildas, spoke of the local rivers as "an abomination and destruction to men, and to which the blind people paid divine honour." The later chronicler, Geoffrey of Monmouth, also placed the Thames in the context of sacred events—it was to the river that Brutus, grandson of Aeneas, came to found Troia Nova. An altar dedicated to Jupiter Optimus was found on the banks of the Thames at Little Wittenham, and the ritual carving of a goddess was excavated by Bablock Hythe. Close by the remains of Reading Abbey lies Hallowed Brook.

The spiritual presence of the river has been attested in a number of different ways. Christ has been pictured by the nineteenth-century poet Francis Thompson, in his "In No Strange Land," walking upon the waters "not of Gennesareth, but Thames!" A similar image was employed by the twentieth-century painter, Stanley Spencer, who saw in the river intimations of the Scriptures. In particular he portrayed Christ preaching from a boat moored by the river-bank. This was beside his local village of Cookham, in which place his images are bathed in the light of eternity. In *Salve Deux, Rex Judaeorum* Emilia Lanier, a poet of the sixteenth century, addressed "sweet Cookham, where I first obtained Grace from that Grace where perfect Grace remained." It was for her "the *Paradice* of Cookham." This has been one of the blessed places of the earth. In 1966 a Polish émigré, Alexander Wozniak, proposed to walk on the Thames from Cricklade to London in order to celebrate one thousand years of Christianity in his native country; for this venture he constructed "skinoes," a hybrid of water-skis and canoes, with which he reached Westminster Pier seven days later.

One of the great celebrators of the river, Kenneth Grahame, for a moment abandoned the childlike animal life of the Thames in *The Wind in the Willows* in order to evoke the holiness of the river's presence. In a chapter entitled "The Piper at the Gates of Dawn," he describes how Mole and Rat approach an island in the middle of the river with "solemn expectation." When they land upon this eyot, Rat whispers: "This is the place of my song-dream, the place the music played to me. Here, in this holy place, here if anywhere, surely we shall find Him." He is the ancient deity of the river, the pagan divinity who is part Pan and part Shiva and part Hapi, the quintessential river-god to whom "the two animals, crouching to the earth, bowed their heads and did worship."

Yet there are some who would claim that these gods, and goddesses, are expressions of the natural divinity of water. The river represents the concept of divine intervention in Nature; it is a token of the perfectibility and redemption of the world. It is the oldest of all nature's forces. The holy waters support life and promote fertility as well as destruction. They represent the mystery, as well as the benevolence, of the natural world. In the forty-sixth psalm it is revealed that "there is a river, the streams whereof shall make glad the city of God, the holy place of the tabernacles of the Most High."

Thus the deity of the river adopts a fluid shape. He is Proteus as well as Pan. There are four gilded statues of the Buddha overlooking the river from their prominence in Battersea Park. In 2004 a Hindu shrine was found beside the Thames near Chelsea Bridge, complete with candles and cymbals of brass. Both Sikhs and Hindus are now pursuing a campaign for legislation that would allow them to scatter the ashes of their dead into the river. On the first morning of the Jewish new year a company of Jews used to meet on a quay by the north bank of the Thames, against the Custom House, and offer up prayers in remembrance of their captivity. The ancient river can be seen as an ancestral home for the faiths of all. It is not too fanciful to notice the pulpits built into Blackfriars Bridge; they have been placed there deliberately to remind passers-by of the monastic traditions of the river at this point.

The Knights Templar settled by the Thames; all physical trace of them has now disappeared, but they have left behind the tokens of their presence in the names of Temple Lock, Temple House, Temple Combe and Temple Mills along the river. The original crossing at Marlow, where a bridge now stands, can be attributed to the Knights Templar of Bisham. In Iain Sinclair's fantasy of the Thames, *Downriver* (1991), he compares the fortifications of the Thames Barrier to "helmeted Templars, flashing with signals, arrows, red crosses—warnings." Not for the first time has he intuited the ancient denizens of the river.

Pilgrims crossed the Thames as part of their journey towards salvation or, at least, towards the remission of sin. There was a pilgrim pathway, from Waltham Cross to Canterbury, that traversed the uninhabited marshes of the Isle of Dogs; there was a pilgrim chapel, too, by the river where the devout could pray for a successful crossing. It is shown on an early eighteenth-century map, with nothing beside it but a few windmills. There was another ancient causeway near the parish of Higham, in the estuary, from which the pilgrims of Essex could make their way to Becket's shrine. Other river-crossings for the pilgrims of medieval England are marked by the number of badges or tokens that have been found in deposits along the foreshore.

There is a church on the river-bank at St. Clement's Reach, near West Thurrock, which is still called the Pilgrim Church. It retains a reputation, albeit of a more secular nature. It is one of the churches used in the successful film, *Four Weddings and a Funeral*. The film is apposite in another sense, since river churches have always been a favourite venue for weddings. In the spring and summer months there is a plethora of such ceremonies, with a clear connection to the fertility magic associated with the Thames. It is the custom for the newly married couple to cross the bridge, if one exists, and to be photographed on the bank opposite the church. It is an emblem of crossing between worlds, one of the many rites of passage with which the river is identified.

To be baptised in the river is also to be reborn, to have crossed the threshold into a new life. On the humpbacked stone bridge at Radcot, the oldest on the Thames, there are the remains of a stone font that was employed for the baptismal rite. There is in Cricklade a traditional place beside a small plank bridge, known as Hatchetts Ford or more prosaically Plank Bridge, where full immersion baptisms were still taking place at the beginning of the twentieth century. An extant photograph shows a woman in white being escorted into the middle of the river, while more than a hundred people are congregated upon the bank to watch the ceremony. It was one of the most ancient rituals of the Thames. There were baptisms by the Isle of Sheppey, close to the seventh-century abbey established by Queen Sexburga. In more recent centuries the villages of the Upper Thames have been well known for their strong Baptist congregations, as if some atavistic memory determined their faith. The Baptist chapel at Cote, near Shifford, may be the oldest Protestant foundation in the country since it is associated with Wycliff and his "poore preachers" of the fourteenth century. The Anabaptists met for worship in a house by the river, at Reading, where they were joined by John Bunyan. There are at least three churches dedicated to St. John the Baptist along the course of the river. And there is a painting by Stanley Spencer, *The Baptism*, which shows Christ being baptised by the waters of the Thames.

Hermits have found sanctuary beside the river. There was a medieval hermitage, known as the Swan's Nest, in the riverside area of Wapping; it was inhabited by John Ingram from 1371 to 1380, and by other hermits at a later date. There was a recluse, known as Annora, who lived immured in a cell beside the riverside church of St. Mary in Iffley. There was within living memory a hermit in the woods by the river at Hambleden, known only as "Judgement Jack." The river offers seclusion, and the stilling of human voices.

Nymphs have always been part of the life of the Thames. There are still memorials of them everywhere. By an old riverside path in Twickenham, just past Eel Pie Island, there are stone images of seven nymphs lying upon some rocks. In the pediment of Somerset House by the river reclines a nymph, brandishing a trident. In his paean to the Thames in *Windsor Forest* (1713) Alexander Pope declares to the river that

> Nor all his stars a brighter lustre show,
> Than the fair nymphs that gild thy shore below.

The nymph was popularly believed to be a healer and a guide to travellers, a caretaker of youth and a source of knowledge. She embodied the natural magic of the river. Of all the local deities, the nymph was the one most revered. In the classical world, for example, almost every spring or fountain had a small altar or shrine. The nymphs were powerful and benevolent spirits, able to diffuse wealth and fertility over the riverine regions that they occupied.

In the sixteenth century John Dickenson, in *Arisbas, Euphues amidst his slumbers* (1594), celebrated "lovely Thamesis, fairest of fair Nereides . . . the faire Nymphs keeping tyme with the billowing of her Chrystall waves, carrying to the Ocean with her ebbe." When Elizabeth I or James I went on royal progress through the riparian counties, the sovereign was generally presented with a masque of the nymph "of the place." It was a way of expressing the particular quality and nature of the area, haunted by water and by springs. It was also a way of honouring native goddesses, deities more ancient than the classical divinities of European Renaissance pageants, a way of maintaining the most ancient traditions of the river.

In 1660 the Lord Mayor's Show along the Thames contained "four virgins cloathed in white loose garments, and their brows circled with sage, representing the nymphs that frequent rivers." It was an enduring popular superstition that did not really fade until the middle of the nineteenth century. But, as T. S. Eliot lamented in *The Waste Land* (1922), "the nymphs are departed." It is the mark of a great transition in which the natural religion of the world has been abandoned.

There were many rituals concerned with the river. In the tenth century the monks of Abingdon put a sheaf of corn and a lighted taper on the boss of a shield; then they launched the shield into the Thames, where it was supposed to trace the contours of disputed land. At Eton, by the river, a group of German travellers were surprised in 1598 by country folk parading a sheaf crowned with flowers. In that same century, on 1 May, the scholars of Oxford assembled by a bridge over the river and chanted a Latin hymn in honour of Mary; whereupon a lamb was roasted and fed to the assembled crowd. In the parish of Cumner, in a ceremony known as the "perambulation circuit," the sum of 6 shillings and 8 pence was brought to the local vicar by the Thames ferryman. He carried the money in a basin of river water, with a clean napkin, and after the vicar had fished for the coins and dried his fingers, he distributed the shillings and pence to the young people who came within his reach. The origin of this custom is quite obscure, although the association of the ferryman with death is an old one. The habit of rinsing hands in river water was replicated by the villagers along the Rhine, who on St. John's Day watched women washing their arms and hands in that river so that, according to the Italian poet Petrarch, "the threatening calamities of the coming year might be washed away." In Rogation week the same villagers of Cumner on the Thames used to cross in the ferry to the other side, and there lay hold upon the twigs and reeds that grew by the bank. This may be some ceremony of possession, as in the beating of the bounds, but it is also intimately linked to the veneration of the *genius loci*.

A similar rite of possession was conducted around "London Stone." This is not the stone now deposited in Cannon Street as the guardian spirit of London, but that established just upriver from the bridge at Staines. It marked the upper limit of the jurisdiction of the City of London over the waters of the Thames, and was first erected in 1280. The ceremony here included a ritual walk around the Stone, and the characteristic scattering of coin to the crowd, but in homage to the egalitarian temper of the Thames the watermen were supposed to "bump" any sheriffs or aldermen who attended the ceremony. There is now a replica of the Stone, hidden by trees upon the northern bank.

The custom of soothsayers and conjurors congregating by the side of the Thames is continued, in attenuated form, by the practice of hydromancy. The eye of the earth is water. If we meditate upon the image in flowing water, we contemplate the future and the past of that image in continual motion. That is one of the reasons why the Thames has been used for divination. There was, for example, the custom of throwing three pebbles into the water and observing the passages of the ripples that spread from them. The number of these circles, and whether they were even or odd, was also deemed to be of importance. The agitation of the water was considered significant in various other rituals. There were adepts who divined messages within the colours of the river from stormy grey to benevolent green. It was important for the adept to remain calm and peaceful; otherwise the vision might be broken. This is also the state of mind needed for water-gazing, which is perhaps just another word for day-dreaming. This is the technique of gazing into the water, or into the stray shimmerings and sudden gleamings of the sun upon its surface, in order to experience scenes or images rising from the depths.

In 2001 some candles and a sheet of paper were found by the banks of the Thames; the name of a man was written upon the paper three times, and inscribed upon the candles. The man was located, and confirmed that these were the remnants of a prayer service designed to protect him from harm. The present author has found on the river wall by Erith the following objects laid out in ritual fashion—a knife with a blue handle, with blood on the blade, a white T-shirt with bloodstains upon it, and a roll of Sellotape.

There are many river omens and superstitions. A coin thrown from the ferry at Bablock Hythe was supposed to return sevenfold to its owner. It was considered to be a very bad omen when a snake was seen swimming in the river. The villagers by the Thames would get out of their boats if a snake swam in front of them. The mariners and fishermen of the Thames had superstitions different from those of the land. A black cat upon a ship was deemed to be the omen of a storm. The spotting of a hare near the boat was enough to call off a coming voyage. Fishermen also refused to carry white stones among their ballast, and a holed stone signified a holed net. If a monk-fish was caught it was nailed to the mast as a means of averting misfortune. This may relate to the superstition that a priest, or monk, should never be allowed on board a Thames vessel. Until quite recent times the backbone and skeleton of the herring were thrown back into the river after the flesh had been eaten as a tribute to King Herring.

One of the most familiar superstitions connected to the Thames, however, was also one of the oldest. Loaves were pitched into the water as a tribute to the local water-goddess; if they sank she had accepted them and would renew her blessings but, if they continued to float, the offerings had been rejected. There is a variant of this ancient practice in water scrying. The person must go to the river-bank with a question, and fling in a piece of bread. If the bread sinks, the answer is in the affirmative; if it floats, the answer is a negative. The same practice has been undertaken with the use of sticks, where their direction in the water conveys their answer. This primitive tradition may be the forerunner of "Pooh sticks," explained in A. A. Milne's account of river life and still played from the many bridges of the river.

CHAPTER 12

Saints of the River

*S*t. *Birinus has long been venerated* as the first and principal saint of
the Thames. In the seventh century he converted the first Saxons
to Christianity by baptising them in the river at places such as
Somerford Keynes, Taplow, Ewen, Poole Keynes and Kemble. He baptised
King Cynegils of Wessex in the Thames at Dorchester; in the same stretch
of river, in the following year, he baptised the king's son. The river had become his fountain of grace. In the early seventh century he is supposed to
have established a church by the river at Hurley, on a previously pagan site
of worship, as well as the church of the Holy Trinity at Cookham. The
graveyard of this church is the scene for Stanley Spencer's painting of the
final resurrection of the dead, completed in 1926. Bapsey Pool at Taplow,
associated with the baptismal ministry of Birinus, is still to be found in the
grounds of Taplow Court. As a missionary bishop he established his see by
the Thames at Dorchester; he is buried in the abbey there, and his shrine became a place of pilgrimage in the Middle Ages. The shrine still survives in
the church, to be visited by modern Thames pilgrims.

St. Alphege is the patron saint of Greenwich. He was Archbishop of
Canterbury at the beginning of the eleventh century, when he was ab-
ducted from the cathedral there by a detachment of Danish invaders and

taken to their court by the river at Greenwich. Here he was murdered by his captors, beaten to death with the bones of oxen, and the present church of St. Alphege was erected by Nicholas Hawksmoor on the site of his martyrdom. There is every reason to suppose that shrines have been placed on this spot ever since his death in 1012.

St. Alban parted the waters of the Thames in front of the blasphemers who murdered him. On his way to execution, on 20 June 304, he was obliged to cross the river. "There," according to the Venerable Bede,

> he saw a multitude of both sexes, and of every age and rank, assembled to attend the blessed confessor and martyr; and these so crowded the bridge, that he could not pass over that evening. Then St. Alban, urged by an ardent desire to accomplish his martyrdom, drew near to the stream, and the channel was dried up, making a way for him to pass over.

In his sixth-century chronicle, *De Excidio Britanniae*, Gildas reported that "with one thousand others, he [Alban] opened a path across the noble river Thames, whose waters stood abrupt like precipices on either side." As a result of fervent prayer "he opened up an unknown route across the channel." Gildas's analogy here is with the river Jordan in the Holy Land.

St. Chad is supposed to have given his name to Chadwell St. Mary on the Thames estuary, in the seventh century, and there is a well here in which he is believed to have baptised the East Saxons to the Christian faith. St. Erkenwald founded the abbeys of Barking and of Chertsey in the seventh century, and so can be considered a tutelary spirit of the Thames. And then there is St. Edmund, born by the river in Abingdon, who was one day wandering in the water-meadows beside the Thames when he was vouchsafed a vision. According to Caxton's *Golden Legend* (1483), "sodeynlye there apperyd tofore hym a fayr chylde in whyte clothynge which sayd, 'Hayle, felowe that goest alone.' " But he is perhaps not so much a saint of the river as the saint of solitary walkers, who find by the moving water peace or solace and quiet dreaming.

There have of course been many female saints intimately associated with the river. St. Frideswide is perhaps the most celebrated. In the late seventh century she fled to the Thames with her two sisters in order to escape the advances of Algar, an Anglo-Saxon prince, and on the Thames near Oxford they found a youth of heavenly appearance, clothed in dazzling white, who seated them in a boat, and within an hour landed them 10 miles downstream at Abingdon. At Abingdon Frideswide performed a miracle and, her presence being known, she sailed upstream to Binsey where she erected a chapel constructed of "wallyns and rough-hewn timber" by the Thames. Here through the medium of prayer she found a stream of water that, in succeeding generations, became a healing well. Hers could be the tale of a river nymph, fleeing from sexual pollution and in the process rendering the water of the Thames sacred. But her principal connection is with Oxford, of which city she remains the divine patroness. She established a monastery in that place which was at a later date transmogrified by Cardinal Wolsey into Christ Church College. She died at Binsey in AD 740, and her shrine is still to be seen in the cathedral of Christ Church. Her most celebrated maxim, according to legend, is that "whatever is not God, is nothing." That part of the Kentish bank known as the Hoo was under the special care and protection of St. Werburgh, daughter of Wulphere, king of Mercia; little is known of this blessed lady except for the fact that she had an aversion to geese.

The abbey at Reading once contained a sacred relic, believed to be the hand of James the Apostle. The bones of a human hand were in fact found in the ruins of the abbey, in the late eighteenth century, and somehow or other they migrated to another church by the river, St. Peter's in Marlow. The Thames has always attracted votive objects. It is suggestive to note, however, that the skeletal cadaver of St. James, buried in the cathedral of Santiago di Compostella, lacks its left hand. At the priory of Caversham, too, many relics were venerated—among them the spearhead that pierced the side of Jesus upon the Cross.

With this litany of attendant saints and relics it is not at all surprising that the Thames is a river of churches. Their history often begins with the wooden constructions of Saxon origin, but almost all of the churches in the Thames Valley had taken their present form by the eleventh century. It represents a remarkable story of continuity. There are some very ancient foundations indeed, still manifest in the long and narrow churches by the river. The presence of the Thames is always sensed within them, if for no other reason than that many of them are built as close to the river as the stonemasons and labourers could possibly manage. The churches of Castle Eaton and Kempsford, near the source of the river, are almost in the waters. The church of St. Mary Magdalene at Boveney, meaning "the place above the island," is so close to the river that it can only be reached by a footpath; it was said originally to have been a chapel upon a wharf. It is now being sponsored by "the friends of friendless churches."

The church of All Saints at Bisham stands upon the river-bank. The church of St. Mary the Virgin stands beside the bridge at Henley, raised upon an embankment so that it can look over the waters. The church of St. Peter, at Caversham, is similarly built upon a steep bank beside the river. The churches of Streatley and Goring face each other across the Thames.

There is some deep connection between worship and the crossing of the water. The church of All Saints at Marlow, built upon a site dating back to at least the twelfth century, is beside the bridge there. The church of St. Leonard at Wallingford is close beside the river and the bridge. The church of St. Mary at Hurley was sited by an important ford, recorded as early as the seventh century. It is likely, however, that there was a significant crossing here in prehistoric times. The church of St. Andrew in Sonning stands beside a bridge. The riverside village of Sonning itself was also the site for the palace of the bishops of Salisbury, dating back to the tenth century; once again the association between the Thames and religious power is maintained.

To visit these churches now is to be made aware of solemnity and old time; there is a palpable stillness within them, a perpetual harbouring of worship. In many of them are the relics of very different styles, from the ninth to the nineteenth centuries, and this heterogeneity of periods is typical of the Thames churches. It is a place where time itself is mingled and confused. From a certain vantage, in the meadows outside Lechlade, the spire of the church of St. Lawrence seems in fact to rise from the water and become an expression of it.

CHAPTER 13

Hail Holy River, Mother of Grace

❧

There is a church of St. Mary the Virgin at Whitchurch-on-Thames. There is a church of St. Mary in Reading, founded by St. Birinus in the early years of the seventh century. In Wargrave there is a church of St. Mary, also of great antiquity. There is an ancient church of St. Mary in Cricklade; on its north wall was a half-length fresco of the Virgin and Child. The original dedication of the church of St. Lawrence in Lechlade was to St. Mary. The church of St. Mary the Virgin at Castle Eaton had a fresco of the Virgin. The most perfect Norman church in the country is that of St. Mary the Virgin perched above the river at Iffley. The parish church of Putney is dedicated to St. Mary the Virgin, as is the church at Bampton. The church of St. Mary the Virgin at Long Wittenham is erected at one end of the village. Among the warehouses of Rotherhithe, beside the Thames, still stands the church of St. Mary the Virgin.

The church in the market place at Wallingford is known as St. Mary-the-More, in distinction to the one of St. Mary-the-Less that was united with St. Peter in the fourteenth century. The ancient church of St. Mary at Eisey, or "island in the river," was built on the summit of the hill; it was demolished in the last century for absence of worshippers. There was on the island of Sheppey, at the mouth of the Thames, an abbey dedicated to the Blessed Virgin; the abbey church of the Blessed Virgin Mary still stands there, at the highest point of the island. The church of St. Mary at Cholsey, or "Ceol's island," was originally built upon a dry place in a marshy area. There may have been some sanctity associated with these refuges from the river. In the centre of the island still known as the Isle of Dogs there was formerly a small chapel dedicated to St. Mary, founded for the purpose of offering up masses for the souls of mariners. It has long gone. London's church of St. Mary at Hill was named because of its position on a steep bank above Billingsgate. St. Mary le Strand stands on an eminence where the Strand and Fleet Street now meet. The river was of course much closer to it, at the time of its erection, than it is now in its present embanked state.

John Stow records that on the marshy bank, opposite Greenwich, stood "the remains of a chapel built of stone" that had been dedicated to St. Mary; it seems to have been connected with the monastery of St. Mary of Graces that had stood near the Tower of London. At Kempsford, Horns Cross, Gravesend, Benfleet, Corringham, Datchet, Hambleden and Teddington are parish churches dedicated to St. Mary. The church of St. Mary at Sunbury lies on the site of a prehistoric settlement. The church of St. Mary the Virgin at Purley is close to that point on the river where a ferry once crossed to Mapledurham. The church of St. Mary at Streatley is also beside the river, as is the church of St. Mary at North Stoke. The ferry that ran between Cookham and Cliveden was known as "My Lady Ferry." The university church of Oxford in the High Street is also that of St. Mary the Virgin. The parish church of Mortlake is dedicated to St. Mary, as are those of Hampton and of Barnes and of Twickenham, of Walton-upon-Thames and of Thame.

There is some dispute whether the parish church of Langford, near Kelmscott, is dedicated to St. Mary or St. Matthew but, as Fred Thacker wrote in *The Stripling Thames*, Mary "was certainly a very favourite dedication amongst these churches." The church of Abingdon Abbey was originally dedicated to St. Mary the Virgin, but in the fifteenth century it was rededicated to All Saints. The church of North Stifford is named in honour of the Virgin. So is the church at Chadwell. These are little-known places, but they are part of a broad sweep of faith. The church of St. Mary at Buscot is beside the river, and contains stained-glass windows designed by Ed-

ward Burne-Jones. The little church by the river at Inglesham has a carving of the Virgin and Child, dated to the early eleventh century, on its
south wall; the sculpted forms are taken from a Byzantine model. St. Mary's
at Staines is erected upon the site of a seventh-century church. The church
of Lambeth is dedicated to St. Mary. A little further along the river, at Battersea, also stands the church of St. Mary.

The abbey at Eynsham, of which now only a few stones remain, was
named in honour of the Virgin. The monastery at Hurley was dedicated to
the Virgin, and was known as Lady Place. Grace's Alley, by Wellclose
Square in the East End, is the only memorial to the Cistercian Abbey of St.
Mary of Graces that stood by the river. The nunnery at Godstow was dedicated "in honour of the Virgin Mary and St. John the Baptist." The priory
at Bisham was dedicated to Mary. The Bridgettine abbey at Syon was dedicated to the Virgin as well as to St. Bridget herself. Eton School, beside the
river, was founded in the fifteenth century as "the College of the Blessed
Mary of Eton, beside Windsor." The cathedral of Southwark was originally known as St. Mary Overie, or St. Mary over the river.

From the downstream parapet of the bridge at Radcot a niche still
projects; it once supported an image of the Virgin that was destroyed during the Civil War. One arch of the medieval London Bridge was known as
"Mary Lock." In the same period the records refer to "the Ymage of our
Lady on the Brydge" and in the church beside the bridge, St. Magnus, a
perpetual chantry was set up in honour of the Virgin where "Salve Regina"
was sung every evening.

The ancient abbey at Barking harboured "the Lady Chapel of Berkyn-
gechirche in London" which became the destination of Marian pilgrims; a
statue of the Virgin here was reputed to possess miraculous powers. At
Caversham there stands Our Lady of Caversham chapel, the only relic of
a great shrine to the Virgin where was erected a jewel-encrusted image of
Mary, again supposed to contain sacred powers, to which pilgrims travelled
from all over the country. When Doctor London, an agent of the Crown,
came to this holy place at the time of dissolution he reported in apparent
disgust that "even at my being ther com in nott so few as a dosyn with ima-
gies of waxe."

When the Saxon kings were crowned at Kingston, the ceremony was
conducted in the chapel of St. Mary; it was in this chapel that John Aubrey,
in his *Antiquities of the County of Surrey* (1718), recorded the presence

of five pictures of the Saxon monarchs. In the grounds of Culham Court, by the river, is a copy of Elizabeth Frink's statue known as "Striding Madonna."

This litany of names and places suggests that there is more than coincidence at work in the association of the Virgin and the Thames. From the churches of the Upper Thames to the churches of the estuary, the dedication to St. Mary far surpasses all others. It might in fact be claimed that the Thames is Mary's river. From the seventh to the fourteenth centuries, the churches in her name sprang up on both banks of the river from the source to the sea. There are more than fifty churches, chapels and chantries devoted to the Mother of God, an astonishing number for a river that extends for only 215 miles.

The connection has not been noticed in books upon the Thames, but it is one of deep significance in the history of a river that has always been associated with the "great mother" of primaeval beliefs that predate those of Celtic myth. There are strange laws of association at work here. In Irish myth Bridget was the goddess of fertility—and also the Swan Goddess—and according to Robert Graves in *The White Goddess* (1948) "in medieval Irish poetry Mary was equally plainly identified with Brigit." The great goddesses of the river in ancient and classical myth, Isis in particular, are thus associated with the Virgin Queen and Mother of God. Isis herself was once the Mother Goddess, the emblem of fertility and the womb of rebirth. It is not a great leap of faith from Isis to the Virgin. There is a strange reference in William Harrison's *The Description of Britaine* (1587) to the church of St. Mary in Reading when he refers to those natives "which call the aforesaid church by the name of S. Marie Auderies, or S. Marie ouer Isis, or Ise." The names become conflated, and substituted. Mary is simply the latest, and perhaps the most powerful, of all the water goddesses. The river was in legend and superstition also associated with the virgin. Virgins would bathe in the Thames so that they might become fertile. It is one of the oldest myths of the river. So who better to bless the water than the Virgin herself?

CHAPTER 14

The Ruins

❧

The Normans, like all previous invaders, understood the benevolent aspects of the river. They had come upon what was essentially a civilised and stable society in the Thames region, in many ways in advance of their own culture, and they did not attempt to alter it in any significant fashion. It can in fact be claimed that the region civilised its new inhabitants. The parish boundaries, and the county boundaries, were preserved. The hamlets and villages by the Thames remained intact, albeit under new lordship; they maintained a pattern of settlement that had persisted for more than a thousand years and perhaps for much longer. Many of the Norman, and later medieval, churches were built on Saxon foundations. There were occasional changes of name, in villages with a French accent such as Kingston Blount and Compton Beauchamp, but the ancient nomenclature was in general respected.

But the Normans did in part alter the appearance of the river. They built palaces, and castles, and fortresses beside it. They built the Tower of London as a solemn token of the king's strength over the adjacent city; in its original state it was essentially the White Tower, *La Blaunche Tour*, made of Caen stone sailed up the Thames from Normandy. They built Baynard's Castle, or Castle Baynard, on the banks of the river near the present Blackfriars. They constructed the castle of Windsor, on a high knoll of chalk, as another example of military pre-eminence. It was here, in 1070, that William I celebrated Christmas. He also laid out hunting grounds in the vicinity, and enforested many other stretches along the Thames.

It can hardly be claimed that the Normans inaugurated the passion for building royal palaces beside the river. In the eighth century Offa had built a palace near the church at Benson, and there was a Saxon palace at Ewelme described by Leland; there was also a Saxon palace in Kempsford. Canute had built at Westminster, and there had been a hall in the place now known as Old Windsor. It can be said, however, that the Normans were the first fully to exploit the connection of the river with royal power. They essentially created the sovereign's river from the Tower to Windsor. The charter of William I declares that Windsor came into the possession of the king "because that place seems commodious for the King, by reason of the nearness of the river, and the forest for hunting, and many other conveniences; being likewise a place fit for the King's Retirement."

These "conveniences" may in part help to explain the ubiquity of royal palaces by the river. From the eleventh to the sixteenth centuries, there were built six others below Windsor. They were Hampton Court and Richmond, Greenwich and Whitehall; there was a royal palace at Bermondsey, erected by Edward III in the middle of the fourteenth century, of which a few stones remain. And then of course there is the Tower of London itself. It can be said, in general, that the towns along the river were designed principally as strongholds or as defensive settlements. Oxford is essentially an island fortress. Windsor Castle itself is set upon an ancient mound that may have been the site of very early fortifications. Cricklade and Lechlade are protected by the Churn and the Leach as well as by the Thames. Wallingford is protected by marsh as well as water. That is why mints were set up in Wallingford, Oxford and Cricklade. They were well known to be secure places. The ancient name for Wallingford was Gallena (Guallenford), from the British words *guall hen* meaning "old fortification." It is not possible to re-create the exact conditions of the earliest warfare, but the heavy settlement along the Thames would suggest that the river itself has always been of paramount importance in time of conflict.

The earthworks at Sinodun, the permanent garrisons along the river associated with the British chieftain Ambrosius, the armed camp on the isle of Sheppey, the Viking encampment at Fulham, the battle at Kempsford between Ethelmund of the Hwiccas and Woxtan of Wiltshire in the early ninth century, the siege of the Tower of London by the Yorkists in 1460, all tell the same story. The conflict between Stephen and Matilda, in the earlier part of the twelfth century, was in part a contest of ownership of the castles along the Thames. The river is the vital link to London and prosperity.

That is why other notables have flocked to the river, among them the secular and ecclesiastical leaders of the country. The Strand, between the City and Westminster, was lined with palaces. York House, Winchester House and Durham House—the residences of the Bishop of York, the Bishop of Winchester and the Bishop of Durham respectively—were built on the banks of the Thames. Lambeth Palace, built as a residence for the Archbishop of Canterbury in 1200, is less than a mile upstream on the opposite bank. As late as 1657, when the Tudor magnificence of the Thames had departed, James Howell remarked in *Londinopolis* upon "the stately palaces that are built on both sides of her banks so thick, which made divers foreign ambassadors to affirm, that the most glorious sight in the World (take water and land together) was to come upon a high Tide from Gravesend, and shoot the Bridge to Westminster." At a slightly earlier date Michael Drayton celebrated the Strand—meaning literally the stretch of land that runs along the river—as expressing "the wealth and bravery of the land."

It is such a familiar pattern of residence that it generally goes unremarked. But why should the leaders of the land wish to live in close proximity to the Thames? Precisely because from the very earliest times it has been the site of power. Notable people have lived by the river as a matter of instinct and of custom. Spiritual leaders, in particular, seem to have claimed the river as their proper home. The same pattern persists in later centuries. The Houses of Parliament are built by the river, despite the risks of riverine attack. County Hall is on the south bank of the Thames, as is the present headquarters of the Greater London Authority. The major public buildings of the city seem naturally to find their place beside the Thames.

There was one other notable contribution by the Normans, and their medieval successors, to the life of the Thames. It lies in the expansion of religious communities by the river. They have all now disappeared, or lie in ruins, but in earlier centuries they were a great presence by the Thames; they included the monastic and conventual establishments of Godstow,

Bisham and Medmenham; the abbeys of Abingdon and Reading and Dorchester, Eynsham, Rewley and Osney, Streatley and Chertsey and Cholsey; the priories of Cricklade and Lechlade; the nunneries of Burnham and Little Marlow.

Certain of them had existed as early as the seventh century, in particular the Benedictine monasteries of Westminster, Chertsey and Abingdon. These establishments were in large part the civilising force within the Thames Valley; with their skill in estate management, their commitment to scholarship, and their connection to the sources of continental learning, the Benedictine monks did more than anyone else to enlighten the early years of Saxon rule by the river. In *The Historic Thames* Hilaire Belloc goes so far as to state that the new country that emerged in the course of the Saxon era "was actually created by the Benedictine monks."

There is of course the historic foundation of Westminster Abbey, which can be dated to the beginning of the seventh century when the first Christian king of the East Saxons, Sebert, patronised a Benedictine monastery here. His tomb now rests in the abbey. The early monastery was erected upon a triangular patch of waste ground known appropriately as "Thorney Island"; this island of shingle and marsh and thorns was bounded by the Thames and by two small streams that issued into the river. It was an unpromising spot, but the black-cowled monks were known for their skill in turning waste and wilderness into flourishing land. The later history of the abbey is better known, with the work of Edward the Confessor in 1050 and the rebuilding of the church by Henry III in the thirteenth century. It has remained a sacred place ever since, a river shrine where all the monarchs of England (with the exception of Edward V and Edward VIII) have been crowned. The area may already have been sacred by tradition, since London antiquarians have suggested that on this island was once a pagan shrine to Apollo. In an eighth-century charter it was described as the "terrible place," the adjective here meaning sacred terror or holy terror. Such places seem to spring up naturally by the river.

In the building of Westminster Abbey the Thames was associated with supernatural visitation. A legend recounts the appearance of St. Peter on the south bank of the river, at Lambeth, from where he asked a fisherman to row him over to Thorney Island. There, with his own hands, Peter performed the ceremony of consecration. At the time of Edward the Confessor, a monk of Westminster was vouchsafed a vision in which the apostle commanded the monarch to restore the abbey church in the place "which I chose and loved . . . honoured with my presence, and made illustrious by my miracles." This church by the river became the hallowed sanctuary of such relics as blood from Christ's side and milk from the Virgin Mary, a beam from the holy manger and a fragment of the true cross. It also became the sepulchral church of England, a vast mortuarium by the side of the river in the spirit of the prehistoric burial sites that have been excavated in recent years.

The origins of the Benedictine monasteries of Chertsey and Abingdon are also surrounded by legends and stories of supernatural intervention, but their immediate and intimate connection with the river is better attested. Both of these foundations were established upon marshy or swampy ground, but both commanded a superior position on the Thames itself. The monastery at Abingdon, for example, was erected a mile downstream from an ancient ford. The monks eventually diverted the course of the river so that it flowed beside their walls; at a later date they bridged the river at two points, and built a causeway to link the two bridges. They were adept at exploiting the possibilities of the river, which is one reason why they originally chose the setting of the Thames. The monastery was also the gateway to the fertile valley that is still known as the Vale of the White Horse.

The consolidation and expansion of the religious foundations of the Thames Valley really began after the Conquest. The abbeys of Westminster, Chertsey and Abingdon were enlarged and reinforced; they were then joined by a sequence of abbeys that grew up along the course of the river. From the mother house of Cluny, in Burgundy, came the establishment of Reading Abbey, of Bermondsey Abbey, and of Osney Abbey. Then there were the abbeys of Eynsham and Rewley, the priories of Lechlade and Cricklade, the abbey and monastery of Dorchester, the Charterhouse at Sheen, the little nunneries of Ankerwycke, Burnham, Littlemore, Goring and Little Marlow, the foundations of Medmenham and Bisham and Cholsey. These are only a selection of the religious communities that sprang up by the Thames, claiming it as their natural territory.

The religious Orders possessed most of the land beside the Thames. It has been estimated that the eight largest religious houses owned between them the manors of Shifford, Eynsham, South Stoke, Radley, Cumnor, Witham, Botley, the Hinkseys, Sandford, Shillingford, Swinford, Medmenham, Appleford, Sutton, Wittenham, Culham, Abingdon, Goring, Cowley, Littlemore, Cholsey, Nuneham, Wallingford, Pangbourne, Streatley, and Stanton Harcourt. These are the names of the upper river, comprising almost its whole length. Closer to London the religious Orders administered and farmed Sonning, Wargrave, Tilehurst, Chertsey, Egham, Cobham, Richmond, Ham, Mortlake, Syon, Sheen, Kew, Chiswick, and Staines. This is of course not to mention their extensive possessions along the banks of the Thames in London itself, nor their possessions within Oxford. They seem almost to be an emanation or extension of the Thames, a spiritual body that rested upon the river.

They became the centre of organised life and of industry; the great abbeys built the bridges that can still be seen across the river, and they supervised the agricultural life of the communities in which they were established. The Benedictines were well known for their agricultural expertise, for example, particularly in cutting back forests and in reclaiming marshes for arable land. These skills were all the more necessary beside the banks of the Thames. They were also the recipients of rich donations and bequests from all over the country, and indeed became the largest landowners in the kingdom. They were in every sense the centre of the life of the Thames. They established the local prosperity of the region and, if the Thames Valley is still one of the principal areas where the economic and technological wealth of the country is situated, it is in some part owing to the efforts of the religious Orders six or seven centuries ago. There was a habit of residence by the banks of the Thames long before the monastic Orders arrived there, but the great foundations materially assisted the process of settlement and cultivation.

We can also provide a working model of an abbey's relationship with the river. The water first pours into the corn mill and then, after moving the wheels that grind the grain, it is diverted into the next building where it flows into the boiler that is heated to prepare the beer for the monks' drinking; it is then drawn into the fulling machines for the shrinking and cleaning of cloth, where it raises and lowers the heavy hammers and mallets employed therein. Then it enters the tannery of the abbey. Other branches and diversions of the river are also used in cooking, watering and washing. Finally, at the close of its labours, it carries away the refuse and scours all clean. The Thames was the Proteus of the working world.

The abbeys were also the centre of national education. One of the abbots of Abingdon was the most celebrated historian of early England, Geoffrey of Monmouth, and in that abbey one of the sons of William the Conqueror was instructed. There are apocryphal reports of Saxon "colleges" being established at Lechlade and Cricklade, near the source of the Thames, but another riverine foundation has a more authentic history. The monastery of St. Frideswide at Oxford was the predecessor of, and direct inspiration for, the university itself. The earliest years of that institution cannot now be recovered, but by the ninth century it had become a centre for learning. Among the earliest to endow it was King Alfred himself, the patron of English scholarship, and Oxford became known as "the fountain whence issued many learned clerks." The king may be said to have restored or re-established it, because there are reports that his nominees as teachers—Grymbald and John the Monk—had to contest for supremacy with "the old students" of the place. By the end of the eleventh century Theobald of Etampes was describing himself as *Magister Oxenfordiae.*" It should be recalled that Oxford is almost entirely encircled by water, and many have noticed what Max Beerbohm called in *Zuleika Dobson* (1911) its "mild miasmal air." As John Wycliff declared, "not unworthily is it called the Vineyard of the Lord. It was founded by the Holy Fathers and situated in a splendid site, watered by rills and fountains, surrounded by meadows, pastures, plains and glades; it has been rightly called the house of God and the gate of heaven."

At the time of the Reformation, and the dissolution of the religious establishments, the organised religious life of the Thames was all but destroyed. The smaller houses were the first to be closed, among them Hurley Priory, Bisham Priory, Eynsham Abbey, Rewley Abbey, Goring Priory, Medmenham Priory, Chertsey Abbey, Cholsey Abbey and Ankerwycke Priory. Then the commissioners turned their vengeance upon the larger establishments, among them Godstow Abbey and Osney Abbey, Abingdon Abbey and the friary at Reading, as well as the friaries and monastic colleges of Oxford. The priories of Lechlade and Cricklade, the nunneries of Burnham and Little Marlow, were also extinguished. Generations of religious observance and ceremony, conducted by the river, were removed at the instigation of a sovereign who cared as little for the sacred history of the river as for the spiritual heritage of the nation itself. Only the abbey of Dorchester, and Westminster Abbey, survived the general destruction and decay. The rest were looted and rifled. The refectory at Abingdon became a malt-house, while the refectory at Hurley became a stable. The religious establishments of Sutton, Bisham and Medmenham became part of private houses. The occasional wall, or fishpond, may survive; there are fragments of graveyards, or cloisters, to be glimpsed. In nineteenth-century studies of the Thames, there are engravings of ruins. But even these ruins have for the most part disappeared.

All that remains of Reading Abbey, for example, are some scattered masses of flint rubble from which the stone facing has been removed; one inner gateway has survived, but it is much restored. In its original form this great twelfth-century foundation would have resembled Durham Cathedral, a splendour of the riverine landscape. Its ruins are now not much visited. It is doubtful if many of the inhabitants of Reading know that they are there. This was the abbey in which Henry I was buried, and in which Henry II was offered the crown of Jerusalem. Thomas à Becket consecrated the church in the reign of that king. Here John of Gaunt was married, and the English parliament assembled three times. In the cloisters of Reading Abbey was written one of the loveliest and most celebrated of all English songs, "Sumer Is Icumen In." This four-part song, the first of its kind, was written by John of Fornsete in the thirteenth century. It is the only part of the abbey that can be said truly to have survived.

Of the nunnery at Godstow, the line of one wall remains. Nothing of the original structure of the twelfth century has survived. Of Chertsey Abbey, William Stukeley the antiquary, wrote, in *Itinerarium Curiosum* (1724), that

> so total a dissolution I scarcely ever saw . . . as if they meant to defeat even the inherent sanctity of the land. Human bones, of the abbots, monks and great personages, who were buried in great numbers in the church and cloisters, which lay on the south side of the church, were spread thick all over the garden, so that one might pick up handfuls of bits of bones at a time everywhere among the garden-stuff.

Of the abbey itself nothing remains but a piece of broken gateway and a few stones from its once encompassing wall.

CHAPTER 15

Liquid History

In the sixteenth century the Thames became the river of royal pomp and procession; this was the river down which Henry VIII, and pre-eminently Elizabeth I, sailed in state. It was the river of pageant—gilt barges decorated with banners and streamers, awnings and tapestries, flags sewn with tiny bells that rang out in the breeze, musicians playing their sackbuts and cornets upon the water, barges and galleys swathed in cloth of gold and arras. It was the river of pleasure, and the river of spectacle. It was the stage upon which the rulers and principals of the kingdom could display themselves to the populace. It was the theatre of water.

Anne Boleyn, dressed in cloth of gold, processed down the Thames for her coronation in 1533; it was said that the barges following her stretched for four miles. On that day, according to contemporary reports, "there were trumpets, shawms, and other divers instruments, all the way playing and making great melody." The barges themselves were "gorgeously garnished with banners, pennons and targets richly covered." The state barge of the lord mayor led the procession "adorned by flags and pennons hung with rich tapestries and ornamented on the outside with scutcheons of metal, suspended on cloth of gold and silver." It was the triumph of the

Thames as much as of the ill-fated queen. The Thames was the appropriate setting for extravagance and conspicuous wealth.

It was the same river that carried Anne Boleyn to her beheading three years later; it was the same route, from Greenwich to the Tower, but the river was now the baleful conduit of death. This was also the river upon which Sir Thomas More, and later the young Princess Elizabeth, were taken to the Tower. It was the river down which the body of Elizabeth was taken to the Palace of Whitehall. In *Annales Britannia* (1615) William Camden wrote that

> The Queen was brought by water to White-hall,
> > At every stroake the oars did let tears fall:
> > More clung about the Barge, fish under water
> Wept out their eyes of pearl, and swam blind after.

It was the river that seemed to curl through the affairs of state, noble or ignoble, bloody or benign, and was an intrinsic part of royal London. That is also why the great palaces of the nobility and the clergy were built on the banks of the river, so that they might be near the ultimate source of power. Although the belief in the water's divinity had apparently been dispelled, the continuing invocation of nymphs and sea gods—not least in the Thames pageants—suggests that there was some residual faith in the deities of the river. It was the river that blessed the monarch, not the reverse.

The Thames was seen as the microcosm of the kingdom, incorporating past and present, the world of pastoral and the world of the city, the centre of secular as well as of religious activities, the site of sports and carnivals. It was considered to be "another Helicon" where Apollo and his Muses had alighted, so that under its benign influence London surpassed Rome and Athens. The excitement and energy of London were the excitement and energy of the Thames.

It was also the highway along which all the traffic of London passed—not just for the fishermen in their coracles, and not just for the merchants in their vessels from Spain and the Low Countries, but for the ordinary citizens who used the Thames as the most convenient means of transport through London. Of course they travelled across the water from north to south, especially when London Bridge was busy and crowded, but also they sailed along the north bank to the various "stairs" where they could alight and continue their journey. The streets of the city were narrow and perilous, and it was considered safer and easier to travel by water. The number of small boats, barges, lighters, tilt-boats and ferries upon the river was a source of perpetual interest to foreign observers. And of course there were hundreds of watermen with their boats for hire, the water continually in motion with their labouring oars. There were many occasions when the press of boats was so great that traffic came to a halt in what became known as a "lock" or "jam." This was the Thames well known and even celebrated for its crowded wharves and busy shores. It is not at all surprising that the citizens congregated along its banks, since in the sixteenth century the majority of Londoners still earned their living directly or indirectly from the river. From a distance, it was said, the Thames looked like a forest of masts. At any one time there were estimated to be some two thousand vessels on the water, as well as three thousand watermen. In a map from the middle of that century the various "stairs" or landing places are depicted as places of great and restless activity. It was the cartographer's way of asserting the primacy of the river.

The Thames supplied London with goods from the known world, with spices and furs and wine; here came the Venetian galleys, with their stock of merchandise from Constantinople and Damascus, joined by the three-masted ships from the Low Countries with their cargoes of fur and timber. But the river also carried the great barges of hay and fuel, without which the city could not have survived. There was a story of an alderman, who had been told that Queen Mary was so annoyed with the city that she intended to remove Parliament and the Courts of Justice to some other place. He asked "whether she meant also to divert the river of Thames from London." On being told that she had no means to do so, he replied that then "by God's grace we shall do well enough at London, whatsoever become of the Terme and Parliament."

It was the river down which the first explorers sailed. Hugh Willoughby and Richard Chancellor set sail from Deptford in 1553, with a letter addressed to "all kings, princes, rulers, judges, and governors of the earth." They were on a voyage of discovery, searching for a northern route to the Indies, but the one surviving vessel landed on the Russian coast; this was the beginning of trade with the merchants of Moscow. When the ships came near Greenwich "the courtiers came running out, and the common people flockt together, standing very thick upon the shoare." At a later date Colonel John Smith left from Blackwall and, after a perilous voyage, established the colony of Jamestown in Virginia. The *Mayflower* sailed from

Rotherhithe. It seemed then that the waters of the world might be interpreted as one extended Thames. The Turkey Company was later established as a result of the trading voyages and, on the last day of the sixteenth
century, the queen signed a charter for the establishment of the English
East India Company. The merchants and adventurers of the Hudson Bay
Company, of the East India Company itself, and of the West India Company, started their travels on the river.

So when Wenceslaus Hollar depicted the river in the 1630s, in his famous panoramic map of London, it was appropriate that he should depict
the banks and stairs, wherries and barges, as combined in a vast network of
activity. In contrast the streets and houses of the city seem deserted, as if
all the energy and business of London were concentrated upon the flowing
Thames. The names of the wharves are clearly marked, for ease of reference, with "Paulus wharfe . . . Queenhythe . . . the 3 Cranes . . . Stilliard . . .
Cole harbour . . . the Old Swan," and the river itself is filled with vessels of
every description. Below London Bridge the great merchant ships are
docked while Mercury, the god of commerce, is pointing to the cartouche
of "LONDON" itself. This vista became the model for many later maps
and representations, so that the prospect of London stretching from the
river became the single most important vision of the city. The Thames represented the city's destiny. It was how London was imagined.

During the early stages of the Civil War the Thames remained a royalist
stronghold along its middle reaches. The river was, after all, the source and
site of ancient or traditional power. Just as it had once harboured old
Catholic families, recusants under Elizabeth, so it acted as a refuge for
those who supported the king in his struggle against parliament. Many royalist and Catholic houses, beside the river and its tributaries, were besieged
by parliamentary troops—among them Mapledurham House, Blount's
Court and Basing House. There were royalist garrisons at Reading and at
Oxford. Oxford became the temporary royal "capital" for Charles I. By
two of the river's most ancient bridges, those of Radcot and New Bridge,
there were battles and skirmishes; at Radcot Bridge, in 1645, Prince Rupert
fought off a parliamentary army. The prize of Kingston was sought by
both sides, with the monarch's troops being ousted by parliamentary soldiers who in their turn were expelled by royalist troops retreating from the
battle of Turnham Green. Then a parliamentary army returned and held
the town until the end of the Civil War. Prince Rupert destroyed two par-

liamentary regiments who had set up a garrison by the river at Brentford; many of the soldiers were drowned in the Thames.

The royal river of course celebrated the return of royal favour. When on 23 August 1662 Charles II was rowed from Hampton Court to White-hall with his bride, Catherine of Braganza, he was imitating the Tudor pageants of Henry and Elizabeth in a deliberate attempt to renew his own majesty. He was associating himself, and his family, with the history of the river. As he sat upon the royal barge with his bride, he was inviting the blessing of the river. He received it in the shape of an actor playing Isis who sang out, accompanied by music,

> Divinest pair! Isis (to meet
> Your unmatched loves) kisses your sacred feet.

The royal pageant had been titled "Acqua Triumphalis" and, according to Evelyn, it was

> the most magnificent Triumph that ever floted on the Thames, con-
> sidering the innumerable boates & Vessels, dressd and adornd with all
> imaginable Pomp, but, above all, the Thrones, Arches, Pageants &
> other representations, stately barges of the Lord Mayor & Companies,
> with various Inventions, musique, & Peales of Ordnance both from the
> vessels and shore.

It was a chance for Londoners in particular to exorcise their previous association with Cromwell and the Protectorate—a London crowd had gathered for the execution of the present monarch's father—and it was also an opportunity for the Thames to be recognised again as the sovereign river of England.

That is why, at the time of the Plague and the Fire, in 1665 and 1666 respectively, it became the instinctive place of refuge. It was part of the river's status as a boundary that it was believed that it might act as a frontier, or defence against flame and disease. In Daniel Defoe's *A Journal of the Plague Year* (1722), written some years after the events described, there is an account of a waterman at Poplar who acted as a carrier and postman for those families who had taken to the river and had secured themselves in vessels anchored in it. "All these ships," he explained, "have families on board, of their merchants and owners, and such like, who have locked themselves up and live on board, closed shut in, for fear of infection." Defoe estimated that there were ten thousand people sheltering on the Thames in this secluded manner. The riverside was lined with boats, too, and many Londoners had decamped to the estuary where they lived upon the barren marshland of that area. The precautions did not in general check the contagion. The plague had been carried into London by the Thames itself, spreading from the *Rattus rattus*, otherwise known as the black rat or the ship rat. The infection reached the ships, creating havoc among the refugees who had believed themselves to be safe. The watermen, who used their boats as houses, were also struck down. They were found dead in their wherries, riding the tide.

Of the Fire a year later Pepys reports that, after watching the flames from the Tower, he walked down to the waterside and hired a boat to take him towards London Bridge. The Thames had already become the scene of intense activity with the citizens and their families removing their household goods by "flinging them into the river, or bringing them into lighters that lay off." The poorer people stayed in their houses until the fire came too close, at which point they began "running into boats, or clambering from one pair of stairs, by the waterside, to another." Later that night he described the Thames as "full of lighters and boats taking in goods, and goods swimming in the water; and only I observed that hardly one lighter or boat in three that had the goods of a house in it, but there was a pair of virginalls in it." But the river once more proved an illusory refuge. Pepys reported that "all over the Thames, with one's faces in the wind you were almost burned with a shower of fire-drops." Evelyn completed the picture in his diaries, with an account of "the Thames covered with goods floating, all the barges, and boats laden with what some had time and courage to save . . . Oh the miserable and calamitous spectacle!" The heat and the smoke became too intense, and those on the river were forced to land on the southern bank and fly to the fields, or sail out of the immediate neighbourhood of London.

The rebuilding of London after the Fire of course greatly changed the prospect of the city from the Thames. It also altered the appearance of the banks themselves. The warehouses and quays, destroyed or damaged, were rebuilt. The streets leading down from the City were also rebuilt, their houses now constructed of russet or yellow brick, and above the roofs rose the gleaming steeples of the fifty-one churches that Christopher Wren, the king's Assistant Surveyor-General, restored or built again. It was a more solid, a grander, riverscape than that of the medieval or Tudor city. This was nowhere more evident than in the reclamation of the Fleet River that flowed down into the Thames by Blackfriars. It had become no more than an open sewer in the heart of the capital, making its noisome way through the Fleet valley, but under Wren's superintendence it was widened and cleaned up. It became a navigable "cut" as far as Holborn Bridge in the centre of the city; it was crossed by newly built bridges and lined with wharves and warehouses. It was a measure of Wren's determination to scour London and the Thames of their past.

The king had decreed that "we do resolve and declare that there shall be a fair key or wharf on all the river side." As a result there emerged a plan for a continuous Thames Quay, a model of progress and efficiency on the north bank of the Thames that would complete London's pre-eminence as a trading nation. It was to take the place of the jumble or warren of wooden sheds and warehouses, stairs and alleys, that characterised the old riverscape. It was to stretch from the Temple to the Tower of London, at a width of 40 feet (12 m); it was to be lined with grand buildings, of which the new Customs House (also designed by Wren) was the exemplar. It was to represent the wholesale transformation of the river: on both sides of London Bridge the Thames was to be overlooked by new building that reflected the spirit of a city awakened and renewed.

It did not quite succeed in the manner intended. Below the bridge, private and unplanned quays had already been erected, before the programme of public works had begun; they had been needed immediately after the Fire, not least to bring provisions and materials for the army of building workers who had migrated to the city in the first stages of rebuilding. It did not seem practicable to begin again. Above the bridge, Wren reported to the monarch that everywhere the area was "inclosed and incumbred with Pales or Brickwalls irregular houses and buildings Piles of Timber Billetts Faggots and heapes of Coles many boarded sheds and several great Laystalls . . . the old Towers of Baynard's Castle yet standing."

The rebuilding was occasional and sporadic. But there were specific accomplishments. A new Fishmongers' Hall, for example, was built. New wharves were constructed at Dowgate and at Puddle Dock. Bridewell was largely rebuilt. Houses were erected along the side of the river in more orderly fashion. Thames Street was widened and the level was also raised 3 feet (0.9 m), to ensure against inundation by water rather than fire. And there were additions to the litany of great buildings along the Thames. Pre-eminent among them stood the cathedral church of St. Paul, with its dome of shining Portland stone. Wren changed the Thames just as he changed London; he designed the hospital at Chelsea for wounded soldiers, and then the hospital at Greenwich for naval men. The official or administrative life of the river was partly his invention.

It was now being celebrated as the calm river, the river that did not rage, the river without extremes, the river that did not generally overflow its banks in excessive vigour. In that sense it became an image of the new dispensation of the renewed kingdom, averse to extremism and the enthusiasm of any faction. The river incorporated the myth of the nation.

PART VI

Elemental and Equal

The island in the Thames where Magna Carta was reputedly signed

CHAPTER 16

The Waters of Life

ater is utterly familiar and yet altogether elusive. That is why it has been described in terms of negation. It is odourless. It is colourless. It is tasteless. It is rarely, if ever, located in its pure state. The epitaph upon the headstone of John Keats, "Here lies one whose name was writ in water," is the token of one who believed that he had left no trace. Water is utterly mysterious. Images of the river, whether in photograph or painting, never really look "like" the river itself. Until a relatively late date the natural philosophers and scientists considered water to be an indivisible element, and only after 1783, through the combined efforts of Cavendish, Watt and Lavoisier was it recognised to be an inorganic compound of hydrogen and oxygen. But still ancient beliefs clustered around the chemistry, with oxygen considered to be the "father" and hydrogen the "mother" of this substance.

Yet water is the matrix and nurse of all life. It is perhaps the oldest thing upon the earth. It has remained unchanged, in every respect, for 3,500 million years. The seas were formed in the depths of pre-Cambrian time, and there is not one drop more or less than at that inconceivable beginning. The water of the Thames may once have fallen from the back of a pleiosaur or filled the bath of Archimedes. That is where the enchantment of the river lies. It is the deep and ancient force, the thrust and stir of creation. The noise of its waters is the sound of burgeoning life. "And all the liquid world," as Abraham Cowley put it, "is one extended Thames."

It is the first element of life in another sense. The child in the womb lives and develops within the embrace of water, growing within the membraneous sac, and of course the human body is itself comprised principally of water. So was Neanderthal Man. So was Cro-Magnon Man. We are all part of the same texture. It has been estimated by biochemists that the amount of salt in human protoplasm, some 0.9 per cent, was precisely that within the ancient seas where life first began. We are born within primordial waters.

The fact that the human body is by weight 60 per cent water may help to explain why the river has been granted human characteristics such as unpredictability and fierceness. What better way is there to symbolise purity, too, than the image of clear and limpid water? It may also help to explain the intimacy with which water is associated. The water is like blood coursing through the veins. And in that consonance between the veins of the human body and the rivers of the earth there is a strange pull of sympathy between the human being and the running water. Motionless waters evoke death, as the poems and stories of Edgar Allan Poe testify. When we look at our reflection in water, we are looking at ourselves in a double sense.

It has also been described as the mother of all elements, with Isaac Newton's belief that "that rare substance water can be transformed by continued fermentation into the more dense substances of animals, vegetables, salts, stones and various earths." That is why the myth of purity is so important, since motherhood and purity are deemed to be cognate in the myths of human origin. It is in fact the attribute of water to be able to purify itself; the river metabolises waste in the manner of a living organism by absorbing oxygen from the air and from plants; the oxygen then "burns" organic waste material.

But in a more general sense water is spiritually pure. It is the renovator and protector of the world. It redeems ugliness. It is the source of health and strength. It palliates the human senses, refreshing to the touch, calming to the eye, and melodious to the ear. There seems to be an instinctive harmony in the life and appearance of the river-bank, for example, at least where the set of the stream and the nature of the soil have not been displaced by human activity. Like white light it contains everything, embodying the paradox of simplicity and heterogeneity. White light contains all colours, and therefore none. Water contains everything, and is therefore transparent. It is the quintessence of everything, and of nothing. It communicates easily with all manifestations of itself, effortlessly becoming one and finding a common level.

So what is its identity? It has been compared with time, death and consciousness, but in that sense, too, it is being compared with everything and nothing. It is of protean appearance, changing its shape from ice to water to steam. Solid, liquid, or gaseous, it is forever elusive. When Coleridge watched the course of a waterfall in the Lake District he was moved to write of "the continual *change* of the *Matter*, the perpetual *Sameness* of the *Form*—it is an awful Image & Shadow of God & the World." But this changefulness, this state of perpetual becoming, is also part of its energy. It is also an aspect of its power. Water can defy gravity by moving uphill. It will wear down and dissolve the toughest metal. It has created the plains and valleys of the earth. It does not abide obstacles. It can destroy mountains. A single drop of rain exerts a force of 2.3 pounds per square inch (0.165 kgf per square cm). A thunderstorm unleashes the energy of a large atomic bomb.

Water never can be wholly still, with the forces of radiation and gravity, heat and movement, all around it. Leonardo noted down in eight folios "730 conclusions on water," of which sixty-four were concerned with water in movement. Among his categories were *polulamenti e surgimenti* (bubblings and surges), *sommergere* (submersion) and *intersegatione d'acque* (intersections of waters). He was considered to be a "master of water" and was employed as an adviser on its power in fields as various as flooding, energy and transport. He understood the might of the river.

He was particularly interested in the formation of the vortex, since there if anywhere is to be found a microcosm of water itself. The flowing river is after all part of what has become known as the "hydrologic cycle," the vortex of the earth, the circle of life. The process, not fully proven until as late as the mid-seventeenth century, has the twin merits of harmony and simplicity. The water evaporates from the sea and land, and is thus drawn into the atmosphere; it falls back as rain or snow or sleet, and thus replenishes the rivers and water-courses that return it to the sea. It has been estimated that, each year, 95,000 cubic miles of water rise into the atmosphere; of these, 80,000 cubic miles ascend directly from the oceans, to which return 71,000 cubic miles. The rest of the falling water replenishes the lakes and streams and rivers or nourishes the land. The trees and plants are of course part of this endless circle, and each day a single birch-tree can transpire some 70 gallons (318 l) of water. Larger trees can disperse hundreds of gallons. One drop of water may spend a few days in a river, or a few hundreds of thousands of years locked within the ground, but that drop is not lost. Eventually it will return.

There is a manuscript map of Kent in the eighteenth-century treatise *Ankographia* (1743), which shows the drainage system of the Thames in the form of a man half-kneeling upon the ground. It is a haunting image, as if the human shape had risen out of the topography like the ghost or spirit of the place. He holds a pail with which he pours the waters into the sea.

The hydrologic cycle propounds another mystery. It is best expressed in the words of Ecclesiastes 1:7: "All the rivers run into the sea; yet the sea is not full; unto the place from whence the rivers come, thither they return again." There is a glimpse here of some divine apotheosis, when that which is filled to overflowing can never contain enough. All flows into the One. Seneca meditated upon the flow of rivers and "thus contemplating them, we should reverence a fountain of Life flowing into Itself . . . simple, self-moved and self-worked . . . a knowledge surpassing every kind of knowledge, and always contemplating Itself, through Itself." The image of bliss, or perfection, may be found in the contemplation of the circle rather than of constant movement. The movement of the Thames itself, restless and heaving as it proceeds downward to the great sea, can provoke such reflections.

It is a beneficent cycle that has affected the metaphors of time and human destiny. It has no beginning and no end—or, rather, the beginning and the end cannot be identified with any certainty. There is no trace of a beginning, and no thought of an end. It suggests some interior harmony that we may extrapolate into the cosmos itself. Plato believed that the human body, like nature, adhered to some universal law of circulation. The process of life is in a constant state of becoming. All of these attributes affect our perception of the Thames itself.

CHAPTER 17

The Leveller

❧

Water is the greatest of equalisers. It is well enough known that water seeks an even level, but this is more than a metaphor. Throughout its history it has been understood that the river is free to all people. In the Magna Carta, sealed by the banks of the Thames, the great rivers of the English kingdom were granted to all men and women alike. A parliamentary committee of the nineteenth century declared the Thames to be "an ancient and free highway" with the attendant right of the public "to move boats over any and every part of the river through which the Thames water flows." The monarch does not own the river, despite many tendentious claims to the contrary, any more than the Corporation of London owns that part of the river that flows through the city. In truth the river belongs to no one.

The water of the Thames was available both to rich and poor, whether for bathing or for cleansing, for cooking or for drinking; the need for it was so universal that it was deemed to be common to all. A pamphlet of 1600 quotes with approval the Muslim belief that "no money nor fee should be exacted for the use of water which God had freelie bestowed on poor and rich." In the same period the Thames provided the setting for the festivals that united the people of the city. The food of the Thames fed everyone.

The riverside was also the home of rich and poor, with palaces and hovels almost literally side by side. As Sir William D'Avenant described the northern bank of the Thames in 1656, "Here a lord, there a dyer, and places of the worst kind between both." In his early drawings of the river Turner contrasts the baroque architecture along the river-banks with the neighbouring waterworks and coal-barges. The river actively worked against hierarchy and division of all kinds, particularly because water is a dissolving and unifying element. The Thames also provided work, and profit, for the diverse people along its banks. At the height of the boating "craze" of the late nineteenth century, the locks and weirs saw the close congregation of lords and cockneys; this resulted in what one observer called "spontaneous gaiety," as if the values of the ordinary world had for a moment been turned upside down. It is this innate egalitarianism that explains the "water language" of the boatmen conventionally directed against their ostensibly richer or more socially superior passengers.

Thus we have the association of the Thames with various levelling movements. In the late fourteenth century the rebellion of Jack Straw, against the exactions of Richard II and the poll tax, was largely instigated by the disaffection of the Thames fishermen along the estuary in villages such as Mucking and Vantage. The first riots broke out in Fobbing, and the county history of Essex records that "the portion of the country most implicated [in the revolt] was along the Thames shore." The river was involved in much of the violent action. There were rebel uprisings in Barking and at Dartford, and there were incendiary riots in Gravesend. One contingent of rebels marched from Blackheath to Southwark and to Lambeth where they stormed the archbishop's palace. The river seems to call forth the defenders of liberty. In the same riverine spirit the bargemen of the Thames were once known as the "Sons of Liberty," albeit in an ironical sense.

In the fifteenth century the sect of the Lollards, opposed to hierarchical tenets as well as the corruption of the established Church, was strongly represented in the Thames Valley. They were well established, for example, at Marlow and at Faringdon, at Abingdon and at Buscot. They were also active in the vicinity of Oxford. The Lollard rebellion of 1431 was in fact crushed at Abingdon itself, where they could expect the most loyal support, but Lollard ideas were still retained in the regions around the river. The Baptists emerged most powerfully, for example, in old Lollard strongholds.

The connection of the Baptist movement with the river itself, not least in the ritual of immersion, suggests how much the presence of the Thames can be felt in the espousal of egalitarian creeds.

The Levellers, the sixteenth-century group of republicans and democrats who emerged in the period of the Civil War and Commonwealth, congregated in the church of St. Mary, by the banks of the river at Putney, in 1647. It was here that they engaged in the "Putney Debates" and put forward an "Agreement of the People" or new social contract. Then, two years later, Walton-on-Thames became the setting for the experiment in living conducted by the Diggers under the inspiration of Gerrard Winstanley; they proclaimed themselves to be "the true Levellers," and proceeded to cultivate the common ground of St. George's Hill. They espoused a primitive form of communism derived from the principles of Magna Carta. So the Thames runs through all of these levelling proceedings. For a short time in the 1990s a village was established by the river at Battersea, named "Land and Freedom," dedicated to the principles of communal equality and ecological rectitude; it was following an ancient calling.

You can feel "free" on the river. Indeed the Thames itself seems to encourage some dissolution of the identity. It encourages various forms of communal revelry, such as the "frost fairs" that were conducted on the frozen river during various preternaturally cold episodes. All classes and sections of London society congregated on the river during these unnatural episodes:

> Straight comes an arch wag, a young son of a whore,
> And lays the squire's head where his heels were before.

Class distinctions seem to disappear in the process of going upon the river, even in its frozen state, and through the centuries the Thames was an emblem of liberty. All the divisions and distinctions of dry land are washed away and erased. As Richard Jefferies says in *The Modern Thames* (1885), "on the river people do as they choose, and there does not seem to be any law at all—or at least there is no authority to enforce it, if it exists." The bargemen, for example, knew no law. They deemed themselves to be as free as the river gypsies. The various pilferers and smugglers who used the river as the focus of their activities genuinely believed that they were doing no wrong. That is why the establishment of the river police provoked such outrage. It is still considered somewhat offensive to ask someone, on the river, to desist from one activity or another. Some of the greatest radical enterprises of English history, in particular the sailors' revolt or "Nore mutiny" of 1797 and the dockers' strike of 1889, have taken place upon the Thames. The river is the zone of liberty.

PART VII

The Working River

Barges at Blackfriars

CHAPTER 18

River Boat

There have been wherries and clinkers, hoys and onkers, houseboats and skiffs, yachts and motor-boats, tilt-boats and shallops, peter-boats and eel-boats, punts and lighters, funnies and cutters, barges and steamships, coracles and canoes, scullers and colliers, barques and schooners, gigs and dinghies, whiffs and randans, rowing boats and dhows and narrow boats. They used to be made out of oak, mahogany and spruce; the fastenings were made with copper, and the bands with iron. They have sailed on the Thames out of ancient times.

When coracles were launched, on certain rivers in India, a sheep was sacrificed and blood sprinkled upon the new vessel. In Madras a pumpkin was placed under the keel of a new boat and squashed upon its entry into the water; the pumpkin was the substitute for a human head. The Solomon Islanders were accustomed to place the head of a slaughtered enemy in the prow of any newly built canoe. We will soon have cause to notice the connection between heads and the Thames, so that some domestic version of this custom cannot wholly be ruled out. This may not be a very long way from the ritual breaking of a bottle of champagne—the "neck" of the bottle is said to be broken—and there is some ceremony still to be observed in the launching of new craft upon the river. Boats are blessed and venerated, in advance of their journeys upon the waters.

The flat-bottomed barge became over many centuries the model for most of the vessels that negotiated the Thames, but there were modifications of the essential structure. The Vikings, for example, introduced a version of "clinker-built" vessels that have been in use on the river ever since; the "clinker boat" is one in which the external planks are overlapping. Large log-boats, or "dug-outs," have been dated to the Saxon period. It is possible that some of them were employed as ferries. The shallow draught of such vessels was important; the log-boat became the punt, which in turn was enlarged to become the familiar "Western barge" with square-cut hull that sailed over the Thames waters. The simple "punt" or "flat," now celebrated as the transport of Oxford and Cambridge, was thus originally a working boat of great antiquity. The "peter-boat" can also claim to be of hallowed age; it is a fishing boat, named after the patron saint of fishermen.

Medieval ships, of approximately the same design, have been reclaimed from the river-bed. One large boat, and a smaller "lighter," were found in close proximity. The larger boat was carrying cereals and other produce; the lighter was transporting stone. It seems likely that they were involved in a collision. The ships of medieval merchants have also been recovered—some of them galleys with masts and oarsmen, and others known as "cogs" with a single square sail and very high sides. There were some twenty-eight types of medieval boat upon the Thames, according to Laura Wright's *Sources of London English* (1996). There was the "skumer" or light ship and the "cock," a workboat sometimes known as "the masons Cokke" or "the Carpenters Cokke." The "farcost" or "varecost" was employed to transport stone, while the "mangboat" was used by fishermen. A "flune" was a small ship, and a "cog" went back and forth across the Channel. There was the "crayer" or "croier" or trading vessel, and there was the "shout" or "showte," a flat-bottomed craft for the transporting of goods. The name itself probably derives from that of the Dutch eel-boat or "schuyt" known from the middle of the fourteenth century; the name persisted until the 1930s, in fact, and is some indication of the Dutch influence on Thames craft.

So the boats of the Thames flowed down from these originals. A statute of 1514 declared that "it had been a laudable custome and usage tyme out of mind to use the River in Barge or Whery Boate." "Tyme out of mind" was a ritual phrase, meaning further back than anyone could remember. The barge was the most familiar craft upon the river, being a variant upon the prehistoric vessels that had sailed along the Thames. It was also synonymous with "lighter," and a parliamentary Act of 1859 classified the lighterman as "any person working or navigating for hire, a lighter, barge, boat, or other like craft." Barges were the work-horses of the river, sturdy, dependable and capacious. It was said of their draught that they could sail anywhere after a heavy dew or anywhere a duck could swim. Certainly, in the upper stretches of the Thames, they needed to negotiate the shallowest waters. They even reached as high as Eynsham, near the source.

They carried every conceivable cargo from stone and wheat to butter and manure and gunpowder. They even carried letters. They had a crew of two men and a boy, and the largest of them could carry cargoes of almost 200 tons (203 tonnes). The average load, however, was between 60 and 80 tons (61 and 81 tonnes). The barges on the middle and upper reaches of the Thames were known by their diminishing size as the "western barges," "trows" or "worsers"; the lighters were known as "dumb barges," perhaps because they had no sails. There were "stumpies," with no top mast, and "stackies" or hay barges. There were also estuary barges known as "hoys," but the name was predominantly associated with Margate. The "Margate hoy" became famous as a conveyance, and is popularly supposed to be based upon the design of the Norman vessels that crossed to Hastings. They were not universally appreciated, however. A report of 1637 remarks that "the hoy, like the grave, confounds all distinctions; high and low, rich and poor, sick and sound, are indiscriminately blended together . . . I would not recommend it to ladies of great delicacy."

There are engravings of barges being towed by ropes through empty riverscapes. The rope was fastened to the top of the mast, to keep it clear from obstructions on the river-bank, and two horses were generally used for the journey upriver. There are also engravings of barges complete with small iron funnels, which might suggest that they had bowed to progress and converted to steam. In fact the funnels were used for the smoke of the fire where the bargemen cooked their food.

There were a variety of barges, of all sizes, designed to cope with the riverine conditions in their particular neighbourhoods. The sails of all of them, however, were a distinct reddish-brown. The exact hue was created with a judicious mixture of cod oil, red ochre, horse fat and sea water. It became the colour of the Thames, to be seen in a thousand paintings. The barges were often gaily painted, with a variety of colour and ornament to accentuate their singularity. They endured for a thousand years, but then, like their sails, slowly mixed with the sunset. At the end of the nineteenth century there were some 2,500 barges still plying their trade upon the river; now there are approximately twenty of them left.

The other familiar and popular craft through the centuries was the wherry, which was noticeable for its shallowness, its broad stern and its sharp stem. It was "clinker"-built with overlapping planks, and was generally equipped with a wooden back-rest on which the boat's name was emblazoned. It was technically a "ran-dan" ferry, because it allowed room for three people rowing at the same time, but it became the sole prerogative of the sometimes surly waterman. It was approximately 26 feet (8 m) in length, with a beam of over 5½ feet (1.6 m), and could hold between six and eight passengers—although there were many occasions when it was overloaded. "To take a pair of sculls" was to be rowed by a single waterman, while "to take a pair of oars" was to be rowed by two. They were employed for carrying light freight as well as passengers, and were often in use as ferries at various points across the river. They could move very quickly indeed, and in 1618 the secretary to the Venetian Ambassador wrote that "the wherries shoot along so lightly as to surprise everyone." There are few, if any, wherries now operating on the river.

The oldest way across the river is by means of ferry. There were "accommodation ferries," intended only for passengers, and "navigation ferries," for livestock and goods as well as people. One of the oldest ferries carried animals and travellers from the north bank at Vauxhall to Lambeth; it is still enshrined in the name of Horseferry Road. There is also a Horseferry Place in Greenwich, from where the ferryman took his passengers to East Ferry Road on the Isle of Dogs. The ferry between Erith in Kent and the north bank of the Thames is first recorded at the beginning of the eleventh century; the route was eventually taken up by the Ford Motor Car Company in 1933 for the ferry between Erith and the Dagenham car works. There was a ferry between Dowgate, in the City, and Southwark on the opposite shore; it survived until London Bridge was constructed out of stone at the beginning of the thirteenth century. There were no less than four

ferry services operating at Cookham, and the ferry at Twickenham was celebrated in song:

> Ahoy! And Oho, and it's who's for the ferry?
> (The briar's in bud and the sun going down),
> And I'll row ye so quick, and I'll row ye so steady,
> And 'tis but a penny to Twickenham Town.

A penny can go a long way. It was reported, in the *London Daily Advertiser*
of 23 October 1751, that "yesterday a coach and four being taken over in a
boat at Twickenham Ferry, the horses took fright and leapt into the water
drawing the coach after them."

The ferry between Tilbury and the opposite shore remains still, with a
history of many thousands of years; the remains of a causeway over
Higham Marshes suggest that the Romans improved what was already an
ancient crossing used by the prehistoric peoples of the region. The ferry
from Higham to East Tilbury was instituted by the emperor Claudius, in
AD 48, for the convenience of foot passengers and for cattle. This was succeeded in the sixteenth century by a ferry from Gravesend to Tilbury Fort.
This was known as the "Short Ferry," while the "Long Ferry" was essentially the journey from Gravesend to Billingsgate.

There is still a free ferry service at Woolwich, established in 1889.
There is a ferry at Hampton, and another at Twickenham. The ferry at
Bablock Hythe has been in existence for more than seven hundred years,
and is first mentioned as "the ferry of Babbelak" in 1279.

The ferrymen were often appealing or reassuring figures. Many seem
to have been old. In 1605 there is a record of Henry Dible, "an Antient
fferry man" at Kew. In Fred S. Thacker's study of the river, *The Thames
Highway* (1914 and 1920), there are some 135 ferrymen listed with names
like Linteboy and Scopeham, Pither and Tibble. Theirs was a profitable
trade, and it was generally kept in the family for many generations. But
their ancientness may be in part a reflection of the veneration in which they
were once held. The ferryman is a figure of myth. In the legends of
Mesopotamia, for example, the ferryman named Arad-Ea took the human
souls across the river of death. In Egyptian myth the ferryman across the
lake of lilies had to be placated if the human souls were to reach the island
of life. In Greek myth Charon, the ferryman, was the son of Nyx or the
night; he rowed the souls of the dead across the river Styx, and for his

services the Greeks left a small coin in the mouth of the corpse. He was generally represented as an old man, with a scowl upon his face. He is the guardian of the mystery, the porter of hell, the guide who conducts us through death. It may be that the figure of Charon is indeed some meta-morphosis of an ancient rite, when the bodies of the dead were lowered into the river. The ferrymen of the Thames have a powerful inheritance.

CHAPTER 19

The Bridges of Contentment and the Tunnels of Darkness

Some verses of Rudyard Kipling, in "The River's Tale" (1911), are pertinent:

Twenty bridges from Tower to Kew
Wanted to know what the River knew,
For they were young and the Thames was old,
And this is the tale that the River told . . .

In the vast period that marks the existence of the Thames, stretching back for unimaginable ages, the bridges are indeed "new." They emerged only in the later stages of the human occupation of this territory.

There are 106 pedestrian bridges on the Thames: seventy-six on the non-tidal river, ranging in height from 7½ feet (2.2 m) to 32 feet (9.7 m), and thirty on the tidal Thames. On the tidal river there are also nine rail bridges and nineteen road bridges (most of which also accommodate pedestrians).

The oldest remaining bridge on the river is that of New Bridge, where the tributary of the Windrush joins the Thames; it was built in approximately 1250. It is pre-dated by some quarter of a century by the bridge at Radcot, but that ancient structure now spans a side stream rather than the river itself. The most recent bridge, the Millennium Bridge that crosses the Thames between St. Paul's and the Tate Modern, was completed in 2000, but not opened to the public until 2002.

There are brick bridges and iron bridges, bridges with many arches and bridges with a single span; there are stone bridges and wooden bridges; there are suspension bridges and cantilevered bridges; there are bridges that join villages and bridges that continue ancient roads; there are bridges that mark the confluence of rivers and bridges that mark the presence of weirs; there are toll bridges and bridges that act as railway junctions.

A bridge across the Thames at Eton has been dated to the Bronze Age, 1400–1300 BC; its wooden posts were over 8 feet (2.5 m) apart, leading from both banks, and they were found in what is now a disused channel. In that previous age, however, it was part of the flowing current. At a later date, in the Iron Age, another bridge was built on the same site. A wooden structure of Bronze Age provenance, interpreted as either a bridge or a jetty, has been found on the Thames at Vauxhall. Twenty large timber posts were lined up in two rows, some of them set at an angle to each other. So the bridges of the Thames are of ancient foundation.

Before that technology had emerged, large stones formed the crossing for the ancient riverine people. It is plausible to see them hurling great rocks into the water, so that they might make a path across the Thames. They might anger the gods, in doing so, but the necessities of natural development led them forward. The construction of the wooden bridge, however, was the seminal event. It was a way of defying, or changing, the natural world. It was even a way of taming the river. That is why the god or gods of the river had to be appeased. Rituals and sacrifices were performed on the erection of new bridges. Shrines and offerings, and chapels, were placed on them. The bridges themselves became sacred. It is often claimed that the Roman name of priest, *pontifex*, derives from the root word *pons* or "bridge." Thus the priests were so named because they performed rituals upon bridges. According to Plutarch in his *Vitae Parallelae* (*c.* AD 100), "their offering sacrifices upon the Bridge, which the Latins call *Pontem*, it seems, being looked upon as the most sacred, and of the highest antiquity. These Priests, too, are said to have been commissioned to keep the Bridges in repair, as one of the most indispensable parts of their sacred office." There is another connotation, equally redolent of sacred terror. In thousands of legends the devil is associated with bridges. In the Swiss legend of the devil's bridge, the fiend agreed to help a man construct a bridge spanning the Reuss near Andermat on condition that he was allowed to keep the soul of the first creature to cross it. It was a dog.

Catherine of Siena, in the fourteenth century, employed what had by that date become a familiar metaphor—"God made a brigge of his sone whanne the wey of goynge to hevene was broken by inobedience of Adam, by the which brigge all trewe christen men mowen overepasse . . . it reacheth fro the erthe upe into hevene." The bridge can be used to cross from death into eternal life, just as the sacred river-crossings of pagan antiquity were a means of moving from life into the dark limbo of death. The turbulent waters beneath the bridge were seen by Catherine as "the fervent see of this wrecchid life," that which passes while the bridge stands firm. The water is mutable and vain—"swift the watir is, and abideth nobody"— where the bridge rises on the stones of Christian piety and virtue. It was Catherine's genius to create a strong metaphor out of the ancient beliefs of the people, in which the river was considered to be the home of dangerous or fickle gods.

That is why the construction of bridges was itself considered to be holy work. Their builders were celebrated because they were helping to tame the pagan gods, who had not wholly departed. The work of building was then accompanied by indulgences, and pious testimonials. Thus in Leland's *Itinerary* of 1540 we have the following verses:

Another blessid besines is Brigges to make,
Where, that the pepul may not passe after greet showers.

Isabella de Ferrers, of the manor of Lechlade, established an alms-house for all those working on the construction of the bridge there. In time it became the Priory of St. John the Baptist. In general the monastic foundations of the neighbourhood were charged with the responsibility for maintaining the bridges closest to them. There was of course a system of tolls for all of the principal bridges that helped to replenish the purses of the abbots and abbesses; there are now only two toll-bridges remaining, those at Swinford and at Whitchurch, as a remnant of what was once an ancient if unwelcome custom. At the beginning of the nineteenth century it cost every foot passenger a penny or a penny-halfpenny; 1 shilling was charged for a four-wheeled carriage, such as a brougham, and 3 pence "for a dog drawing a cart."

There is another aspect of the Christian veneration of bridges. The more pious and wealthy citizens left bequests in their wills for their construction. In the early fifteenth century, for example, the bridge at Abingdon was built largely upon legacies. Sir Peter Bessils gave all the stone from his quarries at Sandford, while Geoffrey Barbour donated 1,000 marks. Both men then left properties in the neighbourhood to pay for the maintenance of the bridge, and the wool merchants of the Abingdon region also contributed money. The Christian panoply of dedication and reverence was then completed when a stone chapel was built on the bridge itself.

The custom of erecting religious houses upon bridges was of great antiquity. There were in fact many chapels and shrines designed both to solace the weary traveller and to pay for the new foundation. There were some places where the bridge actually passed through the chapel, so that the congregation was separated from the pulpit and reading desk by a thoroughfare. The chapel at London Bridge was built within one of its piers, and descended to the water's edge. On the north bank of the Thames, by the site of the head of the medieval bridge, stands the church of St. Magnus the Martyr, otherwise known as St. Magnus Ad Pontem. Reading Bridge found its median point on an island, in the middle of the river, where was placed the bridge chapel of St. Anne. The Angel Inn beside the bridge at Henley was once known as the Angel-on-the-Bridge, and is said to commemorate a chapel that stood upon the bridge itself. In the sixteenth century, according to Leland, there stood at the north end of Caversham Bridge "a fair old chapel of stone, on the right hand, piled in the foundation because of the rage of the Thames." Among the relics preserved here was a piece of the halter with which Judas hanged himself and "the blessed knife that killed St. Edward." It is hard to explain why this one bridge chapel was so blessed with holy tokens. It was rivalled only by the possessions of the church of St. Thomas à Becket, set upon London Bridge. These are a few scattered examples. It seems likely that no bridge was without its chapel, except for the smallest and most remote of them. They were pulled down in more sceptical or revolutionary ages, and plundered for their stone. The Reformation no doubt played a large part in their downfall. And they were never rebuilt. The connection of bridges with sacredness had long since been forgotten. The river was no longer a powerful god. Putney Bridge is perhaps unique for still possessing a church at either end of its structure.

On many bridges, too, there was generally a socket over the central arch in which a stone cross had once been placed as a sign. They were large enough to dominate the bridge itself, and were immune from graffiti and vandalism. There was just such a cross upon Radcot Bridge. It has now been removed but its old socket remains; even in the early twentieth century, baptisms of children were often performed within it. Leland copied a verse inscribed upon the stone bridge at Godstow:

Qui meat hac orat,
Signumque salutis adoret.

"Pray and venerate the token of salvation." The verse suggests that a cross was also erected here. Ritual offerings are still left on the completion of a new bridge, generally taking the form of a set of newly minted coins. It is the modern version of the votive offering.

There is something consolatory about bridges. They are reassuring. They are welcoming. They are tokens of human agency and purpose. They have borne many millions of footsteps, and have thus been rendered holy by time. People tend to take up the same position while resting upon a bridge, their bodies slightly forward, their arms leaning upon the parapet, looking over the water. Bridges reach across the void, prompting the wanderer onwards. They arch above the perilous waters, providing a refuge. That is why there emerged a tradition of "bridge hermits," solitaries who lived in niches or sheds upon the bridge where they begged alms. On the bridge at Abingdon there lived a "hermit carpenter" who was responsible for the maintenance and safety of the structure; he lived in a "hermitage" opposite the little bridge chapel. The hermits responsible for New Bridge, close to Witney, lived at the end of the village of Standlake closest to the bridge itself; in 1462 the hermit here, Thomas Brigges (the name itself meaning "Thomas of the Bridge"), was granted a licence from Edward IV allowing him to demand from travellers "to give of their Goodwill and Favour" for the upkeep of the bridge. By Folly Bridge, in Oxford, there was a "pretty little stone building" where the hermits spent their life in prayer; their principal occupation was continually to dig their own graves, and then refill them, in the perpetual hope and expectation of death. In 1423 another resident hermit, Richard Ludlow, was granted a licence to dwell at the foot of the bridge at Maidenhead and to preserve it by leading a quiet and pious life as well as by soliciting alms. These hermits became a metaphor of pilgrimage, and of salvation. Vagrants also find comfort in bridges; they often sleep beneath them, or even upon them. In the nineteenth century the bridges of London were resting places for hundreds of night wanderers. In 1846 it was reported that Kingston Bridge was "tenanted at Night by Vagabonds and people of the worst description." Perhaps they were claiming sanctuary.

There are more bridges across the Thames than across any other river of similar size. Of necessity they have remained in much the same form over the millennia. They are the only part of the riverscape that has not changed, with the possible exception of the river itself. They have survived, for example, where the fords have disappeared for ever. New Bridge and Radcot Bridge have emerged, intact, from the medieval ages.

The first reference to a stone bridge across the Thames occurs in a document of AD 958 when Eadwig granted to his thegn, Eadrig, the lands "first to the stone bridge and from the stone bridge eastwards along the Thames until it comes to the boundary of the people of King's Hone." King's Hone is now known as Kingston Bagpuize, and the site of the stone bridge is that of the present Radcot Bridge. The requisite skills for the construction of arched bridges were not available to the masons of the tenth century, and so this early stone bridge is likely to have consisted of large flat stones placed upon broad piers of masonry. This bridge was then rebuilt in the early years of the thirteenth century, after King John had requested in 1208 "Our Brother Alwyn to take both men and materials for the reparation of the bridge at Redcote."

The age of arched stone bridges, in fact, can be dated from the beginning of the thirteenth century. The first of them, London Bridge, was erected in 1209. The building of St. John's Bridge, in Lechlade, was undertaken soon after. Before that time there were principally wooden structures spanning the Thames, created out of great posts and piles driven into the river-bed with baulks of timber suspended upon them. The floods of winter often disabled them, and they were in an almost constant state of disrepair. Yet there were still wooden bridges, as late as the nineteenth century, at Marlow and Cookham and Windsor, Maidenhead and Staines, Chertsey and Hampton and Kingston. Until the middle of that century the bridge at Caversham was built half of timber and half of stone.

The thirteenth and fourteenth centuries were the great ages of stone. This was particularly true of the upper reaches of the Thames, where local stone was readily available. Yet only the monks, and the masons associated with the monks, had the skills necessary to build bridges. The architecture of the stone bridges is in fact remarkably similar to that of the old cathedrals, where ribs of stone emerge from the piers and span the openings between them. They resemble the Gothic arches of the churches, and the vaulting of the chapter-houses.

The most celebrated of all Thames bridges, however, must be London Bridge. It is the most frequented of all bridges, the great highway of the city; if we may speak in an Aboriginal sense of a songline, or dreamline, of London then it is represented by this path across the river. It is a great cord of humanity. It creates the great stream of human beings, contracted and innumerable, which in itself becomes a river echoing the Thames. For a brief passage the vehicles and the people are brought into relation with the push and flow of the sea. The wind and the dust, the noise of the traffic and the cry of the gulls, are brought together.

There are no buildings upon it, as there were in past ages of the bridge. Now the pedestrians are outlined against the sky and framed by the water beneath their feet; they are caught between immensities. They become frail and evanescent, a pilgrimage of passing souls suspended between the elements. Over the bridge cross all the varieties of human character with no complicity, or community of interest, between them. They are together but alone; they evince expressions of endurance or of merriment, of suffering or of abstraction. It is the most suggestive of all bridges. It has evoked, in many writers and artists, phantasmal or oneiric images.

There may have been a bridge here beyond the memory of man. It is a familiar and often quoted "fact" that the Romans erected the first bridge on this site, but there is no reason to suppose that such a favoured vantage was overlooked by the British tribes who had previously inhabited the area on both sides of the river. All we can say with any certainty is that there has been a bridge here ever since we know anything of London. A bridge, that is to say, has stood for more than two thousand years. It has taken many forms. Bridges have come and gone, have been erected and dismantled,

have worn away and been rebuilt, above this stretch of water. The generations have passed across them, never considering what came before or what
might come after. In *The Waste Land* (1922) T. S. Eliot contemplated the
crowd flowing over London Bridge, and saw in it the passage of a death
fugue.

The Roman bridge may have been erected primarily for the passage of
goods, or for the movement of troops, rather than for the convenience of
pedestrians. Its superstructure was of wood, and in 1834 some bulky oak
piles were dredged from the river; they had "shoes" of a hard iron that only
the Romans could have made. When the ancient medieval bridge was being demolished, at the beginning of the nineteenth century, specimens of
Roman coinage were found that covered the whole period of occupation.
So the bridge was continually in use. It quickly became the centre of commerce for the entire island, and the point of communication between that
island and continental Europe; it was a crossing, and a terminus, the nodal
point of England itself. The city began to cluster around it, with important
avenues of commerce and of communication on both sides of the Thames.
The growth of London was thus determined by the bridge, and it marked
the centre of the financial and mercantile life of the capital.

It is now generally agreed that there were three succeeding Roman
bridges across the Thames. The first of them was erected in AD 40s, and
connected Fish Street Hill with a section of the bank close to the southern
end of the modern bridge; this was followed by a temporary bridge in AD
85–90 that came out from Pudding Lane. A third and more permanent
bridge was then built, in approximately AD 100, on the same site as the first
of the bridges; this was more securely fashioned with stone piers and a
wooden superstructure. The thoroughfare from the bridge proceeded up
Fish Street Hill and along the present Gracechurch Street, until it reached
the front entrance to the great forum of London. This bridge lasted some
230 years before it fell. There is a commemorative medal, struck in
AD 290s, which displays a warship on the Thames together with gate-
towers on either side of the bridge. It has also been suggested by the students of Roman London that there were several shrines, or altars, upon the
bridge where votive offerings were made to the gods of the river and of the
sea. In Rome itself the *collegium pontifices*, or "college of bridge-builders,"
made a ritual journey each May across the Sulpicius Bridge where images
were thrown into the river Tiber. It is not inconceivable that a similar pilgrimage was undertaken across London Bridge.

The first Saxon bridge cannot be securely dated. The earliest mention of it in the public records occurs in AD 730, when a witch was thrown from its parapet and drowned in the river. There is a reference to a long and low wooden bridge, in AD 994; it was built of thick rough-hewn timber planks, placed upon piles, with movable platforms to allow the Saxon vessels to pass through it westward. It was said to have dissuaded King Sweyn of Denmark from further invasion. The history of the various phases of this bridge is necessarily uncertain. Some historians of London say that a bridge was built at the end of the tenth century, in order to forestall Danish invaders. Other authorities state that a bridge was erected here by a college of priests situated at Southwark.

We can say with certainty only that it was a rickety structure lined on each side with rows of dirty wooden huts. It was broad enough to accommodate two wagons passing one another—the same width, therefore, as the principal London streets—but it was packed with jostling life. Itinerant merchants and dealers in goods spread out their wares on the pathway so that the narrow thoroughfare became another London market; the bridge was also blocked by cattle for sale, and by wagons of provender. It is mentioned frequently in the *Anglo-Saxon Chronicle*, but there is also a compelling narrative in the sagas concerning Olaf Haraldson.

He had sailed up the river with his fleet of Norwegian ships, in 1014, in order to assist Ethelred and the English in their bid to fight back the Danish invaders of London. But Olaf was impeded by the Danish army who had massed upon the bridge with their weapons and missiles. The sagas report that the bridge was itself defended with towers and wooden parapets "in the direction of the river," an apt indication that the bridge itself could be used for defence as well as for communication. Olaf protected his oarsmen against attack from above, with shields and coverings of hide, and proceeded to sail beneath the bridge. Then he fastened great ropes around the piles of the bridge and, with the help of the incoming tide, managed to unloose them from the bed of the river; the bridge, with its Danish defenders, fell into the water. A curious alternative history suggests that Olaf burned down the bridge.

In any event the early Norse poet, or *skald*, Ottar Svarte, composed some verses:

London bridge is broken down,
Gold is won and bright renown.

Here then we may see the true origin of the ancient rhyme, "London Bridge is falling down," which is worth quoting in full in order to measure the true significance of the bridge in the popular memory:

London Bridge is falling down,
 Falling down, Falling down.
London Bridge is falling down,
 My fair lady.

Take a key and lock her up,
 Lock her up, Lock her up.
Take a key and lock her up,
 My fair lady.

How will we build it up,
 Build it up, Build it up?
How will we build it up,
 My fair lady?

Build it up with silver and gold,
 Silver and gold, Silver and gold.
Build it up with silver and gold,
 My fair lady.

Gold and silver I have none,
 I have none, I have none.
Gold and silver I have none,
 My fair lady.

Build it up with needles and pins,
 Needles and pins, Needles and pins.
Build it up with needles and pins,
 My fair lady.

Pins and needles bend and break,
 Bend and break, Bend and break.
Pins and needles bend and break,
 My fair lady.

Build it up with wood and clay,
    Wood and clay, Wood and clay.
Build it up with wood and clay,
    My fair lady.

Wood and clay will wash away,
    Wash away, Wash away.
Wood and clay will wash away,
    My fair lady.

Build it up with stone so strong,
    Stone so strong, Stone so strong.
Build it up with stone so strong,
    My fair lady.

Stone so strong will last so long,
    Last so long, Last so long.
Stone so strong will last so long,
    My fair lady.

Much speculation has been devoted to the identity of the "fair lady," but it seems likely that the phrase describes Eleanor of Provence, wife of Henry III. Her husband granted her the income from the tolls upon the bridge, but she was signally unwilling to spend any of the funds on the maintenance of the structure. For this she earned popular opprobrium, and emerges in the rhyme as the fair lady who will under no circumstances "build it up." It was perhaps appropriate that in 1236, on endeavouring to escape to Windsor from the Londoners who supported the de Montfort faction, she was pelted with dirt and stones from the bridge until she retreated to the Tower of London. We may say, then, that over a long period the poem accrued various images and details related to the bridge; like the bridge itself it was rebuilt over many generations until it had become a thing of harmony and proportion. There are other variants of the rhyme, the most important being the introduction of "my lady Lee" considered to be a reference to the Lea river that runs into the Thames at Wapping. It is in large part a threnody of transience and decay, until in its last two verses it touches upon the salvation of London Bridge in the form of stone.

The wooden bridge was indeed continually being damaged or destroyed by fire, and constantly being rebuilt. Between 1077 and 1136 it was endangered by eight great fires, and the *Chronicle* reports that the city and the surrounding counties were "grievously oppressed" by the taxes levied to maintain "the bridge that was nearly all afloat." In the reign of William Rufus it was swept away in a great flood. Six years later, in 1097, the *Chronicle* reports that once more it was "nearly washed away." In 1130 Geoffrey "Ingeniator" was paid £25 for the construction of two new arches. In 1163 the bridge was completely rebuilt in elm, but the new structure lasted for only thirteen years.

The cost of continual renovation and rebuilding had finally persuaded the city fathers, at the end of the twelfth century, to erect a great bridge of stone. The work was supervised by Peter the Bridge Master, or Peter of Colechurch, and was not completed for more than thirty years. It was built a few yards downstream from its wooden predecessor, so that the original might remain in use until the stone edifice was completed. Its precise dimensions are not known; it is estimated to have been a platform of Kentish rag stone some 900 feet (274 m) in length, with a width said by John Stow to be approximately 30 feet (9.1 m)—rather narrow for the weight of business that would soon press upon it. It was supported by nineteen arches, with great piers, or "starlings," to buttress them, and there was a wooden drawbridge both to prevent invasion from the river and to allow the passage of ships upriver. The drawbridge eventually began to decay, however, and was dismantled in the middle of the sixteenth century.

Peter of Colechurch died in 1205, four years before the bridge was completed. But he was eventually interred in the floor of the bridge-chapel, dedicated to St. Thomas à Becket, so that he found his resting place in his great monument. His burial here may also have been a recognition of the old superstition that, in the foundations of bridges, a human sacrifice must be laid. Peter's tomb was discovered by the workmen demolishing the old bridge in 1834; no reference to the ultimate destination of his remains has ever been found.

The Corporation of London has some medieval documents, making grants of land "to God and the Bridge." So it was treated with veneration. Yet it was also a bridge of motley. There were the wooden huts and earth floors of the poorer residents, together with the stone oratories and stained glass of the chapel, and the battlements of the defences. There were large dwellings divided into tenements known as "Bridge-House Rents." There were shops and ale-houses and cellars. In 1281 the bridge is recorded as having "almost innumerable people dwelling thereon," and in the middle of the fourteenth century there were sixty-two shops on the east side and sixty-nine shops on the west side. There were many apophthegms concerning it. It was said, for example, that "wise men walked over London Bridge and only fools went under it," referring to the strength of current created by the piers. It was also said that "you can never cross London Bridge without seeing a white horse," the origins of which are obscure. Perhaps it was true.

It was never wholly a safe foundation, however. The dwellings on London Bridge were principally built of wood, and there were frequent occasions of fire. Only four years after the bridge had been constructed, in 1213, there was a serious conflagration in Southwark. Crowds of people swarmed onto the bridge from the south bank in order to escape the flames, only to confront another crowd coming in from the north bank to watch, to help, or to pillage. At that point a sudden gust of wind sent the blazing timbers across to the north end of the bridge, where all became consumed; the crowd swayed and hesitated, watching as the southern end then took blaze. In all, some three thousand people were burned or drowned. It was just one of the many disasters that have affected the history and character of the bridge. A royal patent of 1280 discloses that "it hath lately been represented to us, and it grieves us to see, that the Bridge of London is in so ruinous a condition; to the repair of which, unless some speedy remedy is put, not only the sudden fall of the Bridge, but also the destruction of innumerable people dwelling upon it may suddenly be feared." Just a year later five arches collapsed. When in 1399 the crowds gathered to greet the young bride of Richard II, "viii persones vp on London bregge weren crowsed to the dethe." In 1437 two more arches fell down at the southern end. The subsequent renewal took some forty years. Then in 1481 the public privy on the bridge, known as the "common siege," fell into the river, drowning five men.

In its refashioned state of the 1480s and 1490s, however, London Bridge became once more the centre of commerce; its sides were lined with shops and stalls and houses. In a record of the late fifteenth century there are listed 129 "tenements" upon the bridge, among them the shops of "haberdassher, jueller, cultellar, bowyer, armurar, fleccher, taillour, peyntour and goldsmith." It became the most famous sight of all London, the centre of the river, with its unmistakable outline of crowded buildings, irregular arches, and rushing water. A market was held on the bridge itself, but the congestion became so great that it was eventually moved to the dry land of

Southwark where it still remains. It was an engine, as well as a centre, of commerce; tolls were levied on all traffic passing over, and all vessels sailing under, the bridge. The tolls of 1398, for example, are recorded as a halfpenny for a small ship and a penny for a "greater one." "For ships which are filled with wood, one log of wood shall be given as toll." There is also extant an exhaustive inventory of goods that attracted the bridge toll, ranging from "vermillion" and "verdigrease" to almonds and garlic.

In the sixteenth century the bridge acquired another function, of equal significance to Londoners. It became a source of piped water. It had always been the washing machine, and the well, and the public convenience, of London. But in 1580 the first watermill was established on one of the arches closest to the City; from here the water was pumped, through tubes or "quills" of wood, to the adjacent streets. The experiment was so successful that other mills were installed upon other arches.

In his *Britannia* (1586) Camden reinforces the praise of a bridge that "may worthily carry away the prize from all bridges in Europe, furnished on both sides with passing faire houses, joining one to another in the manner of a street." There was then a gateway at the southern end of the bridge, and the bridge itself was by 1603, according to the *Chronicles of London Bridge*, "beautified with statelye palaces, built on the side therof . . . with excellent and beatuous housen built thereon." It was a fashionable address with the houses occupied, according to Stow, by "rich merchants and other wealthy citizens, mercers and haberdashers." On the roofs of some of the houses were built "penthouses" or river terraces. "Over the houses," one contemporary wrote, "were stately platforms leaded with rails and ballasters about them, very commodious and pleasant for walking and enjoying so fine a prospect up and down the river, and some had pretty little gardens with arbours." These terraces or penthouses were known at the time as "*hautepas*." It was altogether a desirable area. Hans Holbein and John Bunyan were two of its residents.

There was even a palace on the bridge, named "Nonesuch House" because of its unique character. It was an elaborate and fanciful affair, made entirely of pieces of wood fastened together with pegs; it was ornamented with turrets and towers and cupolas, with windows and weather-vanes, the whole wooden structure being lavishly painted and gilded. On its south side, facing the water, was a sundial with the emblem "Time and Tide stay for no man." There was still a chapel on the bridge, built on the eastern side above the tenth or central pier. It was a Gothic structure, some 60 feet

(18 m) in length and 40 feet (12 m) in breadth, with a crypt beneath it; its interior was decorated with fourteen clustered columns and eight pointed arch windows. Its crypt could be reached by ascending a flight of stone steps from the pier itself, so that it was of ready access from the water. The chapel was an integral part of the bridge. No one could buy fresh fish on the bridge before Mass had been celebrated at the chapel. In one of the houses above the chapel lived a haberdasher, Mr. Baldwin; he had been born there, and had lived for seventy-one years in that place. When he was eventually ordered to go to Chislehurst for a change of air, "he could not sleep in the country for want of the noise." He had always been used to the roar and rush of the tide beneath the bridge.

The many engravings show it to be a vast hive of human industry and human ingenuity, a monument to the energy and ambition of its makers. It was a vast street arching the water. As Michael Drayton wrote in *Polyolbion* (1622):

> With that most costly Bridge that doth him most renown,
> By which he clearly puts all other rivers down.

In the manner of a street, too, there were shops and alcoves, small alleys and hovels that somehow always managed to emerge among even the grandest edifices of sixteenth-century London. There were many buildings that contained a shop on the ground floor, and lodgings above. Some of these upstairs rooms reached a fourth or even fifth storey, and often touched each other across the thoroughfare at roof level. There was a "cage" or small prison for offenders. In the middle of the sixteenth century a woman was imprisoned and told "to cool herself there" for refusing to pray for the soul of a recently deceased Pope.

In the middle of the seventeenth century there were bookshops at the sign of "The Three Bibles" and "The Looking Glass"; there was a silver-smith with the sign of "The White Horse," and a milliner at the sign of "The Dolphin and Comb." There was a maker of breeches, Churcher and Christie, at the sign of "The Lamb and Breeches"; and a wig-maker, John Allan, at "The Locks of Hair," who "Sells all sorts of Hair, Curled or Un-curled." There was a map-seller "at the Golden Globe, under the Piazzas on London Bridge." When the maid of a needle-worker put a tub of hot ashes beneath her master's stairs, in 1632, she began a conflagration that de-stroyed some forty-three businesses along the northern end of the bridge.

Among them were several haberdashers, grocers, mercers and shoemakers. For some reason the shops were not rebuilt for twelve years. Yet the Bridge escaped the worst excesses of the Great Fire and the Plague. The flames of the conflagration were prevented from crossing the bridge by the speedy demolition of the houses in its path, and during the "visitation" of the epidemic only two inhabitants died. The environment of the bridge was, indeed, considered to be a healthy one. It was open to the cleansing wind, was washed by tides, and was clear of the cesspits and open drains of the crowded city. In prints and engravings of the bridge, there are to be seen buckets being lowered down on ropes from the various windows of the houses.

It was the bridge that acted as the principal highway for royal pageants and processions, and so became the setting for tilts and jousts. "And so the Kinge passed throwe London Bridge," as the *Chronicles* put it, "with his trumpetts blowinge before him":

> To london Brygge thanne rood oure kynge
> The processions there they mette hym right . . .
> To london Brigge when he com right
> Vp on the gate ther stode on hy
> A gyaunt that was full grym of might.
> And at the Drawe brigge that is faste by
> Two toures there were vp pight.

It was the bridge that witnessed the slaughter of invading rebel armies. It was the point of entry for visiting princes. It was the avenue for funeral processions. It was the bridge of pilgrims, who began their holy journey to Canterbury with a Mass at the chapel of St. Thomas on the bridge. It was the sanctuary for beggars and ruffians. It was a meeting place for apprentices. It was the haunt of citizens. It also became a necropolis, where the heads of traitors were placed. For, as Hall said in his account of the deposition of Jack Cade's head, "where men striue against the streame, their bote neuer cometh to his pretensed port." It was the vantage point for remarkable visitations, as on 21 March 1661 when "several Miraculous Sight seen in the Air Westward by divers persons of credit standing on London Bridge between 7 and 8 of the clock at night." The clouds parted to reveal "two great armies marching forth" which, after a sharp dispute, vanished;

then there appeared a cathedral, and then a tree, then various strange beasts.

The bridge embodied all the variety and heterogeneity of the city itself, with its rich and its poor, its mighty and its humble, its sorrowful and its joyous. The German traveller, Zacharias Conrad von Uffenbach, walked across it in 1710 without in fact realising that he had done so; he believed that he was simply walking down another London street. Yet Joseph Addison's patriotic knight, in 1714, declared "that the Thames was the noblest river in Europe; that London Bridge was a greater piece of work than any of the Seven Wonders of the World."

But of course this did not stop it from becoming an object of concern for those who used it every day. By the middle of the seventeenth century there were complaints about the excess of citizens who thronged upon the bridge, with the "irregular passing and repassing of coaches, carts and cars, and the standing of costers and mongers, and other loose people there." To avoid the press of people there were three vacancies opposite each other, between the houses, where people could step out of the thoroughfare and look down at the river. In 1685 the street across the bridge was widened, and the houses pulled down so that they might be reconstructed "in a new and regular manner."

Nevertheless by the eighteenth century the congestion of traffic and people on the bridge had once more become acute. It was still the only crossing of the river in the neighbourhood of the city and, as such, was notoriously over-used. As Thomas Pennant wrote, in *Some Account of London* (1790),

> I well remember the street on London Bridge, narrow, darksome and dangerous to passengers from the multitude of carriages; frequent arches of strong timber crossed the street, from the tops of the houses, to keep them together, and from falling into the river. Nothing but use could preserve the rest of the inmates, who soon grew deaf to the noise of the falling waters, the clamour of the watermen, or the frequent shrieks of the drowning wretches.

Another commentator noticed that "as there was no regular foot-way over the bridge, it was therefore the most usual and safest custom to follow a carriage which might be passing across it." By the middle of the eighteenth century, too, the fashionable residents had moved out; it had become insupportable, with its attraction to all the itinerant traders and vagrants of the city. The southern bank of the river had long had a reputation for noisomeness and excess, and that atmosphere was being communicated across the Thames.

So in 1760 the entire superstructure of shops and houses was pulled down; the bridge assumed a bare and denuded state, except for the presence of little "shelters" where pedestrians might escape from the throng of traffic and of people. In an age that demanded speed of communication, and unimpeded access to the city, it was the only solution. It is perhaps worth recording that three people were employed to direct approaching traffic to keep to the left; this is the first instance of the traffic directions that later played so large a part in London transportation. That traffic was counted on a July day in 1811. It amounted to 89,640 pedestrians and 2,924 carts, 1,240 coaches and 485 gigs, 769 wagons and 764 horses. By the time of its renovation in 1760 another great bridge had already been opened at Westminster, and preparations were being made for the building of a third bridge at Blackfriars. From the success of these bridges sprang all the other bridges over the Thames, culminating in the erection of Tower Bridge in 1894.

The faltering status of Old London Bridge was confirmed, in 1820, when an Act was passed to permit the demolition of the old bridge and the erection of a new structure. One anonymous contemporary apostrophised the fading bridge: "Alas, pass but another twenty years, and even thou stately old London Bridge! Even *thou* shalt live only in memory, and the draughts which are made now of thine image." Work began a few yards upstream from the old bridge in 1824, with the laying of the foundation stone by George IV. It was formally opened six years later, with five arches rather than the twenty arches of its predecessor.

In the nineteenth century this newly built bridge was the most frequented of all points of departure for the ocean-going or seafaring vessels. In his *London* (1872) Blanchard Jerrold remarks on the spectacle of that bridge as the vessel came upstream from the sea:

> It is curious to see the eager faces that crowd to the sides of a steamer from the ocean, when London Bridge is fairly outlined against the horizon, and the dome of St. Paul's rises behind. This is the view of Lon-

don that is familiar to all civilised peoples. "Le Pont de Londres!" the Frenchman explains, carrying his vivacious eyes rapidly over its proportions.

The barges and express boats and "citizen boats" sailed through the arches, dipping their sails and masts as they travelled under the bridge; the parapet was crowded with people, looking out at the scenes of farewell and of general leave-taking, watching the drooping pennants and the gleaming masts and the black-pitched hulls. Behind these crowds were the two lines of heavy traffic, going to and fro across the bridge. Beside the bridge were inns for travellers, porters, cab-men, and all the bustling crowds of a major destination; there were stables, and yards, and alleys, and passages filled with loiterers and officials and customs men.

For Coleridge the experience of standing upon the bridge was that of a "sort of beggarly day-dreaming, during which the mind of the dreamer furnishes for itself nothing but laziness, and a little mawkish sensibility." But there was an air of challenge for those travelling to new places and to new destinies.

The bridge completed in 1830 was, 130 years later, deemed to be sinking. It was sold to an American company, McCulloch Properties Inc., for the sum of $2,460,000. The bridge was then removed, piece by piece, and reconstructed in Lake Havasu City, Arizona. The cornerstone was laid in 1963, and the reconstituted bridge was opened seven years later. The new London Bridge—that across the Thames—was formally opened in the spring of 1973, and has taken its place in the litany of the bridges that have spanned this small stretch of earth and water. For a future generation the bridge now extant will be known as Old London Bridge, and will in turn pass away just like the bridge in the nursery rhyme.

There are other ways across the river. There are more subterranean channels beneath the Thames than beneath any other river in the world. As early as 1798 there had been a scheme to create a subfluminal tunnel between Tilbury and Gravesend, but it was abandoned. The dangers were too pressing; the risks enormous. So it turned out that the Thames Tunnel, dug beneath the river between Wapping and Rotherhithe, was the first underwater tunnel in the world. There had been plans for such a tunnel from the beginning of the nineteenth century, but the first attempts had failed. The river had broken through. In 1823 Marc Brunel was asked by Parliament to advance a new scheme, eventually finished by his son, Isambard Kingdom Brunel, some twenty years later. But the experiment succeeded only at a cost—the waters of the river invaded no fewer than five times. Deaths, however, were caused more by the insanitary conditions of the work than by drowning.

Marc Brunel's diary is filled with foreboding. On 26 May 1838, he recorded that "Heywood (a miner) died this morning. Two more on the sick list. Page is evidently sinking very fast . . . the air excessively offensive. It affects the eyes. I feel much debility after having been some time below . . . All complain of pain in the eyes." They were afflicted by blindness, temporary or permanent, that became known as the "tunnel disease." It may have been caused by the long-soaked sediment and detritus of the river, which had lain undisturbed for many thousands of years.

The metaphor of "sinking" here is also very suggestive, as if the workers were still in some sense caught up in the currents and forces of the river. They were below the river, where Brunel himself considered them to be "sacrificed" to the work of defying the natural world. At the time of one calamity a parson at Rotherhithe deemed it to be "a just judgement on the presumptuous aspirations of mortal men." The building of bridges had once been marked by ceremonies of veneration and propitiation. How much more dubious and dangerous to dig beneath a river, closer to the infernal regions from which it came? In the course of the work it became one of the wonders of London, and attracted eminent visitors intent upon seeing the progress made in burrowing beneath the Thames.

It was a foot-tunnel in its first years, notable for its gloom and dankness. It was 1,200 feet (365 m) long, and was more like a cavern than a tunnel. The American novelist, Nathaniel Hawthorne, left an account of it in *Our Old Home: A Series of English Sketches* (1863) as "an arched corridor, that extends into everlasting midnight. Gloomily lighted with jets of gas at regular intervals—plastered at the sides, and stone beneath the feet. It would have made an admirable prison." The air of hopelessness and weariness, associated with the image of the prison, seems to have haunted the site. *The Times* reported, upon the tunnel's opening in 1843, that "the very walls were in a cold sweat."

There were stalls and little shops along both sides of it, most of them kept by old women, but there were few customers. Hawthorne himself saw only half a dozen pedestrians in its whole length. It may be that most people felt some reluctance and uncertainty, even some primal fear, about walking beneath a great river. In 1870 it was converted into a tunnel for the underground system of the East London Railway Company. It survives still, a subterranean monument to the engineering skills of the nineteenth century. The river has never revisited the site.

In 1869 the Tower subway was dug beneath the river to connect Tower Hill in the north with Tooley Street in the south. It was lined with cast iron rather than with brick, and was designed for omnibuses travelling beneath the Thames. It was not a success. If the omnibus stopped for some reason in the middle of the tunnel, the sound of paddle steamers overhead could distinctly be heard by the passengers. It was then turned into a tunnel for pedestrians, before being entirely replaced by Tower Bridge. It is now what is known as a "ghost tunnel" used to house cables and pipelines. From the cast iron tube the constant noise of the water can still be heard. It has a reputation for being one of the loneliest spots in London. There is a curious fact that might in any case repel any putative visitor. The movement of the tides affects the shape of the tunnel, and under the pressure of high water it becomes slightly bulbous or egg-shaped.

The first purpose-built tunnel for underground trains, or "tube tunnel" as it became known, was constructed in 1890 between King William Street and Stockwell on the south side of the river; it was the first to possess two separate tunnels, one "up" and one "down," beneath the Thames. This was followed sixteen years later by the boring of a tunnel between Charing Cross and Waterloo. There were eventually some six separate "tube" tunnels beneath the river. The Blackwall road tunnel was opened in 1896, followed by the Rotherhithe tunnel in 1908 and the Dartford tunnel in 1963. In the middle of the twentieth century the Rotherhithe tunnel was described as being one of "gas-filled darkness" causing malaise and headache.

The bare and forbidding foot tunnel between Greenwich and the Isle of Dogs was completed in 1902. Those who have walked that distance beneath the river will know that it is an unnerving and even intimidating experience, with the realisation that the great force of the old river is rushing above one's head. At high tide the pedestrian walks some 53 feet (16 m) under the water, and at low tide the depth is 33 feet (10 m). It is one quarter of a mile long, and is always a cool and dank place, like the original Thames Tunnel. The fear is that of all subterranean things—that the forces of the natural world will rush in, overwhelming and unstoppable. The tunnels beneath the Thames are haunted places. They are delving deep into previous eras of the earth's history, reaching further down than the first beds or rivulets that became the Thames. The gods of the Thames cannot reside in such places. The tunnels do not have the animation or restlessness of the river. They are empty, dark, and echoic.

CHAPTER 20

River Law

The river has always been the centre of national law, as well as of national punishment. The Thames has been the focus of power, at Westminster Abbey and at Westminster Palace, at Windsor and at the Tower. At the very end of the sixth century St. Augustine met the Celtic bishops beside the Thames in order to solve some problems of ecclesiastical observance. Cricklade and Down Ampney are possible sites for such collocations. Bede states that one meeting was "at a place which is to this day called Augustine's Oak . . . on the borders of the Hwicce and the West Saxon." The oak was cut down in 1865, and eventually was placed in the churchyard of St. Sampson's church in Cricklade where it mouldered away.

In 747 Eadbert called a synod at "Clovesho" to determine, among other things, the status of the churches in Kent; Clovesho has been interpreted as Cliffe, lying beside the Thames estuary. Later in the eighth century Offa, sovereign of Mercia, held autumn synods at his palaces and churches in the Thames Valley; there was a synod at Brentford in 781 and another at Chelsea in 787 (the ancient waterfront there has recently been discovered). In 890 Alfred the Great held a parliament, or *witenagemot,* at Shifford, on the Oxfordshire bank of the Thames. The convocation was commemorated in a later Anglo-Saxon poem:

At sifford seten thaines manie
Fele biscopes and fele woclered
Erles prude cnihtes egloche.

So "many thanes," "many wise bishops and clerks," as well as "prudent
earls" and "admirable knights," met at Shifford. The location could only
have been chosen because of its situation by the river. There is in the vicinity a Court Close, supposedly harbouring a relic known as "Alfred's
Stone"; there is a "Knight Bridge," a "Kingsway Field," and a path known
as "royal way." In 1008 a *witenagemot* was summoned by King Ethelred to
the riverside town of Eynsham. In the abbey of the Benedictines here, according to the chronicles, "they reasoned and held discourse of many
things concerning the recovery of the worship of the Catholic religion, and
also for the amendment and furtherance of the state of the commonwealth." The river was thus closely associated with spiritual authority.

In 1018 Cnut held an assembly or parliament at Oxford. Here it was
agreed that the laws and customs of the Anglo-Saxons would be employed
to the south of the Thames, and those of the Danes to the north. It is supposed that Cnut had a palace, or more likely an armed fort, close to the
river at the ancient ford of Duxford. On an island in the river near
Kingston, Raven's Ait, a peace was arranged in the early thirteenth century
between Henry III and Louis of France. Then in 1305 the Scots made a
treaty with the English "at the Manor of Sheane on Thames." The presence
of the river, which generally goes unremarked in historical accounts of
these episodes, is consistent and continuous. In the fifteenth century no
fewer than four parliaments were held by the Thames at Reading.

Of course the most notable instance of the river's law-giving is connected with the island on the Thames by Runnymede where, in 1215, King
John ordained the liberties of the British people—or at least of that section
of the populace represented by the noble barons. It is notable that in the
Magna Carta document itself there is a demand that weirs upon the river
be "utterly put down" so that the beginnings of English democracy were
fundamentally associated with the liberties of the river. The name of
Runnymede has been variously interpreted as "council meadow" and as
"meadow of runes." Whatever the precise connotations of the word, it is
likely that the two parties encamped on the opposite banks of the river at
this point before meeting on the island between them.

There were also Mints by the river, where the coin of the realm was produced and distributed. There were Mints at Wallingford, at Oxford and at Cricklade; the most significant of them was beside the Thames in London, just to the east of Tower Hill. It is easy to see the significance of the connection between the coining of money and the flowing of the river, at least in terms of the industrial process, but perhaps there is some more arcane association.

In the sphere of law and authority it is also worth noting that the Thames police were the first regular police force in the country. It was set up after diverse complaints from the mercantile interest that goods and property were being stolen from the warehouses and quays by the river. In 1798 Patrick Colquhoun, formerly a magistrate at Wapping, established the first force that was armed and directed by a centralised organisation (the Bow Street foot patrol was of limited jurisdiction). The river police are in that sense the harbingers of the 1829 Metropolitan Police Act. The river had helped to organise investigation and detection in the capital.

Colquhoun also set up a system of discipline in the new docks. The loose clothing of the labourers and sailors was prohibited, with "no frocks, trowsers, jemmies, pouches, or bags" to be allowed on the premises ("jemmies" were a species of undergarment, with pockets both before and behind). The new Thames police completed the network of mercantile exploitation that was maintained over the river when they became responsible for the payment of wages to the "lumpers" and other dock workers. There were quay surveyors and watchmen and quay guards; there was a special court, and prison cells, at 259 Wapping Old Stairs. The present Wapping Police Station, the headquarters of the Thames Division of the Metropolitan Police, still occupies the site.

Yet how, in the larger sense, can you manage the river? It has been regulated but it has never wholly been tamed. But that has not stopped generations of courtiers, civic leaders and engineers trying to load chains upon the Thames. In the late tenth century "Asser," the biographer and supposed contemporary of King Alfred, reported that the river was already organised within a system of complex rules and principles; in particular there were regulations concerning free access to the water unimpeded by mills, weirs and fish-ponds. This was important in a period when, in a hundred different stretches, the river stood in danger of being converted for private use. The Thames was declared by Alfred and his successors—most notably William the Conqueror—to be a public highway.

There has always been a battle between Crown and City, however, for ultimate jurisdiction over the Thames. Was it a royal river, allowing passage from one palace to the next, or was it the city's river of trade? In 1197 Richard I ceded provisional control of the Thames to the Corporation of London; the authority of the City seems to have endured up to Staines, but no further. Here the stone known as the City Stone was placed. The rest of the river was of no concern to the merchants of London, but the ownership of the lower reaches was always in question. There were many disputes between the Lord Mayor and the Constable of the Tower, the royal representative, over the rights to the water. In the reign of Henry III "the Cityes Jurisdiction over the said River, was set forth and allowed," and then again in the reign of Edward II it was declared that *Aqua Thamisiae pertinet ad Civitatem London usque mare*—"The water of the Thames, down to the sea, belongs to the Corporation of London." In 1613 the Lord Mayor of London was deemed to be wholly responsible for the conservation of "her dearly loved Minion, the river of Thames."

But no judicial proceeding could pre-empt the greed or selfishness of the monarchy. The proposed construction of the Embankments, in the 1850s, precipitated a protracted battle in the courts between Crown and City. The solicitor for the Crown put forward the case that "the Thames being a navigable river and an arm of the sea prima facie belongs to the Crown, by virtue of its prerogative, as far as the water ebbs and flows." The legal proceedings continued for thirteen years. It was eventually agreed that the sovereign owned "the bed and soil" of the river and the seashore, at the same time as the Crown gave a newly established Thames Conservancy the title and right of the management of the river itself. But could Victoria in any meaningful sense be said to "own" the Thames? She might own the land upon which it flowed, but did she have any proprietorial rights over the water that ran into the sea and fell from the sky? Can you own the rain and the snow?

Over the centuries there were sporadic attempts to clear the river of notable obstructions, to control the charges levied by lock-keepers or the proprietors of weirs, and to maintain the towing-paths along the banks. But the local landowners and even the local millers were more powerful than any commission or London authority. The first Thames authority was established in 1695; it was composed of local Justices of the Peace, who were obliged to fix the tolls and thus expedite navigation, but they had little success. They were succeeded by the Thames Navigation Commission in 1751, and nineteen years later the Thames Commissioners were formally appointed. There were six hundred of them, but this somewhat unwieldy body pushed through a programme of new wooden locks and turnpikes. They were in turn followed by the members of the Thames Conservancy in 1857. Then in 1908 the Port of London Authority was created to manage the docks and the tidal river, from a point 265 feet below Teddington, while the Thames Conservancy was charged with the maintenance of the Thames above that point. One of their notices became well known for its general scope—"All Persons Using the River Thames and the Locks, Works, and Towing Paths Thereof Must Take Them as They Find Them, and Do So at Their Own Risk." The Conservancy finally expired in 1974, and passed its powers to the newly formed Thames Water Authority. This august body lasted for only fifteen years before it gave way for the National Rivers Authority. This survived for only six years, and in 1995 was replaced by the present Environment Agency. The river runs on.

CHAPTER 21

The Criminal Element

꘠

There has always been crime on the river. In an account of 13 July 1752, the "Ordinary," or chaplain, of Newgate prison states of one inmate that "he did work upon the River, this is a very suspicious Way of Life, such People being generally looked upon as getting more Money by the bye than by their Labour." His remark confirms the reputation of the Thames for lawlessness. The life of the river for many centuries was quarrelsome and on occasions highly dangerous, boatmen pitched against lock-keepers and millers organised against fishermen. The seamen fought against the Customs, and the wherrymen fought against the sailors, in an environment where land law was not recognised.

Theft was of course the most immediate and obvious transgression. It was estimated by Patrick Colquhoun that there were almost eleven thousand people who earned their living by dishonest activity on the Thames. In his *Treatise on the Commerce and Police of the River Thames* (1800) he described the river as the peculiar territory for "acts of peculation, fraud, embezzlement, pillage and depredation." The Thames had helped to create "a species of systematic delinquency, which in its different ramifications, exhibits a degree of turpitude as singular as it is unparalleled."

While hundreds of ships lay at anchor, waiting for the tide or for a suitable wharf, they were pestered by thieves and wreckers who were intent upon acquiring their cargo. There were smugglers all the way down the estuary, taking on consignments of wool or other merchandise; there were "river pirates," armed thieves who at night cut the mooring ropes of lighters carrying goods and waited for them to drift upon the banks or foreshore. There were "night plunderers," watermen who worked under cover of darkness, and "scuffle hunters" or "long apron men" who specialised in stealing the goods left on the quaysides. There were "light horsemen," who were the renegade mates of ships and revenue officers, and "heavy horsemen," the porters and labourers earning a second living. Some threw over goods at high tide, to be recovered by accomplices when the tide had ebbed.

The "copemen" were those who received the stolen goods, and their operations could be found down any of the myriad alleys and highways of the river city. There was so much life below, in a thousand cellars that were often no more than holes in the ground, that concealment was easy. King David Lane in Shadwell was well known for its receivers. Some of them lived further from the river: a tobacconist in the St. Ann parish of Soho, Mr. Cooper, was a well-known receiver of snuff and tobacco.

Downriver, closer to the mouth of the open sea, there were also "wreckers" who with false lights lured unsuspecting pilots onto the mudbanks. Much of the estuary, with its streams and marshes, was ideal ground for the concealment and carriage of contraband. "Owlers," for example, were those who smuggled packs of fleeces through the marshy terrain. For many centuries smuggling was endemic to the estuary, where watermen would find their route through the waterways or along the tributaries. The beaches under the cliffs at Reculver, or at Whitstable, were perfect havens for their trade. Other smugglers would slip into the river Swale, or the river Medway, or Yantlet Creek, in order to escape the attentions of the revenue men. Pubs and churches were used as convenient storage, and some goods were suspended in the pools and rivulets of the marshes. Of Faversham Defoe wrote, in his *Tour through the Whole Island of Great Britain* (1724–7), that "I know nothing else this town is remarkable for, except the most notorious smuggling trade." It was rumoured that, in Essex, gin was in such large supply that the inhabitants cleaned their windows with it. A parliamentary report noted that, as soon as vessels from the East Indies had entered their moorings along the Thames, "the place which they lie becomes the resort of smugglers, and resembles a public fair." There were also illegal transporters of people as well as of goods, the direct descendants of the human traders who would smuggle renegade Jesuit priests into and out of England in the early sixteenth century.

The amount of goods entering the Port of London was so vast, and so various, that all forms of theft were practised. Before the building of the defended docks at the beginning of the nineteenth century the loss of revenue was estimated at approximately £800,000 per annum. It was supposed that one-third of those engaged in dock labour were practising some form of felony. But, since most of the money found its way into the pockets of Londoners, it was considered by the perpetrators to be a version of fair trade. It was familiar; it was customary. The mud-larks and the scuffle hunters believed themselves to be earning a living from the river with as much right as the mariners and the pilots. To the coopers and lightermen the theft of tobacco from hogsheads was known as "socking," and was preserved as an "old Custom." It is a matter of common sense, too, that many of the merchants and clerks involved in the river traffic were also complicit with the felons. There were "game ships" and "game officers" who were corruptible. It could be said, in fact, that the Thames materially helped to create crime within the metropolis.

The river has been connected with punishment as well as crime. That is why it has been described as angry or even savage. The Thames, composed of immense volumes of water, is itself inherently destructive. When it floods, it wreaks havoc. It can seem harsh, and cruel. Shelley once professed to Thomas Love Peacock that "it runs with the blood and bones of a thousand heroes and villains, and no doubt the water is sour with tainting." The entire history of the river strengthens and confirms his opinion. As a popular ballad, on the flight of King James II's wife in 1688, put it:

> Away they went, through driving sleet,
> Across the angry Thames . . .

The Thames was for many centuries part of the fierce ritual of "ducking." It was a common penalty, dating at least from the early medieval period, but was only infrequently mentioned in the public prints. It was too familiar to need extended description. It was generally inflicted upon women or "scolds"; the term was applied to mature females who used foul language, who nagged their husbands, or who slandered other members of the community. A scold would be strapped in a chair, or upon a stool, and then lowered into the river three times. At Kingston, for example, a beam for that purpose jutted out from the central arch of the bridge. It was first deployed in the summer of 1572, when the wife of the grave-maker, Mrs. Downing, was ducked three times "over hed and eres," and it must have been constantly in demand, since a new stool was ordered by the churchwardens that same year. The last use of this stool at Kingston occurred in the spring of 1745. The *Evening Post* of 27 April reported that "last week, a woman that keeps the King's Head alehouse, Kingston, in Surrey was ordered by the court to be ducked for scolding, and was accordingly placed in the chair and ducked in the river Thames under Kingston Bridge, in the presence of two or three thousand people." That particular stool of punishment had been in place for 173 years.

This penitential, and often fatal, ceremony was connected with the idea of river water as the medium for ritual cleansing. In the early third century a Church Father, Tertullian, recorded the incidence of votaries who were baptised in springs or rivers "as they presumed to think unto redemption and exemption from the guilt of their perjuries." He added that "among the ancients anyone who had stained himself with homicide went in search of waters that could purge him of his guilt." There seems no reason to doubt that similar purgative rituals occurred on the island of Britain. It was a belief that survived for many hundreds of years. The Thames may also have been used as a test for guilt or innocence in another sense. There was a tradition of making suspected persons drink from a well or river; for the guilty the water became contaminated, typically causing dropsy.

If the river was the original home of the gods, it was the source of all justice. In 1646 Cromwell ordered the decapitation of the royalist soldiers who had defended the castle at Wallingford. "Let the river have them," he is reported as saying, "before they corrupt the land as the king corrupted England."

The accounts of life in the villages of the Upper Thames contain many stories of witches and their craft, and indeed more witches were recorded in the Thames region than in any other part of the country. They have names like Bet Hyde and Poll Packer, Minty Frewin and Mother Dutton, Old Margaret and Elizabeth Stile, Urania Boswell and Mother Hibblemeer, Brickie Jane and Granny Pantin. But the fables of these women have more distant roots than the presence of some "wise women" in the immediate neighbourhood of the river. The association of witches and the Thames may in fact be an echo of the belief that female spirits and nymphs were wreathed within the waters, and that the river itself was to be worshipped as the "Great Mother." If female deities were connected with the Thames, then it was perhaps only natural that female demons or female malevolence would form part of the cluster of associations.

There were strong witch traditions in Henley, in Reading and in Wallingford. A fungus growing upon elm trees in the Thames Valley was known in the nineteenth century as "witches' butter," and was said to be caused by the churning stick of a witch. It has been claimed that many of the stiles along the path of the Upper Thames are made of iron, to keep the witches from "crossing over." It was the custom, too, to wear the herb vervain as an antidote to the "owl blast"—the sickness caused by a witch's curse. It is reported that, as late as 1946, some of the older inhabitants of Cricklade carried the foot of a goose in a small linen bag to ward off the attentions of witches. In the late twentieth century there were reports of witchcraft at Kemble, at Appleton and at Reading. The prolonged presence of such customs and beliefs is easy to dismiss as mere hearsay, or historical sensationalism, but the weight and body of tradition cannot be denied so easily.

Trials of witches were generally held by the river itself. One venue was the neighbourhood of "Shrew Ash" in Richmond Park. And of course the trial by ordeal is well known. The suspected witch, with her hands tied, was thrown into the Thames. If she floated the river was rejecting her, and she was deemed to be guilty. If she sank her innocence was proved. But there were more certain punishments. The first occasion on which London Bridge is mentioned in the official records occurs in the *Codex Diplomaticus Aevi Saxonici* for AD 984. It is narrated that a witch was taken up and condemned for creating the wooden image of a man. Thereupon "they took that woman and drowned her at London Bridge." The river was the appropriate form of punishment for supernatural transgression. It is mentioned so much as a matter of course, in the *Codex*, that it may have been the conventional death for those accused of witchcraft. In the thirteenth century two women, with their arms and legs tied together, were thrown into a pool called Bikepool (near the present town of Croydon) that communicated with the Thames. There is some intimate association between the river and what we call "paganism." Something has settled there.

The river in some sense becomes the sacred witness of punishment. It is perhaps not coincidental that the two major sites of execution on land, Tyburn and Smithfield, were adjacent to the Thames tributaries of the Ty-

Chertsey Abbey and its farms in the fifteenth century. For centuries religious communities were a great presence along the Thames valley, but almost all were reduced to ruins at the time of the Reformation. Dorchester Abbey (below) was one of the few survivors.

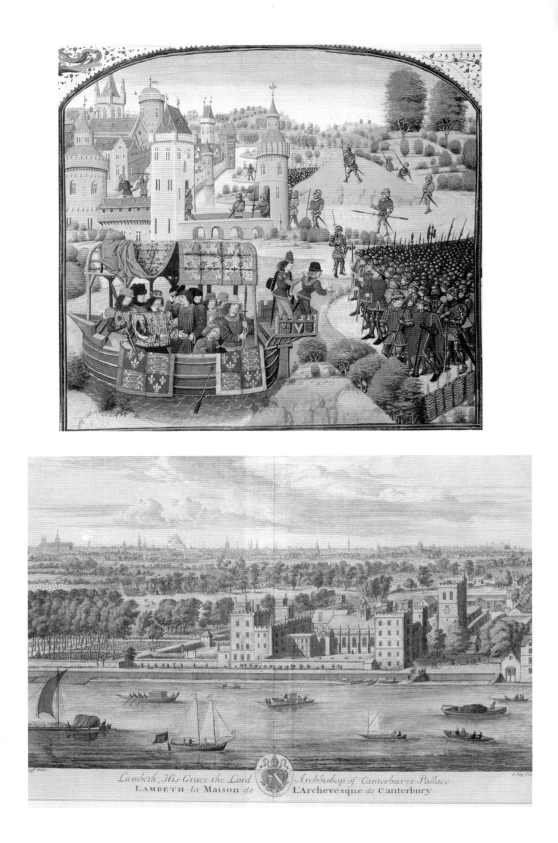

The river has always been a source of power, both sacred and secular. That is why abbeys, monasteries, palaces and parliaments have been erected beside it. Left: the Tower of London and Lambeth Palace. This page: Windsor Castle and Westminster.

The bridges of the Thames are its most enduring human feature. There are 106 pedestrian bridges now spanning the river. Traces of bridges date from the Bronze and Iron Ages, and before that large rocks were thrown into the water in order to form a path. Above: old London Bridge, *c.* 1630; below: the opening of new London Bridge, 1831.

There are now nine railway bridges across the Thames. The Greenwich railway viaduct at Deptford (above) dates from 1836. The millennium footbridge, completed in 2000 and opened to the public in 2002, is the most recent of the Thames bridges.
It links St. Paul's and the Tate Modern.

The various sports and races of the Thames have a long history. There are accounts in the twelfth century of jousting on the river. Doggett's Coat and Badge Race (above, *c.*1820) is the oldest competition still thriving. In 1721 Thomas Doggett, an Irish actor, established a prize of a coat and silver badge for the winner of a race from London Bridge to Chelsea. It is contested by six water-men every year.

Henley Regatta in the 1900s (below). The first Henley Regatta, in 1829, was in fact also the first university boat-race between Oxford and Cambridge.

In the Edwardian period the Thames became the river of pleasure and of fashion. Everyone, from earls to cockneys, liked messing about on the water. It became an egalitarian delight. Above: pleasure boats at Pangbourne; below: Goring lock.

The era of cheap transport heralded the most popular period in the long history
of the Thames. "Day-trippers" became the new sovereigns of the water.

burn and the Fleet. But there is a more direct association. There was a gallows set up by the riverside at Dagenham, and it was in use as late as 1780. There were gibbet posts stretching along the foreshore at Millwall, to be seen in one of Hogarth's engravings from the series on the fate of the idle apprentice. There was a gallows near Greenwich, at a place now known as Bugsby's Causeway; the name may derive from "bug" or evil spirit, which suggests that it was known to be tainted ground. There was another gallows in the neighbourhood of Blackwall Point, and a place by the river (site now unknown) called Hanging Ditch. There is a famous Hanging Ditch in Manchester, which once connected the rivers Irk and Irwell; the connection between execution and running water is not exclusively one for the Thames. Just by Butler's Wharf, close to Tower Bridge, was the mouth of one of London's lost rivers called the Neckinger; the word means "devil's neck-cloth," which is a term for the hangman's rope. We may justifiably speculate, then, that this also was a place of hanging.

The most famous site of riverine execution, however, was Execution Dock. It was never a true dock, of course, except in the sense that the dead were harboured here. The gallows was originally situated by the river at St. Katharine's Dock, but in the sixteenth century it was removed downstream to Wapping. It was then moved from the western to the eastern end of Wapping when the defensive wall was erected. Hence there has been some confusion about its exact location, with at least two public houses claiming that honour. The condemned—who were by tradition customarily those accused of piracy—were taken from Newgate or the Marshalsea and, following a silver oar, were marched to the river. Here they were despatched or, in the words of the river people, they "danced the hempen jig." Their bodies were then tarred and placed in a gibbet by the water. At a later date they were bound with an iron chain, their wrists similarly fastened, and then shackled to a wooden post near the low water mark; here they hung until three tides had passed over their bodies, just as the scolds suffered from three duckings. The hangings at Execution Dock continued until 1834.

Then there were the hulks, a baleful sight upon the Thames for almost a hundred years. These were the prison ships, otherwise disused vessels that were refitted to contain a captive crew; they had been established in 1776, and the last of them did not burn until the summer of 1857. Ships such as the *Discovery*, the *Retribution*, and the *Belliqueux* were used to hold convicts who, as a result of the War of Independence, were unfortunately deprived of the opportunity of being taken to America. Many thousands of them served their sentences at Deptford, at Woolwich, at Chatham and elsewhere, where they were forced to labour on shore-works. They returned to their ships each night, where they were kept in chains. They inhabited the lower decks, some five or six hundred prisoners confined on each—the new prisoners were consigned to the lowest deck of all—where "the horrible effects arising from the continual rattling of chains, the filth and vermin" are better imagined than described. One prisoner explained that "of all the shocking scenes I had ever beheld, this was the most distressing . . . Nothing short of a descent to the infernal regions can be at all worthy of a comparison with it." The river had become a hell. The wharf at Deptford was popularly known as Deadman's Dock. When the inmates died, their bodies were taken to the marshes and perfunctorily buried there. There is a red-flowering nettle that grows along the marshes at Plumstead and the Arsenal; it was once known as "the convicts' flower."

There were other prisons beside the river. The Clink was next to the water at Southwark, while the Fleet prison was erected less than 100 yards (90 m) from the Thames shore. Tilbury Fort was employed as a prison, and the Millbank penitentiary (now the site of the Tate Gallery) was a famous "modern" prison organised on Benthamite principles. The octagonal shape of the gaol is still visible from the air; a sculpture by Henry Moore, "The Locking Piece," marks the point where the prisoners boarded the ships that would take them down the Thames on their way to Australia. The river would be one of their last views of England.

CHAPTER 22

The Workers of the River

n her pioneering survey, *Sources of London English*, Laura Wright has listed the variety of medieval workers who took their livings from the Thames—from the baillies of Queenhithe and Billingsgate, who acted as customs officers, to the ubiquitous and necessary watermen. There were conservators, who were responsible for maintaining the embankments and the weirs, and there were the garthmen who worked in the fish garths or enclosures; there were galleymen and lightermen and shoutmen, called after the names of their vessels, and there were hookers who were named after the manner in which they caught their fish. There were water-bailiffs and sub-conservators to manage the river. The searcher patrolled the Thames in search of illegal fish weirs, and the tideman worked on its banks and foreshores whenever the tide permitted him to do so.

All of these occupations persisted for many centuries, as did those jobs that depended upon the trade of the river. There were always warehousemen and porters, but along the sixteenth-century Thames there were infinite gradations in the status and employments of such people. There were tacklehouse porters and ticket porters, fellowship porters and companies porters. These were the four "brotherhoods," each of which had a special monopoly on certain goods. The ticket porters, for example, had a monopoly on materials imported from Danzig as well as all Irish products. Their hold upon trade of course meant that they received various special privileges and sometimes over-generous compensation. The tacklehouse porters were paid 1 guinea for discharging 100 quarters (1.27 tonnes) of malt, when other porters would have been happy to undertake the work for 8 shillings and 4 pence. The river was always a haven of restrictive practices.

Yet it was not easy work for any of them. They carried most goods upon their backs, since the rough surfaces of the quays and nearby streets were not suitable for wagons or large carts; the merchandise characteristically arrived in barrels which could be rolled from the ship along each quay. If the burden was too great to be carried by a single man, then the goods were slung on poles resting on the shoulders of two men. It was a slow and expensive method of business.

There was also a puzzling change of status. By the late eighteenth century dockside labour was considered to be the most disreputable, and certainly the least desirable, form of work. Before that time river work had been seen in a generally favourable light. For Langland, writing in the fourteenth century, the labourers working on river merchandise "throve the best." The porters of the seventeenth and early eighteenth centuries were obliged to be freemen of the city, and were if anything aristocrats of labour. But in the years from the late eighteenth to early nineteenth centuries there was a marked change in attitude. This was in part because the working river was within the region of the East End, which in this period acquired an unenviable reputation.

It could be said in fact that the first industrial population in England grew up around the Thames. With the dockers and the porters, the engineers and the warehousemen, the watermen and the draymen, the costermongers and the touters, the clerks and the carters, the smiths and the stevedores—as well as the vast assembly of ancillary trades such as tavern-keepers and laundresses, food-sellers and street-hawkers, shopkeepers and prostitutes, marine store dealers and oyster-men—there was a working population of many thousands congregated in a relatively small area of the East End. It has been calculated that, in the neighbourhood of Shadwell, some 60 per cent of men earned their living as seamen or watermen while 10 per cent were engaged in ship-building and repairs. There were more varieties of business to be observed by the riverside than in any other part of the city. As a result, with the possible exception of Seven Dials, the East End was also the most intensively inhabited region of London. The Isle of

Dogs, for example, was in the nineteenth century colonised by the small houses put up for workers and their families by William Cubitt.

In that century, too, dockside work was believed to be the poorest paid, and generally deemed to be the least skilled and the most irregular of employments. None of these charges was in fact accurate. Dockers could earn more than the carmen of the metropolis, for example, and there was plenty of work for those who were fit enough to undertake it. Yet it was also considered to be rough and dirty labour, the province of the lower classes of workers or of those who were otherwise unemployable. The atmosphere of the working river was one of dust and mud, of filth and smoke. The faces of some dockers were blue with indigo or black with coal-dust, their garments smeared with the detritus of the merchandise they carried. There was also some connection with the generally bad reputation of watermen and bargees. The river was linked with licence and bad language. The river was associated with smuggling and theft. To work on, or by, the river was in itself disreputable.

It was a world apart, with its own language and its own laws. From the Chinese sailors in the opium dens of Limehouse to the smugglers on the malarial flats of the estuary, the workers of the river were not part of any civilised dispensation. The alien world of the river had entered them. That alienation was also expressed in the slang of the docks, which essentially amounted to backslang or the reversal of ordinary words. This backslang also helped in the formulation of Cockney rhyming slang, so that the vocabulary of Londoners was directly affected by the life of the Thames.

Other slang emanated from the river. The workers in the grain and corn warehouses of Milwall Docks were known as "toe-rags," because of the sacking they wore over their boots; the word itself then became a synonym for a despised individual. The lightermen in the Port of London referred to their colleagues working downriver as "chalkies" or "carrot crunchers." The stevedores who characteristically worked at the Surrey Docks were named after the Spanish word for a packer, *estibador*.

The reports in the nineteenth-century press reveal a heterogeneous world of dock labour, in which the crowds of "casuals" waiting for work at the dock gates at 7:45 a.m. include penniless refugees, bankrupts, old soldiers, broken-down gentlemen, discharged servants, and ex-convicts. There were some four or five hundred permanent workers who earned a regular wage and who were considered to be the patricians of dockside labour. But there were some 2,500 casual workers who were hired by the shift. Henry Mayhew, in *London Labour and the London Poor* (1849–50), has left an account of those congregated at the entrances of the docks waiting to be chosen for employment—"some in half-fashioned surtouts burst at the elbow, with the dirty shirts showing through; others in greasy sporting jackets, with red pimpled faces; others in rags of gentility; some in rusty black; others with the knowing thieves' curl on each side of the jaunty cap." The work for which they competed had become ever more unpleasant. Steam-power could not be used for the cranes, for example, because of the danger of fire. So the cranes were powered by treadmills. Six to eight men entered a wooden cylinder and, laying hold of ropes, would tread the wheel round. They could lift 20 hundredweight (1 tonne), to an average height of 27 feet (8.2 m), forty times in any one hour. This was part of the life of the river unknown to those who were intent upon its more picturesque aspects.

There were other workers by the river. There were the dredgers or "river-finders" who searched the water looking for articles that had fallen overboard from the argosy of ships going up and down the Thames. The derisory word "tosh" comes from the activity of the "toshers," the group of watermen who dredged the river for flotsam (those articles that are found floating in the water, unattached to any particular source) and jetsam (those goods and articles that are deliberately thrown into the sea, perhaps for lightening a ship in peril of sinking). Then there were the "mud-larks" who worked on the foreshore, many of them very young children or very old women who spent their lives in the filthy water searching for small bits of coal, lumps of metal, or stray pieces of wood. They waited by the stairs until the tide had gone down sufficiently to uncover the banks, and then they scattered in all directions. Henry Mayhew described them silently crouched over the mud beneath their feet and "with a stolid look of wretchedness they plash their way through the mire, their bodies bent down while they peer anxiously about."

They were among the wretchedly poor living in the courts and alleys of the riverside, "scarcely half-covered by the tattered indescribable things that serve them for clothing; their bodies are grimed with the foul soil of the river, and their torn garments stiffened up like boards with dirt of every possible description." These were the people of the river.

There were also many immemorial occupations upon the Thames. The history of the river, for example, is in part the history of the sailor. Their occupation did not noticeably change over the centuries, although there were obvious alterations in their appearance. In the Saxon period the sailors wore red or blue (the Danish sailors were dressed in black) but in the medieval period they wore leather jerkins and costumes of coarse felt. By the fifteenth century they were dressed with quilted jackets and leather breastplates; they were also given leather helmets. In the sixteenth century they wore short coats of white or sky-blue, as well as wide and baggy breeches; they wore fur caps rather than helmets, in the manner of pilgrims. In the late seventeenth century the fashion had changed to one of striped trousers, with short jackets and buckled shoes. In his *New London Spy* (1794) Sir John Fielding, junior, wrote of the sailors at Wapping that their "manner of living, speaking, acting and dressing, behaving are so peculiar to themselves" they formed a quite different race. Then, by the early nineteenth century, they were wearing bell-bottom trousers, waistcoats, and striped jumpers with open collars; their costume was completed with the monkey-jacket and the black silk foulard.

There were more specific Thames "types" among the teeming humanity by the river. These included the porter, the lumper, the holder, the decker and the myriad other divisions of labourer. But more particularly there was the figure of the Thames waterman, renowned in song and story as the epitome of the tidal river. He was deemed to be wild, uncultivated, surly and rough of speech.

The Watermen's Company was established in 1555, but of course the occupation is much older. There is a document of 1293, for example, in which the watermen between London and Gravesend were prosecuted for over-charging—that "they did take from passengers unjust fares against their will," extorting 1 penny each rather than the customary halfpenny. This particular complaint was levelled against them over many centuries. In "London Lackpenny," an anonymous poem of the early fifteenth century, a traveller visits London:

> Then hyed I me to Belynges Gate
> And one cryed "Hoo go we hence"
> I prayed a bargeman, for God's sake
> That he would spare me my expence
> "Thou stepst not here," quoth he, "under II pence."

There was also the problem of overcrowding. Many watermen of the fourteenth and fifteenth centuries were prosecuted for taking more than three people in any one vessel. They were also forbidden to moor on the south bank of the river, in case "thieves and malefactors" took possession of their boats. It is a clear indication of the perceived difference between the two shores, with the river acting as a boundary just as it had once been a frontier between warring British tribes. There were also later restrictions, such as the measures in the mid-seventeenth century prohibiting transport on Sunday; it was considered to be "prophanation" for "any one coming by water to his Lodging on the Lords Day," and soldiers were posted on both banks of the Thames to arrest any malefactors. It is a matter of some interest why travelling by water, rather than by land, was considered to be unholy. There was in this regard, in the nineteenth century, a Society for Promoting Religion among Watermen, Bargemen and Rivermen in general.

There is an important distinction, however, between the boatmen of the river. Watermen were (and are) those who are concerned with the carriage of people upon the river, employing barges or wherries for that purpose, whereas lightermen are concerned with the transport of goods within lighters. As in most riverine trades the skills of the watermen were passed from fathers to sons. They would be trained in the lore of the tides, and the variations within each different reach of the river; they would learn the effects of the wind, where the river changes course, and would learn to gauge the depth of the water at any particular point.

At the end of the sixteenth century there were estimated to be some three thousand watermen, but at the beginning of the eighteenth century that number had risen to eight thousand. By the end of that century the number had risen still further to twelve thousand, two thousand of whom were apprentices. There are other authorities who believe the figures to be much higher—claiming that there were some twenty thousand watermen on the river in the sixteenth century, and some forty thousand in the eighteenth century, but all numbers must be approximate. It is important only to note the supremacy of river traffic and river transport. The energy of the city, and of the country, was the energy of the river. In the nineteenth century, however, their numbers began to fall away as new forms of transport appeared on the Thames and as new bridges were constructed between the shores. Waterloo Bridge, for example, was erected between 1811 and 1817. Mayhew calculated their number, in 1850, as sixteen hundred.

They were obliged to wear a badge upon their arm, for the purposes of identification, but they also wore a distinctive short jacket and hat. Their most celebrated representative, John Taylor, the "water poet," confessed that "there are many rude uncivil fellows in our Company" but then excused their behaviour on account of the provocations they received from their passengers. Thus the "roaring boy" or gallant would "no sooner kiss the cushions, but with a volley of new coined oaths . . . he hath never left roaring, row, row, row, a pox on you row . . . and when his scurviness has landed where he pleases, he hath told me I must wait on him, and he will return to me presently." And of course he never does.

There were other perils facing the watermen. In the seventeenth and eighteenth centuries, for example, they became peculiarly liable for "impressment" or enforced conscription into the navy where their riverine skills were deemed to be useful. So in the late eighteenth century Charles Dibdin wrote a famous song on the woes of the watermen:

> Then farewell my trim-built wherry,
> Oars, and coat, and badge farewell!
> Never more at Chelsea Ferry
> Shall your Thomas take a spell.

Whatever their misfortunes, however, the watermen of the Thames were generally considered to be degraded and reprehensible. There is a famous engraving by Thomas Rowlandson, entitled "Miseries of London" and dated 1807, which shows a group of voracious watermen—recognisable by their hats and badges—harassing an old lady on Wapping Old Stairs. Rowlandson depicts them bawling out "Oars, Sculls, Sculls, Oars, Oars."

More reprehensible still, in the public imagination, were the bargees of the river. They piloted, and for brief periods lived upon, the barges otherwise known as "canal boats," "monkey boats" or "wussers." They were known for their pugnacity and their caustic wit. It was said that Richard Burton, the lachrymose author of *The Anatomy of Melancholy*, was only known to be amused when he frequented Folly Bridge at Oxford in order to listen to the conversations of the bargees. As a chronicler of Oxford put it, "nothing at last could make him laugh, but going down to the Bridge-Foot in Oxford and hearing the Barge-men scold and storm and swear at one another, at which he would set his Hands to his Sides and laugh most profusely." The bargees were also proficient at the more unconventional practices of fishing, and were well known for their skill with the picking and mixing of herbs. They were well acquainted with the places along the bank where certain medicinal "simples" were to be found, and they sold them in the towns through which they passed. Their barges were often brightly coloured, with various riverscapes painted on their sides in the most garish colours; these paintings were known as "cuts." Like the gypsies who once used to encamp along the course of the river, the bargees were a separate and exclusive caste whose members married and intermarried. They mixed rarely with the villagers along the Thames, and indeed the two parties seemed to hold each other in mutual contempt. The villagers in fact classed the bargees with the gypsies, blaming both for misdemeanours and thefts such as the stealing of ducks' eggs. In 1600 they were described as "a fewe dronken and beggerley fellows."

Their reputation for violence was not altogether undeserved. When a system of locks was being created near Reading one of the members of the river's management received a threatening letter in 1725 which ended "only your men must beene all drowned so teake warning before tis too late, for Darn you for ever if you come we will do it. From wee bargemen." They do not often enter the historical record. But then once more, in 1804, the Thames Commissioners passed a by-law concerning complaints "by gentlemen and others, navigating on the river for pleasure, or otherwise" about the threats, obstruction and abuse that they suffered from the bargees.

The labourers of the river were in fact often condemned as savages. As Jerome K. Jerome put it, "the mildest-tempered people, when on land, become violent and blood-thirsty when in a boat." The minutes of a parliamentary committee, considering a Thames Preservation Act in 1884, are indicative of a central aspect of public perception of the Thames:

> CHAIRMAN: What proportion of the public do you complain of in
>   this way?
> SIR GILBERT: That is what I have often wanted to know; whether
>   these people were naturally savages; or whether they become
>   savage when they come on the river.
> CHAIRMAN: What proportion of the public who use the Thames in
>   this way possess this qualification of savages of which you speak?
> SIR GILBERT: I distinctly say it is not the working class . . . I believe
>   that it is a class of savages born on purpose. It is getting more
>   every year that these savages use the river.

The toll-keepers and the lock-keepers along the river were also subjects of much interest and comment. The toll-keeper on the bridge was in particular open to innumerable insults from those who did not wish to pay the fee for crossing, originally a halfpenny for weekdays and a penny on Sundays. Under the cover of night his hand might be filled with mud or pebbles. A tramp would offer his halfpenny and demand that the gate be opened; as soon as it was unfastened a hidden party of tramps would make a rush and pass through. The toll-keeper was never a popular figure. The advent of the motor-car increased his sense of beleaguerment. When a motor vehicle drove over the Maidenhead end of Maidenhead Bridge, and refused to pay the 8 pence charge, the toll-keeper grabbed a cushion from the car and sub-sequently sold it for 3 shillings—returning only 3 pence to the owner after deducting certain expenses. This was the final provocation. At midnight on 31 October 1913, a crowd of five hundred people assembled on the bridge and encouraged workmen from the Maidenhead Town Council to tear down the offending gate. The toll-keepers of the London bridges were known as "tipstaffs." They survived at their posts until 1879, when most of the London bridges were finally declared "free and open to the public for ever."

Unlike the toll-keepers, the keepers of the locks have survived into our own time. There are forty-five locks on the non-tidal river, from the source to Teddington. The first pound locks were erected (with turf sides) at If-fley, Sandford and Swift Ditch in 1635. In that century there was a new emphasis upon utility and experimental progress, especially in relation to the circulation of commerce. There was no reason at all why the Thames should not be organised under the same set of principles. So other locks followed.

Anyone who passed through the lock was obliged to pay a toll, a fee that provoked enormous discontent. It was the old argument whether God and nature provided the water free from charge. The locks subsequently became known as "Thames turnpikes." Then from the 1770s there was a spate of building at several sites along the river, the first of the new pound locks coming into service in 1772 at Boulter's Lock. They were said to have been designed by Humphrey Gainsborough, the brother of the painter; if this is so, then he had more effect upon the vision of the riverscape than his more famous sibling.

The pound lock was, as its name suggests, an enclosed chamber or "pound" with a gate at either end. It was sometimes known as the cistern lock. It is the system still in use, although the equipment has been thoroughly modernised. The gates themselves must be capable of holding back thousands of tons of water. Buscot is the smallest, Teddington is the largest and Boulter's is the busiest. On the south bank of the river at Teddington, the first lock upon the non-tidal river, there are examples of the little skiff lock (otherwise known as the coffin lock), the launch lock and the barge lock. The traffic along this stretch of the navigable river is now so heavy that they are almost constantly in use.

The lock-keepers of the last two centuries, unlike their counterparts in the tolling booths, were generally considered to be cheerful and amiable characters. Their setting, with the lock cottage surrounded by friendly blossom, was highly picturesque. They were associated with the sound of the swinging gate and of the groaning winch, with the lap and gurgle of the slowly ascending or descending water. A character in Elspeth Huxley's *The Flame Trees of Thika* (1962) is posed a pertinent question. "Once he was asked, what, in his heart of hearts he most wanted to be. After some thought, Ian replied that his true ambition was to be a lock-keeper on the River Thames. 'There I would stand amongst my phloxes and snapdragons and watch life go by in an orderly manner.' "

They are the guardians or wardens of the river, keeping it in order and chastening its bounds. There are records of them dating back to the eighteenth century, with names like Caleb Gould at Hambleden and George Cordery at Temple; there were some women among them, Widow Hewitt of Cullum ferry and Widow Walters of Whitchurch being no doubt the relics of past lock-keepers. In March 1831 it was decreed that females could no longer take on the task of lock-keeper, but the regulation seems to have been largely ignored.

Caleb Gould was something of a river legend. He possessed a large oven behind his cottage, and would sell bread to the passing bargemen. He wore a long coat with many buttons, and ate a dish of onion porridge every night for his supper. He may be the origin of the strange phrase of Mole in the first pages of *The Wind in the Willows*—" 'Onion-sauce! Onion-sauce!' he remarked jeeringly . . ." The keeper of Shiplake Lock in the 1880s, known only as Mr. Sadler, was a bee-master, a maker of ornamental beehives and a grower of roses. He was a poet, on the twin themes of bees and roses, who also wrote verses on the life of the river Thames. As he said of the immediate riverine landscape:

From hence the town of Reading
Is just one field across,

> 'Mong other things so widely known
> For biscuits, seeds and sauce.

Some lock-keepers were drowned while on watch. One, at least, was eventually confined to a lunatic asylum.

There were also the keepers, or the guardians, of the weirs. There have been weirs upon the Thames ever since humankind began to use its waters. There is an old English poem with the phrase "weary as water in a weir," suggesting the weariness of long tenure. The people of the river tended to pronounce it "wire." The weir is intrinsically dangerous. It is essentially a dam or fence built across the course of the river to interfere with the flow of the water; it may be used to divert or regulate the current. The earliest weirs were built of timber and brushwood, creating a primitive obstruction that raised the level of the water immediately upstream. Then these obstacles were built in two parallel rows or "hedges," with an infill of chalk or stone. Then weirs took the form of wooden bridges, with a great log of timber or "cill" on the river-bed; between the bridge and the cill were placed vertical wooden planks, so that the whole device resembled a dam. When a craft wished to pass through, the planks were removed, thus causing a "flash" or "flush" as the pent-up water poured through the opening. The keepers of these weirs also demanded a toll, from boats or barges, before they would release the flood of water needed to carry the vessels downstream. They soon became the most hated figures on the water.

There were other types of weir. The one built for the mill directed a strong head of water towards the mechanism for the turning of the wheels. There was also the weir for fish, known as a "fishery hedge," which took the form of a trap. The weirs for the miller and fisherman were indeed the most common in the earliest phases of the river, but from the beginning they posed a threat to navigation. So weirs were condemned by succeeding kings. In the reign of Richard I a charter was granted to the City of London in which it was stated that "all weirs within the Thames be removed, wheresoever they may be." Eighteen years later they were again prohibited in Magna Carta. In the twenty-third clause of that document, sealed alongside the Thames, it was ordered that "all weirs from henceforth shall be utterly put down by Thames and Medway, and the whole of England, except by the sea-coast." The frequency of these edicts suggests that they were never honoured. In the reign of Richard II an order was issued demanding the removal of all weirs from the Thames, but once more the law was not obeyed. In 1405 the Lord Mayor of London, Sir John Woodcock, ordered the destruction of every weir below Staines, but they soon reappeared. Their ubiquity is a token of the extent to which the livelihood of the people depended upon the damming of the waters. Henry VI issued an edict that "no man shall fasten nets to anything over rivers" and Edward IV imposed a fine of 100 marks upon the owner of any weir. The measures were not effective. There is an intense conservatism about the Thames.

In the gentler waters upstream the weir often stood alone, whereas in the lower reaches it was characteristically accompanied by a lock. In the eighteenth and nineteenth centuries there was sometimes a cottage nearby for the use of the weir-keeper, although this residence was often employed as an inn for the weary traveller waiting to pass over the water. There was also often a primitive footbridge constructed over the river at such points. Eventually they became outmoded, and many unnecessary weirs were dismantled in the course of the nineteenth century. Many of them were replaced by locks, although locks and weirs are still often found adjacent to one another. Footbridges were also built upon the ancient site of "flash weirs."

Weirs were such a familiar presence upon the river that they were given names that endured over many centuries—Old Man's Weir, Old Nan's Weir, Rushy Weir, Kent's Weir, Ten-foot Weir, Winnie Weg's Weir, Noah's Ark Weir, Skinner's Weir. There was a weir at Caversham that was known as "the Clappers." But the most famous and ferocious weir along the Thames has always been called "the Lasher." It is located on the river at Sandford, between Oxford and Iffley, and is notorious for drownings. There is beside it a stone obelisk that commemorates some of those who have been lost in its fierce waters. In the flood and cataract can be seen the whirling remains of trees, of old bridges, of debris, even of blocks of concrete.

The millers of the river maintained another immense and vital aspect of its business. Between Oxford and Staines there were twenty-eight mills, fifteen of them being named in the *Domesday Book* and the rest of almost equal antiquity. It is one more example of the conserving power of the river. The watermill itself is an ancient device; the first record of its use can be dated to 85 BC, in a poem by Antipater of Thessalonica. The earliest watermill appeared in England at some point in the fifth century, as far as anyone can guess, and for almost fifteen hundred years the "merrie miller" served his local community. He was not universally popular, however, in his efforts to divert or dam the water of the Thames for his own purposes. The threat to navigation was often serious, and it was not unknown for millers to demand payment before they released the flood. There was an old Arabic saying, "How could we compel the sweet water to turn a mill?" It might therefore be deemed indecent, or immoral, of the miller to harness the pure water of the Thames. Or, as an anonymous Thames poet put it,

> How can that man be counted a good liver
> That for his private use will stop a river?

It has been calculated that there were some forty mills on the Thames; this seems an under-estimate, but no more reliable figure is available. The *Domesday Book* itself records a mill in practically every village along the Thames upriver from Windsor. There were important mills at Marlow and at Hambleden, at Mapledurham and at Hurley, at Temple and at Marsh. There were flour mills at Deptford and at Lambeth. There were also the great enterprises of Hovis at Battersea, Spiller's in the Royal Docks and McDougall's on the Isle of Dogs.

The craft of towing may be as old as the peoples of the river themselves. It was the custom for gangs of men to wait at the wharves and jetties for the opportunity of towing a barge or other vessel along their particular stretch or "reach" of the river. One gang would haul on the line until the tow-path ended on their bank, and at that point they would pass the burden to another gang on the opposite bank. The tow-path was known to them as the "bargewalk." Some of these gangs comprised as many as eighty men. They went barefoot and were accustomed to sink up to their waists in the icy water of the river, bearing on their shoulders a cable that might weigh up to a ton. The cables or lines themselves could reach a length of 400 or 500 yards (365 or 455 m)—a quarter of a mile to be hauled and handled.

It was hard and uncomfortable work and the towers themselves, known as "hauliers" or "haulers" or sometimes "scufflehunters," had an unenviable reputation. There must have been haulers ever since cargo was first carried upon the Thames, and it was not until the latter part of the eighteenth century that the men began to be replaced by teams of horses or (occasionally) of donkeys. Like so many other people of the river the tow-ers were accused of insolence, insubordination and foul language. On many occasions they were described as a "terror" to the riverside commu-nities through which they passed. They drank a great deal, naturally enough, and they evinced all the rougher qualities of the river.

The haulers and the river workers in general were in particular known for their foul language. Of the bargees it was said, by a French traveller of the eighteenth century, that "they use singular and quite extraordinary terms, generally very coarse and dirty ones, and I cannot possibly explain them to you." The oaths and sexual slang of the watermen became famous from the medieval period until the end of their supremacy upon their river. It became something of a tradition. In the *Oxford English Dictionary* the term "water-language" is defined as "the rough language of watermen" with an appended reference to "water-wit." Wit had little to do with it.

Foul language has in fact always been associated with the river. One of the terms for violence and obscenity in speech used to be known simply as "Billingsgate," after the example of the porters and "fish-wives" who worked in that riverside vicinity. The "Billingsgate fish-wife" became a proverbial figure of gross abusiveness.

The bad language also became a matter of public statute. In 1701 the Corporation of Watermen made it illegal to "use immoderate, obscene and lewd expressions towards passengers and to each other, as are offensive to all sober persons, and tend extremely to the corruption and debauchery of youth." The punishment for "swearing or cursing" was 2 shillings, and that of "reviling passengers" was also 2 shillings. It did not stop the flow, and in 1773 there were complaints about "indecent Conversations" as well as "horrid Oaths and imprecations" to be heard at the riverside. When a riverside resident of the early nineteenth century remonstrated with a bargee for tying his rope to a small punt post, "he answered that if he chose, he might fix the Rope to the knocker of my Street door. The Lan-guage used by the Men was very improper to be within the hearing of the Ladies in the House."

The watermen were not the only offenders. Richard Jefferies, the mid-nineteenth-century naturalist and novelist, wrote in an essay entitled *The Modern Thames* (1885) that everyone felt free to swear upon the river and that "on the Thames you may swear as the wind blows—howsoever you list. You may begin at the mouth off the Nore and curse your way up to Cricklade. A hundred miles for swearing is a fine preserve: it is one of the marvels of our civilisation." There were often complaints about the language of the trippers and loafers who hired launches or small boats for expeditions on the Thames; they were known for becoming drunk and for what were called their "impudent" or "beastly" expressions. The dockers of the river swore with such regularity that the obscenities were given no emphasis. The explanation for this endless flood of profanity by the water is perhaps not difficult to find. It has to do with the freedom and the equality which the long history of the Thames induces. Or as Jerome K. Jerome put it in *Three Men in a Boat*, "when a man up the river thinks a thing, he says it."

CHAPTER 23

The Natives

he river can get into the blood. There are families now working on
the Thames whose lineage stretches back for many generations,
families such as the Hobbses of Henley, the Turks of Kingston,
the Cobbses of Putney, the Phelpses of Hammersmith, the Murphys of
Wapping, the Coes of Barking, the Crouches of Greenhithe, the Luptons
of Gravesend, the Fishers of Limehouse, and the Salters of Oxford. It
would seem that there is not one populated stretch of the Thames that does
not have its own presiding family of boatmen.

The Bossom family was associated with the river, at Medley and at
Wallingford, from the eighteenth century until the 1960s. Charles Bossom
was mentioned as a bargeman in 1754, and in 1878 William Morris recorded
that he sailed from Medley to Kelmscott with "Bossom and another man to
tow us as far as New Bridge." There is a photograph of Bossom's Boatyard, near Oxford, taken in 1880 by a famous photographer of the river,
Henry Taunt; Bossom's Boatyard is still there. Sargent Brothers (Thames)
deal in such riverine matters as pilotage and hydrographic services; their
association with Woolwich goes back for three centuries, and Thomas Sargent was a shipwright in the eighteenth-century Woolwich Dockyard.
Their present headquarters are still in Woolwich. The Tough Brothers of

Teddington have been connected with the river since the beginning of the nineteenth century. These are continuities that the river seems to foster, patterns of labour and habitation that persist beside the ever-flowing Thames.

The Freebodys are first mentioned in a document of the mid-thirteenth century as ferrymen and bargemen; John Freebody was a bargeman at Hurley in the early seventeenth century. Peter Freebody still has a boating business at Hurley, and is celebrated for the building of traditional craft. There are other river families, such as the Bushnells and the Woottons, the Parrotts and the Coopers, who began their association with the river as gravel diggers or as bargemen; they have continued that association ever since in their modern incarnation as boat-builders or leisure-boatmen. The Livetts of Gravesend and London can be traced back to the early eighteenth century, when the first Livett arrived in Bermondsey as a French seaman. For the last 150 years the Livetts have been concerned with tugs and towing, but Chris Livett now runs a thriving passenger business on the Thames; he himself married the daughter of a waterman and has already apprenticed their son and daughter to the same trade. The Purdues were associated with Shepperton for five hundred years, although they now seem to have departed.

It has been claimed that there are also regional characteristics shaping, for example, those who live and work along the upper Thames and the estuary. Those who harbour a topographical imagination tend to view the various communities as in some way reflecting the characteristics of the river. The people of the Upper Thames are then considered to be calm and contemplative, almost languorous; the people of the estuary are deemed to be quick and alert, almost mischievous. This is all perhaps fanciful. Yet there is not one area or one community beside the Thames that is not touched in some unique way by the presence of the river. If a riverine family can trace itself back seven or eight generations—as many still can—then the Thames is part of its inheritance.

The population of the Upper Thames was until recent years relatively stable; there was no noticeable immigration into the region after the close of the eleventh century, and with the absence of large towns and cities (with the exception of Oxford) there was little of that spirit of innovation and change associated with the medieval merchant or the modern businessman. Until the advent of the First World War, in fact, it has been claimed that four-fifths of the population of the Upper Thames lived and died within 10 miles of their birthplace. This is of course true of many rural areas, but the relative seclusion of the Thames Valley rendered that isolation all the more noticeable.

There are accounts and histories of the region, most notably Alfred Williams's *Round About the Upper Thames* (1922) and *Folk Songs of the Upper Thames* (1923), that treat the resident population as if it had some tribal force or spirit. In the first of these volumes Williams invokes the Thames as the presiding deity of a place whose "whole life is governed by the river, that operates in a hundred ways, openly and secretly, determining all things, and whose decrees are absolute and irrevocable." He traces the history of the population from the earliest settlements to the period of his writing, and in this progress he touches upon the most local and circumstantial details of the riverine world—from the particular mist or vapour that hangs over the vicinity to the popularity of eel-pie in the various villages of the Thames Valley. There are stories of ghosts, of witches buried by the roadside, and of a certain local "peggy-wiggy" pie made of the stillborn young of the long-eared white sow.

It has been said that the inhabitants of the Thames Valley were once unusually fond of singing, as if Pan were still busy in the reeds; the closer the inhabitants lived to the source of the river, the more strident became their voices. In *Folk Songs of the Upper Thames* Alfred Williams describes the "wassails," for example, held by the source at Thames Head. These exuberant games and dances are of much anthropological interest. Common sense would suggest that they were the surviving elements of very ancient rituals. Williams transcribes the song of Thames Head and observes that "I have not heard it except around the Thames source":

> Here's to the ox, and to his long horn;
> May God send our maester a good crap o'corn!
> A good crap o'corn, and another o'hay,
> To pass the cold wintry winds away.

Williams records more than two hundred songs of the river region, a large number for such a relatively small area. Among them are "When Morning Stands on Tiptoe," "I Once Had Plenty of Thyme," "The Downhill of Life" and "The Husbandman and the Servingman" glossed by Williams as very popular "around the Thames Head at Kemble, Somerford Keynes and Oaksey." Some songs were confined to one village, and indeed to one singer. Thus we have "The Sower's Song," "words of Mrs. Mackie, Lechlade":

> Old earth is a pleasure to see
> In sunshiny cloak of red and green:
> The furrow lies fresh, and this year will be
> As years that are past have been.

If there are constant themes in the songs of the Thames, they are of permanence and of endless renewal. These matters are deeply congenial to the nature of the territory. Some of the songs are obscure, and others are obscene. But they all exude the strong spirit of the locality. They are not in dialect form, curiously enough, and Williams believes that dialect songs were an artificial introduction of the mid-nineteenth century. The songs in his collection are delivered in what might be called simple Saxon English.

Williams suggests that there were once thousands of songs circulating in the Thames region, and "I have frequently come into contact with those who have assured me that such and such a one knew from two hundred to three hundred pieces." At the singing matches in the inns, the competition was not for him who sang best but for him who sang most. One man "commonly issued a challenge to the village, or the neighbourhood, and declared himself able and willing to sing continuously for twelve hours—from morning till night—and to have a fresh piece each time." The competitions then lasted for two days.

In this context Williams mentions Elijah Isles of Inglesham whose songs "were gently humorous and witty" and William Warren, a thatcher of South Marston, who specialised in "the romantic-historical kind." There were also "singing families," such as the Pillingers of Lechlade and the Wheelers of Buscot, all of whom sang and who passed their gift from generation to generation. At Lechlade, too, the songs were taught to the children at school. Certain villages acquired a reputation for song, among them Standlake and Castle Eaton. Before the arrival of the church organ every hamlet or village in the region had its own small band, composed of fiddle, bass viol, piccolo, clarionet, the cornet, the trumpet and something known as "the horse's leg." At the beginning of the twentieth century the most celebrated ballad-sellers of the Thames Valley were a couple, a man and a woman, each of whom possessed only one eye.

Yet the music passed away. It was perhaps fated to disappear in any

case because, as Williams puts it, "a countryman never sings to a stranger."
It seems that the true decline began when the police objected to public
singing in the inns of the neighbourhood, and by degrees the traditions
were lost. The songs died with their last singers. It would be unwise to suggest that the region of the Thames was the only one in which such traditions were maintained for many centuries. But as Williams notes, it is
instructive to recognise that this region, reputed to be "about the dullest
part of England . . . cut off, as it were, from the heart of the great world,"
could create the conditions for melodies that "quickened" the hearts and
feelings of the people who lived by the Thames. By prolonged absorption
in what was then the isolated life of this region, Williams was able to invoke what has now become an alien and immeasurably distant culture. It
was a culture of the river which, with its traditions of communal feeling
and of competitive singing, might hold the key to much earlier phases of
life beside the Thames.

The native people of the tidal river, for example, bear striking similar-
ities to the inhabitants of the Upper Thames. They shared an aptitude for
singing. On New Year's Eve, a few minutes before the change of the year,
the inhabitants of Wapping and of Rotherhithe used to congregate alongside the piers and quays of their river world and there begin to sing. In response the ships and tugs on the river would blow their sirens. Is there some
deep connection between the river and song? The people of the London
river also shared with their upriver cousins the habit of interbreeding between local families. The *Morning Post* reported at the beginning of the
twentieth century that in an attendance register of a school at Bow Creek,
known then as "Bog Island," there were 100 Lammins among a total number of 160 children; the rest were comprised almost entirely of Scanlans or
Jeffrieses.

So the people of the docks were cut off geographically from their
neighbours. As a result they used to evince a strong collective spirit. Even
within the terrain of the docks themselves there were regional variations.
Swing bridges and large gates separated the inhabitants of the Isle of Dogs
from the people of Rotherhithe; there were fierce rivalries between them.
In March 1970, for example, the people of the Isle of Dogs blockaded
their bridge and declared themselves to be an independent republic of
twelve thousand people. The protest, for such it was, lasted only for a day.
Rotherhithe Street, known popularly as "Downtown," was distinct from
neighbouring Bermondsey and Southwark. But they had in common a pre-

occupation with the life of the river. It was the centre of their work, most of it casual, and of their little leisure; it was their means of transport, and their common sewer. It was the centre of their being, their various thoroughfares, streets and alleys leading unfailingly to the quays and stairs and other points of access to the foreshore and the dark water. The children collected pieces of coal and driftwood to light their families' fires. It might seem to the observer that life for the majority of riverside people was the sum of a dark house and a dark street but, where a thousand such houses are found together, there can breathe a spirit of adventure and of wonder.

Those interested in the survival of remote Thames customs might do worse than to study the habits of the river gypsies. In the nineteenth and early twentieth centuries the gypsies were well known for their skill at catching fish, although they were quite devoid of any knowledge of angling; they used the old-fashioned method of a stick and spear, and occasionally employed a blunt instrument like a wooden sword with which they would bludgeon the fish. They constructed rude boats, like canoes, out of willow wood. Their skills were, therefore, of very ancient provenance.

The habitations of the river people have been considered as undesirable as the river people themselves. The small and unsanitary cottages of the Thames villagers were hardly ever deemed worthy of comment; the wharfingers and bargees of Marlow and Henley (the bargees never lived permanently on their barges) inhabited rows of damp and narrow terraces where the more respectable townsmen did not venture. But the conditions of riverside London were always the subject of much morbid description. The world of Wapping and of Rotherhithe was one of decayed streets, dark and malodorous, with an occasional gas bracket, its glass broken, high on a dank wall. The uneven cobbled streets that ran from Tooley Street by the Hole-in-the-Wall to Deptford Docks, or from Tower Street along Wapping High Street to Limehouse and the Isle of Dogs, were marked by taverns and pawnshops and brothels and low lodgings for sailors. It may be that the dwellings of those who go down to the sea in ships will always have a makeshift and temporary air. They are not to be loved—the ship is to be loved—only to be endured. The streets at night, with names like Malabar Street and Canton Street, Amoy Place and Pekin Street, were clothed in an inky blackness broken only by distant or diminished lights. The houses were so uniform that analogies were made with the reefs that grow within water; they were like accretions of coral polyp. The people, and their habitations, are in every sense determined by the neighbouring river. Curiously enough, the Thames was rarely seen; it was the invisible brooding presence behind these mean streets.

The book that most effortlessly and vividly evoked the riverine neighbourhood was Thomas Burke's *Limehouse Nights*, published in 1917. It created a sensation at the time, not least for its intense descriptions of the vice and squalor of an area that no one presumed to explore. It was a world of "mephitic glooms and silences," where an acrid tang hovered in the air and where "every corner, half-lit by the bleak light of a naked gas-jet seemed to harbour unholy things, and a sense of danger hung on every step." It was an over-heated vision, perhaps, but it was balanced by Burke's calmer observations of "the fried-fish shops that punctuate every corner" and the "general" shops that contained assorted rags, and broken iron, and basins of kitchen waste.

There is a special language of the river. In Alfred Williams's books there is a record of the local speech of the Thames Valley, for example, which seems to have been a variant of rural demotic—"Ef thee'st a kipt thi eye and that owl' elm yander, same as I told tha, thee'st a 'ed un right." "Chorus" was pronounced as "chorius" and "breek" was used as "break." It is also worth remarking that "v" was substituted for "w," as in "ven" or "Villiam"; could this usage have migrated down the Thames until it was co-opted into mid-nineteenth-century Cockney vocabulary? When the ground became inundated with flood-water, it was described by the local people as "goggy" or "patey." To be shrewd was "deedy," and snail-shells were "guggles." There may be some trace here of a primordial language long since fallen out of customary use, perhaps derived from the Wessex or Mercian tongues.

It is sometimes claimed, in fact, that the English language emerged among the first communities by the Thames; it was then fashioned into the national speech by Alfred, who was deeply inured to the dialects of Wallingford and of Farringdon. It is not so exotic a suggestion as it may appear. There is a deep connection between the river and language, exemplified by the emergence of written communication in the river-plains of Mesopotamia. The first cities were created by the rivers, and the exigencies of communal expression thus arose in connection with the flowing waters. The rivers were known in the early myths as "the voice of God," and in classical texts the flowers of rhetoric are described as *flumen orationis*, "the stream of speech." So we speak of liquid consonants. Water is the presiding deity of flowing or fluid language, of language without break, of freely associative language, and of rhythmic or harmonious language. The metaphor is a persistent one because it rests upon an ancient association. Ruskin once said of Turner's relationship to the Thames that "he understood its language."

There was one individual inhabitant of the river through whom the spirit of the place spoke. Douglas Chellow was born in 1790 in High Timber Street, Rotherhithe, and for the rest of his life he lived or wandered within the neighbourhoods of the river from Chelsea to Southend. One day he encountered by Blackfriars Bridge the writer and periodical editor, Charles Whitehead, who subsequently described the strange meeting: "He wrung his hands as if finding all hopeless, and then suddenly quietened and was all smiles and concern. It seemed that he wanted only to convey his love of the river to anyone who would listen and I found the interest to hear him many times."

Chellow discoursed on the Romans and Saxons who had commandeered the Thames, on the medieval merchants who sailed through London, and on the monks who built their establishments on the banks of the river; he spoke of Chaucer, and of Tyler. He described the great "frost fairs" that had taken place on the frozen river, and after the *Princess Alice* disaster of 1878 he walked up and down the river-banks with a placard on which was inscribed: "CAN WE BE MASTERS OF THE SEA IF WE CANNOT KEEP A PLEASURE BOAT AFLOAT ON THE THAMES? THE RIVER HAS HAD HER REVENGE." The police records of the period note that he haunted the temporary mortuary and the coroner's court with the same message.

This was indeed his belief—that the river was an ancient deity, sometimes beneficent and sometimes implacable, that had to be appeased. He printed broadsheets entitled "Crimes Against the River Thames," aimed at the river pirates and profiteers, as if the river itself were the injured party. Towards the end of his life he erected for himself a shack or hovel on the river-bank at Greenwich Reach. Each morning he made his obeisance to the river, according to Alan Wykes in *An Eye on the Thames* (1966), by "throwing up his arms and then prostrating himself on the shore, and calling on London's river to claim him as his follower." One morning his body was found, on the foreshore, at low tide.

PART VIII

The River of Trade

The entrance to the West India Docks

CHAPTER 24

The Trade of the World

In *A Tour Thro' the Whole Island of Great Britain* (1724), Daniel Defoe calculated that there were some two thousand vessels on the Thames during any one day. But his principal interest lay in the amount of "revenue" or "income" that the river could generate. For him the "silver Thames" was silver indeed, liquid coin running through the heart of London. It has always been a river of trade. Its tidal reaches, from the Nore to London and its environs, have always been hard at work. The Thames has been touched by sweat, and labour, and greed, and poverty and tears. Its docks and wharves and factories were once the great machinery of empire, but its mercantile history stretches much further back.

By the twelfth century it was already an ancient port. There are some extant verses of that century, written by William Fitzstephen in the preface to his biography of Thomas à Becket, *Vita Sancti Thomae, Cantuariensis Archiepiscopis et Martyris*, describing the wealth of the commodities that the merchants brought by sea:

Arabia's gold, Sabaea's spice and incense,
Scythia's keen weapons, and the oil of palms
From Babylon's rich soil, Nile's precious gems,

Norway's warm peltries, Russia's costly sables,
Sera's rich vestures, and the wines of Gaul,
Hither are sent.

Already there were wharves for wheat and rye and wine, flax and hemp and
linen cloth. In the thirteenth century there was a wharf close to the Tower
of London known as the Galley Quay, since it was the place where the Venetian galleys were moored during their annual visit to London from the
Serenissima; they were protected by a company of archers. The most important export of the period—and one that was loaded onto the Venetian
galleys in exchange for sugar, spices and silken garments—was raw wool.
By the fourteenth century it was estimated that one hundred thousand sacks
of wool were transported overseas each year. There was now so much
trade that in the fourteenth and fifteenth centuries major centres for ship-
building and ship-repairing were established at Shadwell, Rotherhithe and
Deptford—in which quarters they remained for four hundred years. In the
following century the great yard at Blackwall was also opened. The presence of these docks meant in turn that the riverside became populated by
tradesmen such as coopers and sail-makers who joined the porters and
labourers in acquiring their income directly from the Thames. There were
biscuit-bakers and store-shippers in Tooley Street, ship-chandlers at Wapping and famous rope-makers at Limehouse. Other river trades flourished
from the sixteenth century. Gunpowder was produced at the Rotherhithe
water-mills in the Tudor period, and it was later manufactured at the riverine sites of Greenwich and Woolwich. Cannon and lead-shot were also
forged by the Thames.

In the seventeenth century it was declared that "the greatest ships that
ride upon the sea come and unload in London in the very harte of the
towne"; these vessels "either bringeth to it or carryeth from it, all merchan-
dize the world can afforde it or it the worlde." Trade was always brisk. In
1606 James I granted the City of London the right to tax all the coals, grain,
salt, apples, pears, plums and other goods coming by the river. Three years
later these rights were extended to oil, hops, soap, butter and cheese. A
third charter, some seven years later, ordered that all coals be landed on the
legal quays. It was "notoriously known" that the Thames was "so necessary, commodious and practicable" to the continuing life of the city. Certainly, by the end of the seventeenth century, the London quays were
handling 80 per cent of the country's exports, and 69 per cent of its im-

ports. A foreign traveller, Count Magalotti, writing *Travels in England* (1669), observed that there were fourteen hundred large ships between London Bridge and Gravesend, "to which are added the other smaller ships and boats, almost without number, which are passing and repassing incessantly, and with which the river is covered." He had been told that "more than six hundred thousand persons sleep upon the water," which would have made it the largest riverine population in Europe. Yet not all goods began and ended their travels at London. There were shallow draughted vessels that took merchandise upriver to Oxford, and even beyond; the "Western Barges," as they were known, worked between London and Oxford throughout the year.

In the *Carriers Cosmographie* of 1637, by the water poet John Taylor, it is stated that "to Bull Wharfe (neere Queenhithe) there doth come & goe great boats twice or thrice every weeke betwixt London & Kingston: also thither doth often come a Boat from Colebrooke . . . the Redding Boat is to be had at Queenhith weekly." A Lechlade boat-master has left an inventory of goods that he took down the river in 1793, among them "iron, copper, tin, brass, spelter, cannon, cheese, nails . . . and bomb shells." The channel of the Thames between Abingdon and Cricklade was scoured and cleaned out in order to make room for the boats and barges to pass freely upriver. It is estimated that 3,000 tons (over 3,000 tonnes) of cheese each year were transported from Oxford to London. There was of course also the vast amount of hay for the horses of London; they provided the true energy of the city.

The trade of the river altered the appearance of its river-banks. Durham House was torn down and replaced by an exchange and by arcades of shops. Salisbury House was demolished to make way for houses. Arundel House suffered the same fate. Essex House, the possession of Robert Devereux, second Earl of Essex, was purchased by the property speculator Nicholas Barbon in 1674; it was largely demolished, and its stone used for the houses that Barbon built upon the site. It was Barbon who exploited the desire for standardised houses after the Fire. As a direct result of his influence the area between Strand and the river became a network of narrow streets and houses, with the occasional cookshop or tavern in attendance. The waterfront itself was rebuilt in the service of profit and of commerce; where once the gardens of the noblemen had sloped down to the river, there were constructed wharves and jetties for the use of brewers and wood merchants. It was the sign of transition in the river's life.

One foreign observer, J. H. Meister, noted in his *Letters* (1791) that the port had become "an object of bewilderment and admiration to all." In his account he also urged the traveller to "take boat to go down the Thames, and see the bosom of that noble river bearing thousands and thousands of vessels . . . you will then confess that you have beheld nothing that can give you a stronger idea of the noble and happy effects of human industry." If the eighteenth century was the era of expanded and heavily financed trade, it is by no means coincidental that it was also the age in which the first London newspapers emerged. The *Daily Courant* began publication in 1702 and, from the beginning, its purpose was to bring news of overseas trade—and of events that might affect trade—to the merchants of the city. Fleet Street itself was conveniently close to the river. *Lloyds List*, founded in 1734, was primarily concerned with the movement of ships into London and elsewhere. The *Daily Universal Register* of 1785 (now transmogrified as *The Times*) was, as its name suggests, primarily a digest of overseas news. The Rialto of Venice was no busier, or better informed, than the riverside of the Thames.

In his *Tour* Defoe emphasised the vast quantities of timber, of malt and of meal that were carried along the river into the city. The Thames was for him the life-blood of the nation, and the wharves of London "a kind of infinite, and the parts to be separated from one another in such a description, are so many, that it is hard to know where to begin." Further downriver he noted three wet docks, twenty-two dry docks and more than thirty shipbuilding yards. The river was now so crowded with ships that it was possible to walk from one bank to the other on their decks. Defoe himself was part of the commercial river, and owned a tile manufactory beside the Thames near Grays. The eighteenth-century river no longer inspired the poetry of nymphs, but the poetry of trade. Thus James Thomson, the author of *The Seasons* (1726–30), celebrated the fact that the Thames had stirred

> The busy merchant; the big Warehouse built;
> Rais'd the strong crane; choak'd up the loaded street
> With foreign plenty; and thy stream, O THAMES,
> Large, gentle, deep, majestic, king of Floods!

The river created other forms of trade. Along its banks rose mills and manufactories, as well as the infamous "stink industries" that were sited away from the centres of population but were within easy reach of the flowing energy (and disposal outlet) of the Thames. There was a range of potteries in the areas of Lambeth and of Fulham; there were porcelain factories in Chelsea, Bow and Limehouse; there were glass-makers in Vauxhall and Southwark; there were paint, ink and dye manufactories in Shadwell and Deptford; there were sugar refineries at Ratcliff and at Whitechapel. Bermondsey was well known for its leather-tanning and for its vinegar-making, both of them ill-smelling trades that gave the locale a noxious reputation well into the early twentieth century. And of course there were the breweries, carrying on one of the oldest of all trades upon the Thames. The makers of gin and beer could be found at Pimlico and at Southwark; there were breweries at Rotherhithe and at Lambeth, at Limehouse and at Mile End, and then further upriver at Wandsworth and Chiswick and Mortlake. The Hop Exchange was erected in Southwark, where it can still be seen.

The craft carrying hops joined the barges that had been bringing sea-coal into the capital from the north-east of England for five centuries. These barges were in themselves as capacious as great ships, many of them with a capacity of 200 tons (over 200 tonnes). In the words of Thomson once more, "the sooty hulk steer'd sluggish on." Coal was in fact the most important item of merchandise upon the Thames. At any one time some seven hundred colliers were on the river, providing fuel for a million homes. It was the tax upon coal imports that paid for the new churches built in London after the Great Fire, so in a real sense the river trade was responsible for the design of the city, and the coal dust hanging over the port in a permanent cloud was a visible token of the city's dependency.

CHAPTER 25

The River of Immensity

*O*ne of the wonders of the Thames world was its system of docks. The first "purpose-built" dock for cargo in London, the Brunswick Dock, was opened in 1789. Beside it rose a great mast-house, some 120 feet (36.5 m) in height, which for many years overlooked and dominated the area as a token of maritime trade and power. It was the maypole of the commercial deities that had now claimed the Thames as their own. That first dock had a river lineage, of course, deriving from the ancient sites of Billingsgate and Queenhithe. There was a port here in Roman, and in Saxon, times. The warehouses of the Roman period were sturdily built with stone walls and timber floors, the buildings often divided into "units" for ease of storage. The dry land to which the docks gave access was known for many centuries as "Romeland," although the origin of the word is not clear.

The medieval port comprised the principal deep-water harbours of Billingsgate and Queenhithe, then joined by Dowgate a little further upriver. By 1170 the German merchants had their own hall, or place of residence, beside Dowgate; it was known as the Steelyard after the beam used for weighing the merchandise. It seems likely that the Fleet river (otherwise known as Bridewell) was developed in the twelfth or thirteenth centuries. Most of the vessels entering London would have been moored mid-stream, however, and their merchandise taken by barge to the shore.

There had been one principal change that altered the nature of the port. Fitzstephen reports that by the end of the twelfth century the river-side wall, separating the city from the Thames, had fallen into ruin and disrepair; this opened out the area immediately adjoining the banks, where new arcades and warehouses created the conditions of a flourishing market. It grew and grew, in unanticipated and unsupervised ways, for the next five centuries. Gradually the trade became so large that it began to spread downriver and away from the twenty so-called "legal quays" set up, in the reign of Elizabeth I, between London Bridge and the Tower of London, all of them on the north bank of the river. Quays denote those places where ships could be legally discharged and loaded. Wharves were designed to pass goods to and from barges only, but they were eventually being used for merchant ships also. Ratcliff and Poplar became new mooring sites for shipping, known as "sufferance wharves," and the East India Company began to make use of Blackwall. The "sufferance wharves" constructed at Bermondsey were in fact on the site of medieval granaries; so there was a continuity. Another Elizabethan ordinance forbade the construction of private houses beside the banks of the Thames, so that the river could be saved for commerce. It is an indication of the pre-eminence of trade in the river's history.

Docks were essentially small open harbours that were cut into the bank, and could be used by every type of vessel. The first mention of a dock upon the Thames, at least in the guise with which we are familiar, occurred during the reign of Charles II. In his diary of 15 January 1661, Pepys noted that he travelled by boat to Blackwall where he saw a new dock and wet dock holding "a brave new merchantman which is to be launched shortly." Five years after Pepys made his entry, the Great Fire might have put at risk all the achievement and enterprise of the city's port. That Fire in fact began within the precincts of the port, at Pudding Lane, and the contents of the warehouses—including such combustible materials as brandy and sulphur, pitch and resin—materially helped to increase the conflagration. As happened in the Second World War, the marine trade of London helped to bring on the city's destruction. Yet the commerce of the river, already thousands of years old, was not to be thwarted. It increased after the Fire, and continued to do so. In 1696 a parliamentary Bill was passed to create what became known as the Howland Great Wet Dock at

Rotherhithe. It was 10 acres (4 ha) in extent, and held some 288,712 tons (over 292,700 tonnes) of water; it could hold without discomfort 120 of the largest merchant ships then sailing, and it helped to consolidate the possibilities of the area downriver from the Port. It was eventually renamed the Commercial Dock.

Then at the very beginning of the nineteenth century the West India Dock Company Act was passed, and the whole landscape of the Thames at London was changed. The problem was, in part, one of congestion. It has been calculated that by 1800 there were 1,775 vessels using a stretch of water suitable for only 545 ships, and that there were also some 3,500 barges moored in the immediate vicinity. The result was of course the prospect of severe delays. Vessels could wait a week, or even a fortnight, before finding a vacant berth. But there was also the problem of security. With so many valuable cargoes lying upon the river, the vessels were obvious targets for the host of "river pirates," "scuffle hunters" and others who could steal, smuggle or offload merchandise almost at will. There was the additional problem of inadequate storage. The warehouse accommodation for sugar amounted to some 32,000 hogsheads to meet an annual import of 120,000 hogsheads; under favourable circumstances this might be deemed sufficient, but in fact all of the sugar arrived within the same three months.

The merchants and the ship-owners were united in their complaints, and in their desire to seek secure haven for their vessels while in London's waters. Eight schemes were put before a parliamentary committee, with plans for the deepening of the river and for the building of a canal network. There were of course objections from those who had a vested interest in the existing arrangements. There were protests from the porters and the car-men who worked by the bankside; there were protests from the "lightermen" who discharged cargo from the ships moored midstream; there were protests from the owners of the "legal quays" and "sufferance wharves" who would lose much of their business; there was even protest from the Corporation of the City of London, which claimed that any cut into urban territory for the building of a dock would be an infringement of the city's ancient rights and privileges.

But the objections were met, and a Bill for the construction of docks at Wapping and at the Isle of Dogs passed into law on 23 May 1800. It marked the beginning of a new tidal river. It also changed the nature of the city itself, since by the second decade of the nineteenth century London had become unique in the world as the capital city of finance, seat of government and great port; Petrograd, Lisbon and Amsterdam were not competitors in all of those respects.

As a direct result of the new enterprise, the reaches of the Thames between Westminster Bridge and Greenwich became known as "London River." There was an area of the river known also as "London Pool," the "Upper Pool" stretching from London Bridge to Tower Bridge, and the "Lower Pool" from Tower Bridge to Bermondsey. The West India Dock on the northern end of the Isle of Dogs was soon joined by the London Dock at Wapping, the East India Dock at Blackwall and the Surrey Dock at Rotherhithe, thus forming the largest assembly of wet docks in the world. In 1820 the Regent's Canal Dock was built at Limehouse to allow merchandise to make its way inland through the network of existing canals. It was followed by the construction of St. Katharine's Dock in 1828. This was a more controversial site in certain respects, since it entailed the demolition of the ancient St. Katharine's Hospital with its companion church of St. Katharine by the Tower. Many old streets were also torn down in the process, among them such insalubrious riverine locations as Dark Entry, Cat's Hole, Shovel Alley, Rookery and Pillory Lane. The names are an adequate demonstration of the dark world that could grow up in the immediate vicinity of the river.

The effects of the new docks were immediate and profound. The ships were discharged within three to four days, as opposed to a month under the previous dispensation. Security became of paramount concern, and the hatches of all ships were nailed or tied down at Gravesend before sailing upriver. No carts or porters were allowed to enter the new quays, thus preventing casual or systematic pilfering. Even the loose sugar found in the holds was collected and sold for the benefit of the merchant. The walls around the new docks were fixed at a height of 20 feet (6 m). As we have seen, a new police force—the first statutory police force in the country—was established to protect the traffic of the river.

When a new highway was built to connect these docks with the City of London, it was aptly named the Commercial Road, and the foundation stone of the West India Dock was inscribed with the motto "An Undertaking which, under the Favour of God, shall contribute Stability, Increase and Ornament, to British Commerce." Its construction had also been financed by British commerce, and the grand scheme became the largest single privately funded enterprise in the history of the country. It is interesting to note, in this context, that the successor to the London docks—the great planning initiative known generically as "Dockland"—now has some claim to rivalling that achievement. The river attracts money, as Defoe noted many centuries before. It is still liquid silver.

The docks themselves were created in a spirit of immensity. The first brick warehouses to appear on the banks of the Thames were as large as palaces, as well defended as castles. Their principal architect, Daniel Asher Alexander, is perhaps best known for his design of England's prisons, such as Maidstone and Dartmoor, and the docks themselves were a place of maximum security. Yet the river is also a place of vision and in *Georgian London* (1946), Sir John Summerson compares the work of Alexander to the visionary fantasies of Piranesi—"While Coleridge turned the plates of the *Opere Varie* and the young de Quincey drugged himself into Piranesian frenzy, Alexander built these reminiscences of the Carceri into gaols and warehouses."

The tobacco warehouse at Wapping was celebrated for "covering more ground, under one roof, than any public building, or undertaking, except the pyramids of Egypt." The walls of the London Docks were longer and higher than the walls that had once been placed around London. Artificial lakes were built, comprising some 300 acres of water. The marshlands of the Isle of Dogs were drained.

The plethora of engravings and etchings, lithographs and watercolours, tells its own story of pride and achievement over two centuries. *The Opening of the St. Katharine Docks, October 28, 1828* depicts a panorama of great ships, flags and crowds; many of the men are waving their top-hats in the air, while groups of people throng the balconies of the tall warehouses beside the basin. *Howland Great Wet Dock, Rotherhithe, 1700* shows from an aerial perspective a large artificial lake set among fields and marshes; there are avenues of trees along both sides of it, designed not as a picturesque accompaniment but as a windbreak. *Brunswick Dock at Blackwall, 1803* is a wide riverscape by William Daniell that suggests the scale of the enterprise; some thirty masted vessels are shown arrayed in ranks, while the river winds in the distance down to the sea.

Daniell himself finished many aquatints of the new docks, all of them on a large scale, and has some claim to being the artist of that mercantile revolution. His *New Docks and Warehouses, On the Eve of Completion, 1802, on the Isle of Dogs near Limehouse* is the view of a miniature city, itself the size of Venice. His *A View of the London Dock, 1808* is of a great city within a city; but there are as many ships upon the river itself as in the dock. He was an exact draughtsman, concerned with detail as well as perspective, but there is no doubt concerning the grandeur of his conception. A passage from Ezekiel was often quoted by those who wished to emphasise the spiritual as well as physical blessings manifested by the new port—"O Thou that are situate at the entry of the sea, which art a merchant of the people for many isles . . . Thy borders are in the midst of the seas, thy builders have perfected thy beauty." Anything pertaining to the river can elicit a religious response.

And so there emerged Lady Dock and Russia Dock, Albion Dock and Lavender Pond, Greenland Dock and Acorn Pond, Canada Dock and Quebec Pond. What is perhaps most remarkable of all is that, from the river itself, they were all but invisible. They were hidden behind the high warehouses and factories and channels, so that it seemed as if the city itself had swallowed up the ships. But the docks built in the first decades of the nineteenth century were not enough. The use of steamships on deep sea voyages made it necessary to construct ever larger and deeper docks. The largest sailing ship might reach a maximum size of 1,500 tons (1,524 tonnes); but the steamship *Great Western*, which made its maiden voyage across the Atlantic to America in 1838, was already 2,300 tons (2,337 tonnes). By 1855 a great new complex, the Victoria Dock, had been constructed on marshlands between Blackwall Reach and Galleons Reach. It was followed thirteen years later by Millwall Dock. Then in 1886 the new docks at Tilbury were opened. The older docks had to be rebuilt or extended for the larger vessels, and in 1904 a new Greenland Dock was built as part of the Surrey Docks. Some twenty-five years after its own construction the Victoria Dock was joined by the Royal Albert Dock. At a length of 1¾ miles and a water area of 87 acres (35 ha), it was capable of receiving vessels of 12,000 tons (12,192 tonnes). These were all great plains of calm water, lacustrine cities within which floated fleets and argosies from all over the world, moving in and out on every tide; this was a world of masts and funnels, sails and rigging. It was a treasure house and a refuge, a fort and an industry.

In the nineteenth century there was enough rum imported to make the entire city drunk, and one vat in the Rum Quay at the West India Dock held 7,800 gallons (35,450 l). There was enough sugar to sweeten the Thames and enough indigo to dye the river blue. Sealed under bond, in the warehouses, were generally £10 million by cost of pepper, £23 million of tobacco and £51 million of tea. There was rubber, and coffee, and cinna-

mon, and dates and canned meats. A single cold store in the Royal Albert
Dock could accommodate 250,000 carcasses of mutton, and the Surrey
Docks could hold a million tons of timber. The wine terminal at West In-
dia Dock could contain almost a million gallons (over 4.5 million l).

After the construction of the docks, the trade of London grew ever
larger and more exotic. Young elephant tusks known as scrivelloes and
young ostrich feathers called spads were imported from the colonies. The
huge tusks of mammoths, retrieved from the frozen wastes of Siberia, were
shipped to the London Ivory Market. Ambergris came from the bellies of
whales, and liquid aloe was poured into monkey skins where it hardened
into cadaver shapes.

As a result of this trade, much of it highly specific or rare, the old
wharves and quays still flourished in the shade of the great docks. Although
the owners of the docks wished to maintain their monopoly of trade, the
free enterprise of the Thames was a stronger force. It has always been a
levelling river. The lightermen had been granted permission to work in the
new docks but, when the monopoly on the dockyard storing of goods expired, the old wharves redoubled their business. There were seventeen
hundred wharves on the river between Brentford and Gravesend. In the
short stretch between London Bridge and the Tower of London there were
thirty-four wharves, from Fresh Wharf to Brewers Key on the north bank
and from Toppings Wharf to Hartleys Wharf on the south.

Their names, and some of their structures, survive still in the large
apartment blocks on both sides of the river. The configuration of Oliver's
Wharf and Orient Wharf at Wapping, for example, stands as a ghostly
presence within the old and new buildings upon the site. Beyond them
St. John's Wharf, and Sun Wharf, and Swan Wharf, remain almost unchanged. Some of the ancient watermen's stairs, such as Wapping Old
Stairs by the station of the river police, exist still.

The entire system of docks became the province of the poet and the
painter, and the novelist, as much as the mariner or the merchant. Joseph
Conrad, who knew the docks at first hand as a master seaman, wrote an essay on "London River: The Great Artery of England" in 1904; he compared
the great conglomeration of wharves to "a jungle by the confused, varied,
and impenetrable aspect of the buildings that line the shore . . . London, the
oldest and greatest of river ports, does not possess as much as a hundred
yards of open quays upon its river front. Dark and impenetrable at night,
like the face of a forest, is the London waterside." He described how the

"lightless walls seem to spring from the very mud upon which the stranded barges lie." The port was for him a thing "grown up, not made," representing an organic life that obeyed its own laws of growth and change. In that sense the river reflected, or mirrored, the condition of the city through which it flowed.

For him each dock had its own life and character. St. Katharine's Dock evinced "cosiness" and seclusion, while the great London Docks were "venerable and sympathetic" with "an old-world air." He believed that these sites were "as romantic as the river they serve," principally because they seemed to partake of the antiquity of the Thames itself. They had become imagined places, unique places, "by the long chain of adventurous enterprises that had their inception in the town and floated out into the world on the waters of the river." So the sacredness of the river cast its blessing even upon "the vast scale of the ugliness" that the docks created. Even what was then the most modern of them, Tilbury Dock, had for Conrad the indefinable quality of enchantment in its "remoteness and isolation upon the Essex Marsh." The Thames was "an historical river" that cast its spell upon the life and industry of its banks. "The docks are impossible to describe," Verlaine wrote in 1872. "They are unbelievable! Tyre and Carthage all rolled into one!" The protagonist of J. K. Huysmans's novel, *A Rebours* (1884), sees in reverie "vistas of endless docks stretched farther than the eye could see, crowded with cranes and capstans and bales of merchandise . . . gigantic warehouses bathed by the foul black water of an imaginary Thames, in a forest of masts." When Baudelaire saw Whistler's etchings of the wharves and docks between Tower Bridge and Wapping, he remarked that they manifested "the profound and complex poetry of a vast capital." But it is also the poetry of the river.

Just as Defoe employed the poetry of trade in his accounts of the eighteenth-century Thames, so the writers of the nineteenth century vied with each other in descriptions of the docks' immensity. The commerce of the river was somehow touched by the myth and mystery of the Thames, so that its harshness and squalor were consumed in the general invocations of spectacle and magnificence. The sacredness of the river throughout human history also affected the perception of its trading activities; they, too, are described with a vague but evident religiosity.

The engravings by Doré of the London riverside, in his *London: A Pilgrimage* (1872), are preceded by an image of Old Father Thames as some wild and ancient deity with his hair streaming down his back. He presides over a dark world of labour and sacrifice, with the workers of the docks as his votaries. The crowds of small anonymous figures proceed in endless array through yards and warehouses that tower above them. They swarm; they seem to move in rhythm, dimly outlined. They are caught in chiaroscuro, enmeshed in shadow and fitful light, with the thick network of sails and masts and funnels dominating the foreground. The water itself, when it can be seen, is black—black with coal-dust, or hides, or tobacco. *The Docks—Night Scene* depicts a world of frantic activity with a background of mast upon mast like some dark wood from a dream.

So London itself loomed along the banks with its corona of perpetual smoke, its dust, its noise and its smell. At the end of the nineteenth century, too, the first high-voltage power station in the world was built on the banks of the river at Deptford. This was followed by the power stations of Battersea, Fulham and Bankside. There were other tokens of the future world. In 1880 the first consignment of American oil came ashore at Thames Haven; it was discharged from a sailing ship, but the arrival was the harbinger of all the great oil-refineries that would emerge by the side of the estuarial Thames.

At the beginning of the twentieth century it seemed that the commerce of the river would endure for ever, as long as there were oceans and tides. In 1909 the Port of London Authority was created to supervise this continuing project, and in its first programme of works it envisaged new docks and basins at the West India Dock, Millwall Dock and Albert Dock. A scheme of wholesale extension and improvement was agreed, and by 1913 the port was handling 20 million tons (over 20 million tonnes) of cargo each year. In 1921 the King George V Dock was opened in Silvertown, further enlarging a complex of docks that had spread over 234 acres (94.6 ha) of interconnected water. The Royal Albert Dock itself had a basin 1 mile in length, so that it could have been some inland sea. The docks at Tilbury encompassed 106 acres (43 ha) of enclosed water and 4 miles of quay frontage. By 1930 the port and docks of London afforded employment to one hundred thousand people, most of whom lived in the immediate vicinity of the Thames, and handled 35 million tons (35.5 million tonnes) of cargo within its riverine empire of 700 acres (283 ha).

At the beginning of the twentieth century the industries of the river were in fact increasing at what seemed at the time to be an alarming rate. The river at Brentford had become wholly industrial, while there were factories and mills at Lambeth, Nine Elms, Battersea, Wandsworth and Fulham. There were soap-works and rubber-works at Isleworth, manufacturers of roll shutters at Teddington and of motor-cars at Ham. There were saw-mills in Pimlico, which became one of the centres of the timber trade. The vast army of one hundred thousand workers included dockers and stevedores, lightermen and sailors, all of them owing their livelihood to the tides of the river.

In 1931 Virginia Woolf wrote an essay, "The Docks of London," in which she described how the "banks of the river are lined with dingy, decrepit-looking warehouses. They huddle on land that has become flat and slimy mud . . . Behind masts and funnels lies a sinister dwarf city of workmen's houses. In the foreground cranes and warehouses, scaffolding and gasometers line the banks with a skeleton architecture." For her it was a "dismal prospect," and she can perhaps be forgiven for not understanding the imperatives of trade.

The twentieth-century French novelist, Louis-Ferdinand Céline, adopted a more enthusiastic and celebratory tone in *Guignol's Band* (1944) where he expatiates upon the

> phantasmagoric storehouses, citadels of merchandise, mountains of tanned goatskins enough to stink all the way to Kamchatka! Forests of mahogany in thousands of piles, tied up like asparagus, in pyramids . . . rugs enough to cover the Moon, the whole world . . . Enough sponges to dry up the Thames! Enough wool to smother Europe . . . Herrings to fill the seas! Himalayas of powdered sugar . . .

But then, within two generations, all had gone. The advent of large container ships could not have been anticipated in the first half of the century; their cargo could now be lifted from ship to truck, without need of warehouses, and the vessels themselves were too large to be accommodated by the existing dock facilities. The emergence of great ports in other parts of the world, and the restrictive practices of the London dockworkers, only served to hasten the end. The docks fell silent. The East India Dock closed in 1967, after a life of 160 years, while the London Dock and St. Katharine's Dock followed two years later. The West India Dock survived until 1980, after a span of 178 years, but by then the trade of the Thames was depleted beyond remedy. The last of the docks, the Royal Victoria, the Royal Albert and King George V, were closed in 1981. By the end of the

twentieth century the docks had disappeared, vanished as if they had indeed all been a dream—the dream of toil, and suffering, on the banks of
the river.

The author of the official *History of the Port of London* (1921), Sir
Joseph Broodbank, suggests at one point that "with few exceptions once a
great community establishes itself on a site, that site permanently remains
a dwelling place of crowded humanity." He was no doubt inferring that the
dockland of London would remain a centre of mercantile and commercial
activity, which he believed to be "as secure as the future of any human institution can be," but he was correct in quite another sense. Dockland has
once more become a place of "crowded humanity," but not one concerned
with trade. It has become a new city, opening up what is known as the
"Thames Gateway" to create ever expanded communities. Out of the deserted docks, ten years after they had been consigned to weed and ruin,
rose the shining edifices and refurbished warehouses that have become the
single most important extension of London since the growth of the suburbs in the early twentieth century. That is a story for another chapter in
the history of the Thames.

CHAPTER 26

Steam and Speed

The steamship made its first appearance on the river in 1801, when it was used principally for towing larger sailing vessels. The first steam-boat "packet" or small ship was heralded in the London newspapers on 23 January 1815, with the announcement that "the public are informed that the new London steam-boat packet *Margery*, under Captain Cortis, will start at precisely 10 o'clock on Monday morning the 23rd inst from Wapping Old Stairs near London Bridge." Its destination was Gravesend, from whence it would return the following morning at the same hour. The Watermen's Company, understandably concerned with the livelihoods of its members, began proceedings against Captain Cortis. But no force on earth could have withstood the change. By 1830 there were some fifty-seven steam-packets on the Thames. Their arrival heralded the appearance of the "day-tripper," who became a ubiquitous visitant on the waters. The penny steamboat became known as "the omnibus of the river."

Southend was one of the most popular ports of call, and indeed it became known as "London on Sea." There were musical boats, with resident bands, who made their way upriver to Richmond or Kew or Hampton Court; the trippers on these vessels, known sarcastically as 'Arries and 'Arriets, were the especial objects of the wrath of the fishermen and the middle-class artists who believed that the higher reaches of the Thames were their own particular domain. Jetties were erected with the sole purpose of servicing the new vessels. By the 1830s and 1840s there were all the makings of a "boom." There were some seventeen steamers running daily from London to Gravesend, at a charge of 1 shilling for each passenger. The cost of the journey to Greenwich was 5 pence, and from London Bridge to Westminster it was a penny. In 1846 there set sail the "halfpenny steamers" from Hungerford Pier by Charing Cross to the City. But the new style of passenger could also go further; there were steamboats for travellers to Plymouth, Southampton and Land's End; there was a boat to Dover and a boat to Boulogne; there was a Rhine boat and an Ostend boat. The traffic was very large. One steamboat company estimated that it carried some quarter of a million passengers on the Thames each year.

The Margate and Gravesend boats left from St. Katharine's Wharf and from London Bridge; there were many complaints about the fact that the boats of rival companies raced each other downriver, with the consequent swell washing away the banks as well as swamping passing wherries. The water of the Thames became rougher. There was open warfare between the watermen and the steamboats, with accusations of deliberate ramming and obstruction. There were also boiler explosions, fires and accidents; but the progress of the steamship was unassailable.

In one of his early essays under the pseudonym of "Boz," "The River" (1835), the young Charles Dickens depicts the confused scene at the "steam-wharf" as the passengers clamber aboard the "Gravesend packet" or the "Margate packet"; they sit down on the wrong boat, or cannot find comfortable seats, or mislay their luggage. "The regular passengers, who have season tickets, go below to breakfast; people who have purchased morning papers, compose themselves to read them; and people who have not been down the river before, think that both the shipping and the water, look a great deal better at a distance." At Blackwall the wicker hand-baskets are opened to furnish heavy sandwiches, with bottles of brandy and water. One man brings out a portable harp, and plays dance music. Dickens even records some dilatory conversation between passengers on the topic of the moment:

> "Wonderful thing steam, sir."
> "Ah! it is indeed, sir."
> "Great power, sir."

"Immense—immense."

"Great deal done by steam, sir."

"Ah! You may say that, sir."

"Still in its infancy, they say, sir."

Steam was the future. Steam was progress. In the battle for the Thames, steam would win.

But another form of steam-power had arrived, which threw all the plans for boat traffic into disorder. In 1834 an ambitious project, known as the Great Western Railway Scheme, was initiated to lay tracks for the new trains between London and Reading and Bristol. The Thames Commissioners, fearful for the future of river traffic, declared that "all those who reside on the banks of this river, whether attracted there by its beauty, its salubrity or its utility, would lend their aid to prevent the sanction of Parliament being given to so useless a scheme as that of the Great Western Railway." Yet all the forces of the nineteenth century, in its preoccupation with energy and with speed, in its demands for progress and innovation, in its sense of excitement and its appetite for reform, were moving ahead. The railway line was completed between London and Reading in 1840, and there was a branch line between London and Oxford four years later; lines to Windsor and Henley-on-Thames followed.

The "iron horse," as the train was known, had entered the Vale of the White Horse. It was mounted by Isambard Kingdom Brunel, who first jotted down the idea of the railway in 1833; then he organised his plan of campaign, beginning with a complete investigation of the Thames Valley itself. At the age of twenty-seven he set out to understand the terrain thoroughly, and wrote in his diary for September 1833: "started at 6 am . . . examined the ground in the neighbourhood of Wantage . . . breakfasted at Streatley . . . returned to Reading." He marked out in his mind every stretch of the track that he would eventually build, labouring twenty hours a day to bring his vision to perfection.

He already had some acquaintance with the Thames, having taken over from his father the completion of the Thames Tunnel; he knew the power of the river, too, after it had broken in upon his constructions and taken the lives of his workers. Is it possible that he had some desire to tame the energy and authority of the Thames, by creating this modern network of lines and stations all around it? His attention to the scheme was immense, almost overwhelming. He testified to parliamentary committees and helped to draft the suitable legislation; he even acted as a fund-raiser with various interested parties. He planned the nature and development of the railway in the most minute detail, with attention to tunnels and cuttings, stations and viaducts, sheds and bridges.

The Great Western Railway was accompanied by similar projects that impinged directly upon the river. The London and Greenwich Railway opened in 1838; a year later the London and Southampton Railway began its operations, followed in 1841 by the London and Blackwall Railway Company which laid tracks along the north bank of the river from the Minories to Fenchurch Street. In 1848 the first railway crossing was made by the bridge at Richmond, and a second bridge was built at Barnes in the following year. The first city crossing was at Pimlico, opening for railway traffic in 1860. The advance had been immense, with enormous consequences for the commerce and the passenger traffic of the Thames. The Thames Valley itself was changed beyond recognition. The increase of population in riverside towns such as Reading and Abingdon was extensive; instead of being river towns they had become railway towns.

But there was another change, amounting to a social revolution, best exemplified in Turner's *Rain, Steam, and Speed—the Great Western Railway*. The painting is of course a vision of power, with a steam locomotive rushing over the Thames at Maidenhead Bridge. The bridge itself, constructed by Brunel, was a miracle of engineering. It was the largest span of brick building in Europe. It was believed by many that it could not be finished or, once erected, that it could never last. It was thrown across the river in two spans, the central arches meeting on an eyot in the middle of the Thames. The original contractor, distraught at the problems of the enterprise, had asked to be relieved of his responsibilities; it was feared that once the wooden scaffolding had been removed the arches would collapse. Brunel stayed true to his original vision. Those small red bricks have, in the last 170 years, been subject to a pressure that must approach the extreme limit of sustainability; yet they have survived.

Turner's painting is in part a hymn to speed, with Brunel's bridge at the centre of a great exfoliation of energy; there is a brilliancy about the painting, an effulgence of colour and of light, that suggests Turner's deep excitement at the prospect of this relatively new force. Turner the artist is in essence saluting Brunel the visionary. But there is also an attendant loss. The view of the painting is to the east, towards London, associated with the clouds of dirt and disease that were popularly supposed to travel from the city. Anything "out of the east" was suspect in the middle of the nineteenth century. On one side of the canvas, beyond the explosion of colour and of light, there are people boating on the river while a ploughman labours in a neighbouring field. These were the tokens of the immemorial existence, of the ancient life fostered by the river, that the railway seemed about to end. In Turner's painting a hare flees from the path of the rushing locomotive, an image of the retreat of the natural world from the arts of mechanism.

But there was one other example of nineteenth-century enterprise, and innovation, that entailed arguably more important consequences for the Thames. The principal figure behind the "improvements," as they became known, was the civil engineer Joseph Bazalgette whose singular and ambitious vision in the 1860s was to embank and control the river. There had of course been other attempts in the past to control its course, and to protect the shores from the encroaching tides or from the inclemency of flooding weather. It is believed that the walls around Gravesend were built by the Saxons, for example, and that Romney Marsh was created by them.

In the twelfth century there were embankments around Woolwich. In the thirteenth century Plumstead was fortified against the water, with other sea walls being erected at Rainham Marsh, West Ham and Limehouse. In the fourteenth century there were new-built banks at Blackwall as well as fortifications at Stratford and Dagenham. In the sixteenth century Wapping was reclaimed from "a watery waste," even though sea walls had been previously built there in 1324. In the sixteenth century, too, chalk from the cliffs at Purfleet was used to provide defensive walls at West Thurrock. Canvey Island was enclosed in the seventeenth century by workers from Holland, who were believed to have special expertise in such matters.

At West Thurrock itself a chapel was erected by the wall, one of many that were set up on the sites of embankment as a form of divine protection; from these chapels, many of them lonely places amid a waste of fields, prayers were despatched to preserve and maintain the works of defence against the sea. The process of reclamation was in fact considered to be a holy one. To rescue fruitful ground from the tides, to plant crops where once the waves rolled, is akin to a form of creation whereby earth is made out of the sea.

The waters surged forward, canalised and directed; the river had become deeper and swifter, at the same time as its domain was being steadily diminished by the works of man. In the seventeenth century the demand for riverside sites for houses of course meant that parts of the foreshore

were reclaimed; in 1757 the shore in front of Temple Gardens was embanked, and in 1772 the Royal Adelphi Terrace became the first public
riverside terrace. The high promenade of Somerset House was created
four years later.

Yet the nineteenth century was the true century of change, through the
energetic agency of Bazalgette. An Act of Parliament was passed in 1863 to
expedite his progress on new embanking for the Thames. He would create
a vast and intricate sewage network that would carry filth and detritus out
of London, while above the sewers he would be able to create great stone
promenades on the banks of the river that would form a new Thames landscape. Work was first begun on the Victoria Embankment, between Westminster and the Temple, during the course of which some 40 acres (16 ha)
of foreshore were reclaimed. Bazalgette was only assisting a more general
process. In the course of the river's history, from the time of the Celtic
peoples to the present century, the width of the river at Westminster has de-
creased from 750 yards (686 m) to 250 yards (228.6 m).

The Victoria Embankment was soon accompanied by the construction
of the Albert Embankment and then the Chelsea Embankment. It was one
of the largest civil engineering projects of the nineteenth century, including as it did the building of an underground railway system. A memorial to
Bazalgette stands on the Victoria Embankment itself, with the legend *Flu-
mini Vincula Posuit* ("He placed chains upon the river"). It was the old
boast of the pharaohs, and of the rulers of the ancient hydraulic states. If
it seems hubristic, no deity has so far punished it; that would require an inundation as great as the Flood, an event now apparently deemed to be impossible.

For some these strips of granite stone can be seen as frontiers or barri-
ers to the Thames in its city reaches, stripping it of what once remained of
its human dimension. For others they are a necessary precaution and defence against the wayward nature of the river, reclaiming immensely useful
land for the benefit both of traffic and of the pedestrian. On the newly embanked land, too, gardens were planted for the delectation of the citizens so
that the prospect of the banks was immensely improved. The embankments
had the added advantage of harbouring the sewage tunnels that piped the
waste out of the capital. In that respect, too, Bazalgette's work can be considered to have been beneficial. His enterprise was at the time considered
to be one of the new wonders of the world, a welcome improvement upon
the unsightly mud-banks, ruined buildings and dilapidated wharves that

crowded around the riverside—complete with their unsavoury native population who were generally excoriated as "river-dwellers."

At the beginning of the twentieth century, of course, it seemed that the great riverine developments of the previous century were coming to fruition. The docks had never been more fully employed, and the position of London at the heart of a world empire meant that the Thames was in itself the river of empire, the great market to which the merchants of the world paid their obeisance. Books written in the earlier part of the century, such as the three volumes of Sir John Adcock's *Wonderful London* (1920s), F. V. Morley's *River Thames* (1926) and H. M. Tomlinson's *London River* (1925), and a host of others, were in all essentials celebrations of the Thames's life and career as the greatest of all the world's rivers. There were many photographs of the daily life of the docks, and of the great vessels that moored there. There were aerial shots of the vast extent of dockland, and encomia to the gargantuan forces of trade and industry that had helped to create it. The ending of Tomlinson's study records the progress of a great ship down the estuary where her masts "rose above the buildings and stood against the sky, made her seem as noble and as haughty as a burst of great music. One of ours, that ship. Part of our parish."

One of the best accounts of the early-twentieth-century Thames is to be found in H. G. Wells's novel, *Tono Bungay* (1909), in which he records a journey downriver from Hammersmith Bridge to Blackfriars and the City. The area of Battersea and Fulham, as seen from the river, was one of "muddy suburb and muddy meadow," neither city nor country, where the presence of the coal barges is a token of the urban life towards which the river is flowing. From Putney onwards begin the "newer developments," to which he refers as "the first squalid stretches of mean houses right and left, and then the dingy industrialism of the south side"; this was a period when Lambeth, in particular, was the home of riverside workshops and manufactories.

The enthusiasm of Wells's narrator increases, however, when he reaches Lambeth Palace and the Houses of Parliament. Just beyond them is what he called the "essential London" with Charing Cross Railway Station as "the heart of the world," the river itself now flanked by "new hotels," by "great warehouses and factories, chimneys, shot towers and advertisements on the south." This is the bustling river of twentieth-century empire—not a clean place, not even a particularly pleasant or wholesome place, but one deeply involved in all the vital movements of the period.

As he goes further downriver, past Somerset House and the Temple, the narrator feels intimations of the age of the city and of its brooding presence by the Thames. He feels, also, the presence of "original England." It is a matter of some interest to the social historian, perhaps, that in the early years of the twentieth century the river and its territory did still retain the presence of its "aged" past. The atmosphere of the place, despite the presence of the new embankments, was charged with some vivid reminders of eighteenth- and nineteenth-century London in a manner no longer possible at the beginning of the twenty-first century. Too much has changed. The city, and its river, now seem contemporary once again. They are no longer obscured by the patina of past times. But the photographs of the riverside districts in 1909 and 1910 can take you effortlessly back to the London of Dickens, and even to the London of Johnson and Fielding. The alleys were the same; the wharves and the wharfside pubs were the same; the ill-fed and ill-clad people were the same.

Wells's narrator continues his journey where, just by the bridge at Blackfriars, he sees the first seagulls. Above "a rude tumult of warehouses" there looms the great dome of St. Paul's, singular and alone in that earlier skyline, where it presides over the movement of steamships and barges. The turn-of-the-century picture of St. Paul's overlooking the river is now as timeless as that of the wherries and galleons crowding upon the sixteenth-century Thames.

Then the narrator goes further to comprehend "the last great movement of the London symphony," a world of "stupendous cranes" and "great warehouses" and "large ships." It is "the port of the world." And so it seemed for many decades. Just before the beginning of the Second World War the annual tonnage entering the port of London was some 50 million (over 50.8 million tonnes), well above that of any other port. But even then there were more disquieting signs. In J. H. O. Bunge's report on the state of the river, *Tideless Thames in Future London* (1944), there were descriptions of "the dilapidated appearance of the Thames shores" and of "the derelict shabbiness" of the area from Westminster Bridge to Greenwich. The report also mentions St. Paul's, but in a spirit different from that of H. G. Wells. It is described as "smothered shoulder high in formless brick, dirty and black, sprouting from narrow and dark streets without any pretence at modern or convenient style"; it is also obscured by "dismal and inadequate miserly house fronts." So the Thames of the 1930s contained within itself the seeds of decay and, even, of dissolution. One of the chapter-headings of this account lists the "problems"—"of population, food, fuel, sewage, goods and passenger transport, flooding, fire protection, riparian property, prosperity and amenities." It seems exhaustive. The tone is pessimistic.

The Second World War cast a more lurid light on the role and nature of the Thames. Once more the principal highway was employed by an invader to mark his route into the centre of London. It became a river of fire, and a river of blood; it became the river of the inferno, darker and more dangerous than the Styx or Acheron. Throughout its history it has been a most tempting target; along its banks, in the late 1930s and early 1940s, were car works and oil installations, factories and electricity-generating stations. It comprised the world of the City and the world of Westminster, power and finance combined in one great arc of the river. From the beginning of the war there was a strict "blackout" on the Thames and its shores, but magnetic mines were still dropped by German bombers in its waters.

On 7 September 1940, firebombs were launched against the network of the port itself; all the docks and warehouses, except at Tilbury, were consumed in flame. Ships and barges were on fire, drifting dangerously in the tides against jetties and quays. The resources of London's firefighters were not enough to quench the inferno, and the fire burned so brightly that it could be distinctly seen from 12 miles away. The line of fire had another effect—it acted as a beacon for further waves of bombers that arrived on the succeeding night.

At 8:30 p.m. on 8 September, the raiders came in formation over the burning river. It no longer seemed to be the Thames but rather a flow of molten lava from some unknown source. The German bombers targeted any docks or warehouses that had not been destroyed by the previous night's attack, and fire once more encroached upon the river. The water was covered with a thin film of burning oil, and billows of acrid smoke belched out from every part of the shore. The rum was also alight upon the water, the warehouses of wool had become furnaces, and the paraffin wax blazed up. The Pool was a lake of brilliance, and areas like Lambeth and Rotherhithe were bathed in a radiance that was like the light of day.

On that same night, and on subsequent nights, the raiders attacked the dockside communities and towns. The East End was largely demolished, the houses fallen in a fog of smoke and of dust. The attacks on the Thames and its inhabitants went on without a pause for fifty-seven nights. On 8 December, for example, the headquarters of the Port of London Authority was directly hit; the oil tankers at Purfleet were all blazing, and the landing stage at Tilbury was burning out of control. A train was hit while travelling across Charing Cross Bridge, and many ships were sunk at their moorings in the river. It was estimated, at the end of hostilities, that approximately 15,000 high-explosive bombs, 350 parachute mines, 550 flying bombs and 240 rockets had fallen upon the Thames and dockland in the course of 1,400 raids. It may have been surmised that to destroy the Thames was, essentially, to destroy England; but the river, and the country, somehow survived.

By the late 1940s and 1950s, however, the river was slowly closing down for more mundane reasons. It was not being used by its citizens. The holiday-makers of the nineteenth century had gone, together with the steam-packet trippers and the commuters. It had become a silent river, and was described as a "broad, white, empty highway." The reasons for this lack of interest and of attention were various. There were problems of access, because many of the wharves and stairs had been allowed to fall into delapidation; there was the problem of neglect and consequent drabness; and there was of course the appalling problem of sewage. The South Bank had become "a term of despair and reproach." The point was that hardly anyone considered this area of the river at all. Very few Londoners knew anything much about the vast port within the midst of the city, and fewer still had any inkling of the nature or extent of the docks. The Thames had become unknown territory. The city had turned its back upon it.

The collapse of the docks, and the labour and trade associated with them, coincided with the departure of heavy industry from the Thames. There had been works and mills at Lambeth and Nine Elms, Battersea and Wandsworth. There had been factories at Fulham, soap-works at Isleworth and linoleum-makers at Staines. There had been tanneries at Bermondsey, together with the makers of jam, biscuits and chocolates. But that industrial and manufacturing world began to disappear. Vauxhall cars were indeed originally made at Vauxhall, and the aircraft-manufacturers Shorts began their business at Battersea. Ferranti and Siemens were both once based at Greenwich, which has some claim to being the home of electrical engineering. But the companies left or, in contemporary jargon, "relocated." The metal workers, Morgan Crucible, moved out of Battersea in the 1970s. The cable works, the paper works and the engineering works were gradually vacated in favour of more appealing and accessible sites, leaving just a few traces behind. There is still industrial work upon the Thames, especially in the area between London and the estuary, but it is upon a reduced scale.

The connection of water and power, however, remains undiminished. The power stations of Fulham and Lots Road are still in operation. The six great cooling towers of Didcot Power Station are well known to railway travellers; they take their water from the Thames, and then return it to the river. The power station at Battersea, with its four great chimneys, became and still is one of the most grandiose spectacles beside the river. It began to supply electrical power in the summer of 1933, and it was celebrated as a "flaming altar of the modern temple of power" before being put out of commission in 1983. It is now about to become a vast complex of hotels, shops, cinemas and apartments. The Thames was once used to cool the atomic reactors at Harwell atomic energy research establishment; its water was taken from the river at Sutton Courtenay, and returned at Culham. At Culham, too, there is located the "Joint European Torus" (JET) designed to test "magnetic confinement fusion" as an alternative source of energy; the experimental reactors here are known as "Tokamaks," and the project is described by its founders as the world's largest nuclear fusion research facility. This small neighbourhood of the Thames—marked by Sutton Courtenay, Culham and Didcot—is thus a centre of power. The ancient mills and weirs of the river have been succeeded by more grandiose and efficient agents of energy. But there is a continuity.

The river, however, has become a much quieter place. It has been calculated that if the number of vessels presently on the Thames were multiplied ten times, it would still be no busier than it was a century ago. There were, in the 1880s, six thousand steamers and five thousand sailing vessels using the river. Now the loudest sound can sometimes be that of the gulls. To travel down the estuary is to pass across waters that often seem deserted. In the nineteenth century the "brawling loudness" of the river was compared to its tranquil past; that tranquillity, on large stretches of the river, has returned.

There have instead been new forms of regeneration. Between July 1981 and March 1998 an organisation, known as the London Docklands Development Corporation, was dedicated to reclaim and reform the 8½ square miles of riverine space previously covered by the London Docks. The area included Southwark, Tower Hamlets and Newham. Where there had once been a wasteland of scrub and weed, guarded by the crumbling walls of the old docks or by fences of barbed wire, there arose new buildings and new homes. The area of the docks had once been physically removed from the rest of London, and had remained to most citizens an unknown territory. Now one of the first tasks of the new planners was to connect the river and the rest of the city with new forms of public transport. New roads, and new underground lines, were put into service; public transport was encouraged, and cross-river services were introduced. The Isle of Dogs, deemed unlucky in legend, was reclassified as an "Enterprise Zone" to attract investors and new business. It was as if the river were being charged once again with the life and energy of the city itself.

The development has proceeded in a sometimes haphazard manner, governed more by the imperatives of profit than of communal interest. But that is the story of the city. It is also the story of the Thames throughout its history. The first development was of homes and gardens in the area of Beckton and Surrey Docks, but it quickly became apparent that the area of the river itself should be of prime importance. The warehouses, for example, could be converted into the then fashionable "loft" apartments, with significant access to the Thames. The "views" of the river became interesting once again. In the beginning the demand could barely keep pace with the supply and in the narrow refurbished streets between the warehouses, where once porters and barrow boys trod, there were more estate agents than local shops. The interests of the native inhabitants, in particular, were often ignored. There was much agitation among them for more open involvement in the various schemes of development, and, naturally enough, there were also demands that their immediate concerns, such as employment and housing, be met. A long process of accommodation and rehabilitation began, which has not yet ended.

The emergence of the new financial district in the area now known generically as "Canary Wharf" has transformed the social and economic life of the immediate riverine neighbourhood. It coincided with the "deregulation" of the markets of the City, so that it became an emblem of change itself. It facilitated the development of a new railway network known as the "Docklands Light Railway," an extension of the Jubilee Underground line and the development of new Docklands highways. In the process both banks of the Thames were rejuvenated. There are now large blocks of apartments where there were once derelict wharves. The old canals of the docks have been replaced with marinas. Shopping areas, apartments, public houses and walkways are now, for example, situated where once St. Katharine's Dock lay huddled beneath the Tower; having been closed in 1968, it had remained in a broken and dilapidated state before its restoration as a new centre of urban life. In one sense the neighbourhood of the river is recovering its ancient exuberance and energy, and is reverting to its existence before the residents and houses were displaced by the building of the docks in the nineteenth century.

A photographic panorama of the Thames and its banks was produced for the Port of London Authority in 1937. To compare those black-and-white photographs with the setting of the modern river is to see a new world emerged from the old, not necessarily more interesting or more elegant but incomparably brighter and cleaner; some of the landmarks and the buildings are the same, but the smoke and the grime have gone. The picturesque barges and tugs are no longer to be seen, but the water seems fresher and clearer. There are more trees and open spaces. The patina of grey, the murk of riverside life, has been lifted. Many of the new buildings are disappointing and out-of-scale; many are simply functional. But they are simply the first stage in what will now be a continuing process. The spirit of the river has never departed. It has simply taken on a different manifestation.

New forms of architecture have in any case been slowly emerging that take their aesthetic from the Thames itself. The buildings of the river have always in part reflected the nature of the river, if only because they are hewn from the varying local materials of each region. There is limestone around Oxford, chalk and flint around the Berkshire Downs. But the more recent architecture of the Thames has chosen to pay homage to its presence in more direct ways. There are apartment blocks that are in fact refurbished warehouses, but there are also buildings that have been designed to resemble warehouses of the early nineteenth century. It might be called pastiche, but it might also represent a genuine emergence of the *genius loci* in a new guise. There are some buildings that in their profiles recall the shapes of ships riding the waves. Where the free trade wharves once stood at Ratcliff, there are now great complexes that look like ocean liners. The architect of the pumping station at the Isle of Dogs, John Outram, has said that his building was designed to "imitate a river and a landscape, from which the storm-water flowed." The architect of Chelsea Harbour, Ray Moxley, derived his inspiration from the "ships, towers, domes" commemorated in Wordsworth's poem "Composed upon Westminster Bridge."

There are also buildings along the Thames that have been lent a pharaonic or Egyptian appearance, in honour of the fact that in legend the Thames has also been known as Isis. The great skyscraper of Canary Wharf, Cabot House in Canada Square, has been constructed according to its architect Cesar Pelli as "a square prism with pyramidal top in the traditional form of the obelisk." This powerful talisman has now become one of the river's landmarks. There are other Egyptian designs and motifs in the newly built areas of Docklands, but there was already a "neo-Egyptian" office block by the Thames, Adelaide House, erected in 1926. There is a continuity. The pharaonic connotations may have induced a sense of immensity. The gas-holders at Greenwich were the biggest in the world; now the great dome in the same area, known as the "Millennium Dome," is covered by the largest roof in the world and is also the largest fabric structure. The docks of the Thames were by far the largest in the world, now Battersea Power Station is one of the largest brick structures. There are other examples.

The rhythm of the buildings sited on the South Bank, including the National Theatre opened in 1976, has been described as "flowing"; the architect of the theatre, Denys Lasdun, said that he wanted to create the feeling that "the audience—like the tides of the river—flow into the auditoriums. Then the tide ebbs and they come out into the creeks of the small spaces that are made by all these terraces." And of course "terraces" are the most ancient feature of the Thames. It is perhaps not entirely coincidental that the two living architects who have the most powerful presence in London, Norman Foster and Richard Rogers, have their offices immediately beside the river. In fact Foster has now been raised to the peerage with the title of Lord Foster of Thames Bank, and Rogers has been similarly ennobled as Lord Rogers of Riverside. The architects state their identity in terms of the Thames.

The siting of the Olympic Games of 2012 in Stratford, and the rest of the East End of London, will materially help the development and refurbishment of the river as a principal urban resource. There have already been signs of new industries, and new forms of industry, converging upon its banks. In particular the high-technology electronics companies have arrived in the Thames Valley, and there are many industrial "parks" placed beside the river.

There are other schemes. The "Thames Gateway Development" has been asked to secure the future refurbishment of the north bank of the river as far as the Thames Barrier itself. The "East Thames Corridor" will continue the city along the estuary, as far as Tilbury in Essex and the Isle of Sheppey in Kent. The planning agencies have already been concerned with Dartford and Gravesend, with the Medway towns and with Thamesmead, as possible sites for growth. There are plans for new river-crossings, for an extension of the Docklands Light Railway and for a new bridge or tunnel between Silvertown and the Greenwich Peninsula.

London will then once more become a river city. The shift eastwards is against all historical trends. But then the reversion to the river itself was considered by many to be unhistorical. It had become, in the eyes of urban planners, redundant to the needs of the city. It had no future as a means of transport. But if the new city is to follow the line of the Thames, then new forms of river transport will inevitably emerge over the next century. The river will once more become the highway of the nation.

PART IX

The Natural River

Laleham ferry

CHAPTER 27

"Hey Ho, the Wind and the Rain"

he Thames makes its own weather. It is of course marked by the prevalence of dampness, the humidity and dankness associated with the presence of large volumes of water. The air then becomes a dimension of the river, savoured in the upper reaches of the Thames and in the London streets that border it. The phrase for it, in the nineteenth century, was "river-damp." It is only one stage away from the plentiful mists that have always been a feature of the riverscape. There is a quality of soft and shrouding mist that seems unique to the climate of the Thames.

Along the upper reaches of the river the appearance of the mist was a harbinger of that day's weather; if the mist hovered around the summit of the hills it was a token of rain, but if it remained at their base it was a sign of dryness. In the Vale of the White Horse the mist was described as the smoke of the "White Osse's bacca" or tobacco. The mists of the valley were also believed to be responsible for the prevalence of thunderstorms in the summer months. The famous "dew ponds" on the downs, refreshed each night by the influence of the summer fogs, were reputed never to run dry. A naturalist of the immediate neighbourhood, in *The Naturalist on the*

Thames (1902), recorded that summer fogs were very common on the high downs and "are so wet that a man riding up the hills at 4 a.m. may find his clothes wringing wet, and every tree dripping water." It was as if the river had taken momentary hold upon the land itself. In the dryest or hottest summer the vapours exhaled by the river floated above the fields and meadows, enveloping and nourishing everything. The weather then was sultry, or humid. The damp mists emanating from the Thames in late autumn and winter were, however, considered dangerous to visitors of the late nineteenth century; they were conducive to "chills" or to "agues" that in exceptional cases might prove fatal. In the late months these mists could become numbingly cold and a true risk to unwary travellers.

The mists and fogs were reported from earliest times. Tacitus mentions them in his account of Caesar's invasion, and they were commonly described in all succeeding centuries as the natural companions of the river. Many riverine areas, such as Westminster and Lambeth, were built upon swamp land; here the exhalation of damp and mist is more palpable than on the hills of London. The fogs of Westminster were once well known. During certain winters the riverine trees of London distilled pools of water from the circumambient atmosphere. The fogs were particularly thick along the estuarial waters, and a traveller of 1807 in Essex complained of "the thick and stinking fogs" that lurked there. But these were the fogs of nature, created by marshland and swamp, rather than the fogs of industry and waste.

However, that mist, in the nineteenth and twentieth centuries, did indeed become the surly and sulphurous fog. At the turn of the nineteenth century the Port of London was well known for the veil of fog that often covered it, swallowing up the docks and wharves, obscuring the traffic of the great waterway; the sounds of the river were muffled, too, with the call of sirens or of bells or of voices somehow lost in the immensity. There were many examples of pedestrians—even horses and carriages—falling into the river for the very good reason that they could no longer see it; it had been obscured by the swirling grey or grey-green vapours. This was the fog invoked by Dickens at the beginning of *Bleak House*:

> Fog everywhere. Fog up the river, where it floats among green aits and meadows; fog down the river, where it rolls defiled among the tiers of shipping, and the waterside pollutions of a great (and dirty) city. Fog on the Essex marshes; fog on the Kentish heights. Fog creeping into the

cabooses of collier brigs; fog lying out on the yards, and hovering in the rigging of great ships; fog drooping on the gunwales of barges and small boats.

This is the Thames as fog. It does not flow; it drifts like fog. It settles in the valley of London like thick mist in a hollow. It is comprised of fog, and all the vessels upon it are fashioned out of fog. This is the real phantom of the nineteenth-century river. And it persisted longer than anyone could reasonably have expected. As late as the 1960s there were on average about 237 hours of dense fog in, and upon, and about, the Thames each year.

There is a particular wind that scuds across the river. The prevailing wind of London is westerly, and on Waterloo Bridge there seems to be a perpetual westerly wind. Yet the wind of the river seems to be mainly south-westerly. That is one of the reasons why it is faster to travel downriver. A German traveller in 1710, Z. C. von Uffenbach, noted the continuous wind upon the water at London that, as he said, made sad work of men's wigs. The "South-west" can be known for its force, and for its iron cold, although in the winter months there is another particularly cold wind that comes in from the north-east. Everything is restless in the wind—the rushes, the weeds, the water, the swans, even the cows in the neighbouring pastures. The winds can endure, and in November 1703 a storm of winds continued for several days and wreaked havoc upon the river. The ships were blown from the water and lay upon one another in heaps between Shadwell and Limehouse; every other vessel was thrown upon the shore. Five hundred wherries were lost, some sunk and some dashed to pieces against each other; sixty barges were destroyed, and another sixty were sunk. It was impossible to estimate the loss of life upon the river, but some eighteen thousand men perished while on board ship. It has been estimated that the amount of energy released by a summer thunderstorm is equal to that of a 110-kiloton nuclear bomb, and its effect is magnified when it is set loose upon the river.

And with the wind there comes the rain. There is something particularly soothing about water falling within water. To look at rain falling into the river is like watching flames within a general fire; it is the delectation of observing an elemental force mingling with itself, even when the Thames seems distracted and turbulent with what was once known as the "rage of rain." The turbulence may have other causes. In the third century BC

Theophrastus made the observation that "the rising of bubbles in large numbers on the surface is a sign of abundant rain." The lowering of the atmosphere releases the vital gases held by the river. And there is also the curious phenomenon of the "water-whirls," described by one Thames inhabitant as "slender sprites that danced across the face of the broad and rippling Thames." They might indeed have come out of the mythology of the river, but they are essentially whirlpools above the surface of the river or slender whirlwinds made out of water. Extensive investigation has yielded no clue to their nature or their origin.

The rain is vital for the replenishment of the river. The average annual rainfall of the Thames Valley varies from 29 inches in the Lower Thames to 25 inches in the Upper Thames, making it one of the driest regions of the United Kingdom. But such is the power of the natural world that this relative paucity of rain creates a vast average of some 4,350 million gallons of water each day. Half of this supply is exhausted by evaporation or by the absorption of vegetable life; the rest becomes what is known as "residual rainfall" or the "natural flow" that passes into the river itself.

The rain is one of the phenomena that contribute to the sudden emergence of floods, although it should be observed that rain coming from the east and north-west is less likely to cause flood conditions than rain from the south and south-west. Floods are a permanent condition of the river. The first recorded flood along the Thames occurred in AD 9, although of course there were myriad floods and deluges that find no place in the recorded history of our ancestors. Then in AD 38 another great flood is believed to have killed some ten thousand people. Archaeologists have reported a decline of human activity in London, and in the London region, in the 360s; the evidence suggests that this decade of decay was the result of massive floodings.

It is a story of continual encroachment by the non-tidal as well as the tidal Thames. In 1332 Taplow was all but destroyed. In 1768 the water at Reading rose 2½ feet in half an hour. In 1774 the bridge at Henley was washed away. In 1821 the roads beside the Thames became impassable, and in 1841 the high street of Eton was under water. There were great floods in 1852 and in 1874, on both occasions occurring on 17 November. The heaviest flood on the non-tidal stretch of the river was in 1894, when one-third of the annual rainfall fell in less than a month. The river cannot contain so much water, as we have observed, and so it spills out in all directions creating havoc and confusion wherever the water goes. In 1947 the river below

Chertsey was 3 miles wide, and Maidenhead was 6 feet (1.8 m) under water. The area around Maidenhead has in fact always been susceptible to flooding, and at the beginning of this century a flood-relief channel was brought into operation.

It was hoped, at times of flood, that the river would subside gradually rather than suddenly, otherwise the floods would reappear again, and there is an apparently ancient maxim saying "soon down, soon up." A flood in winter was once not of great consequence, unless it reached the ploughed fields and the cottages close to the river. In the flat and marshy districts of the Upper Thames it was not unknown, in the winter months, for the inhabitants to be practically imprisoned for several weeks at a time. That is why the dwellings in these upper regions tended to be constructed out of stoutly built walls and thick stone. Now the proliferation of new homes in low-lying areas, and the pleasant prospect of owning a property near the river, have put thousands of households at risk. In farming areas, too, a flood in summer can create great damage among the grass and crops of the low-lying lands.

The curious nature of the phenomenon, however, is that flooding always seems to be unexpected. Floods are forgotten, until the next one occurs. There is a strange assumption that the Thames Barrier will somehow now prevent the depredations of the river. Leaving aside the obvious point that it will have no impact upon the river below the barrier itself, or on the miles of estuarial shore, the installation will have no effect upon the non-tidal stretches of the river that will be as liable to flood as at any other time in their history. At the beginning of 2003, for example, 550 houses were flooded; the level of water at Mapledurham Lock was only 12 inches lower than that at the time of the disastrous floods of 1947.

Let us assume that the average daily flow of water over Teddington Weir is approximately 4,500 million gallons; on one or two occasions each year it reaches 5,500 million gallons which is considered to be "bank-full" or within the margin of flooding. At the time of the floods of 1947 the daily flow of water surging over Teddington Weir reached 13,572 million gallons. In 1968 it reached 11,404 million gallons, and in 1988 7,650 million gallons. These large volumes of water represent the power, and the destructive potential, of the Thames.

The worst floods are reserved, however, for the tidal river where unnatural weather conditions and tidal surges can coalesce to form mighty walls of water. In 1090 London Bridge was destroyed and carried away by the Thames in tumult, and then nine years later the *Anglo-Saxon Chronicle* recorded that "on the festival of St. Martin, the sea flood sprung up to such a height and did so much harm as no man remembered that it ever did before." This flood of 1099 had one other unexpected consequence. The estate belonging to Earl Goodwin was quite submerged by the overflowing of the Thames, to the extent that it could never afterwards be drained. It became a sandbank, and from that time forward became known as the "Goodwin Sands," still an object of fear to fishermen and mariners. In 1236 the flood waters rose to such a level that Woolwich was "all on a sea," according to Stow, and wherries were rowed in the middle of Westminster Hall. Matthew Parris recorded that this flood "deprived all ports of ships, tearing away their anchors, drowned a multitude of men, destroyed flocks of sheep and herds of cattle, plucked out trees by the roots, overturned dwellings, dispersed beaches." By curious chance this flood occurred on 2 November, or the feast day of St. Martin, as it had done 137 years previously. In 1242 the river overflowed its banks at Lambeth, and the inundation spread for 6 miles around. In 1251 the tides rolling up the Thames were 6 feet (1.8 m) higher than usual. In 1294 extra defences were ordered and the banks were raised by 4 feet (1.2 m) "in respect of the raging of the sea." Then in 1313 Edward II declared in a charter that "the violence of the sea in those parts has grown greater than it had wont to be." In 1324 100,000 acres of land, between St. Katharine's and Shadwell, were under water.

There have been "freak" tides causing devastation in every century. On 4 February 1641, there were, according to a contemporary pamphlet, "flowing Two Tydes at London Bridge, within the space of an houre and a halfe, the last comming with such violence and hideous noyse" that even the watermen were "affrighted." Between the two abnormal tides the Thames stopped moving for an hour and a half, so that it seemed "asleepe or dead." Then the second tide began "tumbling, roaring and foaming in that furious manner, that it was a horror unto all that beheld it." It was "a wonder, that—all things considered—the oldest man never saw or heard of the like." This was a slight exaggeration, however, since eighteen years before, on 19 January 1623, there were three tides in the space of five hours. On 7 December 1663, Pepys wrote in his diary that "there was last night the greatest tide that ever was remembered in England to have been in this river; all Whitehall having been drowned." There was a famous "breach" along the river, just by the village of Dagenham; it had opened in 1707, 100 feet (30 m) long, and was not closed for seven years. On 14 September

1716, a great and persistent wind prevented the flood tide from reaching its destination; the Thames became so shallow that, according to Strype's revision of Stow's *Survey of London and Westminster* (1720), "many thousands of people passed it on foot, both above and below the Bridge."

In 1762 the waters of the Thames were raised so high that "the like had never been known in the memory of man." In less than five hours the water rose 12 feet (3.6 m) in height, and people were drowned in the principal thoroughfares of the city. In the nineteenth century there were six major floods—in 1809, 1823, 1849, 1852, 1877 and 1894—causing much destruction of life and property. The familiar cry from those who lived by the river was "Water's over!" In 1881 the tide reached 17 feet 6 inches at Westminster when, according to *The Times*, "the most heartrending scenes were witnessed."

In December 1927 the tide reached 17 feet 3 inches, but in the following year it peaked to 18 feet 3 inches. The river-banks at Millbank were breached, and fourteen people drowned. On 6 January 1928 a storm in the North Sea created a tidal surge that raised the waters of the river to their highest recorded level. The defensive walls of the Embankment were breached at Hammersmith and at Millbank. Fourteen people were drowned in the basements of Westminster. The other great flood was of March 1947, and in most locks the two high markers commemorate the floods of 1894 and 1947.

The greatest destruction of all occurred on the night of 31 January 1953, when a great tide coming from the North Sea flooded the Thames estuary. It was a cold night, with a howling gale, and at 2 a.m. a vast cliff of water moved steadily forward. The deaths of more than three hundred people were reported, as well as the loss of twenty-four thousand homes and the inundation of 160,000 acres of farmland. Twelve gas-works and two power stations were crippled by the deluge. The island of Canvey was drowned; many of the islanders were evacuated, but eighty-three of them lost their lives. It was the largest disaster since the Second World War. If the water had not spilled into the farmlands of Essex and of Kent, where the earth banks failed, the devastation would have reached London with unimaginable consequences.

The menace of such high tides and high flows meant that the danger to London itself had been growing. Some 60 square miles (155 sq km) of the capital lie below high tide level, and the depth of water throughout the capital could rise to 10 feet (3 m). With that volume of water pouring into the

Underground system, for example, the transport of the city would be paralysed for a very long time indeed. The potential loss of life would also be very large.

The Thames Barrier Act was passed in 1972, and the Thames Flood Barrier itself was completed some eleven years later. It was generally anticipated that it would close three times each year, to mitigate the effects of unfortunate weather, but in the first four months of 2001 it closed on fourteen occasions. In the first month of 2003 it closed eighteen times to counteract the effects of the tide. In that period it was drawn up to protect against the encroachment of fourteen consecutive tides, sure evidence of how dangerous and destructive the Thames can become.

The barrier can hold back fifty thousand tons of water moving forward each second, but this defence will not be enough for the river of the future. It is believed that it will be for all practical purposes redundant or inadequate by 2030. The tides increase in height by approximately 2 feet (0.6 m) every century and, as the ice-caps melt and London itself sinks at a rate of 8 inches per century, new and more sophisticated defences will soon be necessary. A scheme has been proposed to build a barrier 10 miles long from Sheerness in Kent to Southend, for example, with a number of gates that would allow unimpeded access to the normal tides.

There was an unusual condition of the weather that materially affected the life and nature of the Thames in previous centuries. The river had a propensity to freeze at the bottom while the water above continued to flow. The watermen called this ground-ice the "ice-meer," a cake of ice that would often rise to the surface bringing gravel and stone with it. In times of extreme cold, before the building of the bridges, the surface of the river would also entirely freeze. It was a matter of celebration rather than of wonder, however, and the Thames was transformed into the home of an extravagant market and entertainment known as "frost fair." The first "fair" was reported as taking place in AD 695, when booths were erected and a market was held upon the ice. Between the seventh and seventeenth centuries the river froze on eleven separate occasions, the worst being the winter of 1434–5 when it was immobile from 24 November to 10 February and when pedestrians could walk from London Bridge to within a mile of Gravesend. Holinshed recorded that, in 1565, "some played at foot-ball there as boldly as if it had been on the dry land; diverse of the court shot daily at pricks set up on the Thames."

Then in 1683 an anonymous pamphleteer spoke of the "unheard of rendezvous" kept upon the frozen river, with rows of tents and booths and shops, with sledges and caravans and coaches and wagons sliding over the ice, with bull-baiting and bear-baiting being instigated in makeshift arenas, with coffee and ale and brandy and wine for sale together with baked, boiled and roasted meats. There were bakers and cooks and butchers and barbers and prostitutes. There were hawkers with their news, costermongers with their fruit, and fishwives with their oysters. There were also "several amours, intrigues, cheats and humours": honest men were robbed and rogues profited. Hackney coaches continued a handsome trade, and a coach and six horses was driven on "the white path" from Whitehall to London Bridge. There was even a fox hunt. It was a little city on ice estimated to be 18 inches (45 cm) thick. It was considered to be a second Bartholomew's Fair, and was called "Freezeland Fair" or "Blanket Fair." The meat sold was called "Lapland Mutton." Verses were written to commemorate it:

> Behold the wonder of this present age,
> A famous river now become a stage:
> Question not what I now declare to you.
> The Thames is now both fair and market too.

The waters had become the land, and a flood had become a road. Fish could be seen suspended in the ice. The hilarity derived from the sensation of unaccustomed liberty—to walk upon water was a truly miraculous event, and to be able to cross the mighty Thames was in itself a feat worthy of celebration. All the characteristics that have been deemed intrinsic to the Thames—the spirit of egalitarianism and the spirit of licence—were here lent extreme form.

Yet the hilarity was not shared by all Londoners. Those whose livelihoods depended on the river were reduced to the last extremity of want; the fishermen were in particular distress, although the watermen seemed to take advantage of the situation by charging people for the privilege of entrance to the fair. There was no employment for the vast army of labourers who worked in the wharves or docks and, since they and their families could not afford the lavish meats being cooked on the ice, no sustenance. Coal had become too dear to be afforded by the poor. Many perished of famine or of cold.

In the winter of 1715–16 another great ice stopped the Thames in its path, and a city of canvas soon emerged upon its frozen surface. A "great cook's-shop was erected," according to *Dawkes' News Letter* of 14 January, "and gentlemen were as frequently to dine there as at any ordinary." A party of four young men determined to walk up the middle of the river as far as they could, not using any paths hitherto marked out; the *London Post* recorded that "they still boldly went on, and none of them have ever since been heard of." It was not clear whether the cold, or the river, killed them.

Between 1620 and 1814, in fact, the Thames came to a halt on twenty-three separate occasions. But when the thaws came, they came very suddenly. The ice broke up within a matter of hours; when the mass gave way it swept down the Thames, destroying any vessels in its path and severely damaging the bridges that impeded its descent. Some unfortunate people were reduced to lying upon the ice-floes as they careered along the river, while others jumped into barges that were still fastened within the ice.

The Frost Fair of 1814, when a thoroughfare was marked out on the ice and called City Road, was the last. The demolition of the old London Bridge in 1831 marked the demise of the freezing carnival. The removal of its piers, and all the obstructions that had accrued to them, helped to facilitate the tides and the general motion of the river so that it could no longer be rendered immobile. The building of the embankments also increased the flow of the Thames. It is supposed that the tidal river will never freeze again.

CHAPTER 28

The Ancient Trees

❧

*W*hen the East India Docks were constructed in 1790, the remains of a great subterranean forest were found in a state of preservation; the trees were not scattered or dispersed but lay in regular order. Curiously enough, however, the tops of the trees were all turned southward as if they had been swept by some great convulsion of nature coming from the north. Other drowned forests, dating from the end of the last period of glaciation, have also been discovered at Grays, at West Thurrock and at Sheerness. Pepys noted in September 1665 that at Blackwall "in digging the late docke, they did twelve feet underground find perfect trees over-covered with earth, nut trees with branches and the very nuts upon them." The stretch of river by Stoneness Lighthouse is known as "The Roots" because of the submerged forest within it. At Southwark have been found yew and alder that flourished some five thousand years ago. The workmen at Sheerness had to "burn" their way through trunks and thickets in direct contact with prehistory.

The Thames is a river of trees. They are part of every river panorama, an integral aspect of the riverscape. They are a token of its ancientness, and also of its sacredness. There is an ancient yew beside the river by Runnymede in Berkshire, known as the Ankerwycke Yew, which has been estimated to be over two thousand years old; it was more than 27 feet (8 m) in diameter when George Strutt measured it for his *Sylva Britannica* in 1826, and now measures some 31 feet (9.4 m). The yew by Iffley Church is believed to be older than the Norman edifice itself, and to have been planted in approximately AD 700 when there may have been a Saxon church on the same site above the river. There is also an ancient yew to the north side of Holy Trinity Church in Cookham. On top of the burial mound at Taplow, by the river, there was a yew some 29 feet (8.8 m) in diameter. It may have been planted by the Saxon warriors who mourned the passing of the king who lay buried there. Certain of the oaks of Windsor are believed to be a thousand years old.

They are not ancient by the standards of the river, of course, but anyone who has walked through a primaeval forest will be aware of their power. That is why the trees and the river are inseparable. The woods of Cliveden Reach, rising in wave after wave above the river, are the descendants of the primaeval woods that once covered much of the riverine landscape. Biological analysis has proved the existence in the Thames Valley, in prehistoric times, of the oak and the alder, the hawthorn and the ash, the yew and the willow, and many other species. The remains of alder and yew, dating back some five thousand years, have been found in Southwark.

In the gardens along the Thames, sharing the fruitfulness of the terrain, are the weeping willow and the weeping beech, the horse chestnut and the acacia. In the woods and copses of the surrounding countryside are the oak and the plane, the lombardy poplar and the elm. The chalk hills and cliffs are covered with beech. The pollard willows, their tops lightly clad in silvery leaves, cluster along the river-banks. The pine and the cedar, the ash and the alder, also flourish. The luxuriant elms seem ready to break with the weight of their foliage. In May the hawthorn spreads its blossom everywhere. The green islands, also called eyots, or aits (a name that may spring from islet), harbour willow and hawthorn, elm and sycamore.

The poplar has become one of the most typical of the Thames trees. It lends a formal touch to the natural surroundings, as at Bray where poplars stand in a row all of the same height and all equidistant from one another. They are of relatively recent growth, and the lombardy poplars below Henley are supposed to have been the first of their kind ever to be planted in England. They derive from the middle of the eighteenth century. Oaks

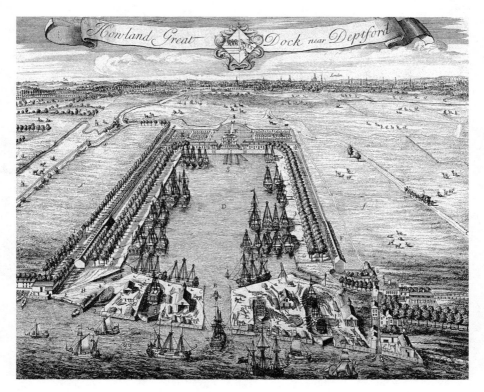

Howland Great Wet Dock, Rotherhithe, shown from an aerial perspective.
A large artificial lake set among fields and marshes, with trees planted as
windbreaks, it was 10 acres in extent and could hold 120 ships.

Perry's Dock at Blackwall.

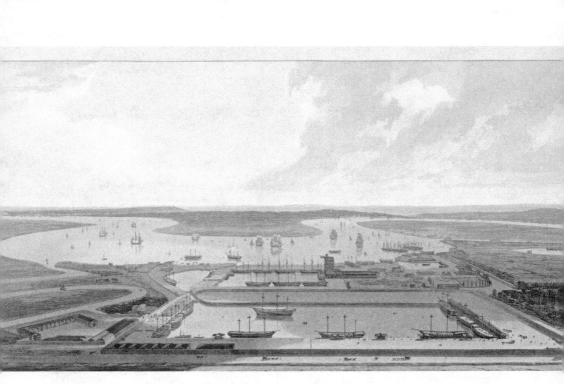

The East India Docks, in use from 1790 to 1967, were constructed on the site of a great subterranean forest of drowned trees.

The docks at Wapping. The tobacco warehouse at Wapping was celebrated for "covering more ground, under one roof, than any public building, or undertaking, except the pyramids of Egypt."

Inside the Docks by Gustave Doré.

The Thames docks of the nineteenth century represented the greatest architectural and engineering enterprise of the period. They were the size of small cities. They housed great inland lakes. They were celebrated by poets and artists as well as by merchants and mariners.

Billingsgate is the most ancient of all London markets. The earliest recorded tolls
for the vessels there can be dated to 1016, but undoubtedly there
was a fish market on that site long before that date.

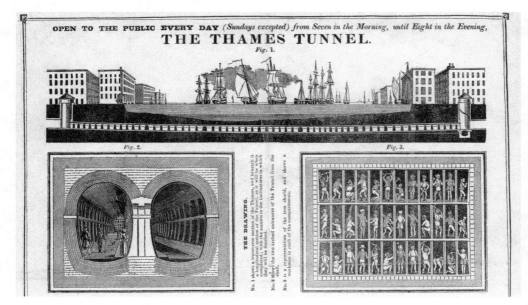

The Thames Tunnel was the first underwater tunnel in the world, begun in 1823 but not
completed for twenty years as accidents and deaths marred the project at every stage.
In 1870 it was converted into a tunnel for the underground system of the East London
Railway Company, and now connects the "tube" from Wapping to Rotherhithe.

FARADAY GIVING HIS CARD TO FATHER THAMES;
And we hope the Dirty Fellow will consult the learned Professor.

The Fleet sewer.

At the beginning of the nineteenth century all the detritus of London flowed into the Thames. The stench was dreadful. It was the centre of contagion and epidemic illness.

The building of the Embankment in the 1860s, at the instigation of Joseph Bazalgette, changed the natural health of the Thames. Beneath the great stone promenades he devised a vast and intricate sewage network that carried the filth out of London.

The supply of endless running water attracted many industries to the banks of the Thames. There were, in particular, hundreds of breweries beside the river. In riverine Reading alone, there were 21 breweries as well as 104 pubs. Above: a smock mill on the Thames; below: Lambeth, showing Goding's New Lion Ale Brewery, Fowler's Iron Works and Walker's Shot Manufactory.

The trade of the London docks was the largest in the world. It was said that there was enough rum to inebriate the whole of England, and enough sugar to sweeten the entire Thames. Above: unloading barrels in the 1930s. Below: the river symbolises power in every sense. Lots Road power station was still in operation in 2002. This photograph was taken by George Woodbine on 26 November 1931.

The Thames Barrier Act was passed in 1972, and the barrier itself was completed some eleven years later. But despite its massiveness, it is not enough. The waters are growing ever higher, and a new barrier will soon have to be constructed to withstand them.

Canary Wharf has become a symbol of the regeneration of the riverside. It stands as a beacon or lighthouse on the borders of the East End, showing the way forward.

are so plentiful on certain stretches of the river that in the nineteenth century they gained the title of the "Berkshire weed."

The tree most often associated with the Thames, however, must be the willow. They are ancient trees, among the oldest of all, and appear with ferns among fossil remains. The *Salix repens* or creeping willow, flourished in the Thames Valley during the interglacial periods; the *Salix herbacea* and the *Salix reticulata*, the dwarf willow and the net-leaved willow, grew in the Thames region during the Pleistocene period. The weeping willow, *Salix babylonica*, is in fact of more recent origin. It was taken from China, not from Babylon, and was planted by the Thames at Twickenham in 1730. The story that Alexander Pope first introduced the weeping willow into the Thames soil, when he planted a twig found in a Spanish hamper, is apocryphal. It serves, however, to continue the connection of that poet with the river. One of William Morris's most celebrated wallpapers, "Willow Bough," came from his direct observation of the trees by the river close to his house at Kelmscot.

The white willow loves the river-bank. So do the weeping willow and the crack willow, which hang over it like Narcissus gazing upon his reflection in the water. The weeping willow in particular seems to be an image of the river's fluidity and flow. In the book of Job these trees are described as the "willows of brook," and in Isaiah as the "willows by the watercourses." They have an especial affinity with water. A large willow will take from the river approximately 1,500 gallons a day (6,820 l), and can evaporate into the air more than 5,000 gallons (22,800 l) per day. Before Ophelia drowns herself in the brook she sings a song of the willow-tree, "sing all a green willow must be my garland," and so the tree has been associated with mournfulness and death by water. Its branches seem to droop in sorrow and pity. It is said to weep. It is a watery tree, but it is like water persistent.

The willow known as the cane osier, or *Salix viminalis*, was cultivated on the islands of the Thames in order to provide the willow rods, or osier rods, that were harvested by the osier-cutters for the manufacture of fish and eel traps, for fencing, for baskets and containers of all kinds, and even for the defences of the river-bank. The osiers were cut in March, having been grown in beds known as bolts or hams, and then placed in trenches of water; when the sap rises in spring they bud and blossom, and in May they start fresh roots. At that point the osier-cutters began to peel their bark, and to draw forth the pliable rods. The lake dwellers of the Iron Age wove baskets out of osiers before the arrival of the Romans, and there is no reason to doubt that the early settlers by the river made use of the same skills. In the eighteenth and early nineteenth centuries it became one of the most important items of commerce upon the Thames, but the trade has now left the area.

It is still possible to see the innate harmony between the river and its trees; they flow and bend, they are both moved by the wind. The sombre green of the yew and the brightness of the beech are reflected in the moving water. The trees take their life and moisture from the water, and in turn afford shade and coolness. It is impossible to imagine the Thames without trees. There is not one river painting by Turner, with the exception of those that depict the estuarial waters, that does not contain trees. They often provide the life and focus of his riverine compositions, with their bright masses reflected in the water, their boughs and branches drenched in variegated green from the light ash to the deep oak. The foliage of the poplar and the willow are green on the upper side, pale on the reverse, lending a shimmer to the surface of his colours. In his paintings, too, they are sometimes dappled with light and with a succession of colours that induces a sense of elation. In his drawings, the fluidity and motion of the trees are evoked in his vibrant pencil or pen. The trunks, the boughs, the foliage have an exquisite flowing line as if they are in communion with the flow of the river itself. In Ruskin's phrase Turner understood the language of the Thames and its surrounding landscape. The trees become the presiding spirits of the river, the guardians of the Thames who stand sentinel by its banks.

Their shade seems to have an especial property of coolness and of seclusion, as if the trees were the sanctuaries as well as the guardians of the river. They help to express that atmosphere of remoteness, and of seclusion, that the river itself induces. In particular Shelley, another poet of the river, celebrated the vast quietness and separateness to be found beneath the boughs of the riverine trees. In a poem he wrote at Marlow on the Thames, *The Revolt of Islam* (1818), he describes those hallowed spots:

. . . where the woods to frame a bower
With interlaced branches mix and meet.

Robert Bridges, in a poem that opens "There is a hill beside the river Thames" (1890), also depicts the riverscape where:

> Straight trees in every place
> Their thick tops interlace,
> And pendant branches trail their foliage fine
>   Upon his watery face.

The idea here is of shadowy retreat, where the wood and the water are in harmony, helping to create an enclave of peace and stillness. It can be a place of secrecy, or of isolation. It can represent a kind of escape. For some people, too, the presence of the trees and water can induce a sense of some earlier and forgotten time before the encroachment of the human world, some sylvan and primaeval state that can never truly be found.

For the ancient people of the Thames region the tree shared the sacredness of water. An early Christian text declared that "No one shall go to trees, or wells . . . or anywhere else except to God's church, and there make vows or release himself from them." The "Shrew Ash" in Richmond Park, close to the Thames, was the place where witches were tried, but it was also venerated for its efficacy in cures. Until at least the middle of the nineteenth century, mothers with sick infants would come to this tree before dawn, and there wait beneath its branches until the sun rose.

There were also sacred woods beside the Thames. There was a grove or wood beside the church at Kemble; it is mentioned in the early Anglo-Saxon charters, and was believed to have been a place of human sacrifice. An ancient cross was placed at the intersection of roads in this vicinity, perhaps as a way of erasing the power of the old rituals. There are woods named the Hockett, Fultness Wood and Inkydown Wood. Quarry Wood, bordering on the river at Cookham Dean, is the original of Kenneth Grahame's "Wild Wood" in *The Wind in the Willows*. Even the title of the book suggests its origin in the music of the ancient trees. In Grahame's story this wood had once been the site of a great city that had been built to last for ever; but it had fallen, slowly subdued by the wind and the rain, until all of its traces had been lost in a wildness of forest trees and bramble and fern. Like the river, the wood erases the traces of human time.

Above the Thames at Dorchester, among a cluster of trees known as the Wittenham Clumps, stands the trunk of a beech-tree known as "the poem tree." On its bark in 1844 was inscribed a poem that, over the passage of almost two centuries, has become indecipherable. It celebrated the ancientness of the riverine landscape and the disappearance of its human settlers:

> Such is the course of time, the wreck which fate
> And awful doom award the earthly great.

It may not be expert verse but it has become part of the literature as well as the landscape of the Thames; the words of the poem are equivalent to the marks that the ancient shamans made in the barks of trees to share their sacredness.

Some trees remained landmarks for generations of river people. Their names and locations survive in designations such as Nine Elms, Pear Tree Wharf, Crab Tree Dock, Orchard Stairs, Willow Wharf and Cherry Garden Pier. The names of several riverside villages also derive from the presence of the trees. Bampton, for example, comes from the Saxon *beam-tun* or "tree enclosure." Curiously enough, in the early twentieth century, it was still called "tree town." Thus do old associations survive even through changes of language. There was an old elm by the river-bank at Teddington; it was known as "One Tree," and stood upon a mound just where the river curved towards the town. There was a lofty clump of trees upon a mound on the south side of the river, beyond Lechlade, known as "Faringdon Folly"; here, it is said, King Alfred left this life.

They are landmarks because they are deemed to be perpetual, with a life as prolonged as that of the river itself. But this is in part an illusion. The destruction of trees has always been the object of complaint in the literature of the Thames. It is as if all of nature were affronted by their precipitate removal. One of Gerard Manley Hopkins's most famous poems, "Binsey Poplars," suggests this theme:

> My aspens dear, whose airy cages quelled,
> Quelled or quenched in leaves the leaping sun,
> All felled, felled, are all felled;
>> Of a fresh and following folded rank
>>> Not spared, not one
>>> That dandled a sandalled

Shadow that swam or sank
On meadow and river and wind-wandering weed-winding bank.

These were the trees that stood beside the river-bank just above Oxford, trees once more associated by the poet with seclusion and shadow, felled in 1879.

CHAPTER 29

"And After Many a Summer Dies the Swan"

Swans exist in many other places, and can be found in locations as far apart as New Zealand and Kazakhstan, but their true territory might be that of the Thames. Here they have been celebrated and commemorated for hundreds of years. The mute swan or *Cygnus olor* has been evoked by Milton and by Wordsworth, by Browning and by Keats. This is the swan that floats in double form, swan and reflection, compounding the visionary poetry of the river; this is the swan whose arched neck is a token of its strength and superiority, the swan who is environed with majesty as it glides upon the waters of the Thames. The most renowned paean to the bird must be Edmund Spenser's *Prothalamion* (1596), which has as its refrain "Sweete Themmes! runne softly, till I end my Song." Here the birds float towards the river from one of its then graceful tributaries:

With that, I saw two Swannes of goodly hewe,
Come softly swimming downe along the Lee;
Two fairer Birds I yet did never see:
The snow, which doth the top of Pindus strew,

Did never whiter shew . . .
So purely white they were,
That even the gentle streame, the which them beare,
Seem'd foule to them, and bad his billowes spare
To wet their silken feathers, least they might
Soyle their fayre plumes with water not so fayre.

The swan here is an image of purity and of innocence, which consorts well with the ancient concept of the river as a baptismal and cleansing force. That Spenser's was not entirely a poetic vision is demonstrated by an earlier report in 1496 from the secretary of the Venetian ambassador in London: "It is a truly beautiful thing to behold one or two thousand tame swans upon the river Thames as I, and also your magnificence, have seen."

Swans are not exactly "tame," nor can they really be designated as "wild" birds. They can on occasions be ferocious, particularly in defence of their brood or of their territory, but the popular legend that one can break a man's arm with its wings is surely apocryphal. They can actually be frightened away by the simple expedient of sprinkling water on them, as if it were not truly their element.

By some power of association, the fact that they are proclaimed by statute to be royal birds may derive from their majestic appearance. By 1295 the monarch had appointed a Swan-master or Royal Swan Keeper whose duty was to protect and conserve the swans upon the river. It was his responsibility to register every one of them; hence the festival known as "swan-upping" or "swan-hopping" which is still celebrated in the third week of July. It must count as one of the most ancient rituals upon the Thames. The royal birds in fact remain unmarked, but those that are marked are deemed to be the property of the Dyers' and the Vintners' Companies; the two guilds were granted that privilege by an unusually generous sovereign. The mark of the Vintners' Company is two "nicks," one on each side of the beak; this is the explanation for the once popular tavern sign, "The Swan with Two Necks" or Two Nicks.

In the time of Elizabeth there were what William Harrison described in *The Description of Britaine* (1587) as "the infinit number of swans dailie to be seene vpon this riuer." In that period there were no less than nine hundred individuals or corporations who owned certain swans, most of the birds being employed for culinary purposes. Or, as Chaucer put it in the General Prologue to *The Canterbury Tales*, "a fat swan lov'd he best of any rost." They are now rarely eaten, the turkey on English tables having re-placed the swan as a savoury dish, and are cherished rather than devoured. In a rectory garden at Remenham, near Henley, there is a simple grave with the inscription:

IN LOVING MEMORY
Died April 26
1956
CLAUDINE
A SWAN

A group of swans is known as a "game" of swans or, in Latin, "*deductus cygnorum.*" They have been surrounded by prescriptions and regulations ever since their first appearance on the river—in one story of their origin, it is said that Richard I brought them from Cyprus on one of his periodic returns from the Holy Land. In these earliest days only those who held property to the value of 5 marks were allowed to keep a swan. There was a strange penalty for stealing them. The ill-gotten bird was hung in a house by the beak "and he who stole it shall, in recompense thereof, give to the owner so much wheat as may cover all the swan."

They make their nests in the eyots or aits of the Thames but, curiously enough, they do not necessarily court seclusion. They seem to be aware of their privileged status upon the river. It has often been attested that the birds, in advance of any flood, will invariably move their nests higher above the level of the encroaching stream. They are intensely territorial, and will defend their district with the utmost ferocity. Once they were said to live for three hundred years but, in a more empirical age, that calculated span has been reduced to thirty.

There is a curious story about the swans that must have the status of legend rather than of historical description. One Italian, Ulysses Al-drovandus, wrote in the sixteenth century that "nothing is more common in England than to hear swans sing . . . every fleet of ships that returned from their voyages to distant countries are met by swans that come joy-fully out to welcome their return and salute them with a loud and cheer-ful singing." It is a beautiful story but does not seem to accord with the general habits of the mute swan. But then there is the testimony of John Dickenson's *Arisbas, Euphues Amidst His Slumbers* (1594), in which he describes "louely THAMESIS" as the "happy harbour of so many Swans, APOLLOS musicall birds, which warble wonders of worth, and chaunt pleasures choice in severall sounds of sweetnesse, pleasant, passionate, loftie, louely. . . ." Could whooper swans, or, more likely, Bewick swans have been identified here? But the sound of mute swans, in the formation of flight, their wings beating in unison, is very thrilling.

The swan in literature is also an image of the nude woman, and the nude woman bathing is in turn one of the fundamental representations of the river established upon the worship of the water goddess. For alchemists the swan was the emblem of mercury. The bird is thus associated with shifting elements and compounds such as the water of the river.

Swans are also associated with light, and with the properties of light. They contribute to the particular luminescence of the river and, as Ruskin put it, "if the reader would obtain perfect ideas respecting loveliness of luminous surface, let him closely observe a swan with its wings expanded in full light five minutes before sunset." In that phrase, the "loveliness of luminous surface," Ruskin has evoked something of the iridescent momentary enchantment of the river itself, so that the swan can truly be said to partake of its being.

The swan is usually joined by the other birds of the river, even though it seems to ignore them. In the area of Dorchester alone two hundred different species of bird have been identified and recorded. In the sixteenth century England was known as a nest of singing birds, but that phrase might more plausibly be attached to the Thames itself. There are, for example, the abundant sedge-warblers and also the less common reed-warblers. In the late eighteenth century the passages beside London Bridge were almost dammed by thousands of dead starlings, which for many years had made the bridge their home. In the nineteenth century, however, carrion crows were the most ubiquitous birds upon the river, where they crowded along the Oxfordshire and Berkshire banks. There is an observation to be made here. The birds of the sea do not sing. Many of the birds of the river do sing. It may be that they imitate the flowing sound of the river. Perhaps they are singing to the river. Perhaps gulls do not sing to the sea.

The humble duck or the common duck otherwise known as the mallard (*Anas boschas*), like the London sparrow, seems to be an inalienable part of its native landscape. On the Thames there are sub-breeds such as the Aylesbury

Duck, the Rouen Duck, the Tufted Duck, and the Labrador or Canadian Duck, but they have also been joined by other species. Mandarin ducks have escaped from captivity, and are now to be seen along the river. Ducks are raucous, energetic and volatile in temperament. They seem to be the children of the river and, in the early twentieth century, they were believed to be under the special protection of the children of any Thames family.

There are more exotic breeds. In recent years flocks of green parrots have been seen along the banks of the Thames, particularly in the areas of Kew and Teddington, but their origin is quite unknown. A glossy ibis has been observed off Swanscombe Point, and a bittern seen in the Lea Valley. Certain birds have returned to the river after an absence of forty years, encouraged by the recent and relative purity of its waters. For some years there were no birds at all along the Inner Thames—except for the various species of gull that fed upon the sewage floating in the water. Within ten years, roughly between 1960 and 1970, the river was cleaned; after that period there returned some ten thousand wildfowl and twelve thousand waders. By the end of 1968 there were flocks of pochard observed at Woolwich; they had been unknown in these waters since the beginning of the twentieth century. The Thames within London, like the city itself, is capable of rejuvenation. The fish-eating cormorant has also returned, now that the Thames once more contains suitable nourishment. A programme to reintroduce red kites in the Chilterns has been successful; now kites drift in the sky above Henley.

It is a matter of dispute how far from the sea seagulls venture. It has been said in the past that swans and ducks give way to them at Twickenham, but in fact seagulls can be seen further upriver at Chertsey and Penton Hook. They have been steadily moving upwards, having made their first appearance beside the London bridges in 1891. They arrived in the severe winter of that year, and it soon became a Sunday recreation for Londoners to feed them with bits of bread or sprats purchased at a penny per box. So the gulls returned and multiplied and flew inland.

In 1658 a large whale was taken on the south bank near Greenwich. The phenomenon was recorded in the same year by John Dryden in "Heroique Stanzas, Consecrated to . . . Oliver Lord Protector":

> . . . first the Ocean as a tribute sent
> That Gyant Prince of all her watery Heard.

A newsletter of that year reported that "it was said to be faeminine, & about 58 foot long and about 12 in thicknesse; She was first discovered neare Blacke-wall, pursued by hideous cries of watermen, strucke first by a fisher man's anchor, throwne from a bold hand. . . ." In his diary for 3 June John Evelyn observed that "It appeared first below Greenwich at low water, for at high water it would have destroyed all the boats, but lying now in shallow water encompassed with boats, after a long conflict, it was killed with a harping iron . . . and, after a horrid groan, it ran quite on shore, and died." A more sentimental age witnessed a subsequent arrival. In January 2006, a northern bottle-nosed whale was seen in the Thames; it swam upstream as far as Chelsea, but attempts to retrieve it and return it to the open sea were frustrated by its sudden death from shock. Its skeleton was exhibited in 2007.

There have been other exotic creatures associated with the river. Richard I returned from the Holy Land with a crocodile, which on its arrival at the Tower promptly escaped into the Thames. Royal bears were also once granted access to the river; they were tied with a chain, and permitted to fish in its waters. In the nineteenth century polecats were observed. Seals have been seen as far upriver as Richmond and Twickenham, where they rest upon the river-banks. A porpoise has leaped beside the Houses of Parliament. In the summer of 2004 a sea horse was discovered in the estuary.

Where mammoths and giant bears, boars and wolves, once roamed, there are now the fox, the bat, the water vole, the otter, the mink and the deer. Otters are increasing in number once more. The beaver has gone altogether, however, despite the fact that Wiltshire was once known as the county of beavers. But the larger change in the species of the river has a further significance. It is the story of how a once grand and majestic river—sometimes tropical, sometimes moving through plains of ice—became subdued into the narrow bounds of its now familiar enchantment. What had been minatory, or overwhelming, has become sinuous and secluded.

PART X

A Stream of Pleasure

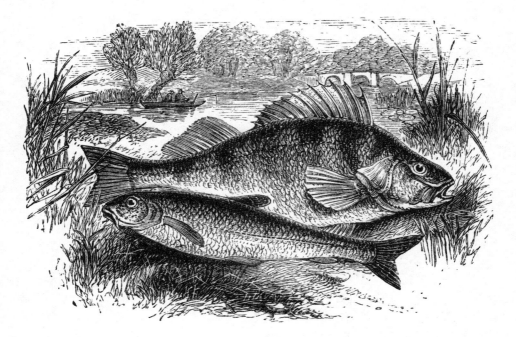

Perch and gudgeon

CHAPTER 30

Drink Your Fill

❧

When a head of Bacchus was found in the river, after the demolition of the arches of Old London Bridge, it served to confirm the connection of the Thames with the rituals of welcome and hospitality. Until very recent years pleasure boats and river steamers did not have to observe the same licensing laws as those that apply on land. That is why drunkenness has been a permanent feature of the river.

Just as Greenwich was famous for its gin-makers, so the Thames was celebrated for its maltsters. At the beginning of the eighteenth century there were in Reading twenty-one breweries as well as 104 pubs. The Anchor Brewery at Horsleydown Stairs, just east of Tower Bridge, was famous for its capacity; it used to produce some two hundred thousand barrels of strong beer, known as porter, each year. The breweries at Mortlake and Henley were equally well known. Fuller's brewery remains at Chiswick, where it has been located since the eighteenth century.

There was an old drink consumed along the Upper Thames, comprised of equal quantities of rum and milk; it was believed to be a "restorative." But there was also a beer made specifically out of Thames water. It was considered to be of good quality, and a pamphleteer of 1657 remarked that

"Thames water beer bears the price of Wine in many places beyond the seas." George Orwell, in *Coming Up for Air* (1939), noted that it had the taste of "chalky water."

But perhaps the most significant association of drink with the river takes the form of the familiar riverside pub. It is familiar because it is of long duration. There have been drinking places by the river—or, more particularly, by the bridges of the river—ever since the first travellers made their way towards its banks. Intoxicating drink was no doubt used in the very earliest rituals by the side of the Thames, and the first pilgrims who made their journeys to the riverside shrines of Bridget or Frideswide would find refuge in the adjacent inns. In the case of the Chequers Tavern at Standlake, the sacredness of the immediate vicinity is well attested. It was here that the village rector would stand beside a barrel of beer and preach a sermon, in commemoration of the fact that the inn was once a religious house and that the barrel marked the spot of an ancient altar.

The Bear Tavern at Southwark was just at the foot of London Bridge, and was already celebrated as ancient in a verse of the late seventeenth century. In fact the entire neighbourhood of Southwark, growing up in the shadow of the Thames, was notorious for the extent and number of its public houses. The Dolphin was immediately beside the Bear, for example, and in the early seventeenth century Thomas Dekker described the high street leading from the bridge as "a continued ale house with not a shop to be seen."

There is the Trout Inn at St. John's Bridge in Lechlade, descended from an inn formerly known as "the Signe of St. John Baptists Head"; this in turn is derived from an old almshouse attached to the priory of St. John in the same location. The Red Lion at Castle Eaton was erected on the site of an ancient castle, and on village feastdays a temporary bridge was built between the inn and the riverside meadows. This is one of the few occasions when an inn actually preceded a bridge. The inn still exists. There also still survives the Three Daws public house at Gravesend, once used as a hostelry by the pilgrims travelling across the river from Essex to Canterbury. It was formerly known as the Three Cornish Choughs, the choughs themselves appearing in the arms of Canterbury. It is reputed to be the oldest public house in Kent and, in later centuries, it had a more secular use as a repository for the goods of smugglers who worked incessantly along the line of both shores. There has been a public house by Radcot Bridge, the oldest bridge upon the river, ever since its erection. It is currently known as the Swan, one of the innumerable Swans upon the river. There is the Lamb at Wallingford, the Beetle and Wedge at Streatley, the White Hart at Sonning, the Trout at Godstow, the Bells at Ouseley, the Ferry Inn at Cookham; all of them are of ancient foundation, and all of them are still in use. It is significant that they were originally on the site of favoured crossing-points. Public houses were also erected in the vicinity of weirs; the Anchor Inn, for example, was situated at Eaton Weir. Both have now disappeared: the weir was "taken up" in 1936, and the inn itself was destroyed by fire. There is a symmetry in their fates. There is now a small foot-bridge, where the weir once stood, and only the foundations of the inn remain.

There are few bridges that do not have a public house attached to them and, in certain favoured locations, there is a pub at either end. Thus at New Bridge, the Rose Revived stands on the northern end of the bridge and the Maybush stands on the southern end. When the times of closing varied between Berkshire and Oxfordshire, the local inhabitants would simply cross the bridge in order to continue drinking undisturbed.

But there is of course another refreshing drink that the Thames provides; it gives up its own water. It has always been a source. There was nothing to prevent individual citizens from taking water from the river, but there were times when it had a brackish or salty taste. By the medieval period water-carriers were organised into the Company of Water Tankard Bearers; at the beginning of the seventeenth century there were four thousand of them engaged in daily trade with the city. They were popularly known as "cobs" and, like other tradespeople associated with the river, were notorious for their combative and churlish dispositions.

At the end of 1582 a Dutchman, Peter Morice, constructed an elaborate water-wheels or mills by the most northern arch of London Bridge, by means of which he was able to pump the river's water into the dwellings of the City. Holinshed's *Chronicles* (1577) reports that the authorities of the City erected a "standard" or pump at Leadenhall "divided there into foure severall spouts ranne foure waies, plentifullie seruing to the vse of the inhabitants neere adioning"; the supply of water "also clensed the chanels of the streets." Already, however, the supply had provoked complaints. It was "a great commoditie" but "would be farre greater, if the said water were maintained to run continuallie."

London Bridge Waterworks remained in operation until the Great

Fire, when its wheels were caught in the general conflagration; but it was rebuilt and by the eighteenth century its four wheels, by each of the four arches nearest the City, were pumping approximately 1 million gallons (4.5 million l) each day. It survived well into the nineteenth century, when it was responsible for conveying some 4 million gallons (18 million l) of river water each day. It only finished its operations when the old bridge was itself demolished in the 1830s. By that time there were many other water companies vying for the trade in Thames water, among them the East London Waterworks and the West Middlesex Waterworks. Other water companies also took their supplies directly from the Thames, including the York works by Charing Cross.

There were perpetual complaints about the salubriousness and safety of the water, but the managers of the various enterprises repeated the claims—made by certain apothecaries at an earlier date—that somehow the water of the Thames had the gift of self-purification. It was "foul" when freshly drawn but, when allowed to stand, it became perfectly clear and "finer than any other water that could be produced." This seems to have been little more than a convenient fallacy, designed to placate customers. There seems to have been some residual belief, however, in the sacredness of Thames water. One of its promoters declared, in 1805, that "Thames water being kept in wooden vessels, after a few months, often becomes putrid . . . and produces a disagreeable smell. But even when drunk in this state, it never produces sickness; therefore it is evident no harm or ill occurs to persons whose resolution, notwithstanding its offensive smell, induces them to drink it." This was mere myth-making—or, rather, a restatement of earlier myth. A paper for *Philosophical Transactions* (1829), however, claimed that during a long voyage the foul water drawn from the Thames was "cleansed" by the fermentation induced by its own impurities. The association between contaminated water and cholera was to be made later in the same century.

Although half of London's supply of water came from the Thames, by the beginning of the nineteenth century, its distribution was fitful and sporadic. It was drawn off by means of wooden pipes, and various regions of the City were given "water-days" when their supply would be turned on. It went into the basements of private homes, and the rest was pumped into public cisterns around which the citizens and citizens' wives gathered with their leathern buckets. The introduction of steam-power, and of cast-iron

pipes, materially assisted the process; but it remained notoriously inefficient until the last decades of the nineteenth century.

The quality of Thames water steadily deteriorated in the nineteenth
century, too, as the sewage and effluent discharged into the river increased
proportionately to the size of the population. There is a famous cartoon of
1827, entitled "MONSTER SOUP commonly called THAMES WATER";
it shows a drop of that water as seen through a microscope, with a full
range of "hydras and gorgons and chimeras dire" swimming within it. It
was found by customers to be of a "brownish" colour, and quite insalubrious as well as unpalatable in its natural (or rather unnatural) state. The
water was in fact a killer, as the diseases of the nineteenth century testify.
It helped to spread the epidemic fevers that were so common in Whitechapel, Shadwell, Limehouse and elsewhere. The river once more replicated the condition of the city through which it ran. While the old edifice
of London Bridge survived, its numerous arches acted as a form of barrier
or *cordon sanitaire*; the fresh water upriver contrasted strongly with the
odours and effluent of the tidal river. When in 1855 it was declared illegal
to take river water "from any part of the River Thames below Teddington," the health of the whole capital was improved.

The establishment of the Metropolitan Water Board in 1902 also instituted a regime of cleanliness and efficiency. The building of vast reservoirs
was begun, most notably the Queen Mary Reservoir erected in 1928. It was
capable of holding some 6,700 million gallons of water pumped directly
from the Thames, from an intake at Laleham, and had an area of water surface covering 707 acres (286 ha). It was the largest water reservoir in the
world. There began in 1991 the construction of the Thames Water Tunnel
Ring Main; it forms a circle around London at a depth of 40 metres (131
feet), punctuated by sixteen great vertical "shafts" from Holland Park to
Surbiton. It provides an average of 284 million gallons of water each day
to almost six million citizens or "consumers." This would suggest that each
person uses approximately 47 gallons (213.6 l) of the precious substance.
All of this water is taken directly from the Thames. The river is still the
protector and nourisher of the city.

CHAPTER 31

Going Up the River

✣

In 1555 a trader in Abingdon organised boating expeditions to Oxford, so that his passengers might see the burning of Bishops Latimer and Ridley at the stake; this is one of the first recorded instances of the "pleasure trip" on the river. In the seventeenth century women and girls used to scull downriver to Rotherhithe on each Trinity Monday; they took with them cannon and trumpets, in order to celebrate the services of the river pilots to the general community. The river offered freedom from the world of dry land, and has always been associated with pleasure and entertainment.

In particular the rising population of London throughout the nineteenth century helped to turn the Thames into a river of pastime and exercise. The upper parts of the river had been almost deserted at the beginning of the century, when the only traffic was that of the commercial barge, but a few decades later the life of the Thames was fundamentally altered. The Thames Preservation Act of 1855 recognised the new situation of the river, when it declared that the Thames "has largely come to be used as a place of public recreation and resort; and it is expedient that provision should be made that it should be preserved as a place of regulated public recreation."

If the river was "free" to everyone, then the enjoyment of its quietude was open to all.

The change can be dated with reasonable precision. It occurred in 1878 and in 1879. By the mid-1880s the river had become a "holiday" destination besieged by thousands of "trippers" who took advantage of cheap railway travel to journey to Henley or Richmond or Teddington Reach. This was the era of the amateur boater, and of the amateur angler who hired a fishing punt for his favourite stretch of the Thames. The decades of the 1880s and 1890s represented the most popular periods in the Thames's long history.

On an average summer day in 1888, 6,768 people travelled from London to Henley on the Great Western Railway for a return fare of 3 shillings and 6 pence. A Thames observer of the time noted that the river was in a continual state of unrest and disturbance "from the wash and hurry and turmoil caused by hundreds of steam launches and the endless procession of every description of floating craft" from the light dinghy to the canoe and even the ubiquitous "houseboat." It seemed that everyone wanted to be on the river, an atavistic movement that has had no parallel. It must in large part be connected with the transformation of the city itself into the first metropolis of the world, with a concomitant need among its citizens to escape into some presumed natural retreat. The phrase, "going up the river," became part of the popular repertoire in music-hall songs and sketches.

This was the age of the regatta and the fête, the river picnic and the river carnival. There were firework displays, and concerts, and processions of every description. Photographs of Henley, taken in the 1890s, record a river so covered by small boats that the broad highway of the water bears more than a passing resemblance to Piccadilly at "rush hour." In one boat are two ladies with parasols, being punted by a gentleman wearing a naval shirt; in another is a man with a pipe, and his dog; in a third is a sculler in the vest and trousers associated with that sport. At times of drought, the river was still employed as a place of entertainment; during one particularly dry spring and summer, in 1885, cricket matches were played on the bed of the Thames at Twickenham.

There were also river fashions observed with rigorous conformity by everyone for whom such things mattered. Gentlemen only appeared on the river if they were wearing white trousers with white flannel shirt, straw hat and striped flannel coat. For the Victorian lady, a dress or skirt of serge was essential; navy and black were deemed the most appropriate colours, complete with long suede gloves and the most elaborate hats. It was also considered advisable to wear woollen combinations, drawers, corset, chemise and bustle of whalebone. It is interesting, however, that jewellery was not approved. It was considered the height of bad taste to wear diamonds in a boat, perhaps on the supposition that the artificiality of sparkling gems did not consort well with the presumed naturalness of a day on the river. In the same spirit profuse flowers were considered to be an essential part of the décor of the Victorian houseboat; the *Thames Tide and Fashionable River Gazette* of 25 June 1892 recommended three rows of plants around the deck as well as hanging baskets of foliage, window-boxes, and large pots as an alternative to "costly furniture or valuable bric-à-brac." The vestiges of civilisation were to be banished in favour of the natural touch of floral decoration. As a result some of the houseboats resembled floating gardens, which was precisely the effect intended.

This embrace of the natural world, however willed and theoretical, was also the context for the universal abhorrence of the steamboat among the ordinary enthusiasts of the river. Dickens's son condemned them as the "curse of the river," and in *Three Men in a Boat* Jerome K. Jerome declared that "I do hate steam-launches; I suppose every rowing man does. I never see a steam-launch but I feel I should like to lure it to a lonely part of the river, and there, in the silence and solitude, strangle it." The new boats were called "river fiends" and "smoking devils." They brought hordes of unwashed cockneys to the relatively sylvan setting of the Thames. They were denounced for their noise, created by the bands and revellers as much as by the engines, and for the continual churning of their "wash" that distracted anglers and wreaked havoc upon the banks. But the principal dislike was for the entrance of the nineteenth-century world of engine and machinery into the ancient landscape of the river; the steam-launch was, if anything, an emissary of the metropolis in regions that the city had not yet reached. It brought "the Smoke," one of the catchphrases for London, in a literal sense. That was why it was unwelcome.

The festivals of the river were once its defining feature. In earlier periods, beyond historical reckoning, there were no doubt water festivals in honour of the gods of the rivers and the sea. In the modern period these ancient rituals have been turned into pageants and regattas and boating races of every kind. The first formal regatta upon the Thames took place on 23 June 1775, just in front of Ranelagh Gardens beside the river at Chelsea. A report in the *Annual Register* noted that

> early in the afternoon, the whole river from London Bridge to the Ship tavern, Milbank, was covered with vessels of pleasure . . . Vessels were moored in the river, for the sale of liquors, and other refreshments . . . The avenues to Westminster Bridge were covered with gambling tables . . . Soon after six, drums, fifes, horns, trumpets etcetera formed several little concerts under the several arches of the bridge.

It seems, then, to have been something of a bacchanalia—which is the nature of the principal river festivities.

The first regatta was followed two weeks later by a second at Oatlands, near Weybridge, at which members of the royal family presided. These early regattas then became the principal summer festivals in many riverside settlements, such as Molesey and Cookham, and included punting and dinghy races, and competitive sports on boats such as tug-of-war and walking-the-pole. In the evening there were generally fireworks and musical entertainments. Visitors mixed with villagers, amateurs with professionals, and barrow-boy fruiterers travelled up from London with their hampers. The regattas were believed to have been copied from the Venetians, but the derivation is uncertain. It seems more probable that these river festivals of the eighteenth century, and later, represented a renewal or resurgence of water pageants and festivities that had fallen into disuse during the Puritan Commonwealth.

There have always been sports upon the water. Fitzstephen's account of London, written in the twelfth century, records what was already an ancient game of tilting on the Thames. A target was attached to the trunk of a tree, fixed in the middle of the river, and in the prow of a boat stood a young man with lance at the ready; he was rowed to the point by several oarsmen at high speed, helped by the current, and then launched his lance at the target. If he succeeded in hitting it and breaking his lance, he was cheered. If he failed, and his lance was unbroken, he was thrown into the water to the laughter of the spectators who crowded upon London Bridge and the neighbouring banks. Since the tide here could be strong, two boats were at hand to rescue the unsuccessful contestants. There was also a tilting match between boatmen. Two wherries were rowed towards one another, with a contestant standing upright in the prow of each; they bore staves, flat at the fore-end, which they drove against each other. One, or both, would end up in the water. It was a contest that endured for at least five hundred years.

There were other contests. The University Boat Race, between Oxford and Cambridge, is sufficiently well known. But its popularity among the general population has perhaps been forgotten. It had been initiated in 1829 as a race from Hambleden Lock to Henley, and this first race led to the establishment of the Henley Regatta. The course was then moved to the stretch of river from Westminster to Putney, but within a few years the crowds at Westminster became too large; the course was in 1845 moved up-river, from Putney to Mortlake, and this venue guaranteed its success. By the middle of the nineteenth century it had become something of a cockney festival, perhaps surprising for a race essentially between what were known as "toffs." On an early April morning every Londoner, and certainly every young cockney, seemed to be involved with the "light blues" (Cambridge) or the "dark blues" (Oxford). The day became a public holiday and the ribbons of variegated blue were fastened around the necks of costermongers' donkeys, tied around dust-carts, fastened to the whips of cab-men, or worn as scarves by match-boys and other "gutter children." It was called the blue fever.

The river was filled with steamers and barges and launches, packed with enthusiastic spectators, and the tow-paths pullulated with mechanics, shop-keepers, street-sellers and the whole panoply of London life. There are drawings and paintings of the railway and pedestrian bridges, packed to the point of danger, with the more courageous spectators perched high above the water on the parapets and arches. It had become a great popular ritual, and the combativeness of the medieval tilt-matches upon the river had been transferred to this university pursuit. It was part of what in the nineteenth century was known as "the battle of life," and there was no reason why it should not be conducted on the Thames.

There is also a race that proceeds in the opposite direction, the 4½ miles from Mortlake to Putney, known as the "Head of the River" race. It is conducted at the beginning of March each year, and comprises more than four hundred "eights" leaving the starting line at 10-second intervals. The course is generally completed in about two hours. It is in fact the largest rowing event in the world, although one still little known to Londoners themselves. With the hundreds of craft resting on the water, the Thames recovers its ancient life for a brief interval.

Four months later the Doggett's Coat and Badge Race continues a tradition of racing inaugurated by the Irish actor, Thomas Doggett, in 1715 in commemoration of the accession of George I. Doggett himself was used to the services of the watermen, ferrying him from the theatres on either side of the river. It is the oldest as well as the longest racing competition in the world, re-emphasising the lines of continuity that mark the Thames of the twenty-first century. Six waterboatmen, members of the Watermen's Company, race with the tide for the 5 miles from London Bridge to Albert Bridge; their prize is the scarlet livery of the company itself, together with a silver badge.

There are individual achievements also. In the summer of 1822 Lord Newry and five of his servants rowed without a break from Oxford to London in eighteen hours. In the summer of 1880 there was a race between a man and a dog. The course was set from London Bridge to Woolwich and the *Illustrated London News* reported that "man and dog plunged into the river at half-past three, cheered by a great crowd of spectators, and went down with the stream; they were eagerly watched by thousands of spectators." The dog, known as "Now Then," soon pulled ahead; the man himself gave up the race at Limehouse, with the animal some half a mile ahead of him. Its owner won the wager of £250.

Blood sports used to be associated with the river. Shooting parties were a regular feature of Thames life, for example, in the nineteenth century when any creature that moved was liable to be killed. There were human victims, too. Bare-fisted knuckle fights were frequently held on the banks of the Thames. There was a notorious spot by Thames Ditton, a common called Moulsey Hurst, where there were on occasion fatalities among the boxers. Bull-baiting and cock-fighting were the sports of Cricklade. Jousting was performed on London Bridge.

One of the most enduring of riverine festivities, until it was transferred to dry land, was the Lord Mayor's Pageant. It was a way for London to proclaim its dominance over the river. The first recorded pageant took place in 1422, but there must have been earlier rituals of a similar nature. On that particular occasion the new Lord Mayor, Sir William Walderne, was taken by water from Blackfriars to Westminster, where he was to make obeisance to the dead king Henry V. It was decreed that "the Alderman and Crafts should go to Westminster with him to take his charges in barges without minstrels." But over the next thirty years the City companies erected and fitted out their own barges—together with minstrels—in as sumptuous a fashion as possible.

In 1453 the new mayor, Sir John Norman, equipped a barge at his own expense complete with flags and streamers. He was "rowed in this barge to Westminster, with silver oars, at his own cost and charge." According to the Harleian MSS, "this yere the riding to Westminster was foredone and goying thider by barge bigonne." Out of this event arose a famous wherrymen's song, "Row thy boat, Norman." A civic rite became a spectacle, and the "cost and charge" soon rose as the companies vied with one another over the extravagance of their ceremonial barges. In 1624 the merchant tailors, for example, spent the unparalleled sum of £1,000 upon their boat.

An observer of the procession in 1660, John Tatham in *The Royal Cake*, described "the barges adorned with streamers and banners, and fitted with hoe-boys, cornets, drums, and trumpets . . . and by the way his lordship is saluted with twenty pieces of ordnance, as peals of entertainment and joy." He also notes the presence of various allegorical and mythological figures such as Oceanus "who is said to be God of Seas and the Father of Rivers." This reverence for the water god suggests atavistic worship of some kind, as if the earliest rites had not wholly been forgotten in the early modern era. Why should not ancient beliefs, and ancient festivals, reappear at different periods of human history?

The Lord Mayor's Procession on water survived for more than four hundred years, until in 1857 the Thames Conservancy took over authority on all matters concerning the river. The barges were either "laid up" or sold to the boating fraternities of Oxford colleges. The public house known as the City Barge, at Chiswick, is named after the winter mooring here of the last of the barges. Yet to this day the mayor is accompanied during his annual procession, on land, by a liveried waterman, in honour of the fact that he retains the title of Admiral of the Port of London.

There were other fêtes and fairs customarily held upon the river or by the riverside; in the latter years of the nineteenth century, for example, there was a passion for illuminated vessels of every kind. It was a taste that emerged from nowhere, and lapsed just as swiftly. At Marlow there were processions of brightly lit boats and "coloured fires" passing slowly down the river, with the town band also in attendance. At Bray a fully equipped schooner of fairy lights or "cardinal lamps" sailed upon the water, while at Ditton an "Eiffel Tower" was carried downstream. At Datchet an illumi-

nated Chinese pagoda proceeded down the Thames, and at Bourne End a
launch was disguised as the Man in the Moon. This was the river as Proteus, conjuring forth a thousand different shapes. It was also a celebration
of the meeting of water and fire, the primal elements in ecstatic harmony
at a time of festival. In Cookham the local fire brigade carried blazing
torches on an enormous punt, together with their manual fire engine and
wooden horses. There were musical evenings, too, with a pianoforte placed
on a barge moored in the middle of the river while the audiences on either
bank could listen to the voices of the tenor or the soprano. By the Thames
was heard "Alice, Where Art Thou?," "Oh Dry Those Tears" or "The
Lost Chord." There were often performances of dance, too, with terpsi-
chorean routines such as "The Tired Swan."

Fairs were celebrated by the Thames, with various "wakes" and "rev-
els" held in the riverside villages of Berkshire and Oxfordshire. One of the
most celebrated of them, Greenwich Fair, was held on Easter Monday and
at Whitsuntide. It was the most famous fair in the vicinity of the Thames,
and a favoured resort of Londoners. It was considered to be a great "Sat-
urnalia" in which all the freedom and the licence associated with the river
spilled over onto the hills and banks overlooking the water. It was frequented by more than a hundred thousand people, arriving by wagon or by
steamboat. In one of his early sketches, Dickens records that "the balcony
of every public-house is crowded with people, smoking and drinking, half
the private houses are turned into tea-shops, fiddles are in great request."
There was also a favourite pastime of young men and young women,
which involved rolling down One Tree Hill at Greenwich and ending up in
a tangle of promiscuous arms and legs. The one tree on One Tree Hill was
blown down in the summer of 1848, but that did not stop the festivities.

The river has always been associated with sexual licence. In the neighbourhood of Southwark alone, there were streets named Slut's Hole and
Whore's Nest as well as the more euphemistic Maiden Lane and Love
Lane. The riverside village of Chiswick was once known as Slut's Hole,
and Maidenhead was described as the "hymen of London" as a result of the
number of unmarried couples who congregated there. Henry Wallington
Wack, in *Thamesland* (1906) depicted the "love dalliances afloat, these lisp-
ings and kissings and spoonings" in the backwaters of the river. It was often reported that male bathers would strip naked, in the presence of ladies,
and then disport themselves in the water. One contemporary wrote of
"a whirlpool of Charybdis with fifty demons in their birthday suits floun-

dering about and yelling red language with fiendish delight." Sexual aggression, and sexual display, are encouraged by the river.

There was one well-known sexual festival by the Thames, centred on a site known as Cuckold's Point by Rotherhithe. Until the middle decades of the nineteenth century it was marked by a pole, a pair of horns affixed to the top of it; the horns were an ancient symbol of a husband who has been wronged or "cuckolded" by his errant wife. The legend or story used to explain this symbol of unfaithfulness concerned the amatory career of King John, who violated the wife of a Greenwich miller; in recompense he offered the miller all the land he could see in one direction, on the understanding that each year he would walk to the boundary with a pair of buck's-horns upon his head. The clear-sighted miller saw as far as Charlton Hill.

The festivities emerging from this pretty fiction, dating from the thirteenth century, had their destination at the aptly named Horn Fair. It was a place of strange tumult and wild mirth, according to observers, where instruments such as saucepans and vessels of horn could be purchased. Such instruments were the usual components of the "charivari," the uncouth serenade used to greet newly weds. So the sexual associations are evident.

The procession to Horn Fair was formed at Cuckold's Point, winding through Deptford and Greenwich before making its way to a fair at Charlton; the male participants wore pairs of branching antlers, and considered themselves free to make advances upon any females in their path. There is an account by a participant in 1700 who recorded that "at *Cuckolds-Point* we went into the House, where the Troop of Merry Cuckolds us'd to Rendesvous; Arm'd with *Shovel, Spade* or *Pick-Ax,* their Heads adorn'd with Horned Helmets; and from there to march in Order, for *Horn-Fair.*" At the fair itself men would dress as women, wear horns upon their heads, carry horns with them or blow them. It became what the authorities described as an "intolerable nuisance" and was suppressed in 1768; but the site, and the pole, remained. The fair was eventually revived, until once more it was closed by official edict in 1872. Yet all is not lost. The fair has been reinstituted annually at Hornfair Park in Charlton. There is still a pillar, representing Cuckold's Point, overlooking the stretch of river at Limehouse Reach.

There are also the less well advertised pleasures of swimming in the Thames. In the seventeenth century it was the common sport of noblemen who lived by the river, along the Strand, and on one occasion a letter was addressed to "the Earl of Pembroke, in the Thames, over against White-hall." But the ordinary citizens of London were less likely to follow, having no particular fondness for water as an element. The Thames was considered primarily as a highway and as a source of food. The idea of swimming in it voluntarily was not taken very seriously. In the early nineteenth century Byron swam from Lambeth through the two bridges, Westminster and Blackfriars, comprising a distance of some 3 miles. He, too, was something of an exception; he may in any case have been helped by the tide.

A. P. Herbert, an aficionado of the Thames in the middle of the twentieth century, used to swim in the river; but he remarked in *The Thames* (1966) that he found its "muddy waters" very tiring. He noticed that at Waterloo, for example, the water "has no buoyancy at all and, so far from supporting the swimmer, seems all the time to be dragging him down to the extremely muddy floor of the river." This is indeed one of the characteristics of the Thames, treacherous and dangerous as it is within the stretches of London. Herbert recalled, as he approached his destination at Westminster Bridge, that his whole frame "seemed subject to some magnetic force relentlessly pulling it towards the bed." This is the experience of the suicide as well, this appetite of the Thames for drawing the human down into its depths. Herbert also noticed that "it tasted very strongly of I know not what." So the Thames has never really been considered a friend of the swimmer. But it is more than the danger of pollution that acts as a deterrent. It is some deep fear of its nature that seems to prevent its use.

CHAPTER 32

Gardens of Delight

The pleasure gardens of Vauxhall, and of Ranelagh, and of Cremorne, sprang up by the side of the river in the seventeenth and eighteenth centuries. Their charm and popularity were in large part the consequence of their riverine location. Once more the Thames created the atmosphere, or setting, for the deliberate licence of the populace. The first of them, Cuper's Gardens, was beside the river in the area then known as Lambeth Marsh but what is more recognisable now as the southern approach to Waterloo Bridge. It was opened in the 1630s, with gardens and bowling greens and serpentine walks as well as the attendant pleasures of a tavern and a supper room. In 1708 the author of *A New View of London*, Edward Hatton, described the venue as that to which "many of the westerly part of the town resort for diversion during the summer season." A musical pavilion was opened in the 1730s, and concerts were performed in front of large audiences. There were also firework displays. These are the constituents of riverside pleasure: food and drink, music and fireworks. Yet Cuper's Gardens also became a haunt of thieves and pickpockets, to the extent that it was refused a licence in 1753 and was closed down seven years later.

The New Spring Garden was close to Battersea and, before the opening of Westminster Bridge in 1750, could only be reached from the more fashionable side of the river by wherry. It had been established just before the Restoration of 1660, in anticipation of happy times, and changed its name to Vauxhall Gardens in 1785. In the seventeenth century it was known for its alcoves, its bands, its comic singers, its illuminated lamps hanging on the boughs of adjacent trees, its greedy waiters and its expensive drinks. Pepys visited the Garden in 1667, and in his diary remarked that "to hear the nightingale and other birds, and here fiddles and there a harp, and here a Jew's trump and here laughing, and there fine people walking, is very diverting." He was not so pleased, however, with the riotous behaviour of the young men who flocked to the gardens for female company. Or as a ballad put it:

> Women squeak and men drunk fall,
> Sweet enjoyment of Vauxhall.

Another contemporary song was rather more discreet about the London citizens who have

> Sail'd triumphant in the liquid way,
> To hear the fiddlers of Spring Garden play.

In the eighteenth century the Gardens were refurbished with supper rooms, artificial ruins, water spectacles and an orchestra large enough to hold fifty musicians. Handel's "Music for the Royal Fireworks" was performed here in front of an audience of twelve thousand people. A statue of the composer was later placed beside the entrance. A rotunda was built, 70 feet (21.3 m) in diameter, with a picture room attached. It has been conjectured that the domes of Vauxhall in fact materially influenced the architecture of the Festival Gardens, erected in Battersea Park in 1951; the scenery of the Thames might then be seen to regenerate itself.

Rowlandson completed an aquatint of the Gardens in 1784, with the unmistakable figure of Samuel Johnson disporting himself in a supper box close to the orchestra. When Goldsmith described the variegated scene as one uniting "rural beauty with courtly magnificence," he might have been remarking upon the influence of the river itself that contains both elements within its progress. Vauxhall was not frequented for its cultural pleasures alone, however, and there were events concerning tightrope walkers, fireworks and the new craze of "ballooning." Fire and air were therefore being celebrated by water. The portions of food served here were considered to be exiguous, however, and it was claimed that a competent waiter could cover the 11 acres (4.4 ha) of the grounds with the slices from one ham.

There were two celebrated pleasure gardens to the north of the Thames, in the neighbourhood of Chelsea, known as Cremorne Gardens and Ranelagh Gardens. Ranelagh was situated in the eastern section of what is now Chelsea Hospital Gardens. It became a commercial pleasure garden in 1742, and survived for sixty-one years on the customary riverine diet of music, balloons, fireworks, food and drink. A rotunda, bigger than the Pantheon in Rome, was erected in its grounds and was subsequently painted by Canaletto; this was a resort, with a great fireplace at its centre, for anybody who "loves eating, drinking, staring and crowding." There was also a Chinese pavilion, and an orchestra where the young Mozart once played. It out-Vauxhalled Vauxhall, and in Smollett's *Humphry Clinker* (1771) Lydia Melford described it as "the enchanted palace of a genio, adorned with the most exquisite performances of painting, carving and gilding, enlightened with a thousand golden lamps that emulate the noon-day sun." It was one of the many pleasure domes of the Thames. Its charms have not entirely deserted it, however, and it is now the setting for the annual Chelsea Flower Show.

Cremorne Gardens was a little further upriver, on the bankside site now largely covered by Lots Road Power Station. It was opened in the 1840s, almost half a century after the demise of Ranelagh, complete with a theatre, a banqueting hall, a dancing platform and a bowling saloon together with various "arbours" and "bowers" and grottoes without which no riverside resort was complete. In 1848 it was the site for the first flight of a "steam-powered aeroplane," which flew some 40 metres (131 feet) before hitting a canvas barrier. There were fireworks and balloon ascents, once more, as well as more dubious pleasures. In *The Seven Curses of London* (1869) James Greenwood described Cremorne Gardens in the "season":

> By about ten o'clock age and innocence—of whom there had been much in the place that day—had retired, weary of amusement, leaving the massive elms, the grass-plots, and the geranium-beds, the kiosks, temples, "monster platforms," and "crystal circle" of Cremorne to flicker in the thousand gaslights there for the gratification of the danc-

ing public only. On and around that platform waltzed, strolled, and fed some thousand souls, perhaps seven hundred of them men of the upper and middle class, the remainder prostitutes more or less *prononcées*.

The Gardens were condemned by the minister of the local Baptist chapel as "the nursery of every kind of vice"; the proprietor sued, but received only a farthing in damages. In 1877, in a fit of mid-Victorian rectitude, the place was closed down. All that is left is a small patch of green, still called by the same name. There were also smaller resorts, such as the seventeenth-century Cherry Gardens at Rotherhithe; Cherry Gardens was then succeeded by tea-gardens, but they were closed down by the end of the nineteenth century. Cherry trees, however, are now being grown upon the site.

There were pleasure gardens, of a kind, upon the water itself. In the nineteenth century an island in the river, known as Walnut Tree Ait for the prevalence of its osiers, was transformed into an island of entertainment by the erection of a hotel and a concert hall. It was purchased by the theatrical impresario, Fred Karno, and renamed the Karsino. Karno then described it as "the hub of the universe for river people," but it did not survive the First World War. The island was then granted another life as the Thames Riviera, with a ferry service from the southern bank, but still it did not succeed.

The first floating restaurant was envisaged in the seventeenth century, when in 1636 John Rookes petitioned the king for the opening of a boat on the Thames that would serve "such provisions and necessaries as are vendible in the Tavernes and Victuallinge houses especially in the summer season." The fate of this venture is not known, but the history of floating inns or restaurants on the river is not a particularly successful one.

There was another ship of pleasure upon the Thames, a large barge or houseboat anchored in the river on the bend where "Cleopatra's Needle" is now to be found, known appositely as "The Folly." It was formally opened in the seventeenth century, and there is an engraving of it moored in the middle of the river with all the appearance of stateliness and respectability. Built of timber and divided into many separate rooms for the pleasures of the day or the night, it was surmounted by a large platform and balustrade, where its patrons could also take the air. It was at first frequented by the men and women of fashion who, dressed in silk and crinoline, would wait

on the bank to be wherried across. It was described by one contemporary
moralist as "a musical summer house for the entertainment of quality
where they might meet and ogle one another." Pepys visited the place on
13 April 1688, where he recorded spending a shilling. But, like most riverside locations, it eventually acquired a reputation for vice and "low" company who seemed to specialise in what was called "promiscuous dancing."
Tom D'Urfey wrote a song in 1719, entitled "A Touch of the Thames," in
which he recorded how

> When Drapers' smugg'd Prentices,
>   With Exchange Girls mostly jolly,
> After shop was shut up,
>   Could sail to the Folly.

A German tourist of the same century recorded that "innumerable harlots
are to be found there and those who resort to them can take them over to
Cupid's Gardens." Cupid's Gardens had become the popular name for Cuper's Gardens, on the opposite bank. So "the Folly" fell into decay, and the
barge was eventually dismantled and chopped into firewood.

There was one perennial complaint about the river gardens that reflected an aspect of the river itself. The population of these places was considered to be too heterogeneous, an unstable combination of the "high"
and "low" in society that could on occasion cause fights and even riots. In
Fanny Burney's *Evelina* (1778) it is said of Vauxhall that "there's always a
riot—and there the folks run about—and there's such squealing and
squalling." We have already had cause to observe the libertarianism, or
democracy, of the river. This also serves to characterise the entertainments
held beside it where the rougher elements of London were in a state of
comparative equality with the nobility who patronised the assemblies.
"There is," one observer wrote, "his Grace of Grafton down to children
out of the Foundling Hospital, from my lady Townshend to the kitten . . ."

There are gardens, as well as pleasure gardens, that seem to emerge naturally along the banks of the Thames. Many of them are sufficiently well
known, including the gardens of the Hospital in Chelsea and the Chelsea
Physic Garden close by. Battersea Park, on the southern bank, stretches beside the river. Opposite the gardens of Syon House, which clothe the world
in green, lie Kew Gardens, once part of Richmond Gardens, praised for

their "wild" or "natural" aspect. A German observer, Count Kielsman-egge, reported that "you pass through fields clothed with grass, through cornfields and a wild ground interspersed with broom and furze, which afford excellent shelter for hares and pheasants." Erasmus Darwin, in *The Botanic Garden* (1789–91), commemorates the world of Kew:

> So sits enthroned, in vegetable pride,
> Imperial Kew, by Thames's glittering side;
> Obedient sails from realms unfurrowed bring
> For her the unnamed progeny of Spring.

This was a reflection of the wealth of rare botanical specimens that were brought to Kew from Britain's colonial possessions. In a similar spirit the Museum of Garden History is still to be found beside the Thames, at Lambeth.

Along the river, between London and Teddington, there were once vast estates of market gardens growing fruit and vegetables for London; raspberries and strawberries, for example, were once an Isleworth speciality. More curiously there was in the eighteenth century a great vineyard on the south bank of the river, not far from the present Waterloo Bridge, which according to Samuel Ireland in his *Picturesque Views of the River Thames* (1801) was "the richest and most diversified vineyard the world can boast" producing liquor "from humble port to imperial tokay."

Throughout its existence the river has been the source of fertility. It supports a rich alluvial soil that is never barren except, of course, where it has been forcibly displaced. The countryside of the Thames is lush and green for all seasons. The rich pastures of North Wiltshire led to the claim that they were favoured by God's presence. In the seventeenth century Thomas Fuller "heard it reported from credible persons that such was the fruitfulness of the [Thames] land, that in spring time, let it be bit bare to the roots, a wand [sapling] laid along therein overnight will be covered with new grown grass by the next morning." Such is the force that, in the words of Dylan Thomas, through the green fuse drives the flower.

Some of the river's green eyots (sometimes spelled as aits or aights) possess names that derive from the Saxon people. "Nettle Eyot" and Dumsea Bushes or Domesday Bushes, near Chertsey, are two of these ancient nomenclatures. Dog Ait at Shepperton is similarly old. Even the smallest islands in the river have names—Headpile Ait, Cherry Tree Ait, Flagg Ait and Teynter Ait are little patches of land on the river near Taplow. They have also been called holts or hams. The subject of names is always most difficult. Some eyots have become public parks, while others remain private. They have been centres of entertainment and places of retreat; they have been used by courting couples, and by hermits. They are somewhere out of this world.

The riverside gardens of the sixteenth and seventeenth centuries played a part in London's destiny. The most famous of them must be that in Chelsea belonging to Sir Thomas More. It was here, just by the water, that he closed the wicket gate, parting from his family for ever, before sailing downriver to meet his interrogators at Lambeth. While there, he was asked to walk down into the riverside garden for further reflection on his refusal to obey the king's commands.

There were great gardens leading down to the banks at York Place, Cardinal Wolsey's London residence, but the only verdant memorials of Wolsey's ascendancy are now the gardens of Hampton Court. There was a large and ornate garden attached to the Bridge House of London Bridge, and there had been royal gardens in the Tower of London since the middle of the thirteenth century. There was an orchard within the walls of the Tower, too, complete with vines and fruit trees. The gardens of Bridewell have long since departed, as have the gardens laid out by Lord Protector Somerset. The gardens at Richmond Palace were said to be "moost faire and pleasaunt" with "ryall knottse aleyed and herbid . . . with many vynys, sedis and straunge frute right goodly besett." There were also many ecclesiastical gardens, like those belonging to the Bishop of Winchester in Southwark. The space between the Thames and the Strand was in fact entirely taken up by the gardens of the bishops, with the Bishop of Exeter's Inn, the Bishop of Bath's Inn and the Bishop of Norwich's Inn. The view from the river was, literally, of back gardens. There still exist of course the great gardens of Fulham Palace and Lambeth. All of these were designed to be seen from the river, as a token of state and of status. But they were primarily areas of privilege, delightful spaces for private discourse and for self-communing. Their gardens seats and arbours were part of a general moral design "whereby they might the more fullie view and haue delight of the whole beautie of the garden" with its fountains and knot beds and paved alley-ways. They were devoted to "recreation" in an intellectual and civic sense. That is why their position by the river was so essential to their success.

The gardens of Ham House have been restored in accordance to their seventeenth-century design, and the villa of Marble Hill stands in its garden setting. The parks of Bushy and of Richmond reach towards the Thames. Along this part of the river, roughly between Richmond and Hampton, there are in fact many celebrated English gardens designed by Alexander Pope, Charles Bridgeman, William Kent and of course "Capability" Brown. The luxuriousness and fecundity of the riverine setting ensure their survival. The flowing or serpentine line, adumbrated by William Hogarth in his *Analysis of Beauty* (1753), has always been an intrinsic aspect of the English aesthetic. It is known as the "line of beauty," curved or curling, like the sinuous grace of the river itself. The landscape of the gardens by the river was, from the eighteenth century, subdued by the "peculiar curve, alike averse to crooked and to straight" that is a reflection of the movement of the Thames. At Syon House and at Strawberry Hill, in Richmond and Isleworth and Twickenham, emerged the "undulating line." It is the line of the river.

CHAPTER 33

Filthy River

❧

The Thames has variously been described as a grey, dirty, smutty, sooty, smoky river. These are not nineteenth-century epithets. It has always been thus. In the period of the Roman invasion and occupation it was first employed as the city's public sewer; wooden pipes under the large complex of Roman buildings at Cannon Street prove that effluent was already pouring into the waters. In 1357 Edward III proclaimed that "dung and other filth had accumulated in divers places upon the banks of the river with . . . fumes and other abominable stenches arising therefrom." A public lavatory on London Bridge showered its contents directly onto the river below, and latrines were built over all the tributaries that issued into the Thames. The Black Friars and the White Friars complained that they were being poisoned by the stench of the river running beneath their walls; the "putrid exhalations" of the water "had caused the death of manie Brethren." Even the prisoners of the Fleet delivered a petition lamenting the fact that they were being slowly killed by the surrounding waters. A monk recorded his journey on the river, from London to Chertsey, in May 1471—"a smel ther was as grete as deth, but for no berien [burial] was it mad."

In 1481 there were complaints about the wharves where "at every Ebbe of the water there remain the Intrails of bestes and other filth and Carion of grete substaunce and quantitee." The words for such river filth varied, according to its nature—carrion, draff, dung, entrails, garbage, issue and rubbish. The effects were sometimes local and well defined, as in a complaint made in 1422 of the "filth that cometh doun the Trinite lane and Cordewanerstrete by Garlekhith and goth doun in the lane by twix John Hatherle shop and Ric Whitman shop of whiche dong moche goth in to Thamise." We may imagine an ill-smelling stream of excrement and urine, debouching directly into the Thames beyond the shops of Mr. Hatherly and Mr. Whitman. There were Dunghill Lanes at Puddle Dock, Whitefriars and Queenhithe, while Dunghill Stairs was located to the front of Three Cranes Wharf. Great mounds of excrement were from thence cast into the water. In the fifteenth century, too, a "house of easement" or "long house" containing two rows of sixty-four seats (for men and for women) was erected at the end of Friar Lane where the waste matter was washed away by the tides of the river.

In 1535 an Act was passed by Parliament to prohibit the casting of excrement and other rubbish in the Thames since "till now of late divers evil disposed persons have habitually cast in dung and filth." This is the same century in which Spenser had in "Prothalamion" extolled the "sweet Themmes," demonstrating that the myth of the river was still more powerful than any quotidian reality. In the seventeenth century John Taylor composed a litany of the same rubbish still to be found in the river, including "dead Hogges, Dogges, Cats, and well flayd Carryon Horses" as well as "Stable dunge, Beasts guts and Garbage." Pudding Lane was not named after any savoury dish, but after the "puddings" of excrement that were dispatched from it to the dung boats moored on the Thames. In the same century an Italian traveller, Orazio Busino, remarked that the river was "so hard, turbid, and foul, that its smell may be perceived in the linen which is washed with it."

The Thames was able to imitate or to embody the various conditions of the city, therefore, and these included the darker and more squalid aspects of eighteenth-century London. The river by Wapping, for example, was a squalid and malodorous place, dangerous for the unwary, where, according to Henry Fielding in *The Journal of a Voyage to Lisbon* (1755), could be heard the "sweet sounds of seamen, watermen, fish-women, oyster-women, and of all the vociferous inhabitants of both shores." It was a lawless area, beyond the jurisdiction of the City, but it was also the site of

Execution Dock where those accused of crimes upon the "high seas" were given their final bills. It was a place of brothels and "low" taverns, of tenements and stinking alleys, of vagrants and impoverished sailors and out-of-work labourers. The river for them could be a curse.

There were other accounts of the eighteenth century that reflected the less salubrious aspects of the river. The eighteenth-century traveller, Thomas Pennant, left a diary of a journey from Temple Stairs to Gravesend in the spring of 1787. He notes that Greenland Dock, on the south bank near the Isle of Dogs, is the place where "blubber is boiled at a fit distance from the capital." Of Woolwich he records "the sight of the multitude of convicts in chains labouring in removing earth; eight are employed in drawing each cart."

In 1771 Tobias Smollett complained, in *The Expedition of Humphry Clinker*, that

> if I would drink water, I must swallow that which comes from the river Thames, impregnated with all the filth of London and Westminster. Human excrement is the least offensive part of the concrete, which is composed of all the drugs, minerals and poisons, used in mechanics and manufacture, enriched with the putrefying carcases of beasts and men; and mixed with all the scourings of all the wash-tubs, kennels, and common sewers, within the bills of mortality.

The "bills of mortality" were published weekly in the parishes of the city, detailing the causes of each death, primarily as a warning for the onset of plague; but that mortality was in some part due to the pervasive deadliness of the Thames water. In an area of the foreshore on the edge of Limehouse there was a common sewer known in the eighteenth century, and no doubt for many centuries before that, as "the Black Ditch."

But by the middle of the nineteenth century the situation had become far worse. The sewers of all London were flowing into the Thames, breeding epidemic disease among the urban population. Numerous small gas manufactories were set up along the banks, since they needed water to produce the gas itself, and their waste residues entered the Thames. The by-products included spent lime, ammonia, cyanide and carbolic acid, which were not conducive to the health of any marine life.

All the excrement and pollution of the largest city in the world flowed within the Thames. The sewage of three million people bubbled in the tide, and the river had become no more than a vast open sewer. Drapes soaked in chlorine were hung against the windows of Parliament. But they were not enough. In the words of a contemporary report the Chancellor of the Exchequer left a committee room in disorder "with a mass of papers in one hand and with his pocket handkerchief clutched in the other, and applied closely to his nose, with body half bent, hastened in dismay from the pestilential odour." In the words of that Chancellor, Benjamin Disraeli, the river had become "a Stygian pool reeking with ineffable and unbearable horror." When Victoria and Albert embarked upon a pleasure cruise upon the river, the smell drove them back to the banks within minutes. Yet even the foreshores were caked with shit. As far upriver as Teddington Lock, the sewage was reported to be 6 inches (150 mm) thick and "as black as ink."

The water itself was turgid and dark, with a viscous quality created by the mountains of sludge poured into its depths. Its distinctive smell, readily invoked in any account of the "great stink" of 1858, was that of hydrogen sulphide created by the removal of all the oxygen from the water; this in turn caused the water to become black with deposits of iron sulphide. And this was the water with which the citizens made their tea. A contemporary publication, *The Oarsman's Guide*, described the Thames as "the sludgy compromise between the animal, the vegetable and the mineral kingdoms" and described the nineteenth-century riverscape thus: "Feeble rays from a clouded sun glimmer through the murky atmosphere, and play with tarnished glister over the dingy flood." For mid-Victorians it was the fatal harbinger of "the terrors of a new and warmer world." The unnatural warmth of the river, created by the chemical reactions within its depths, suggested a calamitous destiny.

In 1858 *Punch* magazine described it as "one vast gutter" in which the leavings of the city were dumped, which included in that century a host of materials from the lime of Vauxhall to the bone deposits of Lambeth and the slaughter-houses of Whitechapel. It has always been in danger of "silting up," when the alluvial mud gathers in large enough quantities to obstruct the flow of water. There is also the risk of "retention," or the extent to which the river holds on to its contents. If you were to drop a plank or oil drum into the river at London Bridge, it would take from three to eleven weeks to travel the 40 miles into the embrace of the open sea. This was once also the situation of the sewage trapped within the banks of the Thames.

The blackness of the Thames was once taken to be an image of unnaturalness and sterility. Henry James, in *English Hours* (1905), describes how a "damp-looking, dirty blackness is the universal tone. The river is almost black, and is covered with black barges; above the black house-tops, from among the far-stretching docks and basins, rises a dusky wilderness of masts." Black water seems somehow to be the opposite of true water. It is disturbing. It is hard. It is rancid. It is restless. It is the image of London, as if London had drowned in its depths and its sightless eyes were looking up from the water. It is sour, with the sourness of metal and industry somewhere within it. It could not quench your thirst. It will smell of dank and forgotten things.

There were four great epidemics of cholera in the nineteenth century—those of 1832, 1849, 1854 and 1865—in which many thousands of people died from the state of the polluted water extracted from the various city pumps. By the end of 1849, for example, some fourteen thousand Londoners had expired from the infection. Dr. John Snow became celebrated as the man who first demonstrated that cholera was an intestinal disease propagated by infected water; he proved his point in the epidemic of 1854 by the incidence of death within a 250-yard (230-metre) radius of the drinking pump at the corner of Broad Street in Soho. That pump led directly back to the Thames. It is believed that in 1861 Prince Albert died from typhoid spread by the foul waters beneath Windsor Castle. In "The Adventure of the Dying Detective," set in 1890, Sherlock Holmes is deemed to have contracted a deadly contagion, simply by walking down an alley in Rotherhithe close to the water; his eyes are feverish, and his lips are caked with sores.

At a later date the effluent from the power stations located along the river had a further effect upon the condition and healthiness of the Thames. The water, its temperature artificially raised, lost oxygen. It was no better by the middle of the twentieth century. Most people preferred to use the pedestrian tunnel rather than confront the smell caused by the churning of the Woolwich ferry. In the late 1950s the surface of the Thames was observed to heave and bubble with the discharge of methane gas beneath its surface, and the poison ate holes in the propellers of the river boats. The gilded buttons on the officers' uniforms would turn black within two or three hours.

Even in the twenty-first century, the Thames cannot entirely disavow its immediate past. There is still a regular stream of untreated sewage entering the Thames after even moderate rainfalls, and in wet weather many thousands of tonnes of sewage and storm water are discharged from pumping stations at Chelsea, Hammersmith and Lots Road. On one day in the summer of 2004 freak storms meant that a million tonnes of raw sewage were discharged into the river, causing the death of more than ten thousand fish. Rowers on the Thames were advised not to venture onto the water for four days, and after that time they were asked to cover up all cuts and grazes in advance of their outings. In the month of August, in that year, five million tonnes of sewage were released into the upper reaches of the Thames. From the beginning of 2001 to the end of 2004, some 240 million cubic metres of raw sewage were emptied into the river. As a result there have been calls for the construction of a new "interceptor tunnel" to complement the arrangement of London's existing sewers. The river will never be pure.

CHAPTER 34

"*All Alive! Alive! Alive, O!*"

For most of its human history, the river has been a primary source of nourishment. In the medieval period the Thames was a great reservoir of fish, the home of "barbille, fflounders, Roches, dace, pykes, Tenches and other." Clams, "otherwise called wormes pranes," were collected in great numbers. Eels were perhaps the major food, and there were names for six species from the pimpern-eel to the stubble-eel. But there were also gudgeon and mullet, salmon and smelt, cod and bass, plaice and sole and whiting. All of these are still to be found. Other medieval varieties of Thames fish, including lamprey and sturgeon, turbot and mackerel, are now quite rare.

In the thirteenth and fourteenth centuries there was a fish-processing site on Canvey Island. In the sixteenth century William Harrison asked

What should I speake of the fat and sweet salmons, dailie taken in this streame, and that in such plenty (after the time of the smelt be past) as no river in Europa is able to exceed it. What store also of barbells, trouts, cheuins, pearches, smelts, breams, roches, daces, gudgings, flounders, shrimps etc. are commonlie to be had therein . . . this famous riuer complaineth commonlie of no want, but the more it looseth at one time, the more it yeeldeth at another.

He deplores "the insatiable auarice of the fishermen," however, and exclaims: "Oh that this riuer might be spared euen one yeare from nets etcetera! But alas then should manie a poore man be undoone."

In the eighteenth century William Maitland expatiated on the worth of the fish

which *this* River only nourishes and supports. How remarkably good is its Salmon! What fine large Flounders, Smelts, Shoals, Trout, Graylin [there then follows an extensive list] . . . (too many to mention), are there caught above London Bridge . . . And, withal, how many other Kinds of Salt-water Fish . . . with several sorts of Shell-fish . . . are there caught below Bridge, even within the Jurisdiction of the City of London!

A water-bailiff wrote in an essay of 1746 that "though some of our northern counties have as fat and large Salmon as the River Thames, yet none are of so exquisite taste."

The fishermen of the medieval period tended to live and work on the river-banks by Charing Cross but, as that neighbourhood became more select and selective, they migrated across the river to Lambeth which in the eighteenth century had the reputation (and atmosphere) of a particularly squalid fishing village. By that time, too, the fishermen had colonised most parts of the river-bank in the immediate vicinity of the markets of London; by 1798 it is reported that some four hundred earned their living between Deptford and London Bridge.

The principal market was of course Billingsgate, the most ancient of all London markets. The earliest recorded tolls for the vessels there can be dated to 1016, with a halfpenny being charged upon a "small" ship, and a penny for a greater one "with sails." There was, however, a market on the site long before that time. It seems very likely that eel and herring were brought ashore in the earliest periods of human occupation; one of the salient characteristics of the river, even within its urban fastness, is the continuity or persistence of certain chosen locations. The name itself may be derived from Belinus, a Celtic god, which would in turn suggest that there was a market here for fish and other goods in the Iron Age. The "gate" refers to one of the two within the Roman defensive wall, the other being Dowgate. It became a "free" market, without tolls, at the end of the seventeenth century. Indeed it flourished for many centuries largely because of its favourable position below London Bridge, and was not finally moved from its ancient site until 1982; its central position, for more than a millennium, testifies to the importance of Thames fish in the London diet and the London economy. For many hundreds of years it remained an open space by the river, dotted with booths and sheds as well as a row of wooden houses with a piazza on their western end. Only in the middle of the nineteenth century was a wharf built here for the fishermen and the merchants; before that time they were obliged to manoeuvre two gangways linking the boats and the shore.

In the nineteenth century the average volume of fish sold in the market, each day, was some 500 tons (over 500 tonnes). The market was permitted to operate even on Sundays, when mackerel were allowed to be put on sale before the hours of divine service. There are innumerable reports, from that period, of the confusion and bustle of the market immediately after its opening at five in the morning. The porters, and costers, and merchants, and fishermen—together with all the vehicles and carriers of their trade—clustered around this small spot off Thames Street and Fish Street Hill, crying out for custom and trade. Henry Mayhew transcribed some of their calls that might have been replicated at any period in a thousand years—"Ha–a–an' some cod! Best in the market!," "Yeo, ye–e–o, here's your fine bloaters," "Here you are—here you are—splendid whiting," "Turbot, turbot! All alive, turbot!," "Fine soles, oy, oy oy!," "Hullo, hullo here! Beautiful lobsters, good and cheap!," "Who'll buy brill, O, brill, O!," "Fine flounders! O ho! O ho!" The most famous cry was one that was taken up by Londoners themselves as a catchphrase, "All alive! Alive! Alive, O!" These were the sounds of the Thames at work.

The "fish-fags," or "fish-wives," were native to this site; they carried the produce in straw baskets balanced on their heads. They wore strong "stuff" gowns and quilted petticoats, smoked clay pipes and took snuff. There were the fish porters, who wore helmets of hide. And there were fish salesmen, who wore straw hats in even the most inclement weather.

At the beginning of the nineteenth century there were productive fisheries at Chelsea and at Fulham, at Chiswick and at Petersham, where salmon could be caught in season. At Blackwall the fishermen took away many dozens of fine smelt. Anglers fished from London Bridge for perch and roach, and such was the interest that at Crooked Lane by the bridge there were a number of fishing-tackle makers. Roach were also caught near a bed of rushes by Temple Gardens, and at another spot by Westminster Bridge. The docks were also a favoured haunt for fishermen. London was swarming with fish. There was also a phenomenon known as "eel fair," when the river was bordered with a dark line of eel fry; people came down to the banks with sieves or nets, and caught these small creatures for an especial kind of fish cake. In the nineteenth century the "peter-boat men," one of the most ancient trades on the river, would "gravel" for eels buried in the mud and sell them at the eel-market of Blackfriars Stairs on Sunday morning. There were so many lobsters to be found in the Thames that regulations were introduced for their capture.

Then everything changed. In the latter half of the nineteenth century fishing in the tidal river—that is, the river below Teddington—came almost to an end, with the only catches being those of whitebait and shrimp. The middle and upper waters retained their population of perch and roach, carp and chub and barbel and bream and the other species of freshwater fish that had always flourished in the river. But then the tidal river died in a flood of pollution. The salmon vanished. The lobsters disappeared. The flounder was extinct. The shad and the smelt were no longer to be seen. At the height of the river's pollution in the late nineteenth century there was a sad warning in Richard Jefferies's novel, *After London* (1885), that the Thames would become

a vast stagnant swamp, which no man dare enter, since death would be his inevitable fate. There exhales from this oozy mass so fatal a vapour that no animal can endure it. The black water bears a greenish-brown floating scum, which for ever bubbles up from the putrid mud of the bottom . . . There are no fishes, neither can eels exist in the mud, nor even newts. It is dead.

In fact the prophecy, to all intents and purposes, was fulfilled by the middle of the twentieth century. No fish could live in the river, and no birds came.

The river remained in this dreadful condition for more than a hundred years. In the 1950s it was reported that there were no fish in the Thames from Gravesend to Kew, a distance of some 48 miles. But then, by the late

1960s and early 1970s, there was a manifest drop in the level of pollution as a result of more efficient means of neutralising or purifying waste. In 1976 a salmon was found beyond Teddington Weir, the first in the non-tidal Thames for 140 years. In the following year a salmon was seen at Shepperton, and then at Boulter's Lock where the last salmon had been caught in 1824. These are small and local examples, but they signify a giant transition. The Thames was returning to life once more. Since the early 1970s, too, smelt have returned to the river in large numbers. Flounders reappeared then after an absence of fifty years; the first flounder was caught at Strand-on-the-Green in late October 1972. Eels and sea-trout are also to be found in great quantities. The Thames estuary is now the largest spawning ground for sole in England. One of the most curious new arrivals in the river was the minatory piranha, many thousands of miles from its home in the Amazon. It had apparently been dropped, recently dead, by a seagull. It is not known how it arrived in the relatively cold waters of the Thames, but it is suspected that it was released by a nervous owner. No other sightings have been reported.

The Chinese mitten crab became established in the Thames in the early 1970s, but now its numbers have greatly increased until it has become a threat to the native flora and fauna. The crabs damage embankments with their habit of burrowing, consume the eggs of other fish and are in direct competition with the native crayfish. They are now so common that the juvenile crabs can be picked up along the Thames Embankment in London. But the history of the Thames is the history of assimilation and accommodation. There seems to be no way of stopping the growth of the mitten, unless quantities are harvested as the ingredients of Chinese cooking. Then it may compete with its enemy, the crayfish, as a river delicacy.

There are in fact now 118 species of fish that are native to the river, with roach over clean gravel and carp in the deeps, chub in the shadows, gudgeon on the bottom, trout and reed mace in the weir pools, perch and pike in the backwaters. Bottlenose dolphins have been seen at Blackfriars, and porpoises at Wapping; grey seals have been observed at Greenwich and at Rotherhithe, and long-finned whales at Southend. Even the shy sea horse has returned to the estuary. Their presence is of course complemented by the return of wildfowl and other birds, creating what can once more be considered a living river. It is now also a cleaner river than at any time in its history. It is claimed, in fact, that the Thames is the cleanest metropolitan river in the world. It is a miracle of rejuvenation. What had been dead, has once more come alive. That regeneration has sometimes taken unexpected form. There is much more vegetation along the banks of the Thames. A study of Turner's sketches, for example, will reveal that in the artist's lifetime there were far fewer trees in the river landscape. Now the tow-paths are often obscured by trees and bushes, and in recent years there are stretches that have become impenetrable through the sheer volume of greenery.

There is another kind of fishing, as ancient and as venerable as that of the professional fisherman. It is the pleasure of the individual upon the bank, the solitary figure with rod and net who is to be found on every stretch of the Thames as if in implicit communion with the water. He or she (and, despite popular belief, there are female anglers) understands the river in a different sense. In its essential state it must be the simplest and oldest form of food-gathering that still exists in the industrialised world, and its techniques have not altered beyond recognition over the millennia. It is a token of ancientness or, rather, the fact that ancient customs still persist without fundamental change. It is somehow appropriate that they should also be connected with the river. In the Christian eras the eating of fish was associated with penance and with purification; hence its prevalence in the time of Lenten fasting. The creatures of the Thames share the ritual purity of the flowing waters.

It is likely that the earliest settlers along the Thames, going back at least twelve thousand years to the Mesolithic era, used hooks and lines and nets to trap the fish in the river. There must also have been the very early construction of weirs, or fences placed across the flow of the stream to catch or guide fish into small pools or nets. At a later date these were known as "kidells," "hedges" or "stops" and were sporadically outlawed by the sovereign. Thus in the eleventh century they were deemed to cause a hindrance to river traffic—which indeed they did—and Edward the Confessor ordered their destruction. At a slightly later date Edward I established a number of regulations to protect young salmon from being taken up. The size of the nets and the mesh was ordained by law. By 1558 the minimum size at which a salmon could be captured was 16 inches. There were a variety of other fishing devices that had their origin in remotest antiquity, among them the eel baskets or "bucks," the fishpots, and the eelpots or "grigpots"—the "grig" being the Thames name for the eel itself.

There have been many stories concerning the fishes of the river. There existed a strange aversion to the eel among certain Thames people. Some believed it to spring from mud, or from the decomposed remains of any animal. Others believed that it was created when a horse-hair was suspended in the water. Yet it remained the staple food of Londoners for many centuries. It is now not often consumed. The barbel was primarily sold to the Jewish population of London, for reasons now impossible to discover. Roach were believed to congregate around the Thames at Marlow, and to be most easily caught in autumn when the water of the river was "coloured" by rain. It was said in the early nineteenth century that you could take up haddock by hand, at London Bridge, because the fish were so blinded by the spray and spume of the fast water that "they cannot see whither they swimme." The tench was believed to be excessively tenacious of life. Perch were considered to be sociable so that, when one was caught, others were sure to follow. According to Izaak Walton, in *The Compleat Angler* (1653), "they are like the wicked of the world, not afraid, though their fellows and companions perish in their sight." The carp was believed to have been imported from China, but this may only have been the inference from their golden scales. They were easily tamed, and could distinguish between an acquaintance and a stranger.

The angler must be in deep sympathy with the fish and with the water. There is a kind of intimacy at work. That is why Thames anglers will tend to go back to the same spot at which they fished before. They are the votaries of the Thames, the guardians of its quietness and peacefulness. In her *Treatyse perteynynge to Hawkynge, Huntynge, Fysshynge and Coote Armiris* (1496) the prioress of the nunnery of Sopwell, Dame Juliana Berners, praised the avocation of the Thames angler since "at the leest, he hath his holsom walk, and mery at ease, a sweey ayre of the swete savoure of the mede floures that makyth him hungry; he hereth the melodious armony of fowles; he seeth the yonge swannes, herons, duckes, cotes, and many other fowles, with their brodes." This is the Thames as *locus amoenus*, the privileged place, the pastoral setting of natural seclusion complete with birdsong and running water and, of course, fish.

There is a charming work, A. E. Hobbs's *Trout of the Thames* (1947), that exemplifies such easy familiarity with the river and its sometimes elusive occupants. The narrative is filled with the stories and memories of the fishers of the Thames, who form a community as tangible as that of the fishermen downriver. "We knew that a big trout had his home in a very deep spot of the pool," Hobbs writes, "and we had seen him a few times when he was after a large dace or roach, but had never an opportunity to get in touch with him." These anglers knew the fish as individuals. "He or she—for convenience we will say he—was unmistakable, for he had a wall eye."

The prime of the angling clubs was undoubtedly the last decades of the nineteenth century, when it was estimated that some thirty thousand Londoners had become members. A great many of these Cockney sportsmen, as they were derisively known by the more traditional anglers, came up by Great Western trains to their favourite stretch of the Thames. Some of them, according to the *Lock to Lock Times*, "are very liable to become abusive when disturbed, as they generally have heavy bets on the weight of fish they catch . . . generally lavish with slang abuse, which if you have ladies with you is by no means pleasant." This was known as water language.

But there were also clubs in the major riverside settlements such as Marlow and Henley where local competitions were held. Night-fishing, and netting, were disallowed. But eel bucks, woven of osier rods, were a common aspect of the river. Anglers were almost single-handedly responsible for the temporary demise of the otter. Otters were considered great pests and fish-eaters; they were shot on sight as a nuisance, and in the late nineteenth century a reward of 10 shillings was offered for every dead otter proved to have been killed beside the river.

There were of course poachers, not deterred by the prospect of arrest and fine, who subscribed to the ancient belief that the river belonged to no man. As one of them said to the water-bailiff, "Don't the fish belong to me as much as to you? What were they sent for then?" There was also a prolonged struggle, at the end of the nineteenth century, between private owners and public anglers with the former exerting their rights over stretches of the river. The matter was never conclusively argued one way or another, and various local disputes were settled by compromise and accommodation. There were, however, cases of extensive legal disagreement, with the foundation of the Thames Fishing Defence Fund and the popularity of a piece of verse:

> If man or boy the law condemns
> For taking fish from out the Thames,
> What, pray, should be that person's dish,
> Who takes the river from the fish?

PART XI

The Healing Spring

St. Anne's well

CHAPTER 35

The Healing Water

The Thames has always been allied with healing. It is a river of comfort and of restoration. Since it has been customarily associated with baptism, and with other purification rites, its regenerative powers are easily transposed into the realm of physical health. What can be more health-giving than pure water? Water is the nutritive element, the maternal fluid, the milk of nature. Since the water is guardian and preserver of health, the Thames itself becomes a healing sight. It is also a site for the healing of eyes. Ever since St. Augustine performed miracles near the Thames at Cricklade, persuading the blind to see, the wells and springs beside the river have been commonly supposed to cure diseases of the eye. Glaucoma was more popularly known as "water of the eye." There are some twenty-six healing springs known to be sited by the Thames, and of course there are many more that have faded from the view of more sceptical centuries.

The spring is perhaps the purest and brightest of all natural phenomena. It is always fresh and always renewed, emerging from the subterranean depths like the source of life itself. The polluter of a spring was, in all cultures, deemed to be accursed. The divinities of the ancient world congregated by springs, and each spring had its tutelary god or goddess.

Those once dedicated to the ancient goddess Tan have now been renamed St. Anne's Well, or perhaps St. Catherine's Well, but the old mystery survives. As an early Christian bishop, Martin of Braga, put it—". . . to put bread in a spring, what is that but the worship of the devil?"

There is an everlasting spring beside the Thames, in the wood below Sinodun Hill. A shrine to one of the earliest Christian saints of the Thames, Birinus, was erected here for sick cattle. The spring at Cricklade was situated in a meadow to the north of the river, and in previous centuries the people of Gloucestershire and Wiltshire would resort here and fill their bottles with its treasured water. It was reported by those in the neighbourhood that it was "good for the eyes." By 1910, however, it had ceased to be employed as a curative. The spring is now covered over with concrete. There was a spring, known as Assenden Spring, which ran into the Thames at Henley; it was believed to possess the medicinal properties of carbonated water, but it has now disappeared or been forgotten. There were a number of springs and wells (it is sometimes difficult to distinguish between them in the old accounts) close to Pangbourne; there was a spring dedicated to another riverine saint, Frideswide, on Frilsham Heath. A curious superstition was attached to this place. It was customary for courting couples to walk here and drink the waters of the old well; if the young man's intentions were not honourable, a toad would appear and spit at him.

There were of course wells close beside the Thames, and many of the names of the villages near the riverside bear testimony to their presence— Brightwell-cum-Sotwell, or Sweet Well, Ewelme meaning "wells," Mongewell and others. The well must be one of the oldest of all human devices, and there are wells in the Indus Valley that have been dated to 3000 BC. In the pictographic script of Sumeria, that home of great rivers, a circular symbol is believed to denote a well. The wells of London owe their origin to the tributary streams running down to the river—Clement's Well, Clerkenwell, Bagnigge Wells, St. Pancras Wells, Sadler's Wells, Skinner's Wells, Faggeswell, Monkwell, St. Agnes Le Clair (which became Anniseed Clear), and Blessed Mary's Well (that was renamed Black Mary's Well or Black Mary's Hole at the time of the Reformation).

There is some confusion over Chadwell or Shadwell, in addition to the downriver village of Chadwell St. Mary; it might be supposed that they were named in honour of St. Chad, the seventh-century bishop, but he is the local saint of Staffordshire rather than of the Thames region. The names of imported saints are infrequent, and Chad-well may instead simply mean "cold spring." Nevertheless at Shadwell itself, just by Wapping, there was in the eighteenth century a mineral spring that was known as Shadwell Spa; it was said to be impregnated with sulphur, vitriol, steel and antimony that were efficacious against diseases of the skin. It was approached by means of Well Alley, opposite the New Stairs of Wapping; at the back of this alley were the Old Swan Tavern Fields. Here was the mineral spring.

There are other holy wells in London. The Chelsea and Lambeth waterworks, not coincidentally, were built on the site of Seething Wells. St. Bride's Well, or St. Bridget's Well, of course became Bridewell. These once holy sites are directly related to the passing of the river through the city. There was a mineral spring, known as the postern spring, on Tower Hill. There was another spring, and a consequent number of wells, upon the north side of what is now Queen Victoria Street a few yards from the river at Blackfriars; Roman ritual offerings have been found there. There were other offerings in wells at Southwark, by the south bank of the river. There was a famous phrase set in stone beside a marble fountain in Rome and equally apposite for London: NYMPHIS LOCI BIBE LAVA TACE. "The places of the nymphs—drink, wash and be silent."

One of the most celebrated wells was located at Binsey, beside the river outside Oxford. This also was associated with the river goddess or Christian saint, Frideswide, who "by her prayers, caused it to be opened." It was known as St. Margaret's Well, just by the west end of the chapel erected here by Frideswide in 730; the well had a stone covering, as well as an image of Margaret or Frideswide, and flowers were placed beside it. The water was reputed to work miracles; two blind sisters of Eynsham, Jurkiva and Rilda, were supposed to have regained their sight after their pilgrimage here. Such was its efficacy and repute that its water sold for a guinea a quart (1.1 litres); the neighbouring village of Seckworth was transformed into a large town with twenty-four inns for priests and pilgrims as well as eleven churches. In the oratory of Frideswide's chapel, the crutches and bandages of the healed were hung about the walls.

By the mid-nineteenth century, however, the waters had vanished beneath the earth. Seckworth itself disappeared in the twelfth century, leaving only a few cottages behind, and now lies forgotten under pasture land. In the later nineteenth century Frideswide's well was rebuilt and then entered English literature in another guise. One of the ancient words for healing substance was "treacle" or "triacle." Lewis Carroll, who knew Binsey very well, created the treacle well for *Alice's Adventures in Wonderland*. The holy well of Frideswide has by strange indirection acquired legendary status once more.

There was a spring of healing beside the Thames at Goring. It was known as Spring-well, and in the seventeenth century it was reputed to be a cure for skin disorders, ulcers and (once again) sore eyes. In the early eighteenth century the water was bottled and marketed as "Goring Spring water" and a "valuable specific" for various ailments. But it lost its reputation, and thus its efficacy. There was another celebrated spring by the bank near Moulsford, close to the Leather Bottle Inn. It is possible that the inn itself acquired its name from the vessels used to take the water. There was a healing spring at Chertsey, known as "St. Anne's Well," beside which an ancient chapel was built; there is a nineteenth-century engraving of this almost hidden spring, with relics of stone beside its shallow water. Lambeth Wells were known as a curative. There is still an old "Physic Well" hidden among trees by the Thames bank at Cumnor. By the village of Shorne, close to Gravesend, was located a chalybeate spring, containing iron salts, that was considered to be highly effective in the cure of scurvy. Along the same stretch of the Thames there was a spring at West Tilbury, from which issued "canary water" used in the treatment of diabetes and internal haemorrhaging. In the eighteenth century it was bottled as "Tilbury Water." There was a holy well by the river at Reading, "between a field called the Mount and a lane called Priest's Lane." Beside this well stood a mighty oak-tree, which was also held in great veneration. Downriver there was a health spa known as Richmond Wells.

In the village of Eastleach Turville there was a mineral spring of strongly "cathartic" character, and in Bampton there was a holy well that once possessed a wide reputation for healing the eyes. There is a well in the north-western corner of the churchyard of St. Mary Magdalen, North Ockendon, that is connected with the baptismal ministry of St. Cedd, when he came as a missionary among the East Saxons; popular belief supposes that its spring originates in Kent and then travels under the river to come forth in Essex. The village was in more ancient times known as Northockendon Septfontaynes, of the seven springs, but all trace of these has long since disappeared. They may be compared, however, to the "Seven Springs" that are considered to be an alternative source of the Thames.

The water of the Thames itself was once generally reported to have semi-miraculous properties, and in particular the gift of self-purification.

The water by Hampton Court was also believed to possess medicinal properties, and in 1794 it was described as "efficacious in the gravel [for kidney
stones], excellent for drinking and washing, but unfit for culinary use" because it turned the vegetables black. It is certainly true that the area of
Hampton Court enjoyed an enviable reputation for many centuries; it was
a matter of common report that it escaped the epidemics of sweating sickness, plague, smallpox and scarlet fever which were raging in its immediate
neighbourhood. This immunity was also ascribed to the protection of
the river.

The waters at Marlow were reputed to be good for alleviating the
symptoms of gout. The riverine neighbourhood of Streatley also had a
reputation for its health-giving qualities. There is hardly a stretch of the
upper and middle river, in fact, which does not possess some real or symbolic properties of healing. When in 1568 the Jesuit George Napier was
hanged, drawn and quartered, his butchered body was thrown into the
Thames at Oxford; but the river reunited his severed parts and by the time
it reached Sandford the corpse was entire again. It is no more than a story,
a superstition of the river, but it is maintained by the ancient belief that by
immersion in the river the body can become whole again.

There were many hospitals established by the river, as if in implicit
communion with its curative properties. There was an old hospital at
Abingdon, erected during the reign of Henry V on the site of an ancient
monastery dedicated to the Holy Cross, suggesting the implicit connection
between piety, water worship and healing. A hospital dedicated to St. John
the Baptist was established at Cricklade during the reign of Henry III; part
of the present parish of St. Sampson is still called "Spital" in its memory.
There are many other examples of these ancient foundations by the
Thames, but it is perhaps more instructive to look at their more recent incarnations. A tour downriver, along the London stretch of the Thames in
the twenty-first century, will reveal the Cheyne Hospital at Chelsea, once
known as "the Little Hospital by the River," the Lister Hospital by Chelsea
Bridge, St. Thomas's Hospital, King's College Medical School and the
London Bridge Hospital. There is still an association.

A number of mental hospitals or asylums were placed beside the
Thames. Close to the river, in the church at Swanscombe, was an altar famous throughout the region for the cure of madness; here, in previous centuries, a great number of suffering pilgrims were brought by their friends.
Beside the river at Sonning, before the Reformation, there was another

chapel of great repute in the cure of madness; as Leland put it, "there is an Old Chapelle at the Est ende of the Churche of S. Sarik, whither of late tyme resorted in Pilgrimage many folks for the Disease of Madness." There was a ritual enclosure here in the Neolithic period, and there may be some distant but distinct connection; the church still stands. Chiswick House, beside the Thames, was once a private asylum. A few yards from the village of Moulsford, by the Thames, was until recent years the Berkshire Mental Hospital. There was a mental hospital by the river at Littlemore, once the parish of John Henry Newman. The path of the Thames now passes the park and mansion of Higginson, once the residence of Dr. William Battie who specialised in the cure of mental illness. Some of the river's tributaries reflect its power. The river Hogsmill, which enters the Thames at Kingston, runs close to what was a complex of five mental hospitals in Epsom; its source was at Ewell where stood the Ewell Mental Hospital. It had been established in 1903 as the Ewell Epileptic Colony, but became a mental hospital from 1930 until 1962.

In Gerarde's Herball *(1597)* there are many descriptions of the flowers to be found beside the banks of the river including the comfrey "which joyeth in watery ditches, in far and fruitfull meadows" and the water-betony that "groweth by brookes and running waters, by ditch sides, and by the brinks of rivers." It is clear from the title of his book that these river flowers are supposed to have medicinal and curative properties; they share the general atmosphere of cleansing and purification that surrounds the flowing water. Many of the plants and flowers by the Thames are in fact still used as alternatives to conventional medicine; the yellow bedstraw is used for infections of the feet, while the marigold is efficacious for the eyes and the skin. The flowers of the river, like the river itself, can heal. The purple and yellow loosestrife has received its name from its ancient property of taming wild animals and quelling discord among beasts. So the calm and quietness of the Thames are carried by its native plants. The sweet sedge, that grows in the waters of the Thames, was scattered upon the floors of houses and churches to render them fragrant.

The Thames also fosters herbs that have the especial repute of healing. There is the eyebright, which might be considered the guardian plant of the Thames since according to the popular verse "eyebright makes the blinde to see":

Thank ye God with alle your soule
For ye herbe that makes sicke eyes whole.

Another herb to be seen in great quantities beside the Thames, the mead-
owsweet, has similar effects. Nicholas Culpeper, the seventeenth-century
herbalist, states in *The Complete Herbal and English Physician* (1653) that "a
water distilled from them is good for inflammation of the eyes." In this
context we may mention the Chelsea Physic Garden, bordering on the
river, where medicinal herbs were once grown for simples and for oint-
ments. It was established by the Company of Apothecaries in 1673, specifically as a botanic garden for medicinal plants, and was relinquished by the
apothecaries only at the end of the nineteenth century. The spot was chosen precisely because of its proximity to the Thames. It has been suggested
that this was the result of the more favourable "microclimate" which the
water provides, but there may be more ancient affiliations. Health,
"physic," and the river have always formed a close association.

There are many other river herbs. The great water dock was believed
to have curative properties, and in the eighteenth century its astringent root
was widely used as a medicine. St. John's wort is a cure for depression, and
the bugleweed is a sedative. The comfrey is employed to allay ulcers. The
flower-heads of the reeds that decorate the banks of the river were considered to be useful in relieving bilious complaints. The common yarrow or
milfoil, known to the inhabitants of the Thames as "thousand leaved
grass," was reputed to close up wounds and to prevent swelling or inflammation. It was widely used by bargemen, susceptible to bruising and injury,
as an astringent. Another riverside plant, agrimony, was applied as a sedative. The villagers of the Thames also held tansy in great repute as a
remedy for gout and for intestinal worms; the herb was also sold in apothecaries' shops under the name of "Athanasia," the Latin equivalent of the
Greek word for immortality. Tansy may also be, or may be related to, the
herb once known as arginteria. In his *Description of Britaine* William Harrison notes that "it is a world to see what plenty of Seraphium groweth
vpon the Kentish shore . . . whilest he giueth foorth the herbe Argentaria
for Seraphium."

The willow is a great frequenter of the river and its banks; its bark and
leaves were once used as an astringent, and the bark itself was crushed or
powdered as a medicine for what was once known as the ague. Since the

ague was particularly prevalent in the marshy regions of the Thames Valley, and especially in the Thames estuary, it is an example of the local plants offering local remedies for the people of the river. The inhabitants of the Thames did in fact favour a number of native plants for common ills. The gypsies of the river, that now extinct group of travellers who followed the course of the Thames in their wanderings, were known to favour a drink made out of dock-root. For rheumatism and other ailments they made use of the bark of oaks growing close to the river; it was boiled and drunk as a kind of tea. The bark of pollard ash-trees, so common by the banks of the Thames, was also used as a concoction for the health of the liver. Marsh-mallows were good for the toothache. These herbs and plants are by no means unique to the Thames, of course, but they are an inalienable aspect of the healing powers it was once presumed to possess.

This aura of healing also attracted doctors, or "quacks," to the river. In the mid-nineteenth century there was an establishment between Richmond and Kingston, Sudbrook Park, that specialised in what became a famous "water cure." In the 1770s a doctor named James Graham set up a Temple of Health by the river at the newly built Adelphi; the walls of this establishment were decorated with walking sticks, crutches and orthopaedic equipment discarded by thankful patients. Just upriver at Hammersmith the artist and occasional healer, Philippe de Loutherbourg, set up a practice for curing a range of ailments and complaints. He employed a form of animal magnetism, and pretended to heal all diseases by the simple expedient of laying his hands upon the body accompanied by prayer. It is perhaps not strange that in the early eighteenth century a resident of Teddington, Dr. Stephen Hales, made much progress on the circulation of the blood.

But there were other types of "cunning men," as the experimental philosophers were once known, who made their home by the Thames. It is a curious fact, or singular coincidence, that by the river in Lambeth there dwelled over various periods John Tradescant, Francis Moore, Simon Forman, Elias Ashmole and an astrologer known as Captain Bubb. Simon Forman was the Elizabethan astrologer and doctor of physic, whose diaries have revealed the extent of sixteenth-century superstitious beliefs; he noted in one of his many recondite volumes, "this I made the devil write with his own hands in Lambeth Fields, 1569, in June or July as I now remember." Lambeth Fields was then adjacent to the Thames. Forman is buried in Lambeth Churchyard, by the river. His contemporary, Captain Bubb, dwelled in Lambeth Marsh where he "resolved horary questions astrologically."

Kew Gardens: Pagoda and Bridge. Richard Wilson's canvases display an idealised river, an aesthetic version perhaps at odds with the reality.

Westminster Bridge, with the Lord Mayor's Procession. Canaletto brings to the river the light and life of his native city, Venice, and makes the Thames a symbol of majesty.

Artists of every generation have been drawn to the Thames. It is the most painted river in the world.

Left: Abingdon (top), painted by Turner in 1805, and *Rain, Steam and Speed*, Turner's vivid impression of the Great Western Railway bridge at Maidenhead. Turner lived and died by the Thames, painting it in all its aspects. The river was an instrument of his vision and a source of his inspiration.

This page: Turner's *Willows* and Rossetti's *Water Willow*, with the Thames at Kelmscott in the background.

Whistler drew the maritime life of Wapping—
"a world of mud, and planks, and bales"—but, later
in his career, he celebrated the Thames with
crepuscular images of night and twilight.
Above: *The Little Pool*; opposite:
Grey and Silver.

William Blake painted this watercolour of Old Father Thames to
adorn the text of Thomas Gray's
"Ode on a Distant Prospect of Eton
College." Blake was always
drawn to ancient deities.

Baptism. Stanley Spencer's true subject was always the river flowing beside the village
of Cookham, where he was born and where he lived until his death. The Thames became
for him a token of Eden, like the original rivers that flowed throughout the world.

"As if she were part of the refuse it had cast out, and left to corruption and decay, the girl we had followed strayed down to the river's brink, and stood in the midst of this night-picture, lonely and still, looking at the water . . . There was that in her wild manner which gave me no assurance but that she would sink before my eyes." *David Copperfield.*

Trading in the corpses of the drowned: "The girl rowed, pulling a pair of sculls very easily; the man kept an eagle look-out. He had no net, hook, or line, and he could not be a fisherman." *Our Mutual Friend.*

Clockwise from top left: *The Water Babies*: Tom and the dragonflies; *Alice in Wonderland*:
the pool of tears; *The Wind in the Willows*: Ratty and Mole;
Three Men in a Boat: on the Thames.

Dickens was familiar with the tides and the currents of the Thames. As a boy
he had worked in a blacking factory beside it, and he knew that
it was a river of darkness and suicide.

Later novelists have seen the river as a less sinister place. Lewis Carroll and
Kenneth Grahame, for example, made it the setting for fantasy and fun.
The work of Charles Kingsley and Jerome K. Jerome, too, is filled
with the freedom and infantilism of the river world.

Sheerness in wartime: *Barrage Balloons* by Eric Ravilious.

Hadleigh Castle: the mouth of the Thames—morning after a stormy night, by John Constable. This is where the song of the river ends and it flows into the sea.

Moore was an astrologer and author of the famous compendium of prophecies, *Old Moore's Almanack*, that was first published in 1697 and has continued ever since; he lived at the north-east corner of Calcott Alley. John Tradescant and Elias Ashmole were experimental philosophers and accumulators of natural curiosities; among their collections were the feathers of a phoenix, salamanders and dragons 2 inches (25 mm) long.

Further upriver, at Mortlake, dwelled the celebrated John Dee. Dr. Dee was both conjuror and mathematician, alchemist and geographer. He, too, seemed to relish frequent communion with the river or with its spirits; he dwelled in a house by the waterside, just west of the church. It was here that by his own account the angel Uriel appeared at the window of his study and presented him with a translucent stone; with this stone, or magic crystal, he proceeded to summon other angels and to converse with them. At Mortlake he built his own laboratory and amassed the largest private library in the country. He was the magus of the Thames. Mortlake itself, like Lambeth, became associated with magic and even with the practice of the black arts. Here also dwelled Francis Partridge, the magician and astrologer who in the early eighteenth century circulated his predictions in the public prints. Partridge was buried in Mortlake churchyard, while Dee lies somewhere beneath the chancel of the church.

There was a curious event in Battersea Fields, adjacent to the river and just upstream from Lambeth itself. It was here that "the spirits" carried a cunning man known to posterity only as Evans the astrologer; he was taken in the air along the Thames, and then left to his own devices at Battersea Causeway. The reason for this extraordinary conduct seems to be that he had vexed the same spirits by not offering enough "suffumigation" or incense, but their choice of Battersea is still perplexing.

In the vicinity of Walton, on the Surrey bank of the river, dwelled the astrologer William Lilly, known as a "cunning man" whose greatest triumph, in the eyes of posterity, was to predict the Great Fire of London:

> That deals in Destiny's dark counsels,
> And sage opinions of the moon sells . . .

He was born in 1602 and, having gained both fortune and reputation in London, removed to the parish of Walton. He lived there for forty-five years, before moving to the neighbouring hamlet of Hersham. He was an habitué of the river. Even when he had dwelled in London as a young man, his main employment was to "fetch water in large buckets from the Thames: I have helped to carry eighteen tubs of water in one morning." In his riverine retreat, however, he was visited by many people, intent upon securing news of the future, and was even consulted by the House of Commons. In the spring of 1644 he published an almanac in the name of "Merlinus Anglicus Junior." Did he know that Merlin was popularly supposed to have lived by the Thames? He cast his own spells in the immediate neighbourhood. He reported that he told a friend of the magic charm, "*O Micol! O tu Micol! Ergina pigmeorum veni.*" When the friend repeated it, in the little wood behind Lilly's house in Walton, there appeared the queen of the fairies whose effulgence was so bright that he was obliged to ask her to leave. She was, perhaps, one of the fabled nymphs of the Thames in another guise. In the church of Walton-on-Thames, St. Mary, there is a monument in Lilly's memory.

It is perhaps significant that the sixteenth-century essayist and natural philosopher, Francis Bacon, wished to purchase a house by the Thames in Twickenham Park for his own researches. He stated that he "experimentally found the situation of that place much convenient for the trial of his philosophical conclusions." So the immediate presence of the river was considered to be an advantage. He had notable predecessors. In a set of chambers by the river, at St. Katharine's Hospital, the alchemist and hermeticist Raymond Lulli was in the early fourteenth century intent upon making gold out of brass and iron. A little further downriver, in apartments within the Tower of London, Raymond of Tarragona was engaged in the same alchemical exercise. The "silver Themmes" was well named.

But the most famous natural philosopher, dwelling by the Thames, is undoubtedly Roger Bacon. Friar Bacon's Study, the thirteenth-century tower in which he is reputed to have undertaken his experiments, was sited at one end of Grandpont, also known as South Bridge and a previous incarnation of Folly Bridge, above the river at Oxford. It was here that the friar was believed to have held conversations with the devil, and to have constructed the famous brazen head that could prophesy. It is reputed to have uttered some phrases by the agency of the devil—"Time is," "Time was" and "Time is passed"—but it is more than likely that Bacon was able to create sound-effects by applying the principles of natural philosophy. His tower stood until 1779. There was a legend that the building would fall if a wiser man than Bacon passed beneath it. Since it survived intact for five hundred years after his death, it was considered to be a standing reproach to the abilities of the students of Oxford. But there was a warning given to undergraduates on their arrival at university, "Do not walk too near to the Friar's Tower."

The friar is variously stated to have invented gunpowder and the magnifying glass, but his claim to these achievements is open to question. In *The Famous Historie of Fryer Bacon*, published in 1627, he is reported to have prophesied that "chariots will move with an unspeakable force, without any living creature to stirre them" and that "an instrument may be made to fly withal." He also noted that "by art an instrument may be made, wherewith men may walk in the bottom of the sea or rivers." He also looked upward. One of Bacon's principal occupations, in his study by the river, was to climb onto the leads and examine the affects of the night sky. There is in fact a curious prevalence of observatories by the Thames. We could note here an early paradigm: the ritual sites of the prehistoric peoples by the river might in part have been constructed and designed in response to the movements of the fixed stars and wandering comets. Certainly all the "cunning men" who lived by the Thames, from Old Moore to Lulli, consulted the patterns of the firmament.

There is some continuing association between astronomy and the river, perhaps best exemplified by the presence of the Greenwich Observatory on a hill by the south bank of the Thames. It was established in 1675 and, under the administration of the first Astronomer Royal, John Flamsteed, it became the centre of stellar and planetary observation. Flamsteed's principal work, the *Historia coelestis Britannica* (1725), was published six years after his death and provided the most accurate star maps of the period. Greenwich is also known as the site of the meridian, that zero point from which all measurements of longitude are taken. From the period when the first causewayed enclosures and cursus monuments were erected by the river, the Thames has been associated with the measurement of time and space.

The author of *Oriental Despotism* (1957), Karl A. Wittfogel, has traced the role of priests and seers of the riverine civilisations of the East; they are associated with the rivers because they serve what he calls "hydraulic regimes" of Mesopotamia or the Nile Valley dependent upon the uses of water. So

> the operations of time keeping and scientific measuring and counting were performed by official dignitaries or by priestly (or secular) specialists attached to the hydraulic regime. Wrapped in a cloak of magic

and astrology and hedged with profound secrecy, these mathematical
and astronomical operations became the means both for improving hydraulic production and bulwarking the superior power of the hydraulic
leaders.

Everything depended, therefore, on the perceived "power" of the river. It
is the best context for assessing the significance of the Neolithic monuments
as well as the location of the observatory and meridian in Greenwich.

The Thames had other observatories along its banks. The observatory
of Roger Bacon, where the friar took "the altitude of the stars," has already
been described. There was also an astronomical observatory beside the
Royal Mint, on the north bank of the river above the Tower of London.
There is still an observatory at Kew, on the south side of the river in Old
Deer Park; it was also known as the King's Observatory, and was built in
time for George III's observation of the transit of Venus in June 1769.
There is some echo here of pharaonic star-worship by the banks of the
Nile. The observatory was in fact erected on the site of an old monastery,
thus preserving the ritual connection with the river. In its grounds are three
obelisks, one of them on the tow-path leading to Brentford, which were
employed as meridian marks for the astronomical instruments in use. Here,
too, the "time" for London was once set. The observatory then fell into decay until it was revived for "the maintenance of magnetic observations at
Kew," and it is now used for the study of the weather.

There was another observatory beside what is still known as the
"Dutch House" at Kew. It was employed by James Bradley, the Savilian
Professor of Astronomy at Oxford University, and the site of the building
where he undertook his star-gazing by the Thames is now marked by a sundial. Here Bradley made two important discoveries: of the aberration of
light and of the mutation of the earth's axis.

But perhaps the most unexpected, and certainly the least-known, connection of the river and astronomy is to be found at Slough. It was here that
Sir William Herschel and his sister, Caroline Herschel, set up their own observatory. They had previously scanned the firmament from a small house
in Datchet, also by the river, so they must have found some reassurance or
assistance in the immediate neighbourhood of the Thames. Brother would
call out the data gathered from the telescope, and sister would note down
the precise time of the observations. It was here that William Herschel discovered the planet of Uranus, and observed "the island universe" of the

Milky Way; at Datchet, too, Caroline Herschel first noted the presence of three nebulae and discovered eight comets. In some respects they found the weather of the Thames uncomfortable. William Herschel noted that "not only my breath freezes upon the side of the tube of the telescope, but I more than once have found my feet frozen to the ground." Yet some strange affinity survived.

CHAPTER 36

The Light of the Thames

hat are the colours of the Thames? There are the green banks of the upper river, broken not monotonous; there are always successive tints and shades in the colours within the river, fluctuations as subtle as the movement of quiet waters from the brightest to the palest green. The colours ripple and unfold, break apart and yield one to another. The green of the bankside, for example, is striated with golden moss and the yellow stars of the hawkweed, by wild geraniums and by wild strawberries; there is the sulphur of the toadflax, and the purple blue of the skullcap. The predominant colours of the river flowers are yellow and blue, to be seen, for example, in the fleabane and the dewberry that haunt the banks.

In the spring and autumn the riverside is sprinkled with yellow, with a gentle strain of white flowing through the mixture; in the spring, too, the trees are groaning with the weight of their blossom. The fields beside the Thames are white and yellow, with the river flowing between bank upon bank of blossom. In the summer months the purplish pink of the willow-herb and the loosestrife tends to predominate. This may subliminally change the mood of the river from one of optimism to one of meditation, but the general effect is that of natural congruity. There are no inharmonious colours in nature. The dark blue of the dewberry, together with the yellow head of the fleabane, are more deeply satisfying than the blue and gold of any painter.

The Thames has other colours. There is the silvery sheen to be observed at dawn or dusk in the estuary, an emanation of the light breaking through cloud onto the flat landscape. And there are the varied colours of the water itself. It can be the deepest green and the palest silver. In the colder months it can become wonderfully clear, and in its deeper reaches acquires the bluish green tint of spring water. It can be turbid, and muddy brown. In the shadow of a bridge it will sometimes seem to have become blue. Then, from a distance, its reaches seem like a thread of white. Its colour can sometimes be perceived by contrast; there are localities where a tributary, entering the river, is of a much darker hue than the Thames itself.

There are also local variations. At Oxford the water is deep green tinged with brown; downstream, at Radley, it has become dark blue. From Putney onwards samples from the river have a cloudy colour. In the reaches of London it can seem black, or sometimes a dark copper colour. It can become ash grey. And of course it is a mirror to the colours of the world. It reflects the life upon its surface, with the blue of a sail or the rusty vermilion of a barge. When storm clouds pass across it, it turns to the deepest grey and charcoal. The colours change perpetually in implicit communion with the wind and with the sky, with the sunlight and the scudding clouds. It can be silky green in summer, and blue in spring. But there are also times when the sky is brilliant enough and the river itself seems to be in shadow.

Any river can become black. But the Thames is not so much black as dark. It has always been called the "dark Thames," but darkness is not a colour or even the absence of colour. Perhaps the river has no colour. Which is as much as to say that, if it partakes of all colours, then perhaps it is colourless. There are times along the upper Thames when the absolute clearness of the water is its most surprising quality—"as sweet as milke, as clear as glasse," as the water-poet John Taylor put it in 1640. When the water settles it is generally clear at the top, sandy-brown in the middle, and a dirty olive colour at the bottom. And what colour do you call it when the plash of water beneath your boat seems to be amber—but then becomes dark green by the bank? What are the colours *between* the two? It is not amber or green, or black or grey, or even opal. It is a colour that no one can name. Some have called it the colour of death, all-enveloping. It is,

perhaps, the colour or no-colour of oblivion. Just as white light is the emanation of all colours, so the transparency of water is the quintessence of
everything. It is the natural presence of the world. It is unique but it has no
identity. It becomes what it beholds.

The light of the river is something that will never be seen on sea or
land. It can transform the landscape. At twilight the light of the river is a
soft grey, a lacustrine light, sometimes touched by the saffron tints of the
setting sun. Deep water emanates a light different from shallow water. The
river can appear a broad sheet of light, in some places and at some times,
while at others it is murky and confused. Sometimes the water within the
estuary of the Thames seems to be covered by a skin of phosphorescence,
and the brilliant surface of the water breaks into a thousand points of light
when it is disturbed.

The artists of the river are considered in the next chapter, but it is
worth remarking here that they have always been interested in these kinetic
qualities of Thames light. Stanley Spencer's *The Resurrection in Cookham
Churchyard*, just beside the Thames, is a hymn to light; the light on the wall
of the church seemed to Spencer to be the light that he saw when swimming
underwater. In other paintings, *Swan Upping* and *Christ Preaching at Cookham Regatta*, the light on the Thames is granted a mystical significance. It
is the holy presence or the substance of the river. Spencer once suggested
that the excitement of the holiday-makers in *Swan Upping* was that "for
them the climax in heaven lay in the sunlit continuation of the marsh meadows beyond the bend in the river."

In *Sunset on the River*, and other paintings of the Thames, Turner registers an impression of the overwhelming effect of the light lingering in the
sky; it is a continuation of the river or, rather, the Thames itself is a continuation of that effulgent and radiant light that inhabits creation. There is
no river in Turner without sky, the two sources of light reflecting one
another in a thousand fugitive and evanescent ways. For Turner the river
was an experiment, or a study, in light. That is why he was so deeply drawn
towards it. That is why it is the central subject of his art. Light was at the
core of the river. It was part of his purpose to elicit it and thus to celebrate it.

Yet how to paint water? It was a subject about which he thought hard
and deeply. It is no less than moving light, and therefore cannot be rendered as fixed and immobile upon a canvas. Water looks "like" movement.
When it is painted, it becomes some other thing. It is a question that Turner

only resolved when he scattered the world into a prism, into a mist of colour whose wreaths continually change tone and hue. When light becomes the transcendent fact of his painting, then the river acquires its natural power. The light of the Thames can be considered "pure" in implicit analogy with its waters. When Dorothy Wordsworth stood upon Westminster Bridge she noticed, in her journal for July 1802, that "the sun shone so brightly with such a pure light" that it entranced her. It was the river, even here, that made it pure.

As the Thames moves and mingles with London it becomes the most interesting light in the city. At night, with the reflection of the myriad lights above its surface, it comes alive. Then we have that phenomenon of the glitter of the river, that fugitive and mercurial scattering of light that is peculiar to water. The "silver Themmes" can become quicksilver, scattered across its shifting silver surface, and reflected below by streams of easy brightness descending into the ooze. The effect is that of stars, or constellations of stars, in the night sky. For some this is a cold light, a distant light, as cold as the depths of the waters themselves. This light is different in depth and texture from the soft light of the Upper Thames. The glittering is a warning not to come too close.

But, at night, the river can also become a pool of sleeping blackness. Once it has lost its sheen of silver, it becomes ink-dark and viscous. It is silent. It is as still as a river of the dead. In midstream it has a greenish hue, but the rest is purple or black. The shadows of the riverside buildings lend another tone of darkness, and the colour has faded from the city itself so that it is lost in the obscurity of the sky. This was the river, at least, for many centuries. Now, at the beginning of the twenty-first century, it is never wholly dark as it winds through London. The street-lights, and the lights blazing in innumerable buildings, keep it illuminated. Down by the estuary the vivid flaring lights of the treatment plants and refineries are like giant torches guiding it on its processional way to the sea. Only in the Upper Thames, and on certain stretches of the river by the marshes, is still the perfect pitch of darkness; only there is the water still black and silent.

The sounds of the river are as various as those of the natural and human worlds. It might seem unnaturally quiet in the estuarial region. Where once the river was filled with life and activity, there is now very little business upon the water. It has become in part an empty river, which imparts the illusion of silence. But there is still the flurry of the wake of tankers and of

small-engined boats crossing the flat surface like water-beetles. A little upriver, in the neighbourhood of Greenhithe or Tilbury, the noise of the
Thames is that of clangour or loud lament, with the sound of cranes and
other machinery fighting against the lap of the water and the raucous cries
of the seagulls.

In its upper reaches the Thames partakes of that peace which is always
associated with quiet or isolated waters. In that way it can be a balm and
restorative. Thoreau believed that by looking into water, the "earth's eye,"
"the beholder measures the depths of his own nature." This is the context
for the presumed silence of the river. It is a place for inward contemplation.
But it can never wholly be silent. The sounds of the world surround it—
the innumerable callings of birds, the wind in the branches overhanging the
water, the occasional splash of a fish, all these sounds have accompanied
the course of the river for millennia upon millennia before the onset of human time. If we could by an act of sympathetic magic return to that
unimaginable epoch, would the sound be the only familiar element?

Once the sun has set, the sounds of the night surround the river; the
leap of the fish is then more like a pistol shot than a splash, the leaves fall
upon the bank with a definite crack, the wind is louder and the noises of the
creeping creatures of the night seem very close.

In the human river, and in those stretches of it moving within London,
there is perpetual sound, even if only the waters lapping rhythmically
against the side of old wharves and docks. In the river of London, too,
there is the noise of the tide running against the banks. In the days of the
great docks the noise of commercial activity never stopped, night or day,
upon what was principally an industrial waterway. The hymn of the river
was then the bumping of bales and the hissing of steam, the riveting and
the scraping of keels, the shouting of orders through the night. On the
Embankment itself there were the boom of fog signals and the muffled
roar of motor-cars mixed with the whistle of the trains and the ringing of
the bells of the City churches. These were also the circumambient sounds
of the river, as if the Thames itself had become the echo-chamber of
the city.

It is sometimes forgotten how noisy the river once was in the centre of
the capital. In previous centuries, at night, it would have been heard in most
of the streets within the walls. George Borrow, in his novel *Lavengro*
(1851), dwelled upon the cacophony of the Thames:

there was a wild hurly-burly upon the bridge which nearly deafened me. But if upon the bridge there was confusion, below it was a confusion ten times compounded . . . Truly tremendous was the roar of the descending waters, and the bellow of the tremendous gulfs, which swallowed them for a time, and then cast them forth foaming and frothing from their horrid wombs.

The river had become a "roaring gulf," like the roar of the city all around it. In the same period Henry Mayhew chose in *London Labour and the London Poor* to hear the more soothing sounds of the Thames, with the airs of the "four bells" upon the ships mixed with "the tinkling of the distant purl-man's bell"; the "purl-man" was a purveyor of beer who worked upon the river, selling his product to the sailors and labourers. Mayhew also heard "the rattle of some chain let go" and "the chorus of many seamen heaving at the ropes" with "the hoarse voice of someone from the shore bawling through his hands to his mate aboard the craft in the river." This is the human voice of the river; its waters seem monstrous and "horrid," but its devotees or inhabitants issue a more sympathetic sound.

The smells of that earlier river, in the nineteenth and twentieth centuries, were legion. Some of them survive still. There was the smell of mud, exposed on the foreshore at low tide, strong and pungent. There was the smell of smoke or, rather, of the smoke-laden vapours that travelled up-river from the Port. It is not an unpleasing smell for those who savour the various products of humankind; it is redolent of energy and labour, somehow mixed with the melancholy pleasure of the bonfire. When people returned to London by way of London Bridge or Westminster Bridge, they were greeted with a familiar smoky aroma. There was the evocative scent of tar, always associated with shipping; it was the smell that Thomas Carlyle noticed when he first moved to Chelsea. By the dockside the odour of tar was mingled with those of hemp and of tow. And then there was always the scent of beer (or, shall we say, of barley and malt and hops) emanating from the huge breweries beside the Thames; the smell still lingers in Wandsworth, and fugitive odours have been gathered on the south bank near Southwark like the spectres of ancient manufacture.

The land of the Thames docks was the land of multitudinous odours. The atmosphere of pungent tobacco was succeeded by the more soporific aroma of rum; in some quarters the air was filled with the stench of hides, or of binfuls of horn, while from other parts emanated the smell of coffee or the savour of nutmeg and cinnamon. There are corners of Cinnamon Wharf, now a complex of apartments, where fugitive phantoms of that smell seem still to linger. The smell of softwood timber came from the Surrey Commercial Docks, while from Shad Thames came the smell of dog biscuits and the odour of Seville oranges. On the North Quay of the Isle of Dogs there was the smell of sugar, and on the South Quay of dates and tea. There was the smell of wine, and its various incarnations of sherry, port and brandy; there was the smell of oakum and of wool.

The upper reaches of the Thames are, in contrast, filled with the perfume of creation. Along the banks of the Upper Thames comes the smell of grass and of meadows, mingled with the peculiar dank richness of the water-meadows. It is an intoxicating mix of moisture and of growth. Here can be sensed the aromatic odour of sweet sedge and the sharper scent of the osier bark.

Does the river itself have its own smell? If it does, then it is an ancient one. Water itself has no smell, but all the associations and affiliations of the Thames have their own particular odour. It is, perhaps, the odour of the old. It smells of mud and weed and forgotten things. It smells of mould and of fungus. It smells of rotting wood. It smells of engine oil. It smells of metal. It is sometimes sharp. But it is also sometimes refreshing. It smells of the wind and the rain. It smells of storms. In some places it seems to smell of the sea. It smells of everything. It smells of nothing.

PART XII

The River of Art

Alexander Pope's villa at Twickenham

CHAPTER 37

Thames Art

❧

The earliest artists came to the river. There is a fifteenth-century engraving of the Thames beside the Tower, with London Bridge in the background; it is in fact one of the earliest engravings of London itself and this image of the turbulent water, with craft of all sizes upon it, is the harbinger of many representations of a river city. There can be no London without the Thames, and the first artists of the capital placed the river at the heart of their design. In 1558 Anthony van der Wyngaerde executed his panorama from the south bank; it showed the city from the Fleet River to London Bridge but, perhaps more significantly, it linked the north and south banks of the river with various lines of harmony. The city is seen to be flowing with the Thames. In his panorama there are boatmen and fishermen, as well as travellers waiting by the stairs at Stargate Horse Ferry. The "Braun and Hogenberg" map of the 1560s shows a representative group of Tudor Londoners looking down upon the Thames; the skiffs and wherries float upon the water in natural formation, while the line of the streets seems once more to reproduce the flow of the river. It was the best way of conveying the riverine nature of the city.

There is a woodcut by Abraham Saurs, dated 1608, which also depicts the river as the dominating presence; a three-masted galleon is sailing upriver towards London Bridge, and so are many smaller vessels. In 1616 Nicholas Visscher completed a view of London from Southwark. He also chose the Thames as the ground of his composition. In fact there is not one representation or panorama of London that does not yield the palm of significance to the Thames. The most famous of those panoramas, executed by Wenceslaus Hollar in the mid-seventeenth century, displays the river as the centre of activity and energy. The Thames itself is a great band of light uniting the composition, lending an air of power and monumentality to the city itself.

In the eighteenth century artists as diverse as Richard Wilson and William Marlow derived their inspiration from the river. Wilson portrayed the Thames at Richmond and at Twickenham, where the poets congregated, but he also completed a view of Westminster Bridge in the process of construction. His work displayed an idealised river, in much the same spirit as the sylvan verse of the period. He may be said to be the principal artist of the "London School," which might as well be renamed the "Thames School"; it included other eighteenth-century painters such as Samuel Scott and Marlow himself. There is a celebrated work by Scott, *The Entrance to the Fleet River*, which brings all the principles of elegant harmony to what was in reality an incommodious and insalubrious neighbourhood. The wherries and the barges lie in perspective formation, the reflection of their sails in the ruffled water; there are discreet hints of trade, with some bales of wool being transported downriver, but the general atmosphere is one of calm enjoyment. This is the river of Sir Richard Steele, too, who in an essay for the *Spectator* of 1712 dilated on the pleasures of riverine trade where "the banks on each side are well peopled, and beautified with as agreeable plantations, as any spot on earth; but the Thames itself, loaded with the produce of each shore, added very much to the landscape."

The work of Marlow and of Scott had in part been influenced by the Venetian master, Canaletto, who brought the light and life of his native city to the river. For much of his residence in London he stayed at the Duke of Richmond's house in Whitehall, and from that vantage completed many views of the river. He transformed the Thames into a luminous token of elegance and dignity, a force for civilisation comparable to the Tiber and the Seine. Two views painted in the 1740s, *The Thames from the Terrace of Somerset House, Westminster in the Distance* and *The Thames from the Terrace of Somerset House, the City in the Distance*, have become the emblems of calmness and clarity, magnificence and dignity. His was essentially an aesthetic view that removed the more heinous prospects of mercantile commerce and the business of trade, but it was a fitting adjunct to Pope's pastoral tribute in *Windsor Forest* (1713):

> No seas so rich, so gay no banks appear,
> No lake so gentle, and no spring so clear.

More than any other artist he fixed the image of the Thames in the eighteenth-century imagination. And his influence has not faded yet. One contemporary architect, Theo Crosby, wished to re-create the banks of London in accordance with what he described as "the Canaletto Axis" from the terrace of Somerset House. Canaletto set the seal on the notion of the Thames as a river of civilisation, a graceful and harmonious river not untouched by intimations of grandeur. It was the river tamed by aesthetics.

That vision is evident in the celebration of the "picturesque Thames," popularised by the publishers of albums and subscription volumes with titles such as "Tours of the Thames" and "Views of the Thames." There were three very popular collections of river prints in the latter half of the eighteenth century—Boydell's *Collection of Views* (1770), Ireland's *Picturesque Views on the River Thames* (1792) and Boydell's *History of the Thames* (1794–6)—which were largely concerned with the riverine views to the west of London Bridge. This was the area that had been partially reconstructed by Wren and had benefited from the eighteenth-century renovation of London itself.

Samuel Ireland's *Picturesque Views*, in which a series of charming drawings is accompanied by an anodyne text of no great literary or historical value, is sufficiently representative. But studies of this nature prompted a new generation of English travellers to explore the river, just as the "Grand Tour" of European sites was going out of fashion. Europe was effectively closed to English travellers in the 1790s, and from 1805 to 1815, and in these periods the delights of the national scene became even more apparent. To see the Thames was to understand an aspect of burgeoning national identity. The vogue in the late eighteenth and early nineteenth centuries for paintings of the Thames was the single most important dimension of the relatively new notion of painting from English nature. The Thames might even be said to have been the harbinger of "naturalism" in English art.

William Hogarth could not be accused of lending false enchantment to the Thames. He is more readily associated with the urban rather than the riverine world, but he chose to live in Chiswick by the banks of the Thames and was interred in the churchyard there. He depicted the Cockney river, of ribaldry and punishment. In one of his series of engravings, *The Effects of Industry and Idleness* (1747), the idle apprentice is shown by a Thames waterman the spectacle of Execution Dock, on the north bank of the Thames at Wapping in the East, where a dead pirate hangs in chains to await the tides. In retaliation the apprentice, Tom Idle, points out the stretch along the Thames known as Cuckold's Point and formerly Cuckold's Haven.

It was entirely characteristic of Hogarth's love of the more rumbustious river of the eighteenth century that, with a party of four friends, he made a river excursion from Billingsgate to Gravesend that seems to have been an extended drinking bout. They went down the river in a tilt-boat, shouting and drinking, exchanging jokes with the watermen and singing indecorous songs at the top of their voices; this can justly be described as a quintessential Thames scene. Thomas Rowlandson is in the same tradition, and his sketches of watermen in particular lend full weight to the reputation of Thames boatmen as coarse and expansive.

The name of Constable is not generally attached to the river, but he completed at least one painting of the Thames, in a view of the river upon the opening of Waterloo Bridge in 1817. The pre-eminent artist of the river remains J. M. W. Turner, who devoted much of his voluminous work to depictions of the Thames in all its manifold appearances from the calm serenity of the upper river to the dangers of the estuarial waters. There is hardly a part of the river that he did not paint—Folly Bridge, the London Pool, Nuneham Courtenay, Lambeth, Abingdon, Staines, Windsor, Wallingford. The whole world of the river came within his purview. He painted from boats and, while living at Ferry House in Isleworth, he built his own skiff for his Thames excursions. To re-employ a phrase of John Ruskin, he understood its language. It was the language of his painterly career.

Turner lived by the Thames all his life; he was born in 1775, in Maiden Lane, just off the Strand, from where a short stroll took him to the riverside. In *Modern Painters* (1843–60) Ruskin described his youth among "black barges, patched sails and every possible condition of fog . . . Forests of masts, ships with the sun on their sails, red-faced sailors with pipes appearing over the gunwales." From his earliest days Turner understood the human life and labour associated with the river. That is why in his depiction of the workers of the Thames, and of the farm labourers upon its banks, there is a deep consonance between the human figures and the riverscape. Even in his earliest studies he was intent upon describing what might be called the heterogeneous or egalitarian temper of the river; he noted the contrasts between the mansions and the waterworks, the yachts and the coal barges, the "silver" Thames and the grime.

He died by the river, in a bankside residence at Chelsea, and in the years between he moved between Brentford and Isleworth, Twickenham and Chiswick. His earliest biographer, Thornbury, noted that "on the banks of the Thames Turner began his art, on the banks of the Thames he lay down to die." He did literally begin his art by the river. His earliest exhibited picture, shown at the Royal Academy in 1790, was of a *View of the Archbishop's Palace, Lambeth*. In the last days of his life he was accustomed to sit upon the flat roof of his house in Chelsea, and watch the river in dawn light and in twilight. Towards the east was what he called "the Dutch view" and towards the west, upriver, "the English view."

He loved the river but, more importantly, he needed the river. It was an instrument of his vision and source of his inspiration. Turner was entranced by moving water, and by the reflections in water; he fixed for ever in his canvases the various lights that seem to emanate from the regions of the Thames. The luminous quality of his painting has often been remarked, and it is possible that his early experience of the river helped to formulate his mature sensibility. The light of the hour before twilight, the golden hour, is the one that he most conscientiously sought.

His watercolour sketches of the river look as if they had been imbued with the light of the Thames, as if the water had washed over the paper and left its radiance there. He manages to evoke, too, the quickness and fluidity of the river; a cloud passes across the sun, a tree rattles in the breeze. The flow of the natural world—the flow of his paint—reproduces the flow of the river. In that sense the river becomes a unifying force, connecting the artist and the landscape. In some of the sketches there is nothing but the river glowing on the page of the sketchbook, an image of tranquillity and purity. It has been said that Turner was "rebaptised" by his artistic immersion in the water, and it is true that in his sketches he traces the old association between the river and spiritual grace.

His oil paintings are generally of a more majestic temper, however, so that *England: Richmond Hill, on the Prince Regent's Birthday* offers the view of the river as an emblem of national harmony and abundant peace. From his experience of the Thames he acquired a sense of history; he was naturally of an antiquarian temper, loving ruins and ancient stone, and in the sheer presence of the river he could discern the contours of old time. The Thames prompts within him intimations of ancientness, which is why he could place Dido and Aeneas upon its banks. On some occasions he even calls the Thames "Isis" in veneration of that ancient deity. But he also goes further back. In some of the sketches the river seems to revert to its prehistoric origins, with its marshes and its ancient trees.

So he had a deep, and instinctive, notion of the river. When he painted nymphs beside the Thames he was intuitively following one of the archetypes of the river; they have always been the attendant spirits or divinities of the water, honoured by the Hebrews as well as the Greeks and Romans. The mythological as well as the natural aspects of the Thames guided his pencil and his brush; he could see into the heart of things. He had dreams, and visions, by the river.

William Etty lived for much of his life, in the early decades of the nineteenth century, in a house on the corner of Buckingham Street; he overlooked the Thames, and one of his most celebrated paintings is that of the Thames at Chelsea. When he was in Italy he confessed that he "could not bear to desert old father Thames." He had an affection for the river that generally touches those who live beside it. "I love to watch its ebb and flow," he once said. "It has associations connected with life not unedifying." But is it not life itself? There are numerous other nineteenth-century painters who depicted the river—Collins, Callcott, Stanfield as well as a whole genre of "marine painters" who took as their special inspiration the congregation of vessels small and large around London Bridge and its environs.

Other painters did not necessarily portray the Thames, but were nevertheless drawn to live beside its banks. Zoffany lived near Kew, and is supposed to have used the fishermen of the Thames as the models for the Apostles in his depiction of the Last Supper. Kneller retired to Twickenham. Holman Hunt spent his last years in the Thameside village of Sonning. It seems deeply appropriate to spend old age by the Thames and to die beside the ever flowing river. Thomas Gainsborough never lived beside the river, but he requested that he should be buried by the Thames at Kew.

The Pre-Raphaelites—among them Dante Gabriel Rossetti, John Millais and Edward Burne-Jones—all lived by the river for some period of their artistic careers. But of that generation only James McNeill Whistler can be deemed a riverine artist who, in his series of *Nocturnes*, cast the veil of troubled twilight over the London waters. His is the river of mystery, the river that inspired the novelists of the nineteenth and early twentieth centuries with intimations of enchantment; it is the river as reverie, as inspirer of dreams lending a fitful luminescence to the city itself. Yet in his series of etchings, *Thames Set*, he illustrated the working banks of the river from a characteristically low viewpoint, as if he were standing on the foreshore or sitting in a wherry experiencing all the dirt and pungency of the commercial Thames. From this vantage it is a world of mud, and planks, and bales, and what Charles Baudelaire described as "wonderful tangles of rigging, yardarms and rope." Whistler had in fact been inspired by Baudelaire's challenge to create "a new art of the river" as part of the art of the city. Baudelaire had been referring to the Seine, but for Whistler the archetypal urban river was the Thames.

He dwelled for many years by the river in Chelsea, at various addresses, but on his arrival in England he lived among the sailors and dockers of Rotherhithe and Wapping. He drew the longshoremen and the prostitutes of the area, so that he might be said to have created an entire riverine world quite apart from the nineteenth-century city. The river changed his style, too, from the realism of the *Thames Set* (1860s) to the aestheticism of the *Nocturnes* (1870s). It is reported that for the latter he would be rowed to a point in the Thames that he found suitable; he would then contemplate the watery scene, and memorise its composition, before returning to his studio and starting work. It is perhaps significant that he is now buried in the same churchyard as William Hogarth, beside the river at Chiswick.

The river can itself be deemed a work of art. A German traveller of the eighteenth century, Karl Philipp Moritz, found the banks of the Thames "fascinating"; what made the riverine scenery "so magically beautiful" was "the blending of everything into a composition that ensures a peaceful prospect. There is no spot on which the eye does not long lovingly to rest." In his *History of the River Thames* (1794–6) William Combe wrote that the hills of the Thames landscape "rise not to the clouds, but sink into the pastures, or pursue each other in pleasing perspective . . . and alluring shade"; between Greenwich and Woolwich there is the prospect "of bold undulating ground." In nineteenth-century studies it was recommended that

Thames walkers stood in certain pre-arranged positions in order to view the most appropriate scene—so that, for example, a lock might "compose well" with a weir. The villages along the Thames were also known for their "picturesqueness." Many professional painters earned a competent living by specialising in Thames "views," and of course there were hordes of amateur artists who spent their holidays sketching and painting by the banks. Some places, such as Shiplake Lock, were painted over and over again; Shiplake, according to the early Thames photographer Henry Taunt, had "all the makings of a picture in its composition." There is every reason to believe that the Thames is the most painted river in the world.

The Thames was "captured" many times by professional photographers from the nineteenth century forward. Photographs of water scarcely resemble water; the liquid element cannot be "frozen" in time, because of course it loses its essential being. The nature of reflections in water, however, favours photographic reproduction; the stillness supports them, and the immobility maintains them.

One of the moods conjured by the river is that of melancholy or nostalgia, so it is perhaps not surprising that many anthologies of Thames photographs have somewhat wistful titles such as *Forgotten Thames, London's Lost Riverscape* or—more optimistically—*London's Riverscape Lost and Found*. There is still much interest in Victorian photographs of the river, with images of wooden locks long since dismantled, of "shooting parties" on the water, of ancient weirs, and of mills demolished more than a century ago. The Thames was of course then more heavily used and populated, with an enormous number of craft to be seen upon its waters, but there is still the intense pleasure of continuity. There are many stretches where the view remains precisely the same, and this is nowhere more apt than in the images of the ancient bridges that cross the upper Thames.

The river has also been compared to a scenic theatre, and there are river scenes at Abingdon and Nuneham that have been described as closely resembling some stage-set of the early twentieth century. According to Charles Harper's *Thames Valley Villages* (1910) the riverine view is almost "impossibly picturesque," with the illusion that behind it is "merely canvas and framework." In that sense the aesthetic effects of the river may be said to divest it of its life.

The list of twentieth-century artists who have painted the Thames is endless—from Monet and Kokoschka to Pasmore. Some contemporary artists paint nothing else. As one Thames painter of the late nineteenth century, Walter Greaves, put it, "I never seemed to have any ideas about painting. The river *made* me do it." Paul Nash was enchanted, not to say obsessed, by the two hills overlooking the Thames known as the Wittenham Clumps. He wrote that "ever since I remember them the clumps have meant something to me. I felt their importance long before I knew their history . . . they were the pyramids of my small world." He first depicted them in 1912, and continued to paint them. They emerge in such paintings as *Landscape of the Summer Solstice*, *Landscape of the Vernal Equinox* and *Landscape of the Moon's Last Phase*. He believed the area of Wittenham by the river to be a "beautiful legendary country haunted by old gods long forgotten," and sensed a "Pan-eish enchantment."

Of all twentieth-century artists, however, Stanley Spencer is the one most associated with the river. His enduring and everlasting subject is Cookham, a small village by the banks of the Thames between Marlow and Cliveden. The Holy Trinity Church was first erected here in 1140, on the site of a Saxon foundation; the inn, the Bell and Dragon, was established in the early fifteenth century. A wooden bridge was built in 1840, but was replaced by an iron version in 1867. Spencer was so identified with this place that, as a student of the Slade School of Fine Art, his nickname was "Cookham." He took a phrase from William Morris, another artist of the river, and called the neighbourhood "an earthly paradise." The river became a token of Eden, like the original rivers that flowed throughout the world.

Spencer was also one of those artists of the Thames characterised by a profound egalitarianism—not the socialism of William Morris or the Cockney pugnacity of Turner, but what might be called the spiritual democracy of the humble soul. He had a reverence for the human form in an almost Blakean sense, and understood the holiness of creation. This, too, is part of the inheritance of the river. He said of his youthful experience that "we swim and look at the bank over the rushes. I swim right in the pathway of sunlight. I go home to breakfast thinking as I go of the beautiful wholeness of the day. During the morning I am visited, and walk about being in that visitation." The allusion here to the sunlight reaffirms Spencer's concern with the nature of light; some of his paintings, like those of Turner, are imbued with its sacredness. The river emanates light, both as a material and as an intellectual power. The light brings fertility, and lends form, to the natural world; but it is also the symbol of the understanding. The river *is* light; it is liquid light. For Spencer, as for Turner and other riverine artists, it is the halo of eternity.

His immersion in the river, in the waters of the path of sunlight, reawakens his sense of the sacred. It has justly been said that in his work, and in his observations, Spencer is reverting to some pagan source of the Christian faith. But by what more appropriate agency than the river itself, that has welcomed pre-Christian and Christian ritual? He wrote to Edward Marsh, who had purchased his painting of *Cookham 1914*, that he was aware of "a new and personal value of the Englishness of England"; his life by the Thames awakened that sense.

Spencer always recalled his childhood by the river. *Swan Upping at Cookham*, depicting one of the ancient rituals of the Thames, seems to have the clairvoyance and over-brightness of childhood memory. He himself said of the work that "when I thought of people going on the river at that moment my mind's imagination of it seemed to be an extension of the church atmosphere." So the Thames becomes a church, just as its status as a sacred place is maintained in paintings such as the unfinished *Christ Preaching at Cookham Regatta* and *The Baptism* in which Christ is being baptised in the holy river. One of his earliest drawings shows a fairy, or faery, sitting on a water-lily leaf upon the Thames. His sister recalled that the place chosen was part of the bank where the Spencer children once played; his infant vision is restored.

In *The Resurrection, Cookham* the Thames is seen in the top left-hand corner as a band of light—a "bar of gold," to use William Blake's phrase— upon which a group of travellers sail towards the dawn sun. Of the passengers in the steam launch Spencer said that "the climax in heaven lay in the sunlit continuation of the marsh meadows beyond the bend in the river." This is very much like his childhood memory of swimming in the path of the sunlight, and suggests how much his own experience of the Thames formed his mature artistic vision. So what is the nature of his work? He combines a dream-like extravagance with a visionary simplicity and a sense of timelessness. All of these attributes are elicited by the river. The artist Isaac Rosenberg once wrote of Spencer that "his pictures have that sense of everlastingness, of no beginning and no end, that we get in all master- pieces." Rosenberg here might be defining the river itself, without begin- ning and without end; the congruence suggests that the river is the form as well as the content of Spencer's inspiration.

Artists such as Greaves and Spencer are as closely associated with the river as their seventeenth- and eighteenth-century counterparts; if the river represents continuity of any kind, it represents continuity of inspiration. In all of its manifestations it is the same river, with demonstrably the same banks and the same dimensions; yet it has become so various in its manifestations that, like Proteus, it seems to change its identity without changing its essential nature. It is as if the artist saw a true reflection in the moving water of the Thames.

CHAPTER 38

The Words of the River

༘

The literature of the river is voluminous. Some of it is skittish and whimsical, some of it profound. There are many books, inspired by the Thames, that are explicitly or implicitly written for children. Once again the river is associated with innocence. The river elicits dream narratives. It also encourages stories of embarkation and separation. And of course it provokes the themes of time, fate and destiny. There seems to be a tendency, in the writers of prose, to break into verse in the course of their narratives—as if the river itself elicited a less than prosaic response. The actual descriptions of river journeys are in fact more eventful, more replete with meaning, than the calm physical experience of the Thames. In that sense it has become a river of words, endlessly created and re-created by the writers who have voyaged upon it.

The writers of the early twentieth century use the river as a commentary upon the ravages of time and the decline of earlier values—even though the modern world which they abhor has, in turn, become a blessed past of which we regret the passing. Thus in the second volume of *Thames Valley Villages* (1910) Charles G. Harper excoriates the sounds of the contemporaneous world impinging upon the calm of the Middlesex bank of the river with "the strains of a piano organ, the cries of the hawkers, or the squeaking of tramcar-wheels against curves." Who, in the twenty-first century, would not like to hear those sounds? The sighing of the wind through the trees, and the splash of water by the banks, remain simply the same. The noises of another age would in contrast be deeply exciting. The Thames plays strange tricks with time.

The prose accounts of rivers have an ancient history. The first volume entirely devoted to the subject seems to have been that of Ctesias, court physician to Artaxerxes Memnon, who was writing at the beginning of the fourth century BC. Three hundred years later the first Chinese study of the rivers appeared, and was eventually to be known as "the Waterways Classic"; when the book was revised in the sixth century AD, it had grown immeasurably in length.

We may date the first English accounts of rivers, however, to the sixteenth and early seventeenth centuries in the works of Leland, Camden and Harrison. There had been incidental references to the Thames before that time by historical chroniclers, such as Bede and Gildas, but there had been no serious or sustained account of the river. John Leland may be described as the first professional traveller, whose *Itinerary* became a model and an inspiration for his contemporaries. In the spring of 1542 he progressed along the Thames Valley, and left observations upon the riverside towns of Maidenhead and Reading, Faringdon and Wallingford. His was an anecdotal and perambulatory style, a collection of notes rather than a coherent narrative. Nevertheless he contributed material of immense interest to those who are concerned with the history of the Thames:

> Two or three miles after crossing the River Burne I came to the timber bridge over the Thames at Maidenhead. A little above the bridge on this bank of the Thames I saw a cliff overhanging the river with some bushes growing on it. I conjectured that this had been the site of some ancient building. There is a large wharf for timber and firewood at the west end of the bridge . . .

Leland has some claim to being the progenitor of modern English history, but he was also the first English writer to formulate the river poem in *Cygnea Cantio* (1545). He wished to create a river that would coexist on the levels of mythology, literature and history. In this poem the Thames is described as *"nympharum gloria prima"*—the "most glorious of the nymphs" descended from Hesiod and from Homer.

That is why the introduction of the Thames in his *Itinerary* is more than the product of incidental observation; after the Dissolution of the Monasteries he became Henry VIII's court antiquarian, charged with the labour of preserving fragments and records of what had already become a ruined history. It was this, perhaps, that eventually drove him to madness. But his especial love and regard for the river, as an historical as well as a literary force, prompted him to invest great symbolic significance in the very fact and course of the Thames. For him it represented an historical landscape that still existed, flowing beside the ruined abbeys and the churches and maintaining the identity of the kingdom. The Thames became a witness to the past that was in danger of being altogether destroyed.

This gives all the more power and poignancy to his prose descriptions of the Thames in the *Itinerary*:

> three miles above Maidenhead on the Berkshire bank of the Thames is Bisham Priory, and a further mile upstream is Hurley, a cell of Westminster Abbey. On the Buckinghamshire side there was a priory of nuns at Little Marlow, two miles above Maidenhead . . . One mile up the river above Bisham, on the Buckinghamshire side, is Medmenham, a cell of Woburn Abbey in Bedfordshire.

Bisham Abbey was "dissolved"; the priory of Hurley was suppressed; the last prioress of the nunnery at Little Marlow, Margaret Vernon, had gone by the early 1540s; Woburn Abbey was granted to Sir John Russell in 1547. As Leland observed, and wrote about, the sacred edifices of the Thames they were being destroyed or converted or pillaged. Only the Thames offered continuity.

Leland's notes, unfinished by reason of his lunacy, were then taken up by John Camden and William Harrison. Harrison in the *Description of the Islande of Britayne* (1587), and Camden, in his *Britannia* (1586), continued Leland's topographical work in a more voluminous and extensive manner. The eleventh chapter of the *Description of the Islande of Britayne* is entitled "The Description of the Thames, and such Riuers as Fall into the Same." Of the Thames Harrison writes that "I must needs content my selfe with such obseruations as I haue either obtained by mine owne experience, or gathered from time to time out of other mens writings." His is a notably more restrained account than that of Leland, eschewing mythic complexity for the pleasures of observation. He dismisses legends, and the work of armchair topographers such as Polydore Vergil. He relies to a large extent upon the poetry of fact. Harrison is the first, for example, to give an accurate account of the double tides upon the Thames. He also adds incidental detail which is all the more convincing for being apparently random—"after a great landfloud, you shall take haddocks with your hands beneath the [London] bridge, as they flote aloft vpon the water, whose eies are so blinded with the thicknesse of that element that they cannot see where to become." He describes the "infinit number of swans daillie to be seene vpon this riuer," and imparts the interesting information that there are two thousand wherries and small boats upon the Thames that maintain some three thousand poor watermen. He is the first accurate chronicler of the Thames.

In his *Britannia* Camden moves between landscape and riverscape and history so that all of them cohere within his central vision of the Thames as the agent of unity. His narrative crackles with history and with historical reference; whereas Leland's vision was one of barely suppressed dissolution and dismay, that of Camden is replete with references suggesting that the past is still enshrined within the contours of the present. So he will state that "crossing the river, and returning to the source of the Thames and the mouth of the Severn, shall visit the DOBUNI who formerly occupied the present Gloucester and Oxford shires." He is identifying the river with the ancient past of England. The Thames becomes a principle of historical order no less than an aspect of English topography.

It is impossible adequately to quote from a narrative so dense and specific, with the allusions moving rapidly from the ancient tribes of the regions to the reigns of Henry V or Edward III, from the derivation of the names of towns to the quality of the local pastureland. It is an encyclopaedia, a compendium and an anthology rather than a topography, but it has one clear theme—the Thames is the great unifying force which encompasses everything. It makes everything cohere.

The river also acts as the line of narrative, so that Camden will follow its course from county to county in order to rehearse the events that happened along its shores. The Thames leads him forward, prompting him into speech and celebration. Like so many writers of the river Camden introduces verse within his prose narrative, and in one section composes a poem entitled *De Connubio Tamae et Isis*—"On the Marriage of the Thame and Isis." In this poem Camden's Muse travels from Reading to Windsor, from Richmond to Kent, and from Gloucester to Oxford. It is not topographically accurate but, in terms of Camden's concern with natural progress and historical change, it is imaginatively precise. The fact that both Leland and Camden use a mixture of verse and prose to elucidate the meaning of the river is in itself interesting—it suggests that their work can accommodate the poetry of vision and the prose of history, and that somehow the river itself is full and vital enough to embrace both concepts. The river of vision and the river of history are thus the same river, running through their books.

From his prison window in the Tower Sir Walter Raleigh could see as far as Blackfriars Stairs, and the stretch of the Thames from there to the place of his incarceration. He spent twelve years in close association with the river, having been sentenced in 1603, and in that long period of forced propinquity wrote his *History of the World* (1614) in which the river becomes a central part of his design. In the beginning of his study, the four rivers of Paradise are a metaphor for separation, and for decline from the source or Eden; yet the flowing water is also an emblem of historical destiny or what at a later date would be called historical necessity. The rushing water is an image of fate. In his historical account the progress of humankind is the progress of the river. Nimrod tells his followers "to resort and succour one another by the river." The first cities of the world were built by rivers so that "Nineveh, Charran, Reseph, Canneh, Ur in Chaldea, and the other first peopled cities, were all founded upon these navigable rivers, or their branches." In this profound intuition, he has subsequently been proved correct. Noah, surmounting the Flood, is the paradigm or archetype of later men who "lived safely upon the waters." The river thus becomes the central fact of human history, and it might be observed that Noah in his Ark resembles Raleigh in his prison cell overlooking the waters of the Thames. In his eight volumes he had only reached 130 BC, but within those volumes he had charted the flow of history.

His nickname, given to him by Elizabeth I, was "Water." While living at Durham House, overlooking the Thames, he had dreamed of the rivers of the golden Americas. The Thames might have become for him the Orinoco. For Raleigh the sixteenth-century Thames was an image of human destiny and of modern life. Who came there but sovereigns, and travellers, and explorers, and merchants? So the image of the river as the highway of life deeply imprinted itself upon his imagination. There is one irony. The river affected Raleigh's own history in a highly individual manner. After a period of house arrest, as a result of the failure of the expedition to find Orinoco gold, he attempted in 1618 to escape downriver from Tower Dock to the open sea. But he or his mariners had miscalculated the tide; they could not reach so far as Gravesend, returned to Greenwich and, floundering there, were taken. He had been thwarted by the Thames itself.

There are many stray literary associations with the Thames. Samuel Richardson lived in a house by the river at Parson's Green; Fielding wrote *Tom Jones* at Twickenham, by the river in Holly Road, while Francis Bacon lived in the original Twickenham Park in 1593. R. D. Blackmore wrote *Lorna Doone* while living at Teddington, and Gay wrote *The Beggar's Opera* at Ham. Edward Gibbon was born by the river at Putney; he went to school there and at Kingston-upon-Thames.

The characters of fiction—outcasts such as Magwitch and Dr. Fu-Manchu among them—also live and have their being beside the river. Of Fu-Manchu, Sax Rohmer wrote, in *The Book of Fu-Manchu* (1929), that the Thames was "his highway, his line of communication along which he moved his mysterious forces . . . Always he made his headquarters upon the river." It is not generally recalled that sections of Bram Stoker's melodrama, *Dracula* (1897), are set in the estuarial regions of the Thames. Dracula crossed at this low stretch of the river, on his way to Bermondsey after being denied access to his house at Purfleet. He would have hastened down Purfleet Stairs and taken the ferry at low tide to the south bank at some time before one o'clock in the morning. It was of course said of the vampire that "he can only pass running water at the slack or the flood of the tide." The Purfleet Stairs remained, near the Royal Hotel, until recent times.

It is from the vantage of the estuary that Stoker described the setting for one of the undead, with "the wonderful smoky beauty of a sunset over London, with its lurid lights and inky shadows and all the marvellous tints that come on foul clouds even as on foul water." Jonathan Harker had found for the count a house at Purfleet, on a by-road, surrounded by "a high wall, of ancient structure built of heavy stones"; in its grounds were many trees as well as a "deep-dark-looking pond or small lake, evidently fed by some springs." This is the landscape of the estuary.

Some of the greatest writers of the Thames in fact belong to the nineteenth century. We may refrain from placing Pierce Egan in their company, although his *Pilgrims of the Thames* (1839) was exceedingly popular in the author's lifetime; it is a mixture of prose and verse that, as we have seen, is the inevitable literary accompaniment to the Thames. And it is couched in Egan's vivacious and picaresque style, perfectly suited to the taste of the early nineteenth century public for whom "the THAMES—Old Father Thames—and his next door neighbour, the Ocean, combine every thing that must please and attract the coldest spectator; but to a cockney, a man born in London, if you like the expression better, unutterable delight and satisfaction."

For the true music of the nineteenth century we must turn to the great symbolic novelist of that century, Charles Dickens. For Dickens the Thames was essentially a river of tears and of darkness. In his earliest journalistic essays, when he was in fact imitating the style of popular urban writers such as Pierce Egan, he described the "fun" of the Thames in accounts of steam excursions and other riverine escapades. But his experience of the river was deeper and darker than that of any willed optimism. He had lost his hope beside the Thames. At the age of twelve he was put to work in a blacking factory by the river, Warren's Blacking of 30 Hungerford Stairs. It is not too much to say that this "crazy, tumbledown old house, abutting of course on the river," as he described it later in a private memoir, haunted his imagination. It becomes the mouldering house in *Nicholas Nickleby* (1839) beside a Thames wharf; it becomes the summerhouse overlooking the Thames in *The Old Curiosity Shop* (1841), "sapped and undermined by the rats"; in *Oliver Twist* (1838) it becomes Bill Sikes's lair at Jacob's Island by Bermondsey.

The river runs through Dickens's fiction just as it runs through the city itself. This is the river which in an essay, "Down with the Tide" (1853), he characterises as "lapping at piles and posts and iron rings, hiding strange things in its mud, running away with suicides and accidentally drowned bodies faster than midnight funeral should . . . this river looks so broad and vast, so murky and silent, seems such an image of death in the midst of the great city's life." No previous writer had so well captured the lachrymose and minatory aspects of the river. It was the river of secrets, the river of mist and fog, the river of night and thus the river of mystery. In *Bleak House* (1853) the Thames "had a fearful look, so overcast and secret, creeping away so fast between the low flat lines of shore: so heavy with indistinct and awful shapes, both of substance and shadow: so deathlike and mysterious." It carries the weight of London somewhere within it, so vast and so dark and so wild, and in "Night Walks" (1860), an essayistic threnody of the city gloom, Dickens describes how "the very shadow of the immensity of London seemed to lie oppressively upon the river."

It is hard to think of a single novel by Dickens where the Thames is not present, carrying the weight of the novelist's obsession; yet he understood its nature intimately, too, and you could always be sure he knew in which direction the tide was moving. It is an important element of *Great Expectations* (1861). He once wrote that he was concerned to present "the romantic side of familiar things" but his vision of the Thames goes beyond romance and melodrama. By instinct or indirection it is linked with the ancient history of the Thames as a grave and as a place of sacrifice.

In this context the most powerful of his riverine novels is *Our Mutual Friend* (1865), with its opening on the Thames between Southwark Bridge and London Bridge. Gaffer Hexam and his daughter, Lizzie, are in a "boat of dirty and disreputable appearance"—the girl rowing while her father looks out for the corpses of the drowned. The surface of the river is covered with "slime and ooze," and its waters are dark. Lizzie looks upon it with "dread or horror." This is the primaeval river, alien to human life; Dickens might have been describing the Styx or Acheron. In another of his essays, "Wapping Workhouse" (1861), there is a description of a young man staring across the water at Wapping Old Stairs "with a puffed sallow face, and a figure all dirty and shiny and slimy, who may have been the youngest son of his filthy old father, Thames." He seemed like an "apparition" to Dickens, and indeed there is more than a resemblance here to the figure of the drowned man taken from the depths. The "apparition" has become a guardian spirit, or votary, of the river. *Our Mutual Friend*, too, is a story of resurrection—particularly of resurrection from the waters of the river. Some are lost in its depths; some rise again. The significance of Dickens's understanding of the river lies in his conflation of ancient myth and urban reality, so that the old powers of the Thames (perhaps perceived by Dickens when he was a small child) are given expressive reality in the context of the polluted and miasmal river of the nineteenth century.

His only successor in the late nineteenth, and early twentieth, centuries was Joseph Conrad, who understood the darker aspects of the Thames. He had a working knowledge of the river, having been employed as a merchant seaman for many years, but for him the river was the guardian of older secrets. As Marlow said in *The Heart of Darkness* (1899), when looking at the waters of the Thames by Gravesend, "this, also, has been one of the dark places of the earth." It is an abiding memory of the Thames. In a more recent novel, *Downriver* (1991), Iain Sinclair invokes the "wooden stumps in the mud. The ruin of a jetty. The tide was turning: a slime-caked causeway, plastered in filth and sediment, pointed at Gravesend. He often boasted, without much justification, that Magwitch faltered here, escaping from the hulks; and was brought to shore." To the wary traveller, the stretch of water here is filled with ghost images, treacherous and hazardous, out of Conrad and Dickens and all those who have sensed the darkness of the Thames.

In Conrad's novel Marlow and his companion looked at the river "not in the vivid flush of a short day that comes and departs for ever, but in the august light of abiding memories." The air above Gravesend was "dark, and farther back still seemed condensed into a mournful gloom"; the gloom lay above London, as an impression of that city, but still "the very mist on the Essex marshes was like a gauzy and radiant fabric, hung from the wooded rises inland, and draping the low shores in diaphanous folds."

In his volume of "memories and impressions," *The Mirror of the Sea* (1906), Conrad devotes many pages to the experience of the Thames estuary. For him it evinced a "strange air of mysteriousness" which is associated with its historical presence; it was that part of the river first glimpsed by Roman galleys, and indeed by those first visitors from the newly estranged landmass of the European continent. On the banks of the estuary Conrad observed "slightly domed roofs . . . as if it were a village of Central African huts imitated in iron." There is another intimation here of *The Heart of Darkness*, suggesting that the Thames still possessed a primitive or primeval aspect. So Marlow, in that novel, expands on the darkness.

He imagines a Roman citizen voyaging along the river for the first time. For him the Thames would have seemed "the very end of the world, a sea the colour of lead, a sky the colour of smoke . . . sand-banks, marshes, forests, savages." In these terms he invokes the riverscape as one of horror "in the midst of the incomprehensible, which is also the detestable." And it has a fascination, too, that goes to work upon him. "The fascination of the abomination—you know, imagine the growing regrets, the longing to escape, the powerless disgust, the surrender, the hate." The alien nature of the river has never been more powerfully evoked. It might almost be the river before human memory.

Conrad believed that, of all the rivers of Britain, the Thames "is the only one I think open to romantic feeling"; in his lifetime the banks downriver were largely deserted, provoking "the suggestion of mysterious vastness caused by the configuration of the shore." It was a sensation all the more acute since, no more than 25 miles away, there stood the largest city on the face of the earth. It is a sensation that can still be enjoyed, in the early morning or evening light, if you sail down from Gravesend towards the open sea. In the vastness of the river by the estuary Conrad observed that the "traffic of the port," the myriad craft on the water, "becomes insignificant"; in more recent times, when that traffic has diminished beyond reckoning, the sense of emptiness is almost overwhelming. There are occasions, particularly late at night, when you may believe yourself to be aboard the only boat on the river.

The other chroniclers, or votaries, of the late Victorian and Edwardian river are imbued with a sense of mystery rather than a sense of savagery or of terror. This may be in part due to the new role which the Thames played in the consciousness of the age, as an avenue of recreation rather than of trade; but it must be in large measure because Kenneth Grahame, Lewis Carroll and Jerome K. Jerome had moved upriver from the estuary and the Pool of London with their attendant shadows.

Jerome was essentially a comic chronicler in the *Punch* mould, but one who all his life was affiliated with the Thames. He lived along stretches of the river at various times of his life. In the 1860s he lived in Narrow Street, Limehouse, for example, and then in later life moved to a new apartment block a few yards north of Battersea Bridge. In his memoirs he wrote that "most of my life, I have dwelt in the neighbourhood of the river," and indeed he is another of those who need to remain close to the Thames. He asked that his ashes be buried in the churchyard at Ewelme, a small village not very far from the river in Oxfordshire.

His *Three Men in a Boat* (1889) was originally supposed to be a topographical and historical guide to the Thames, but by indirection or design it turned into a comic masterpiece. The three travellers embark at Kingston for the journey upriver. But although it is predominantly a voyage of farce and pantomime, there are elements of the dream fugue within it as Jerome meditates upon the historical past and upon the spirits of the river. The rain falling upon the water has "the sound as of a woman weeping low as in some dark chamber" while the woods alongside the river "stand like ghosts upon the margin . . . a spirit-haunted water through the land of vain regrets." There are stretches of the river that for him are replete with "van-ished forms and faces." It is that note of regretfulness, of loose and senti-mental nostalgia, that keeps on breaking through the overt gaiety of the narrative. That is why, throughout the book, the adults behave like children.

Childhood is often associated with the river. The water nymph, Leu-cothea, was also the patroness of childbirth. In Charles Kingsley's *The Water Babies* (1863), the Thames becomes a perpetual playground for chil-dren. Its refrain is "Play by me, bathe in me, mother and child." In early photographs of the river, particularly in its London stretches, there seem always to be children upon the foreshore—playing, swimming or search-ing. In the 1937 panorama of the river, commissioned by the Port of Lon-don Authority, there are the figures of children to be seen at Gun Wharf and Eagle Wharf, Foundry Wharf and Snowdon's Wharf; there seems to be a tiny mud-lark scrutinising the river at Wapping New Stairs. Wherever there was access to the river, the children gathered. There used to be a plea-sure beach beside Tower Bridge, where the children also played. And at low tide, Gabriel's Reach in Southwark still possesses a stretch of sand where children meet.

But of course there are dangers in the river. By the early twentieth cen-tury access to the river by means of the ancient watermen's stairs had been largely denied, for fear of the children drowning in the sometimes treach-erous waters. There is a notice still to be seen at the top of some stairs, "Children Must Not Play on These Steps." There was a legend, at Eton, that a boy would be drowned in the Thames every third year. The bodies of children have often been dumped in the river. Innocence, and the death of innocence, are part of the story of the Thames.

Infancy is connected with the return of involuntary memories. That is why the river of remembrance is also the river of childhood. In Carroll and in Jerome and in Grahame it is the river of infantilism and of reversion to an earlier state of enchantment. If we may employ the language of the late nineteenth century, it is the gate into a far-off land. In the immediate vicin-ity of the river, adults may become children again. The Thames becomes the nurse, or the mother, in whose embrace the old can dream of bliss. So on the cool and rather wet afternoon of 4 July 1862, when Charles Lutwidge Dodgson took the three small daughters of Dean Liddell boat-ing upon the Thames, upriver from Oxford to Godstow, he began to ex-temporise a story on the adventures of Alice underground. Instead of his

customary clerical black he wore white flannel trousers, like T. S. Eliot's
Prufrock.

A companion on this trip, Robin Duckworth, who rowed stroke as
Dodgson rowed bow, recalled that "the story was actually composed and
spoken *over my shoulder* for the benefit of Alice Liddell." "Is this an extem-
pore romance of yours?" Duckworth asked. "Yes," Dodgson replied, "I'm
inventing it as we go along." Dodgson and the children would sometimes
picnic on Lock Wood Island, an eyot in the middle of the river, and sometimes in the bankside woods of Nuneham Park. Alice Liddell explained in
later life that "most of Mr. Dodgson's stories were told to us on river expeditions to Nuneham or Godstow." There "we were told stories after lun-
cheon that transported us into Fairyland." If she had been acquainted with
the mythology of the river, she would have known that she was there
already.

And so the narrative begins: "Alice was beginning to get very tired of
sitting by her sister on the bank . . ." The original version of *Alice's Adventures in Wonderland*, a manuscript story entitled "Alice's Adventures Under
Ground" (1864), had made more specific reference to its origin. The pool
of Alice's tears, in the first chapter, becomes by some strange process of association a version of the Thames; it becomes a river "fringed with rushes
and forget-me-nots," just like the Thames at Godstow, so that we may
speak of a river of tears.

At the conclusion of the original version, too, Alice has a vision of the
Thames at Oxford. "She saw an ancient city, and a quiet river winding near
it along the plain, and up the stream went slowly gliding a boat with a
merry party of children on board—she could hear their voices and laughter like music over the water . . ." The kinship of the river and innocence,
of the river and purity, could not be better expressed. But this vision of the
river is touched by regret and nostalgia as "the boat wound slowly along,
beneath the bright summer day, with its merry crew and its music of voices
and laughter, till it passed round one of the many turnings of the stream,
and she saw it no more." The allusion to the "ancient city" prepares the
reader for this river of time, time passed and time passing, so that within
the enshrinement of childhood there are intimations of age and experience.
The children pass out of sight.

Yet the Thames was also the cradle for books in which, as Virginia
Woolf put it, we must become children. And on the river Dodgson himself
could become a child again, as he often wished—his persistent stammer

gone, his adult logic transcended. *Alice's Adventures in Wonderland* (1865) and *Through the Looking-Glass* (1871) are narratives of dream and vision and nonsense. One part of the enchantment of the river lies in the hope of escaping from time. The author once reminisced about "the cloudless blue above, the watery mirror below, the boat drifting idly on its way, the tinkle of the drops that fell from the oars. . . ." This is the river as stasis, a paradisal moment prolonged within the eternity of inspiration. There is another connection with the Thames. William Morris once described the experience of boating on the river in terms of "the smallness of the scale of everything, the short reaches and the speedy change of the banks, [that] gives one a feeling of going somewhere, of coming to something strange, a feeling of adventure I have not felt in bigger waters." Is this not an apt description of Alice's own adventures? The river seems to encourage the foreshortened perspective and idiosyncratic detail of dream narratives:

> And home we steer, a merry crew,
> Beneath the setting sun.

The same spirit of nostalgia and of dream fills Kenneth Grahame's *The Wind in the Willows* (1908), another book ostensibly for children that has become the reading of adults. The book was, for example, a favourite of Stanley Spencer. By curious coincidence Grahame was sent as a child to live with his grandmother in Cookham itself. At the age of six he explored the river-bank there, and observed the otters and other animals that lived beside it; his uncle, the curate of Cookham Dean's church, took him boating upon the river to Bisham and other riverside haunts. Forty years later Grahame returned with his wife and son to Cookham, and inspired by this place he began telling the stories of Toad and Badger to his child. But, like the river, from small beginnings it grew and grew. After the suicide of his son he left Cookham, and retired some miles upriver to Pangbourne where he remained for the rest of his life. After his death, the local children decorated the parish church with willows gathered from the river-bank. On his grave were inscribed the words "To the beautiful memory of Kenneth Grahame, husband of Elspeth and father of Alastair, who passed the River on the 6th July, 1932." He would have agreed with Rat's encomium upon the river. "It's my world, and I don't want any other. What it hasn't got is not worth having, and what it doesn't know is not worth knowing. Lord! The times we've had together!'

In *The Wind in the Willows* there is no Alice, the "dream child," but there are dream creatures of another kind. Yet Mole and Badger live in a recognisable riverscape. The old ice house in Bisham Woods is popularly supposed to have been the model of Toad's dungeon, and the Edwardian boathouse on Bourne End Reach has similar claims to being Toad's boathouse. Toad Hall is modelled upon the watermill by the river at Mapledurham, or perhaps upon Lullebrook Manor; the Wild Wood of the novel is certainly an image of Quarry Wood by the Thames near Bourne End. This was the wood that, in Grahame's vision, was once the site of a great and powerful city that had been built to "last for ever." But its inhabitants left, or were forced to leave, and the city itself was slowly levelled by "the strong winds and persistent rains." We have noticed before that the river encourages, if it does not actually inspire, such meditations on vanished cities and civilisations. It is as if the cultures of the people who once lived beside its banks—with their cursus monuments and their stone barrows— have left their traces in the consciousness of humankind. As Grahame puts it in the first chapter of his novel, "the river still chattered on to him, a babbling procession of the best stories in the world, sent from the heart of the earth to be told at last to the insatiable sea." Grahame had heard the call of the sacred Thames.

CHAPTER 39

The Song of the River

✤

There was a great celebration when, on 17 July 1717, a royal barge carried George I and some of his companions from Lambeth to Chelsea. He was accompanied by another barge filled with musicians, who played a piece of music especially commissioned from Handel. It was called *Water Music*, and is without doubt the most famous composition associated with the Thames. It has in a sense become the music of the river. The *Daily Courant* of 19 July reported that the king enjoyed the music so much that

> he caus'd it to be plaid over three times in the going and returning. At Eleven his Majesty went a-shore at Chelsea where a Supper was prepar'd, and then there was another very fine Consort of Musick, which lasted till 2; after which his Majesty came again into his Barge and return'd the same Way, the Musick continuing to play till he landed.

It has often been claimed in retrospect that the music was played in order to drown out the vulgar abuse of the Thames watermen, their egalitarian sentiments hallowed by tradition on the river, but that was not in fact the reason for *Water Music*. It was an attempt to associate George from

Hanover with one of the sources of English identity and English power. The combination of the Thames and the music was so powerful, in fact, that it was used to introduce Humphrey Jennings's wartime film entitled *Words for Battle* (1941). The myth of the Thames runs deeply through the national psyche.

There is another music of the river. What is the song of the Thames? Its endless melody may be glimpsed in all the poetical legends and myths of the river. It is the place where many of the English stories of time and history have their origin—in Spenser's *Faerie Queene*, in Drayton's *Polyolbion*, in Pope and in Milton, in Marvell and in Shelley. In Spenser, the river came to represent the identity of the nation. The Thames conflated genres and forms to create a complete statement. It embodied harmony, and unity. It was an emblem of innocence, and benevolence, and prosperity. It became a metaphor for poetry itself. So there have always been the poets of the river. There has always been a poetry of the river. The name and nature of water have always been fluid, created with liquid consonants: water— *aqua—apa—wasser—eau*. Water is the mistress of flowing language, of language without interruption or surcease. The river has been said to sing as it makes its way towards the sea; it harbours what in *The Revolt of Islam* (1818) Shelley called a "sound like many voices sweet."

The first poet of the Thames is arguably John Gower, of the fourteenth century, who is reputed to have financed the building of St. Mary Overie (presently Southwark Cathedral) on the south bank of the river where he lies buried. He is the earliest poet to mention the Thames, in lines from the prologue of *Confessio Amantis* (1386–90). He explains how he encountered Richard II upon the river:

> As I came nighe
> Out of my bote, when he me syghe
> He bade me come into his barge.

But the true poet of the Thames, in that century, must remain Geoffrey Chaucer; he was born by the river, lived by the river, and earned his living from the river. His house lay in the street that ran parallel to the river in the ward of Vintry. He cannot be imagined without the background of the Thames. He would have seen, and heard, it every day of his life in London. He chose to live near or by the river until his death, retiring first

to Greenwich or Deptford and then later to Westminster. He mentions the
first two riverine settings in the prologue to "The Reeve's Tale" of *The
Canterbury Tales* (1392–1400):

> Lo Depeford, and it is half-wey pryme!
> Lo Grenewych, ther many a shrewe is inne!
> It were al tyme thy tale to bigynne.

Chaucer was the supervisor of the custom tariffs at the Port of London, in
which capacity he heard all the stories of the river and the sea. He was one
of those poets who seem destined to be part of the river, which flowed
through their being as powerfully as it flowed through the city itself.

There is indeed something stirring about the relationship of London
poets, and London writers, to the Thames. We may think of Chaucer himself, of More, of Milton, of Pope, all haunting the same riverside streets—
all living at various epochs within a hundred yards or so of each other, and
all living in later life by the water. There is the artist, Turner, too, the great
Londoner and observer of the river; we can trace Turner quoting Pope on
the Thames, Pope quoting Milton, and Milton quoting Chaucer. There is a
continuity, inspired and maintained by the river itself.

And in that hallowed London company we can also glimpse the form
of William Blake, for whom the Thames was the river of eternity. He lived
beside it at Lambeth, where at Hercules Buildings he could see over the
marshes to the water. He crossed the newly built Waterloo Bridge every
time he wanted to enter the city, and particularly marked the presence of
the Albion Mills on that bridge's approach. They became the "blackened
mills" of his poetry. He died by the river, too, in Fountain Court off the
Strand. Visitors to his lodging there remarked upon the river gleaming at
the end of the alley. Blake himself described it as "like a bar of gold." A
twentieth-century poet, George Barker, was made aware of Blake's presence on the river. In *Calamiterror* (1937) he records a vision of

> The figure of William Blake, bright and huge
> Hung over the Thames at Sonning.

An early poet of the river was William Dunbar who, in "In Honour of the
City of London" (1501), greeted the Thames as triumphant:

Above all ryvers thy Ryver hath renowne,
Whose beryall stremys, pleasaunt and preclare,
Under thy lusty wallys renneth down,
Where many a swanne doth swymme with wyngis faire;
Where many a barge doth saile, and row with ore,
Where many a ship doth rest with toppe-royall.

The poetic myth of the Thames is here given one of its first rehearsals—its "beryl" streams, its fame, its swans, and its association with royalty. This is the river sanctified by the poetic imagination.

In the later sixteenth century there was a plethora of Thames poetry. This was the age when one of the principal landmarks of the Thames, Bankside, became the occasion or setting for the greatest of all English poetry. The association of Shakespeare with the Thames is generally neglected, but it was one of the highways of his invention. He lived beside it, first at Southwark and then later at Blackfriars. He crossed it continually, and indeed it became his primary means of transport. His plays were performed beside its banks, either at the Globe or at the indoor theatre in Blackfriars itself; when he writes of the tides, and of the merchant ships, he is considering the life of the Thames. "Tut, man, I mean thou'lt loose the flood, and in loosing the flood, loose thy voyage." So speaks Panthino in *The Two Gentlemen of Verona* (1592), but he is referring to the tidal rhythm of the Thames rather than the Adige river. The Thames is the rough cradle with which Shakespeare was well acquainted.

Edmund Spenser has been invoked at various points in this narrative, for the very good reason that he is the principal eulogist of the Thames. He is the celebrator of "wealthy Thamis" and of "silver streaming Thamesis." He can in fact be described as the "river poet" of the sixteenth century, and his intended composition of "Epithalamion Thamesis" in 1579 confirms his identification with the Thames. He uses the river to suggest greatness, and the passage of English history; he adapts the river to elegy and to prophecy; he associates the river with nature and with art. It is a theme that Michael Drayton took up, in a contribution to *England's Helicon* (1600), where he apostrophises "thou silver Thames, O clearest crystal flood." The sixteenth-century river indeed survives in poetry and historical legend as the silver Thames, the crystal Thames, the sweet Thames. It was reported that the oars of the London watermen, in that century, could become entangled with water-lilies while they kept stroke "to the tune of flutes." The myth of England's glittering destiny, under the aegis of the Virgin Queen, was deeply implicated in such presentations of the Thames as the river of magnificence. It was an image that reappeared in the poetry of later centuries, with the "silver-footed Thamesis" of Herrick and the "silver Thames" of Pope.

In the seventeenth and eighteenth centuries the reaches of the Thames by Twickenham and Richmond were haunted by the poets. In the more an-tique guide-books of the river there are phrases such as "here Cowley wrote," "here Pope took the air in a boat," "here is Thomson buried," "here Denham stood when he imagined the beautiful eulogium upon the river which has been so often quoted," "here Swift was shown by King William how to cut asparagus in the Dutch way." The Thames became the new Helicon, the favoured home and haven of the Muses.

It has been said with some truth, however, that there has been no great poem devoted to the Thames; the river has no bard. There have been at-tempts at such a composition, among them John Denham's "Cooper's Hill" (1641). It is in fact Denham's one famous poem, endlessly quoted and an-thologised since its first publication. A poem of moderate temper, and of unmatched technical ability, it was considered to be a model of English poetry, with its gentle cadence and its elevated diction, its chastened im-agery and its generous sentiment. The Thames is described as gentle and spacious, a source both of wealth and of pride. It renders "both Indies ours," in terms of trade, and its "fair bosom is the world's exchange," em-phasising its most important value in the seventeenth century. It was pub-lished immediately before a period of unprecedented English turmoil, the Civil Wars, and can be read as an invocation of calmness or moderation. The Thames itself was described as temperate and bountiful; it was never provoked into extremes, never impetuous or unpredictable. Thus it became a wished-for paradigm. In the middle of the struggles of the 1640s the poem might then be read as a nostalgic homage to a golden period of peace; in subsequent decades it was interpreted as an eloquent restatement of the central English principles of moderation and equity. It had a talismanic quality, all the more arresting for its use of the Thames itself as an image of good order:

O could I flow like thee, and make thy stream
My great example, as it is my theme!

Though deep, yet clear; though gentle, yet not dull;
Strong without rage, without o'erflowing, full.

In the same decade Robert Herrick wrote a lachrymose elegy to the river, "His Teares to Thamasis" (1648), in which he bids its waters *"fare-ye-well for ever"* after his removal to a country parsonage. He sends the river his sweetest kiss, regretting that he will no longer take a barge to Richmond or to Kingston:

Nor in the summer's sweeter evenings go
To bathe in thee (as thousands others doe) . . .

This is one of the few references to the evident fact that the river was used for swimming or bathing by "thousands" of citizens. He laments his departure from "my *Beloved Westminster*" and explains that he was born near the banks of the Thames in "*Golden-cheap-side.*" Those who are born by the river, like Turner in Maiden Lane and Milton in Bread Street, claim an especial affinity with it.

The life of John Milton is evidence of this. Every citizen of London was then also a citizen of the river. As Milton wrote in *Damon's Epitaph* (1639), *Thamesis meus ante omnes*—"my Thames above all the rest." After university he resided from 1632 to 1638 at Horton, close to the place where the river Colne is in confluence with the Thames; here, on the banks of the tributary, he composed "Il Penseroso" and "L'Allegro," "Lycidas" and the masque of *Comus*. In *Comus*, for example, there is a reference to that place:

By the rushy fringed bank,
Where grows the willow and the osier dank.

In "Lycidas," too, there seems to be some inspired memory of the river's territory:

Ye valleys low, where the mild whispers use
Of shades and wanton winds and gushing brooks.

In the seventeenth century Horton was altogether a watery region, with rivulets running through the meadows among rushes and water-plants; by

the sides of the roads there were slow runnels in place of ditches, in which
it was still possible in the nineteenth century to see minnows. Milton, like
Shelley, enjoyed the presence of water to the extent that the Thames may
be considered to be a primary agent of his imagination. He invokes the
river when he contemplates the theme of a British epic, and considers it to
be a river of cultural memory. "*Thamesis meus*"—my Thames—suggests
an act of identification or appropriation at once intimate and ultimately
unidentifiable. It suggests almost infantine closeness.

When Boswell took a sculler with Samuel Johnson to Greenwich,
"we were entertained with the immense number and variety of ships that
were lying at anchor, and with the beautiful country on each side of the
river." Once they had arrived at their destination, Boswell took from his
coat-pocket a copy of Johnson's poem "London" (1738), and read out the
lines:

> On Thames's banks in silent thought we stood:
> Where Greenwich smiles upon the silver flood.

This is the mythical river, the picturesque river of the eighteenth century
that by dint of association and tradition remained the paradigm of the
Thames in a period when it was in fact undergoing a fundamental alteration.

The pattern of riparian habitation is nowhere more apparent than in
the life of Alexander Pope, who stayed close to the river all of his life. He
was born in the old City of London, within sight and sound of the Thames;
at a later date he had a study in Battersea, facing the Thames, where he
wrote "An Essay on Man." He then lived on the margins of Windsor Forest, and then briefly at Chiswick by the river. But his most famous riverside
residence was at Twickenham where the garden of his "villa" reached
down to the north bank of the Thames. He purchased the house in 1718 and
remained there until his death in 1744.

His favoured work here was the building of a river grotto, and in a letter to his friend Blount he described how

> from the river Thames you see through my arch up a walk in the
> wilderness to a kind of open temple, wholly composed of shells in the
> rustic manner; and from that distance, under the temple, you look down
> through a sloping arcade of trees, and see the sails on the river passing
> suddenly and vanishing as through a perspective glass.

He deemed the river to be a sacred place, worthy of a "temple" in honour of its deity, and placed shards of glass and polished shells within the grotto so that it shone like an icon of holiness upon the bank. He composed an inscription, too, for:

> Thou who shalt step where Thames' translucent wave
> Shines a broad mirror through the shadowy cave,
> Where lingering drops from mineral roofs distil,
> And pointed crystals break the sparkling rill . . .

In the eighteenth book of Malory's *Le Morte D'Arthur* (1469–70), Lancelot retreats to Windsor Forest, where he inhabits a hermitage beside a spring. It is a prologue to Pope's residence at his father's house in Binfield, close to Windsor Forest and the river Loddon which decants into the Thames; upon one of the trees in an enclosure there was carved "Here Pope Sung." He could never get away from the river; he had to live beside it, like one of those classical deities whose existence depended upon the calm ministrations of the rivers of Greece. He declared once that there were "no scenes of paradise, no happy bowers, equal to those on the banks of the Thames." The river was his Arcadia, a sylvan retreat, to which he addressed his muse:

> Fair Thames, flow gently from this sacred spring
> While on thy banks Sicilian Muses sing . . .
> Blest Thames's shores the brightest beauties yield
> Feed here my lambs, I'll seek no distant field.

The City—Battersea—Windsor—Chiswick—Twickenham: that is the odyssey of Alexander Pope's life, a journey along the banks of the Thames from which he never deviated. He was truly the *genius loci*.

There are other votaries of the river. James Thomson, the once famous author of *The Seasons* (1730) that became the pastoral bible of the eighteenth century, included the Thames within his capacious view. He wrote part of that naturalistic epic by the river at Hammersmith, in the Dove Coffeehouse (now the Dove public house). In it we will find the lines:

> Slow let us trace the matchless vale of Thames
> Fair—winding up to where the Muses haunt . . .

Beside the river at Cliveden he wrote the masque, *Alfred*, which has the sole distinction of containing the song "Rule Britannia!" He constantly haunted the Thames, managing to live and die and be buried by the river. The Thames could be said to have killed him. Thomson caught a chill when sailing in an open boat from London to Kew, and never recovered.

With Thomson we may place Thomas Gray. In his "Ode on a Distant Prospect of Eton College" (1742), he asked "Father Thames":

> Who foremost now delight to cleave
> With pliant arm thy glassy wave?

To which the only answer must be, the same boys as you and your companions once were. Again the river prompts matters of time and memory. To provoke melancholy seems to be one of the more enduring attributes of the river.

But Pope's true successor as the river poet, the poet haunted by the river, must be Percy Bysshe Shelley. The river entered his head. His verses flow with it. He grew up by the river, at Syon House Academy in Isleworth, at Eton and at Oxford, and that early acquaintance seems to have affected his destiny. All his short life he loved rivers, and the poets that sang of rivers. He emulated Pope by living on the borders of Windsor Forest in the summer of 1815; while here he engaged in his favourite pastime of boating on the Thames, and explored the stretches of the river from Windsor to Cricklade in a wherry. He was on a pilgrimage to the source of the river. He was able to navigate as far as Inglesham, where the river vegetation and all the attendant weeds impeded his progress. It was a common enough occurrence. This was the point where the water barely covered the hooves of the cattle.

He was accompanied on this river journey by Thomas Love Peacock who had already written *The Genius of the Thames* (1812). Theirs was a school of river poetry. Peacock lived at Chertsey when he was a child, and was eventually buried at Shepperton. The beginning and end of his life were associated with the Thames, in a pattern that seems to have dominated many lives. Peacock left a portrait of Shelley, on this journey, in the novel *Crotchet Castle* (1831) where he depicts "Mr. Philpot" who "would lie alone for hours, listening to the gurgling of the water around the prow, and would occasionally edify the company with speculations on the great changes that would be effected in the world by the steam navigation of rivers . . ."

They stopped for two nights in Lechlade, and the path between the church and the river there is still known as "Shelley's Walk." So does a poet of the river impress himself upon his surroundings. Inspired by the fifteenth-century church itself Shelley composed "A Summer Evening Churchyard." The changefulness and variousness of the Thames perhaps prevent the composition of a great poem in its honour; it is made up of small scenes and images like that of the Lechlade churchyard. It cannot inspire an heroic measure, or a sense of the sublime; it encourages the poetry of shadow and of seclusion, of rest and of retreat. These are not epic themes.

Yet on his return from Lechlade Shelley composed *Alastor, or the Spirit of Solitude* (1815), in which he invoked the immediate landscape of the upper Thames:

> The meeting boughs and implicated leaves
>   Wove twilight o'er the poet's path . . .

In it, too, he compares the true pilgrimage of a poet to a journey upriver; the voyage into the past, the voyage into the recesses of the imagination, is a river voyage. The river itself becomes a tremulous deity. "Rivers are not like roads," he wrote to Peacock, "the work of the hands of man; they imitate mind, which wanders at will over pathless deserts, and flows through nature's loveliest recesses." The being of a man was "like a river whose rapid and perpetual stream flows outwards." For Shelley, then, the river was an image of human consciousness. It represented in particular the flow of being that was one of the poet's principal characteristics. That is why William Hazlitt wrote of him that "his bending, flexible form appears to take no strong hold of things, does not grapple with the world about him, but slides from it like a river." It is the clearest possible description of the consonance between man and river, and one man in particular who always desired to be near the river which represented part of his being. Shelley was at peace on the Thames.

Three years later after his river pilgrimage with Peacock, Shelley rented a house at Great Marlow, on the river in Buckinghamshire, where he wrote *The Revolt of Islam* (1818). From this vantage he made many

excursions to his favoured places of the river, to Bisham and to Medmenham, to Henley and to Maidenhead. He wrote much of *The Revolt of Islam*
in Bisham Woods, or while floating under the beech groves of Bisham-on-
the-Thames in a boat called *Vaga*. The images of that poem are directly associated with the river, and there are lines that call up the immediate setting
of its composition:

> Waterfalls leap among the wild islands green,
> Which framed for my lone boat a lone retreat
> Of moss-grown trees and weeds . . .

This is the landscape of the Thames, which Mary Shelley believed to be
"distinguished for singular beauty."

In one of his letters Shelley remarks upon the tyranny of places; he
complains that, though you think you have left them, you still inhabit them.
In their absence you still frequent them. This seems to have been his deep
response to the regions of the Thames, and in the cadence of his poetry it
is still possible to trace the movement of the river. Yeats wrote of him that
"a single vision would have come to him again and again, a vision of a boat
drifting down a broad river . . . there is for every man some one scene, some
one adventure, some one picture, that is the image of his secret life." And
of course Shelley died in the open sea, in the watery element to which he
had dedicated his life.

William Morris was born at Walthamstow, on the edges of the northern
marshes of the Thames, and some of his most famous designs were given
the names of the tributaries of the river, such as "Evenlode" and "Kennet,"
"Wandle" and "Wey." But for most of his life he inhabited Kelmscott
Manor, lying a few yards from the river near Oxford, and Kelmscott House
beside the river at Hammersmith. He would journey by boat between the
two houses, like some medieval wherryman. The journey itself, at a slow
pace, took some six days; it took him between two worlds which he commemorated in some introductory verses to the "June" stories of *The
Earthly Paradise* (1865–70):

> What better place than this then could we find
> By this sweet stream that knows not of the sea
> That guesses not the city's misery,

This little stream whose hamlets scarce have names,
This far-off lonely mother of the Thames?

Wordsworth regarded the Thames with almost as much veneration as he
gave to the Lake District or the Alps. The sonnet upon Westminster Bridge
is sufficiently well known, but there are other intimations of the river's
imaginative potential. There is the poem, written upon the Thames near
Richmond in 1790, in which he cites the "lovely visions" that are vouchsafed to him by the banks of the river:

Till all our minds for ever flow
As thy deep waters now are flowing.

In this poem, and in the sonnet composed upon Westminster Bridge, he alludes to the calmness of the Thames. It possesses a "quiet soul" at once
solemn and serene. In the mechanical and artificial chaos of the early-
nineteenth-century city he saw in the river a site of vital communion with
the natural world, perhaps the only vestige of natural life left in the capital.

Yet there is for Wordsworth the intimation that the river encompasses
both origin and ending, source and surcease, and can thus become an emblem of the eternal world. But that is perhaps too easy a formulation. In his
Essay upon Epitaphs (1810) he remarks that

origin and tendency are notions inseparably co-relative. Never did a
Child stand by the side of a running Stream, pondering within himself
what power was the feeder of the perpetual current, from what never-
wearied sources the body of water was supplied, but he must have been
inevitably propelled to follow this question by another: "Towards what
abyss is it in progress? What receptacle can contain the mighty influx?"

There is here the poet's fascination with darkness and non-being. A poem
upon the river Duddon, composed in 1820, alludes to the Thames as the
larger and mightier river; yet both of them move ineluctably towards the
"Deep" where they will lose both name and nature. What can be salvaged
from the process of non-being, except the "Commerce freighted or triumphant War" which are maintained by the Thames? The historical
process is then balanced by the natural process, achievement beside the
"abyss" of loss, in a radically unstable equilibrium. It is one of the more

unsettling visions of the river, doomed perpetually to lose itself while the wreckage of time lies beside its banks.

Matthew Arnold observed all the aspects of the river's life—"who knows them if not I?"—and his poem "Thyrsis" depicts the white and purple fritillaries that are the natural bounty of the water-meadows in the upper reaches of the Thames. He was pre-eminently the poet of the Upper Thames, and he alludes to Wychwood and to Cumner. There is also the place commemorated in "The Scholar Gypsy" (1853):

> Crossing the stripling Thames at Bablock Hythe
>   Trailing in the cool stream thy fingers wet.

Arnold was born, and eventually buried, at Laleham almost within the sound of the river. He lived by the river for the last fifteen years of his life. He was married by the river, too, so that the most sacred ceremonies of his life were conducted by the Thames. For him it was a token of permanence:

> And life ran gaily as the sparkling Thames,
> Before this strange disease of modern life . . .

It is in fact remarkable how many writers of the river do comment unfavourably on "modern life," whether it be in eighteenth-, nineteenth- or twentieth-century versions; the riparian traveller of 1745 is just as likely to condemn "improvements" as the walker of 2007. The river induces a mood of nostalgia, perhaps, for that which never was and never could be. It imposes a sense of time, or a perspective, that would otherwise not occur to the wanderer. It is therefore an easy receptacle for false feeling and for ill-founded sentiment.

The most curious of the Thames poets has been left to last. John Taylor, known in his lifetime as "The Water Poet," was a Thames wherryman who had immortal longings. He was the self-appointed guardian and muse of the river, the Dante of the Thames. He was born in 1580, by the Severn, and attended the Gloucester grammar school there without noticeable success; he came to London, and became apprenticed to a waterman before being impressed into the navy. On his return from service, in the late 1590s, he resumed his Thames trade and began a long career ferrying between the two banks. The Thames haunted him. Like many of his poetical predecessors his first inspiration came when floating on its waters; one evening he was reclining in his boat and reciting some lines from Marlowe's riverine poem, *Hero and Leander*, when he experienced his epiphany. The Muse of the Thames called him. From that time forward he became "the water poet." His collected verses were eventually published in an edition of eight volumes but he also composed riverlogues, tavern reports, and political polemics. He even wrote a reference book, entitled *The Carrier's Cosmographie*. Some two hundred works have been ascribed to him. Pope called him "swan of Thames," albeit ironically. Taylor said of himself:

> Some through ignorance, and some through spite,
> Have said that I can neither read nor write.

He organised river pageants, and royal battles upon the water; he collected the taxes on wine being transported upriver; he was asked to prepare plans for the cleaning and the dredging of the Thames. He became a celebrated London figure and, according to Robert Southey, "kings and queens condescended to notice him, nobles and archbishops admitted him to their table, and mayors and corporations received him with civic honours." He represented what was then a flourishing popular culture around and about the river. He was the plebeian voice of the Thames, itself a potentially levelling and disruptive influence. He was bawdy and humorous in turn, a parodist of other poets, a quick-witted adventurer whose doggerel verse embodies the coarser virtues of the London riverside.

He also arranged what would in the modern world be called a series of "publicity stunts." He built a boat out of brown paper and with another boatman attempted a journey down the Thames from London to the Medway; the paper boat was supported by eight inflated pigs' bladders and the oars were made out of stiffened stockfish:

> The water to the paper being got
> In one half hour began to rot.

After an heroic thirty-six hours afloat, they staggered ashore with the remnants of their craft in their hands. In his later years he wrote an allegorical poem, entitled *Thames-Isis*, and began calling himself the "Acqua-Muse." *Thames-Isis* is in part history, and in part travelogue; he used as his model Michael Drayton's topographical poem, *Polyolbion*, and the Latin poem by

John Leland entitled *Cygnea Cantio*. He was attempting to place his work in the long tradition of riverine epic, where he believed that he truly belonged. He retired to manage a public house in Phoenix Alley by Long Acre, but he was not so successful on dry land. He died in 1653, and there is one report that he starved to death. In Winstanley's *Lives of the Poets* (1687) he was granted this epitaph:

> Here lies the Water-poet, honest John,
> Who rowed on the streams of Helicon;
> Where having many rocks and dangers past,
> He at the haven of heaven arriv'd at last.

PART XIII

Shadows and Depths

Medmenham Abbey, where the members of the Hell Fire Club
established their base

CHAPTER 40

River Dreams

*L*ewis Carroll concluded *Through the Looking Glass* (1871), a narrative in part inspired by his journeys upon the Thames at Oxford, with the refrain:

> Ever drifting down the stream—
> Lingering in the golden gleam—
> Life, what is it but a dream?

The Thames inspires dreams, or what we may also call reflections. Theodore Hook, at Thames Ditton in the early nineteenth century, wrote verses in celebration of "the placid waking dream" he experienced by the riverside. Gaston Bachelard, in *L'Eau et Les Rêves* (1993), wrote that "I cannot sit down beside a river without falling into a profound reverie, without looking back over my happiness."

There is an anonymous poem, also, of the water "under wistful willows wending":

> Why so swift to grasp the dream,
> Mad to learn the story's ending?

In *The Earthly Paradise* (1868–70) William Morris recounted his own dream by the river at Kelmscot:

> And dream of London, small, and white, and clean,
> The clear Thames bordered by its gardens green.

So the river does not only create dreams; it appears within them. It is an ancient presence. In the Aboriginal art of Australia—in Walbiri circle line designs—the image of concentric circles is an emblem of water or of a water-hole, from which dreamings emerge or into which they enter. The water and the dream are of the same element. That is why, in Jerome K. Jerome's *Three Men in a Boat*, Sonning is an area of the Thames "in which to dream of bygone days, and vanished forms and faces, and things that might have been." By the river Turner dreamed of classical and mythological pasts, and some of his sketches are a form of painterly day-dreaming with evanescent shapes of things that are and are not. Dido and Aeneas are to be found at Richmond, saying eternal farewell; Portia laments the departure of Brutus at Isleworth. There are triremes on the water, and elaborate palaces beside its banks. These are dreams of majesty.

And who can tell dreams from visions? Wordsworth understood the power of the river very well, in some "Lines" (1790) written by Richmond-upon-Thames:

> Glide gently, thus for ever glide,
> O Thames! that other bards may see
> As lovely visions by thy side
> As now, fair river! come to me.

The prospect of the river running down to the ocean has prompted many visionary conceptions; the light upon the water, the bridges across the river (the bridges of contentment), have been the agents of the imagination. The river obscures conscious thought and erases memory; the sound and move-ment of water lay to rest the powers of observation, like some watery nar-cotic. It may be the source of visions. That is why it has been commonly associated with the twentieth-century notion of the subconscious. It is water itself that dreams.

. . .

Reflect upon the nature of reflections. They throw a curious light upon the boundary between shadow and substance. When the swan floats upon the water it seems as if it were to float double, swan and shadow of some other swan. At the still hour of the evening—often about half an hour before sunset—every riverside object may be perfectly reflected from the surface of the water, and the reflection or shadow is often seen more distinctly than the object to which it owes its existence. In that state reality seems to depart from the actual and impart its power to the unreal; in the process the most familiar objects become unfamiliar and novel. It is like observing some new world. Water does not in that sense become a mirror. It is gentler, more capacious, and more inviting, than a mirror. It naturalises, and idealises, the other within the depths of itself. It makes the reflected world profound—more profound, perhaps, than the actual world above the water. The reflection is in that sense more real than the reality. Yet this may induce bewilderment, and a form of vertigo; when you gaze at the inverted landscape, you may be half-afraid of becoming lost within it—of being swallowed up by the profound below.

Thomas Traherne, the poet and mystic, was rector of St. Mary's at Teddington and dwelled close to the river there. In a poem, "Shadows in the Water," perhaps composed in the early 1670s, he meditates upon the nature of its reflections:

> By walking Men's reversed Feet
> I chanc'd another World to meet;
> Tho it did not to View exceed
> A Phantom, 'tis a World indeed,
>   Where Skies beneath us shine,
>   And Earth by Art divine
> Another face presents below,
> Where People's feet against Ours go.

The river is filled with such strange reversals and pairings. The river encourages doubling. It can also represent the "world turned upside down," that ancient phrase representing the libertarian and egalitarian power of misrule. We will discover that the river is the setting of liberty in all of its aspects.

There is a significant feature of the ancient cursus at Lechlade. The smaller cursus site here is paralleled by a larger cursus complex on the other side of the river at Buscot Wick. There seems to have been some attempt at pairing, therefore, with the Thames acting as a natural boundary between the two monuments. This phenomenon is to be found elsewhere along the Thames, as, for example, at the adjacent cursus sites of Dorchester, and it acts as a curious harbinger for the emergence of "twin towns" linked by the river—Streatley and Goring, Pangbourne and Whitchurch, Reading and Caversham, Putney and Fulham. Is it possible that the pairing of towns has some prehistoric origin in the siting of monuments? Is it part of some atavistic impulse when humankind contemplates the river? There is some vision of doubleness, connected to the nature of reflecting water itself.

There are more fanciful examples. The echo under the bridge arch as you walk along the tow-path at Maidenhead is well known for its strength. There used to be an inn-sign on the tow-path at Twickenham, for the Barmy Arms, showing the angry Duchess from *Alice in Wonderland* painted upside down. Since *Alice in Wonderland* is itself set in a reverse world inspired by Carroll's sojourns on the river, the sign may be hailed as a true Thames vision. There have been many ghosts observed along the banks of the Thames, but perhaps they have the reality and the nature of reflections in the water. To the poem of Traherne we may add the poetry of Pope, from *Windsor Forest*, on the reflective Thames:

Oft in her glass the musing shepherd spies
The headlong mountains and the downward skies,
The watry landskip of the pendant woods,
And absent trees that tremble in the floods;
In the clear azure gleam the flocks are seen,
And floating forests paint the waves with green.

CHAPTER 41

Legends of the River

*T*here are local myths of the Thames. It used to be said that towns still existed beneath the river; an earlier Tilbury, for example, was believed to lie beneath the waters of the estuary. The area beside Dagenham was according to local belief the site of the original Deluge. There were stories of miraculously created stone trees beside the banks. One of them, at Godstow, was the token of a nun's apotheosis; she used to point to a tree that, she said, would be turned into stone when she was with the saints in heaven. Pilgrims, as late as the early sixteenth century, venerated this tree. It is now of course realised that stone trees do exist by, or in, the Thames; but we have another explanation for their petrifaction. At Fairford, beside Inglesham, there was a sudden invasion of frogs and toads who made their way to the house of the local Justice; here, according to a pamphlet issued in 1660, "they divided themselves into two distinct bodies, and orderly made up to the House of the said Justice; some climbing the walls, and into the Windows and Chambers." When the Justice made his peace with the Nonconformists of the town, the creatures "strangely and unexpectedly vanisht away." There have been rumours of black magic at Cookham and at Burnham Beeches—and of course in connection with the "Hell Fire Club" located at Medmenham Abbey.

There were deep holes by the Thames at Culham, one of them being known as "Gleddie's" or "Glady's" Hole. The people of the neighbourhood believed that a fisherman by the name of Gleddie fell within it and was drowned; it is said that the bubbles that rose from him to the surface of the water exploded as loud curses. There was an eyot beside Binsey known locally as "Black John's Pit" from which, it was said, a goblin sprang who kept the heads of children under the water. The legend in these cases is clearly concerned with the fear of drowning but also, perhaps, of being lost in some strange underground world of chasms and caverns that is deemed to exist beneath the path of the river. It is the Otherworld of ancient reverence, revived in local stories that have never entirely been dissipated.

There was an area on the southern bank of the river, between Westminster and Hungerford, that in the seventeenth century was known as "Pedlar's Acre." The land was owned by a pedlar who, on his death, left it to the church of St. Mary at Lambeth. It is said that he was once granted shelter in the church, and bestowed the land upon it on condition that he and his dog should be commemorated in a stained-glass window. There is indeed stained glass in that church showing a pedlar and his dog, to which is attached a notice that "This window by tradition represents a benefactor who about the year 1500 left to this church a piece of land later known as Pedlar's Acre on condition that his image be placed in the church and repaired from time to time. Mended in 1608; renewed 1703; transferred to this chapel 1884; destroyed 1941; renewed 1956." There is nothing to dispute the legend. A marking stone, inscribed "Boundary of Pedlar's Acre 1777," was found when the area was being excavated. It was being prepared for the building of County Hall, which still stands on the ancient acre of ground.

It is perhaps only to be expected that the river, so anciently a home of spiritual forces, should in later days be associated with the more conventional forms of the supernatural; the presence lingers, even in predictable or risible forms. Books have been written about the ghosts of the Thames. There are reported sightings at Windsor and at Slough, at Maidenhead and at Oxford. There are supposed ghosts at Henley. There was a grey lady of Ladye Place in Hurley; the ghost of Lady Hoby has been seen at Bisham Abbey. A "lady in white" is reported to haunt a room of the George Hotel in Dorchester-on-Thames, and a small lady flits around the fifteenth-century Cockpit bar at Eton. At Kempsford a ghost looks out of the window of the ruined abbey. There is a little grey lady who, at Dorney Court, sits in a bedroom and weeps. And it is perhaps predictable that monks have been glimpsed within the precincts of the ancient abbey at Dorchester. There are many such stories, perpetually restored in legend.

Every local history of the Thames Valley, and of the towns and villages along the river, has accounts of spiritualised visitants. There seem to have been many such apparitions at Cookham, seven of them at the latest count, including a young man in a leather jerkin at Cookham Dean, and a little girl at Strande Water. Two thoroughfares by the Thames have in fact been named after their ghostly pedestrians—Monks Walk in Medmenham, and Whiteladyes Lane in Cookham. It is also said that, down Whiteladyes Lane, there can be seen on dark nights a phantom coach with headless horses. In the neighbourhood of Cookham, too, were to be found the haunts of Herne the Hunter; he is the Celtic figure, half-man and half-beast, that inhabited the popular imagination for many hundreds of years. He was reported to be seen, in the shape of a white stag, in Whiteladyes Lane itself. In legend the eponymous white lady, with streaming hair, was said to accompany Herne's wild hunt. Similarly Herne was said to drive a wagon. So all the constituents of the ancient myth—the white lady, the horned god, the coach—appear as "ghosts" in a late variant of the same story. They are not ghosts at all, but images of lost belief. Such are the workings of the human imagination.

It is perhaps worth noticing that many of these apparitions have been described as comprising a white or semi-white vapour. In Lower Basildon by the Thames, for example, there were independent reports of a "silvery form" and a "white, mist-like figure." At Bisham there was reputed to be a ghost "which spreads itself across the river in a thin, white mist which means death to those who try to penetrate it." At Sonning a "grey lady" floats across Sonning Lane. Another "grey lady" walks through the grounds of Danesfield, on a bluff above the river just beyond Hurley. At Streatley a "white lady" is seen in her "night-dress," and at Marlow "a lady in a cloak . . . her apparel all in grey" is observed. At Abingdon, according to ancient testimony,

it is most certain that there is a visible Ghost, which walks in the shape of a Christian, and most probably in woman's shape . . . in the daie time it is seen only as a woman's head of hair upon the top of the water, in the night it constantly passeth over the bridge, it's all white . . . it onely hisseth as a Snake or a Goos.

A "white lady without a head" has often been seen in an avenue of elms at Cliveden. These are presumably clusterings of water mist, wraith-like forms of mist emerging from the surface of the water or collocations of vapour that have been taken as human forms. The phenomena are generally said to be sobbing or sighing, and at Caversham the sound of invisible oars is heard. We may assume these to be the natural sounds of the river. The stories do at least emphasise the power that the Thames is still believed to possess. The river is haunted by its past.

PART XIV

The River of Death

The remains of Chertsey Abbey. "Human bones . . . were
spread thick all over the garden"

CHAPTER 42

The Offerings

꩜

The river itself is a reliquary. It once contained the bodies of the dead, long dissolved. It still contains weapons, and dwellings, and ornaments. Water is permanent; water is destructive; everything returns to its depths. Ornaments and jewellery, razors and tweezers, sickles and chisels, rapiers and axes, shears and flesh-hooks, have all been discovered. A cup of Trojan origin—a stemless *cantharos* manufactured between 1000 and 700 BC—was found by two dredgermen at Barn Elms near Hammersmith Bridge. A Greek *rhyton* of the second century BC, a curved vessel used to aerate wine, was found at Billingsgate; a *hydria* or water-pitcher of the sixth century BC was discovered in Barking Creek. There are also examples of objects from Cyprus and Mycenae. It would be a mistake to think of the pre-Roman tribes as in any respect "uncivilised"; their culture was undoubtedly as rich and as complex as any other that has flourished beside the Thames.

Other significant archaeological findings are directly related to the Thames, with the evident fact that over half of the Bronze Age spearheads in the Thames region were found in the river itself. The distribution of metalwork clusters along the line of the river, with the finds of socketed axes, palstaves, swords, spearheads and side-looped spearheads all found in or by the water. This clustering seems perfectly to imitate the patterns of Neolithic axes also found in the Thames, particularly in the area between Reading and Staines, and suggests that the river was once more the focus of ritual activity.

The weapons are unlikely to have been lost there by accident; there are too many of them, in too many significant groupings, to be explained in that manner. It seems possible to surmise, therefore, that they represent votive gifts despatched into the running waters as a way of appeasing the river-gods. There may have been occasions of flooding which demanded divine intercession. There were steadily wetter conditions throughout this epoch, and there is evidence of periodic inundation that would have affected the level of the river. That is why it has been suggested that there was a change of worship from the gods of earth and sky to the gods of water. It is also possible that weapons and other goods were deposited in the flowing water to render more powerful the river's role as a boundary. It has already been noted that frontiers and territories took on more importance in this era of population growth and more intensive settlement. The river itself was the most significant natural boundary to be found in the region, and it is likely that its role as protector was sanctified by gifts and offerings.

Ritual deposits have been an aspect of the river's life for many thousands of years. They have been assumed to diminish in the late medieval period, but there is some evidence to suggest that such rituals have not yet entirely disappeared. The veneration of the river is universal. Achilles threw a lock of his hair into the river Spercheios as an offering. The ancient Trojans threw live horses into the Scamander, and at a later date they sacrificed animals upon altars set up by that river's banks. The Algonquin Indians threw tobacco into the waterfalls of their territory as an act of propitiation. The Greeks cut the throats of animals, suspended above the river, and allowed the blood to mingle with the flowing waters.

The earliest Thames deposits, of flake flints and animal bones, derive from the Upper Palaeolithic and Early Mesolithic periods. They suggest that the worship of the river, if such it is, is of immense antiquity. There are also many artefacts, including burnt flint pebbles and pottery and tools of flint, from the Neolithic period. A hoard of Neolithic axes has been found within the Thames, while a group of Cornish axes from the same epoch has been discovered in the Thames estuary. The river has also divulged a large number of mace-heads. In a survey of the river undertaken thirty years ago, some 368 Neolithic axes were listed. They were in good condition, and appear not to have been employed for any of the ordinary purposes. If stone weapons were an emblem of power, it may have been a significant way of augmenting the authority or prestige of anyone who left them in large numbers. They may have been gifts of worship or propitiation, or sacrifices on behalf of the dead.

Deposition seems to have been the most important ceremony during the Bronze Age, and as a result that period remains the single most fruitful in the history of riverine deposits. Various types of artefact had their own especial places. Tools were left in dry, and weapons in wet, locations. This would suggest that the more expensive and highly finished artefacts were consigned to the wet rather than to the dry. In the river itself the offerings of bones, of weapons, and of ornaments, were kept separate and distinct. Could it be that the spirit of each stretch of the river had a different purpose? By the river at Eton, for example, groups of skulls have been found; just as significantly, there are no traces of metalwork. Metal has been found in large quantities elsewhere. It has also been surmised that some parts of the river were devoted to female objects, and that other parts of the river were the repository of objects associated with the male.

One collector from the nineteenth century, Thomas Layton, found twenty-eight rapiers of the Middle Bronze Age, thirty-three Late Bronze Age swords, thirty-four spearheads and six bronze sickles. There seem to be some people, attuned to the spirit of place, who divine drowned hoards. Layton may simply have been fortunate, but he may have read the signs as some of his predecessors read them—a sudden passage of turbulence, where two streams crossed, or a zone of quietness in the generally disturbed flow of the water. There are many river-finders or "mud-larks" still to be seen on the foreshore, when the tide goes out, scrutinising the layers of litter and debris left by the water. The Society of Thames Mudlarks has approximately seventy members, each of whom seems to have an intuitive association with the river. They are often especially favoured. One finder discovered the small bronze tail of a peacock figurine; then, a year later, he found the rest of the figurine in another part of the river. Other stories of coincidental finds abound. It is one of the most characteristic aspects of the Thames. The river may heal that which is broken.

The deposition of Bronze Age weapons in the river has many significant associations. There is one theory that in an act of worship they were being returned to their origin, since water was an important element of "quenching" in the process of smelting. The vision of the sword Excalibur, rising from the surface of the enchanted lake in Arthurian legend, is a significant reminder of what was once the widespread presence of water worship. The weapons may have been deposited in the river as a form of offering to ancestors, or to the spirits of the underworld. The weapons may have been symbolically "killed" in their immersion and disappearance beneath the water, in an act of expiation or thanksgiving. Five imitations of Bronze Age daggers, carved out of bone, were also discovered in the Thames.

The ceremonies of water are connected with the discovery of wooden platforms or causeways by rivers and fens. A large causeway, made out of wooden posts and planks, has been found at Flag Fen near Peterborough. There is a stone and timber ford across a channel of the Thames in Oxfordshire, where metal offerings were found beneath its surface. But the most important riverine site is that upon the Thames itself, in the area of Vauxhall. A plaque now marks the spot on the southern bank where the early settlers constructed a causeway, dated to approximately 1400 BC, that extended over the water. It may have acted as a platform for ceremonial activities, and allowed the participants to throw their votive objects into deeper waters. But since the structure led to a small island, it has also been classified as a bridge. It is comprised of twenty large timber posts in two rows, creating a pathway into the Thames. If it is indeed a rudimentary bridge, then it may rank as the first such structure ever to be built across the river. Two spearheads have been found within its piles.

There are also later offerings. An Iron Age sheath and dagger have been taken from the Thames at Cookham. The evidence of Iron Age water worship comes from the similar tribes in Gaul, in the first century BC, of which Strabo writes that "it was the lakes most of all that afforded the treasures their inviolability, into which the people let down heavy masses of silver and of gold." Coins, and iron bars used as currency, were also deposited in the Thames in a manner which suggests that votive deposits were in some way connected with distinct tribal boundaries. An Iron Age wooden tankard, with bronze handle and casing, was taken up from the river; similarly an Iron Age bowl, with a small circular hole in the bottom, was found. It is suggestive that the objects are generally confined to short stretches of the Thames, such as that between Brentford and Battersea or between Teddington and Twickenham, since these happen to be the areas where Neolithic and Bronze Age artefacts have also been found.

There was an efflorescence of activity towards the end of the Iron Age from which period have been recovered a magnificent horned helmet as well as swords and ornamental horse-trappings. At Battersea an Iron Age shield was trawled from the river-bed, richly embossed and completed with red enamel studs. At Battersea, too, were found cauldrons, battle-axes, and an iron scabbard decorated with the Celtic emblem of a dragon pair. A similar scabbard, with the dragon motif, was found in the river near Hammersmith Bridge. The increase in river worship may have been part of a generally heightened awareness of danger connected with the advance of the Roman legions towards the unknown island in the west. In a world of wars, and rumours of wars, there was a resort to the oldest and most powerful gods.

But the Romans themselves were also inclined to venerate the waters. The number of votive offerings, dating from the Roman settlements by the river, is large enough to suggest that they adopted or imitated the customs of the ancient British tribes whom they conquered. There have been finds of brooches and of lamps, of bronze statuettes and imported red Samian ware. Some of this may be attributable to loss or spoilage, but by no means all. The Roman weapons are often "doubled back" or twisted out of shape, so that they would be rendered useless before being consigned to the river. It was a way of emphasising that their life in the human world was over.

In the same spirit bronze figurines, taken from the river, were found to have been deliberately mutilated; their limbs were amputated, or their heads severed. An image of Mercury, with his right arm removed, was found at London Bridge; so also was a figurine of Apollo, his legs amputated. This is a perplexing phenomenon along the Thames. It has been suggested that the statuettes of the pagan gods were deliberately mutilated by the early Christians before being despatched to the water; in their mythology the underworld, with which the river had associations, had become Hell itself. So, according to this theory, the Thames would transport the heathen idols to the realm of the devil. But the act of water worship, involved in consigning images to the river, works against the assumption. Surely the devotees who left gods in the water were not denying their power or their existence—unless the river itself was seen to be a greater god from whose capacious embrace the deities might not return? The objects may have been ritually killed before their deposition, just as human beings were sacrificed in earlier ages of the world. It was another form of augmenting the power of the river.

A large number of Roman artefacts have been revealed during the various excavations and improvements upon London Bridge. It is the primal site for the deposition of votive objects, and we can assume that it was the place favoured for those looking for the guardian spirit or god of the Thames. When it is recalled that a bridge itself is considered to be an affront to the god, it requires a double form of propitiation. There have been discovered, beside the old timbers, figurines and statuettes, lamps and pots, bells and knives, spindle-whorls and glass and jewellery. There have been discoveries of many hundreds of coins, which are concentrated in a position immediately opposite the second arch of the present bridge; this suggests the close presence of a shrine or altar on the original bridge itself.

There are other deposits that replicate the human form, and in 1834 the brazen head of Hadrian was found near London Bridge. There were also other treasures taken up from the river. An altar, with its resident genius or god, was discovered at Bablock Hythe. At Greenwich were found a lamp with a ram's head and a human mask. A votive plaque, carved in the shape of an altar, was found in the Thames. By London Bridge was retrieved a bronze pair of ritual forceps dedicated to the Mother Goddess, Cybele. These are stray finds over the centuries, but they testify to a continuing interest in cult practice.

The Saxons and the Vikings have left plentiful evidence for their presence in the riverine landscape. Coins bearing the image of Alfred the Great were found in the mud of the Thames at Queenhithe, and in the water itself have been taken up axe-heads and spearheads, swords and spears. There are significant finds of Saxon material at Bray, at Windsor, and near Maidenhead. There are early Saxon spearheads in areas as diverse as Cliveden and Wandsworth, while later Saxon weapons are common in all stretches of the river. The evidence does again support the theory of ritual activity. One Saxon sword, found in the river above Shillingford Bridge, had its tip removed as an act of ceremonial "killing"—perhaps on the death of its owner. There are also many Viking battle-axes, spearheads and swords. At the last count, twenty-four Viking swords had been retrieved from the Thames. The appetite of the river is inexhaustible.

There was no diminution in the scale of medieval piety towards the river. The faithful, returning from Canterbury or from other shrines, had a custom of throwing their pilgrim badges into the waters; on one small area of the foreshore, just east of Blackfriars Bridge, some 250 pewter badges were discovered by what appears to have been a jetty. Among them were the wheel of St. Catherine, the scallop-shell of St. James of Compostella and the rose of St. Dorothy. The river also contained wooden reliquaries and bronze statuettes. The pilgrims were imploring the protection of the saint, perhaps, but the ritual also suggests that they were no less interested in the pagan deities of the Thames. Crucifixes have been found in the Thames with the head of the Christ removed; there are numerous effigies of the saints on the pewter badges, again with the heads broken off. At Wapping was discovered a brass reliquary designed to contain a skull. It may have been a form of sympathetic magic, to protect the head and neck of the owner of the deposit, but it preserves the spirit of ancient rituals.

Two silver pennies from the reign of Henry I were found near the foreshore at Billingsgate; they were bent together in symbolic manner, similar to the ritual clipping of weapons or amputation of votive figures. Many hundreds of medieval inn tokens have been taken up from the river, all of them bent and twisted out of shape. One elaborate and beautiful pilgrim badge, of the Madonna and Child, had been folded up several times before being despatched into the Thames. A lead *ampulla* or small vessel, depicting the martyrdom of Thomas Becket, was found at Toppings Wharf. Hundreds of communion "tokens" have also been recovered. They were all sacred offerings, their broken form attesting to their removal from the natural world of use. But to whom were these offerings made?

Many daggers, spears, swords and other weapons from the twelfth to the sixteenth centuries have been found in the river, many of them bent or broken in the manner of the offerings of weapons from the Bronze Age. Some of them bore inscriptions to whatever god, or power, would welcome them: *Ave Ami* ("Hail, friend") and *Ecce Edwardus* ("Behold Edward") among them. Miniature weapons, made of pewter, were also cast into the waters in the same spirit as the weapons of bone from the Iron Age. Tiny cannons and guns, as well as jugs and cauldrons, have also been found; a small medieval frying pan, complete with miniature fish, has also been recovered. These have been classified as medieval toys, lost by some unlucky child on an expedition down the river, but historians of the Thames may pause before accepting such an attribution. They may not be toys at all but the imitation of real objects designed for another purpose.

How had such knowledge of the river's customs survived for more than three thousand years? It was not written in any medieval book of practice. It must have been preserved in legends and memories that were associated with the Thames. Even as late as the nineteenth century, pins were folded or bent before being thrown into the water. It is an extraordinary example of the persistence of custom and ceremonial. No less significant are the animal offerings made to the river. In the foundations of a fourteenth-century quay, at Trig Lane, two halves of a sheep's jaw were laid in alignment with a wooden beam. It was a way of protecting the structure from the depredation of the waters. Beneath the foundations of the second arch of Blackfriars Bridge, laid in the 1760s, was found a tranche of animal and human bones. Old customs do not seem to disappear. In the nineteenth century it was still customary for ships' captains to throw a penny into the river in order to "buy wind."

The sacred or magical activity of the river is attested by a stranger form of artefact known as the bellarmine, or witch's bottle. In the sixteenth and seventeenth centuries they were used as a precaution against witchcraft, and contained iron nails, scraps of cloth, partly burnt coals and other small items. They have been found at Paul's Pier wharf and at Stepney, at Westminster and at Lambeth, at Gravesend and at Chiswick; many more must await discovery, and they are practical evidence of the close association between the river and the supernatural. It is a link that has remained unbroken since the dawn of the Mesolithic.

The Thames seems to contain the debris of the world—bird-cages and urethral syringes, watches and wooden stools, pipes and phials and wig-curlers. German pottery lies above Venetian glass. A flint hand-axe might share the same stretch of river-bed with a sixteenth-century pot and a nineteenth-century bicycle wheel. A German bomb may lie beside a miniature horse-pistol, and a fragment of Roman statuary beside a blackened relic of the Great Fire. A medieval carpenter's axe may end beside a Roman cooking pot and a nineteenth-century coin-box. In the ancient river all time is redeemable, past and present suspended together in intimate association. The river defies time. The thick mud and silt of its waters lack oxygen and therefore prevent organic decay. Ironwork can be retrieved which, after washing, shines as brightly as the day of its manufacture. Bronze and brass still gleam in the depths. A nineteenth-century clay pipe, found on the foreshore, looks as if it had been discarded a moment before. The river is a great depository of past lives; it is still the home of past cultures that flourished beside its banks.

CHAPTER 43

Head of the River

❧

There is a curious connection between the Thames and severed heads. Of course the heads paraded on London Bridge are the most obvious tokens of this association, but they are a relatively late manifestation of an ancient phenomenon. Heads were deposited in the river from the earliest times. Recent research confirms that almost three hundred skulls have been discovered in the river itself, dating from the Neolithic to the Iron Ages, and that they had been placed there in a "defleshed" condition. This would mean that the flesh was physically scraped from them or, more likely, that they were left to rot until the flesh had fallen away. Only fourteen of them included the mandible. But these are only the documented remnant of what seems to have been wholesale practice. Neolithic skulls have been found placed in pits beside the river; one such pit, at Sutton Courtenay, contained ten human skulls. In some instances the lower mandibles had been removed prior to burial. Marks on a cranium found at Staines suggest that the head was indeed severed from the body at an early stage. Recent excavations have also uncovered a number of human skulls, dating from the Bronze and Iron Ages, that were deliberately placed in riverine locations. Whether this was for the purposes of punishment or of veneration remains unclear.

From the Celtic or Early British period a large number of Roman and British skulls have been discovered in the river below Chelsea Bridge. It might be surmised that these are simply the remains of a more than usually bloody battle, but of course this does not explain why only the skulls have been recovered. It seems more likely that they were severed from the bodies before being placed in the Thames. The stretch of the river at Battersea Bridge was once known as a "Celtic Golgotha," a place of skulls. A paper, published as early as 1857, was entitled "On the discovery of Celtic crania in the vicinity of London." At Strand-on-the-Green, over one hundred human skulls were discovered in the late 1920s. There have been similar finds at Kew and at Hammersmith. The preponderance of the skulls dates from the late prehistoric period, and we may wish to conclude that at some point in its history the Thames was in certain respects a charnel house. The majority of these finds were made between London and Oxford, with particular concentrations in the stretch of the river between Richmond and Mortlake. This may reflect the patterns of population by the Thames, or it may be that these areas are simply the ones that have been most extensively dredged in recent years.

Ritualised heads have also been discovered in the river, perhaps the most notable being that of the emperor Hadrian that was thrown into the Thames close to London Bridge. The marble head of a woman was also found in that stretch of the Thames, and the bronze head of a girl close to the foreshore by Fish Street Hill. And then there is the phenomenon, in the waters of the Thames, of statues with their heads deliberately removed. Some small bronze figurines, for example, were found in the river without heads. Was this some form of communication with the underworld of spirits or with the deities of the river?

The significance and sacredness of the human head were undoubtedly part of ancient British ritual worship. The British believed that the soul resided in the head, rather than the heart, and it may be that in depositing the head the worshippers were also offering up the soul to the other world of which the river was an emblem. Tacitus relates that the Saxons, long before they colonised Britain, were prone to drowning their enemies in the river as sacrifices to the god Nerthus. The Celts severed the heads of both enemies and fellow countrymen for ritual purposes before, like the Saxons, dropping them into the river. It was not simply a pagan practice, however. There have been numerous finds of Christian saints' effigies missing their heads. In the nineteenth and twentieth centuries, as we will discover, both

severed heads and headless corpses have been recovered from the waters of
the Thames.

There is a story connected with this phenomenon, to be found in one
of the Celtic *dindshenchas,* or ballads. It concerns a hero, Riach, who built
a "house" or temple over a well in which he placed the severed heads of
warriors killed in battle. The aura or power of these decapitated heads excited the water to such an extent that it became dangerous, and Riach was
forced to erect a more steadfast structure above the well in order to contain
it. It was of no avail. The waters rushed over him, and he was drowned.
Here the connection is explicitly made between the severed heads of warriors, and the presence of sacred water. The water in some sense responds
to the *mana* of the heads. Is there here some remote explanation for the ritual of depositing human skulls in the Thames? Camden believed that the
name of Maidenhead was derived from the veneration of the head of a
British maiden, said to have been one of the eleven thousand virgins martyred with St. Ursula on the banks of the Rhine.

There are other myths of the head, marking even closer associations
with the Thames itself. The universal Celtic god, Belinus, was charged
with the duty of taking the heads of the sacrificed and of transporting them
to the underworld. It has already been suggested that Billingsgate, the market by the Thames, was named after Belinus. The etymology may or may
not be fanciful; but it is suggestive, if Belinus was indeed considered to be
one of the ancient deities of the river. Another legend of the river is
equally interesting. The British giant, Bran, having been mortally wounded
in a battle with the Irish, ordered that his head be carried down the Thames
and placed by the river at Tower Hill as a bulwark against invasions. As the
rowers progressed down the river, the severed head uttered prophecies
about the island's destiny. The ancient poems claim that King Arthur removed the head, believing that the country needed no other defender than
himself. That is why London, and England, became the victim of Roman
invasion. Bran also means "raven" in modern Welsh and in ancient Bry-
thonic. So Charles II was merely reviving an ancient tradition when he
placed the ravens in the Tower.

Another relatively recent discovery has confirmed the pattern of ritual
killing. Towards the end of the twentieth century a collection of forty-
eight human skulls was found in the Walbrook, one of the tributaries of the
Thames that entered the river near Cannon Street. Ten human skulls were
also found in another London tributary of the Thames, the river Lea.

There are no doubt many more still to be discovered. The Walbrook heads were once believed to represent the victims of Boudicca's invasion of London in AD 60, or perhaps the remnants of some other conflict between the Romans and the British. But the question then remains, why only the skulls? They are of young adult males and, more pertinently, they all appear to have been defleshed before being deposited in the running water. Their mandibles are also missing.

The heads on London Bridge, therefore, take their place in a long tradition. They were deposited there over a period of many centuries; sometimes they were tarred, and sometimes left in their natural state of decapitation. They were stuck upon pikes or poles, and left to rot in the sun and the rain. At the beginning of the fourteenth century, when the first heads are recorded, they were placed on a tower or gate on the northern side of the bridge nearest to the city. The first known instance is the head of Sir William Wallace. Then at some later date, not recorded, the site was changed to the great stone gate nearest Southwark on the south side of the river. This became known as Traitor's Gate. A German traveller counted some thirty heads in 1598, and a map of 1597 shows them clustered together like grapes in a bunch. In fact the heads were not the only human members placed in that position. The legs and "quarters" of convicted traitors were also exhibited there, so that the gate was said to resemble a butcher's shambles. Those engaged in this gruesome practice, however, were participating in a ritual more ancient than they could ever have imagined: they may not have been punishing the dead but, rather, offering up their souls to the Otherworld which is the Thames.

CHAPTER 44

The River of Death

In the spring of 2004 an exhibition was held on the south bank of the Thames, in London, that excited much public attention. It was entitled "Missing," and it contained the photographs of some eighty people who had simply disappeared. No more appropriate spot could have been chosen for such an exhibition. The Thames is a river of the disappeared. In the registers of the National Missing Persons bureau, out of the first eighty unidentified bodies noted, some fourteen had been found in or beside the Thames: "found in the Thames near Erith . . . found in the Thames near the Millennium Wheel . . . found in the Thames at Rotherhithe . . . found in the River Thames near Hammersmith Bridge." And so the litany goes on. It is not at all unusual in the history of the river.

There is some force, perhaps what Dickens called the attraction of repulsion, that still calls many people to the river. There have always been vagrants and beggars sleeping or living beneath the bridges, or huddled in the "pulpits" or passing ways on the bridges themselves. The poorest outcasts of both sexes are known to have employed the seats of the Victoria Embankment, from Westminster Bridge to Blackfriars Bridge, almost as soon as it was constructed. Their enduring fascination with the river is a matter of speculation. Has it to do with the prospect of time, thankfully, passing?

Has it to do with the possibility of immersion? Or does it represent the more mundane desire to be near others suffering the same distress and discomfort? The Thames may call out to the forlorn and to the neglected because it has always been touched by sweat, and labour, and poverty, and tears. The solitaries and vagrants are moved by the same need and loneliness. The river is a great vortex of suffering.

Its darkness has meant that it has been associated with the devil. In the sixteenth and seventeenth centuries there were men in the pageants who dressed themselves as demons, and spouted red and blue fire from their mouths across the waters of the Thames. "Terrible and monstrous wild men they were," Stow wrote, "and made a hideous noise." There was a river-front building on the marshes near Barking, close to the foreshore at Galleons Reach, that was known at the end of the eighteenth century as "the Devil's House"; it was long in a ruinous condition, and was used as a shelter for cattle. Just above Radcot there was a stretch of the river that was known as "Hell's Turn," the meaning of which remains unclear.

The Thames is in many respects the river of the dead. It has the power to hurt and to kill. The figure of the Thames wherryman, and that of the ferryman crossing the river at Lambeth and Gravesend and other localities, seems ultimately to derive from Charon. There were steps known as Dead Man's Stairs at Wapping where, by some accident of tide and current, the corpses of the recently drowned tended to congregate. There is a U-bend between the Isle of Dogs and Deptford, where the drowned may be delayed in their course towards the sea. It was once known as Deadman's Dock, the name given because of the number of corpses that were found there when the dock was being constructed. If the body missed these fatal junctions, and drifted down in its decomposing state past Lower Hope Reach, then there was no hope. It would disappear for ever. There was also Dead Man's Island, lying near Tailness Marsh in the estuary, so called because the corpses of cholera victims were buried there; the bodies came from the prison ships, or "hulks," that were moored in the vicinity during the Napoleonic Wars. Bodies from more recent periods have also been found there; one of them, according to a local waterman, "had shrimps coming out of his eyes, his mouth, his nose. . . ."

It has always been a treacherous river, with its hidden tides and dangerous currents silently working beneath the calm surface. It is extraordinary how quickly a person can go under, sucked down as if grabbed by unseen hands. In the areas beside the old docksides the water would sometimes

simply appear, without steps or wharves, and the unwary pedestrian would
have to start back violently to escape falling into its depths.

The river has always possessed an attraction for suicides, but certain
stretches seem most favoured. In the late eighteenth century a French
writer, Pierre Jean Grosley, explained that the banks of the Thames were
crowded with wharves and manufactories in order to shield the river from
the population considering "the natural bent of the English, and in particular the people of London, to suicide." There is a recent example of one
young woman who travelled from Paris in order to drown herself in the
Thames.

Water is indeed the melancholy element, with its appearance of transitoriness. The water dissolves and passes. It is the material out of which the
house of despair might be constructed. There is always the sense in which
the flowing water induces repose and forgetfulness, but what if that repose
and forgetfulness were to be indefinite? What if the charm of isolation and
withdrawal were to attach itself to the swirling dark water itself? This is
the way of the suicide.

From the medieval period there are several accounts of suicide in the
river, despite the fact that it was considered to be a mortal sin deserving
hell. That is why the suicides were always considered to be insane. Alice de
Wanewyck, for example, "drowned herself in the port of Dowgate, being
non compos mentis." Other Thames suicides were "in a mind other than
their rightful mind." There were of course many medieval citizens who
found their quietus in the river for other reasons: many were simply killed,
and thrown into the water. There are also accounts of drunken Londoners
slipping down the water-stairs and falling into the river.

Most of the suicides in the Thames have remained anonymous and un-
lamented—it was perhaps for that reason that they chose the river in the
first place—but the historical records have documented a few individual
cases. In his diary for 24 February 1666, Pepys records that "going thro'
bridge by water, my waterman told me how the mistress of the 'Beare' tavern, at the Bridge-foot, did lately fling herself into the Thames, and drown
herself . . . it seems she has had long melancholy upon her and hath endeav-
oured to make away with herself often." In the 1680s the son of Sir William
Temple, then Secretary of War, hired a waterman "to shoot the bridge"; in
other words, to go beneath London Bridge at the time when the tide downriver turned into a torrent through the arches. Just as his boat was crossing
beneath a narrow arch, Temple flung himself into the water and immedi-

ately sank. It was discovered later that his pockets were filled with stones, but they were hardly necessary. Hundreds of tons of water drove his body to the bottom where it rotated, rose and was then beaten down again. If he had survived the fall he would no doubt have become enmired in the mud at the bottom of the river which acts as a kind of quagmire for those who land upon it. If that did not kill him, then the cold of the water would have destroyed him within six or seven minutes. In the history of London crime there is not one recorded example of a criminal swimming across the river to escape from his pursuers. It is too daunting a barrier.

The water itself is black; even modern divers can be disoriented by the fact that there is no visibility. At the point where Temple jumped, the waters were known as the "maelstrom," especially in the vicinity of the middle arch, which according to George Borrow in *Lavengro* (1851) was "a grisly pool which, with its superabundance of horror, fascinated me. Who knows but I should have leapt into its depths—I have heard of such things . . ." The darkness and the turbulence of the river exercise a fascination over the unwary, so that you might as it were commit suicide out of instinct rather than determination. If the water in London were clear, and delightful, then it would be much more difficult to jump.

It is also often suggested that deep and silent water provides a potent source of fascination for those who intend to take their own lives. In earlier ages of the world still or stagnant water was considered to be the abode of evil spirits, and perhaps enough of them linger in the quiet stretches of the Thames to lure the unwary to their deaths. Suicides do not normally wish to be seen, or to be found. They wish to make their exit. It is a way of disappearing, perhaps without trace and even without pain. It is possible to imagine the discomfort, but not the pain, of drowning. There are some who claim that it is a peaceful death; but how would they know? It was said that women floated face up, and the men floated face down, but this was no doubt a myth of the river-men.

In 1756 Stephen Duck, a country poet who became a target of ridicule, flung himself into the Thames behind the Black Inn at Reading; perhaps his surname had drawn him towards the river. Another eighteenth-century poet, William Cowper, had chosen the same path to oblivion. He confided later that

not knowing whether to poison myself, I resolved upon drowning. For that purpose I took a coach, and ordered the man to drive to Tower

Wharf, intending to throw myself into the river from the Custom House quay. I left the coach upon the Tower Wharf, intending never to return to it; but upon coming to the quay I found the water low, and a porter seated upon some goods there, as if on purpose to prevent me. This passage to the bottomless pit being mercifully shut against me, I returned back to the coach.

The "bottomless pit" is itself a good phrase for that stretch of the Thames in London.

The nineteenth century was, however, the most fruitful for suicides. A young footman at Hurley became depressed after the death of his own brother by drowning; before he threw himself into the river he dressed in a bathing costume, so that his clothes might be left to his relations. He sought companionship with his brother through a similar death, as if the water were the harbour of lost souls. In another suicide at Hurley, a young man tied a 56-pound (25-kg) weight around his neck before plunging into the water. There are times when the simplest token is the emblem of death. When the hat of a retired stationer was found floating down the river at Bray, the worst was feared; his corpse was later reported to be "comfortable" at a public house. The cap of a baker's boy was found in Bray weir, but his body was not recovered until three weeks later.

Newspaper reports from the nineteenth century furnish a number of similar stories. There was a brewer's labourer who, owing his employers £13, stood in the winter river at Marlow until he died of exposure. Another labourer, having lost his child, somehow managed to bind his own hands and feet before throwing himself into the river. There were two suicides recorded at the Thames in Windsor within a short time of each other; one was the former manager of a theatre, and the other was a butler. The director of a London laundry, before jumping into the river near Windsor (his body was later retrieved by a Windsor eyot known as Monkey Island), had said to his daughter, "Look into my eyes, you can see death there." There is some sense here of the reflections in the river—you can perhaps look into the water and see death there.

Windsor was in fact a favoured spot for those who wished to die. A young woman was witnessed running towards the Thames at Windsor shouting out "William!" and "God help me!" The phrases of other suicides have also been recorded—"Leave me alone. I want to die. I am mad!" "Let me die! Let me die! No one wants me. I would be better out of the way!"

"Take a look at my face. You will never see this face again!" Many putative suicides have been dismayed by their rescue, and have tried to enter the water again at once. It exerts a profound fascination for those who wish for death. There are others who will jump again and again, having been retrieved on each previous occasion. There are watermen's songs about drowning, particularly when they concern the fate of star-crossed or betrayed lovers. These tend to be local in sentiment and in inspiration.

The paradigmatic death of Ophelia has emphasised the poetical nature of suicide by drowning, and those who rush to their deaths in the Thames seem to have been in part guided by tradition. It may be that there is comfort to be found in joining the legion of other Thames suicides, and that somehow the awful oblivion of an individual death is sanctified or hallowed by association. Even in the comic narrative of Thames voyaging, *Three Men in a Boat*, Jerome K. Jerome cannot help reciting the story of one who was then known variously as a "wronged woman" or a "fallen woman," and describes her eventual death in the Thames.

> She had wandered about the woods by the river's brink all day, and then, when evening fell and the grey twilight spread its dusky robe upon the waters, she stretched her arms out to the silent river that had known her sorrow and her joy. And the old river had taken her into its gentle arms, and had laid her weary head upon its bosom, and had hushed away the pain.

There is for Jerome something devoutly to be wished about this fate, as if the prospect of death within the Thames offers comfort and consolation. And that may be so. We suspect that for many thousands of years it was used as a gateway for the dead to their final destination. Who knows but that we are simply following our ancestors?

To the "dead houses" along the banks of the Thames were brought the bodies which, in the words of the ubiquitous posters, had been "found drowned." It is estimated that three or four corpses were recovered each week, although it is an open question whether some deaths were accidental or induced, rather than deliberate. There was a swing bridge by Old Gravel Lane, in the London Docks and close to St. Peter's Church, which was also known as the "Bridge of Sighs" because of the suicides there. There is no apparent reason for the incidence of self-slaughter on this spot, unless it be the sheer weight of example. After Waterloo Bridge was opened, in the summer of 1817, it was known variously as "Lover's Leap," "Arch of Suicide," "Bridge of Sighs" or "Bridge of Sorrow." It was at times a relatively isolated place; the penny toll, issued at either end of the bridge, deterred many pedestrians. In the middle of the nineteenth century the average number of suicides each year from this vantage was thirty. In the latter part of the century there was an especially designed "jumpers' boat," moored by the bridge, with a roller across its stern to help the recovery of the subject in the water. This was a necessary precaution since the act of retrieval could itself be dangerous; the putative suicide, struggling, may pull the rescuer into the water. This boat was succeeded by a floating police station.

It has been suggested, in fact, that there is a quality in the immediate neighbourhood or in the local atmosphere of Waterloo Bridge that encourages suicide. When the German poet, Heinrich Heine, came here one late afternoon in 1827 he recorded later "the black mood which once came over me as toward evening I stood on Waterloo Bridge, and looked down on the water of the Thames . . . At the same time the most sorrowful tales came into my memory." This is perhaps a testimony to the power of the dark Thames. He went on to declare that "I was so sick in spirit that the hot drops sprang forcibly out of my eyes. They fell down into the Thames and swam forth into the mighty sea, which has already swallowed up such floods of human tears without giving them a thought."

Charles Dickens was fascinated by the suicides along the river and by this bridge in particular. In one of his essays as an "uncommercial traveller" or wanderer, "Night Walks" (1860), he crossed Waterloo Bridge from where

> the river had an awful look, the buildings on the banks were muffled in black shrouds, and the reflected lights seemed to originate deep in the water, as if the spectres of suicides were holding them to show where they went down. The wild moon and clouds were as restless as an evil conscience in a tumbled bed, and the very shadow of the immensity of London seemed to lie oppressively upon the water.

For Dickens the river was inextricably bound up with the consciousness of death.

Curiously enough the eldest son of Charles Dickens was also intrigued by the nature and extent of Thames suicides, and interviewed the toll-keepers on Waterloo Bridge as the experts upon the subject:

This is the best place! If people jump off straight forwards from the middle of the parapet of the bays of the bridge, they don't kill them-selves drowning, but are smashed, poor blighters, that's what they are . . . But *you* jump awf from the *side* of the bay, and you'll tumble true into the stream under the arch . . . what you've got to do is mind how you jump in.

As the opening scenes of *Our Mutual Friend* (1865) testify, there was also a thriving trade in retrieving the corpses of the dead. Gaffer Hexam goes out at night in his small boat to find anything "which bore some resemblance to the outline of a muffled human form" and to pick up what spoils he can from the bodies and clothing of those who were sufficiently buoyant to be found floating in the dark water around Limehouse. There is, as is always the case with Dickens's urban scenes, more than an element of truth in this account. In the late nineteenth century, for example, the authorities on the Surrey side of the river paid 5 shillings (a crown) for every body recovered while those on the Middlesex side paid only half a crown. That is why most of the corpses were taken to Surrey. Here they were photographed and re-moved to the parish "dead house" rather than to the police station. When the unclaimed corpses were eventually buried, on the order of the coroner, their clothes were preserved to assist any later identification.

Just a few yards away from Dead Man's Stairs, at the headquarters of the river police in Wapping, can be found the Book of the Dead, or "Oc-currence Book," the registry of those whose bodies have been taken out of the river. In the entry for 2 July 1966, for example, there is a report that wit-nesses

noticed an elderly, respectably dressed man on the pier . . . A few sec-onds later they looked again and were in time to see the man splash into the water, where he drifted down with the ebb-tide . . . During the time the man was in the water he was in constant view of the rescuers who did not see him struggle or hear him call out.

On 26 May 1948, under the heading of "Suicide Alleged," is a report of a witness: "I heard someone shout 'Goodbye!' I looked around and saw a man's legs disappearing over the port side aft." A river policeman added that: "I launched the dinghy and rowed out to try and save him but, as I was holding him, he struggled so violently that he pulled himself free from my grasp and before I could catch hold of him again he sank." He did not wish to be rescued. A little while later a "gent's brown soft felt hat was found floating by."

There are certain days that prompt suicide. Thus on the last day of 1986 there were two suicides within hours of each other. At 8:34 a.m. the police "recovered the dead body of a female from south foreshore"; then at 13:15 they "recovered the lifeless body of a male at Battersea Reach off Falcon Wharf."

So there was no diminution of numbers in the twentieth century. They had become known as "jumpers," a slight word for so momentous an act, or in the mid-twentieth century as "stiffs." In the long period of river pollution, however, those who jumped were as likely to be poisoned as to be drowned; a stomach pump was part of the routine panoply of rescue equipment. In 2002 the Royal National Lifeboat Institution was joined with the River Police and HM Coast-Guard in order to deal with those who had jumped or fallen into the Thames. Within the space of one year there were almost four hundred incidents. There are more suicides in winter than in summer. It is a curious fact, perhaps, that the majority of those found dead in the Thames—and that could be identified—came from beyond the borders of the capital itself. The mother of one young suicide, living in Streatham, told a *Guardian* journalist in December 2004, "There was no reason for him to be there. The river is haunted—it draws people in."

Some other examples of suicide in the last century are no less unusual. One man was found with £3,000 strapped to his chest, so that he could pay for his own funeral. In another incident the body of a man was found weighed down with a dictionary, and almost £200's worth of coins. On another occasion a man who had weighed himself down left a series of claw-marks upon the mud on the bankside; he had attempted to change his mind. Two young girls—two sisters—tied themselves together before throwing themselves into the water. The explanation for their conduct is not known. Some young men were struggling in fun beside the bank of the Thames, and threw one of their number into the river; the man in the water grabbed hold of the first solid object he could find. It was a corpse. I am indebted for these fatal details to one of the most interesting books on the Thames published in recent years, *Another Water* (2000) by Roni Horn.

Bodies decompose more quickly out of the water, when the hair and skin become particularly fragile. But they are exposed to assaults within the tidal river, also, where they can be buffeted by boats and attacked by seagulls. Dickens noted that the bodies of the drowned are seared and discoloured as if they had been the victims of fire rather than of water.

The coroner, when asked to pronounce judgement upon the drowned, will tend to deliver an "open" verdict; there can never be any certainty, in such cases, that the deceased had intended to take his or her own life. It is in any case a wise precaution, since there are not only the bodies of suicides in the river. It has always carried traffic in the victims of murder. There were the mass slaughters of ancient battles when, according to one fourteenth-century chronicler, the river was dyed red with blood. But from the earliest times the Thames was the most convenient and expeditious way of depositing corpses. The medieval city records contain many cases of persons discovered dead in the water. In the sixteenth century it was reported that "there were robberies and murders done nigh Radynge [Reading], and divers men found slain and drowned in the Thames." The highwaymen and footpads who frequented the high road from Hounslow Heath to Colnbrook, in the seventeenth century, used the river near Datchet as a convenient dumping ground for the corpses of those whom they had robbed and murdered; these were placed in sacks, weighted down and deposited in the water. As a result this stretch of the river became known locally as "Colnbrook churchyard."

In the eighteenth century the Thames and its London tributaries became notorious as a means of dispatch. There was a tavern overlooking the Fleet river, or Fleet ditch as it had essentially become, where the criminal fraternity gathered. Here, in a cellar room, was a trap-door that opened immediately above the water; it was used as a refuse disposal point for the corpses of those who had been inveigled to this place and met their death. In the early nineteenth century the bodies of rival gang members were often found in the river, too, and thirteen of their number were recovered from the Thames in one year.

The vast majority of these crimes remained unsolved, no doubt because the Thames itself acted as a great dissolvent of motive and locality. The fact that few murderers were caught, however, might lead to the irrational suspicion that the river was itself somehow responsible. There can be no doubt that in the newspaper reports of the nineteenth century, the Thames itself was often depicted as a baleful presence in the sagas of guilt and crime. There were popular catchpenny volumes with titles such as *The*

Secret Thames and *The Mysterious Thames Murders* that capitalised upon the somewhat eerie reputation of the Thames in the mid-Victorian and late Victorian periods. In one later volume, Elliott O'Donnell's *Great Thames Mysteries* (1928), there is a report of three cases of dismemberment in the neighbourhood of Putney; the author then goes on to suggest that "the murderer had some particular attachment to the neighbourhood"; of another stretch of the river, near Dagenham, he records that "cries of murder from the waterside were of frequent occurrence after dusk, and those who heard them, if alone, merely shivered and hastened on."

The history of Thames murders is embellished, too, by the fact that many of the victims found floating in its waters had been dismembered. There are reports from 1828 of a head found at Shadwell; in 1873 a dismembered body was found at Battersea, and in the succeeding year two bodies in a similar condition were partly retrieved at Putney and Vauxhall Bridge, leading many citizens to think the worst of their river. As O'Donnell puts it, "no mystery associated with the Thames up to that time gave it a more sinister reputation or made it more dreaded, and it was long ere the horror of it faded from men's minds." The killer or killers were deemed to manifest "a hideous fascination for the Thames." The familiar river, the silver-streaming Thames of previous centuries, had become the object of dread and superstitious fear. It may have been reviving its ancient powers.

One of the most famous cases, or series of cases, were the torso murders that occurred in 1887, 1888, 1889 (two bodies were found in that year), and finally in 1902. The first body was found by the river wall at Rainham, in Essex, with the dismembered head and limbs wrapped in a piece of coarse sacking. Other parts of the same body were found at Temple Pier, and at Battersea. According to the *Essex Times* of 8 June 1887, "great excitement was caused on the Victoria Embankment." Murders on the river do in fact create "excitement," if only because there seems to be some instinctive link between death and flowing water. In the following year a woman's arm was found in the river mud near Pimlico; the discovery of other parts followed, leading one newspaper to describe "a carnival of blood." In 1889 the various parts of two bodies were found at St. George's Stairs, Albert Bridge, Battersea, Wandsworth and Limehouse; a "small liver" was discovered at Wapping. Only one of the victims was ever identified. It was rumoured at the time that these crimes were the work of the killer known as "Jack the Ripper," but the claim was never substantiated. It was also counteracted with the report that "the Ripper" had in fact been drowned in the Thames—another indication, perhaps, how the river was instinctively associated with the darker forms of crime. In the opening shots of Alfred Hitchcock's film, *Frenzy* (1972), the body of a strangled young woman is seen floating down the Thames.

There were many famous river murders of the twentieth century. In the early months of 1964 the bodies of two prostitutes were found in the vicinity of Hammersmith Bridge; later victims were found on dry ground, but in the riverine neighbourhoods of Chiswick and Brentford. In 2001 the remains of a human torso were found in the water; it turned out to be the body of a young African boy who was given the name of "Adam" by the police. The killers have never been found, but it is believed that the child was murdered as a result of some form of magical ritual. In the same period the police discovered seven half-burnt candles, wrapped in a white sheet, washed up on the southern bank. It is less generally known that, only nine months before, another dismembered torso had been found in the river; it was that of a young woman named Cathy Dennis. The intestines and leg of another victim were found in the river by Silvertown. On another occasion in very recent years the head and limbs, but not the torso, of a man were found in the Thames. On 8 July 1999, a human head was found in the mud at Lower Pool; it had been skinned to avoid identification. Other parts of the body, including the torso, were found in other parts of the river. The Thames has always harboured an affection for severed heads.

There are other forms of death within the river. There are the accidental drownings. In the parish register of Henley Church, beside the river, are records of such incidents: "8 April 1563. Ignotus quidam viator. Sepultus . . . 24 May 1601. John Smith, a stranger, drowned. Sepultus . . . 30 April 1611. James, a bargeman, called Sweetapple, being drowned. Sepultus." The registry of every church by the banks of the river will have similar testimony to the dangers of the Thames. At Marlow Lock in 1585 "the Streams there were so strong, and the Water had such a dismal Fall, that Four men within a short time were lost, three whereof drowned, and a Fourth had his brains dasht out." It is a signal reminder of the sheer power and brute force of the water. The river along this stretch was so rapid that it became known as "Marlow Race," and one poet complained that it

... hath made many a Child to weepe.
   Their mothers begg from dore to dore
Their ffathers drowned in the deepe.

The river can be a ferocious, as well as a turbulent, god.

A pamphlet of 1647 bears the long but graphic title of "Sad and deplorable news from Oxfordsheir and Barksheir, being a true and lamentable relation of the drowning of about sixty persons, men, women and children, in the lock near Goring in Oxfordsheir, as they were passing by water from Goring feats to Stately [Streatley] in Barksheir." It seems the waterman took his crowded boat too close to a weir where, by the force of the water, it was drawn in and overturned. Even by the standards of the river this was a sizeable loss of life. One of those eventually rescued from the waters reported that some of the drowning creatures were "sprawling about like frogs" on the river-bed. Other victims of drowning seem to have put up no struggle at all, and are found lying upon their backs as if they had fallen asleep.

In 1763

a Boat, with ten people in it, going through London-Bridge, in order to go down the river, overset, and three People were drowned . . . On Tuesday night a Barge, heavily loaded with Timber, coming through London-Bridge, ran against one of the Starlings, and by the shock John Herbert, one of the Bargemen, unfortunately fell overboard and was drowned.

Four years later "On Monday night, a little before ten o'clock, a boat with three women and two men going through London-Bridge overset, and all perished." And so it goes on. It was estimated in the eighteenth century that some fifty people were drowned, on average, each year beneath the bridge. This was largely, or wholly, the result of "shooting" upon the departing tide. There was some interest in compiling these early statistics not least because, as A. J. Church put it in *Isis and Tamesis* (1886), "The Englishman dearly loves to spice his pleasures with the sense of danger . . . and the river fascinates him most when he can discern a prospect of being drowned." This consorts well with the belief that the English were a nation of putative suicides, and suggests the somewhat macabre presence of the Thames in the national life. It has been celebrated by limericks as well as by poems and songs, like this of Edward Lear in his *Book of Nonsense* (1846):

> There was an old person of Ems,
> Who casually fell in the Thames,
> And when he was found,
> They said he was drowned,
> That unlucky old person of Ems

There were many other deaths by drowning in the nineteenth century, when boating for sport and for recreation became the most popular of all pastimes. The long dresses of the ladies made them particularly susceptible to the currents of the water if they fell in. Some people out punting thrust their poles into ballast holes, while others had drunk too much to keep a safe footing. Some ate too well, and were caught by cramp while swimming. Others were fatally captivated by the pleasures of the river; they stayed out too late, when the fog and the evening closed down upon them; they were capsized or overturned in moments of unusual jollity, or they were simply not accustomed to the dangers of the apparently peaceful Thames. The *Daily Mail* of June 1896 interviewed one lock-keeper who had in the course of his service seen a dozen drownings, including "a whole boatful upset by moonlight and their bodies come up one after another and float about in the lock."

Even the professionals of the river were unsafe. The ferryman at Cookham overbalanced in a rain-storm of 1881, and in 1893 the ferryman and his wife at Shillingford were also drowned. The lock-keepers at Hurley, at Whitchurch, at Pinkhill, at Abingdon, at Caversham, at Shiplake and at Hambleden were all drowned in the period from 1871 to 1890. This is a large loss of life among those who were in essence the guardians of the Thames. We are reminded of the words of Isaiah, "Watchman, what of the night?" Yet it is perhaps not so extraordinary that the people who worked and lived by the river also made up a large proportion of those found drowned; sheer propinquity to the water must increase the risks of being caught within it. The frequency of mortality, however, does suggest the treachery and the unanticipated dangers of the river. The area of Temple Lock and Temple Mills seems to have been peculiarly fated; two small daughters of lock-keepers, as well as a son of twenty, were drowned in the waters here.

The worst Thames disaster of that century took place on 3 September 1878. A pleasure paddle steamer, the *Princess Alice*, was returning from

Gravesend to London in the early evening of that day. As the steamer turned the bend between Crossness and Margaret Ness, in the area down-river at Galleons' Reach now known as Thamesmead, she encountered a steam-collier, the *Bywell Castle*, proceeding in the opposite direction. There seems to have been some confusion over signals, and "right of way," since the vessels collided. The captain of the *Princess Alice* was heard to call out: "Ease her! Stop her! Where are you coming to? Good God, where are you coming to?" The collier ploughed into the paddle steamer and broke her apart. One surviving passenger said that it was "like the side of a ware-house" crashing down upon the much smaller ship.

As the stern and bows rose into the air, the *Princess Alice* began to sink. She was beneath the water within four minutes, drowning all but a few of the crew and passengers. A diver sent down to survey the condition of the wreck reported that the doors to the saloon were jammed with the bodies of pas-sengers, most of them still erect and packed closely together. The master of a ship close to the scene stated that "I can compare the people to nothing else than a flock of sheep in the water"; the *Princess Alice* herself was "nothing else than a cloud. One moment she was there, and the next moment clean gone. The river seemed full of drowning people." It was reported that the Thames was "like a sarcophagus," not for the first time in its history.

Some of those who might have been able to swim to shore were in fact overcome by the pollution of the Thames. An hour before the collision, the outfalls of the sewage pumping stations that Joseph Bazalgette had recently built at Crossness and Barking discharged 75 million gallons (341 million l) of waste. According to a chemist writing in *The Times* after the collision, this effluent consisted of "two continuous columns of decomposed fer-menting sewage, hissing like soda water with baneful gases so black that the water stained for miles, and discharging a corrupt charnel house odour." There had also been a fire in Thames Street that afternoon, sending oil, tur-pentine and petroleum into the water. It was noted that the bodies retrieved from the river were covered with a kind of slime. When it was washed off, it simply reappeared. Clothing was discoloured, and rapidly began to rot. The corpses of the victims were unnaturally bloated, requiring especially constructed coffins, and they decomposed too quickly. Some survivors died later from unknown causes. Two weeks later it was reported that sixteen of the rescued "have since expired and many more . . . in a precarious state."

It was later estimated that approximately seven hundred people were killed, representing the largest peacetime disaster upon the river. Some 160 bodies were never claimed, and they were eventually buried in a mass grave in Woolwich Cemetery. One of the few apparent survivors was a young woman named Elizabeth Stride, who later claimed (perhaps falsely) that she lost her husband and three children in the accident. Hers in any case was not to be a death by water. She became the third victim of "Jack the Ripper." It was said that she took to prostitution as a direct result of the family's tragedy.

The only comparable event in recent times was the sinking of the pleasure boat, the *Marchioness*, between Southwark Bridge and Cannon Street Bridge on 20 August 1989. She had collided with a dredger, the *Bowbelle*, of 1,457 tons (1,498 tonnes) against the 90 tons (91 tonnes) of the pleasure boat. On that occasion fifty-one people drowned. The Attorney General of the time, Lord Williams, asked at the inquiry into the disaster, "How is it that if so many people had known for so long of the risk of a serious collision on the Thames, such a thing could still happen?"

The writers of the nineteenth century, unlike their counterparts in the twentieth century, seemed to linger over descriptions of death and mortality. G. D. Leslie, in *Our River* (1881), was one of the many riparian travellers who could not resist the narration of a good drowning. He recounts an incident, at which he was present, when the son of a Baptist minister was caught in the "back suck" of a weir. Leslie relates how "the poor father, half-dressed, kept walking around the edge of the weir, calling to his child, at times bursting into prayer." When the corpse of the child was eventually brought to the surface in a fisherman's drag it seemed to Leslie to be "quite beautiful in death, not being marred or injured in any way." So the child looked "beautiful" in death; he had retained his purity, not being marred, and indeed that purity had been reinforced by his premature demise in the river.

There is in fact a noticeable association in Victorian texts between child and Thames and death, as if this trinity of concerns was an emblem of the ambiguous attitude of the Victorians towards childhood and innocence. They were lamenting the loss of children even as they were consigning them to death in the manufactories and unhealthy streets of the cities. There is the curious story at the opening of *The Book of the Thames* (1859), by Mr. and Mrs. Hall, concerning young Emily who in their hearing refused to cross a simple wooden bridge between Kemble and Ewen. She screamed out that she was afraid. It transpires that she and her grandmother had been crossing this bridge when they both fell into the water. Emily was rescued but "Nanny"—"a fat, merry little thing" according to the family—was never recovered. If Emily ever looked into the Thames, "everything she sees bright on the water she says is Nanny's face— Nanny's face looking up at her." Innocence is threatened, even stained, by the bloated visage of the corpse and by the insidious menace of the river. It is a curious prelude to a book on the Thames, perhaps, and is followed a few pages later by the drowning of Jabez Lloyd, a boatman, who fell face down into a bed of lilies and died before he could be extricated from "the meshes of the golden-chaliced flowers and their broad leaves." Death can emerge in beauty. In Victorian literature concerning the Thames there is always a moral to be drawn, even if it is preserved quietly beneath the surface of the writing.

There is a strange mural monument in Cookham Church to Sir Isaac Pocock, carved in the early nineteenth century; he is seen being caught by an angel while falling into the Thames from a punt, with an inscription that he was "suddenly called from this world to a better state, whilst on the Thames near his own house." Perhaps he is one of those to be seen rising from the dead in Stanley Spencer's painting of Cookham Churchyard.

There is that curious phrase, "to set the Thames on fire." One explanation has to do with a sieve, or "temse," that was used for sieving flour. It was believed that a vigorous workman could make it ignite with constant friction against the flour-bin, and of an inefficient workman it was said that "he will never set the temse on fire." It is so prosaic a theory that it has the ring of truth. But the Thames has also been associated with deaths by lightning, and along the upper reaches of the river it is possible to see lightning-blasted trees. There is one on the summit of Sinodun Hill. Such trees were commonly considered to be sacred. Ash-trees, in particular, were believed to attract fire. In *The Book of the Thames*, there is the story of a fisherman who sat patiently by the riverside "until a flash of lightning deprived him of his sight." In the seventeenth century Dr. Robert Plot recalled a great lightning storm over the river at Oxford when two scholars of Wadham College were struck into the water from their boat, "the one of them stark Dead, and the other stuck fast in the Mud like a Post, with his Feet downward." Just downstream of Radcot, there is another lightning-blasted tree on the very bank of the river. Fire and water are not necessarily antagonistic.

PART XV

The River's End

Thames and Medway

CHAPTER 45

Downriver

❧

It is a mysterious, and an ambiguous, place. Where does the river end and the sea begin? The estuary is the brackish zone, combining salt water and fresh water in equal or unequal quantities. It remains largely unknown and unvisited. The river has changed its nature. It is coming ever closer to the sea, which is always hostile to mankind. There is an area of the estuary, used for the dumping of London's waste, that is still known as the "Black Deep." The waters can be treacherous here, and the waves of the estuary have been known to reach a height of 7 feet. It is a deeper and darker river. Joseph Conrad believed that it appealed strongly "to an adventurous imagination."

The estuary is some 250 miles square and has a length of 30 miles, reaching from Gravesend to the Nore where the Thames becomes the North Sea. At that point of transition, its width is 10 miles. There are three principal approach channels, one of which is the Black Deep, and a score of subsidiary channels or "swatchways" with names like "the Warp" and "the Wallet." The light-ships that dip and swing in the tide are called *Mouse* and *Tongue* and *Girdler*. This is the poetry of the river. The sands and shoals are given names such as "Shingles" and "Shivering Sand," "the Spell" and "the Oven." "Sunk Sand" runs between the Black Deep and the

Barrow Deep. But the names are in one sense deceptive. The "sands" are part clay and part black viscous mud.

The estuarial marshes beside the river are liminal areas; they are neither water nor dry land. They partake of two realities, and in that sense they are blessed. That is why the Thames estuary has always been considered a place of mystery and of enchantment. At times of low tide the sands and shoals become islands, with the false promise of a haven. In the poems of the Anglo-Saxons it is a landscape of nightmare. The "flats" form a dull and monotonous expanse, low ground crossed by paths. The sky seems larger, and closer, here. The tide-washed mud-flats reflect the changing light. For many centuries this land was largely uninhabited and uninhabitable. As such it exerts a primitive and still menacing force, all the more eerie and lonely because of its proximity to the great city.

There is a sense of strangeness and melancholy here at dusk. Charles Dickens understood it very well, and in *Great Expectations* described how "the dark flat wilderness beyond the churchyard, intersected with dykes and mounds and gates, with scattered cattle feeding on it, was the marshes; and that the lower leaden line beyond which the wind was rushing, was the sea." Magwitch could hide here, making his secret way along the network of hidden planks that used to traverse the mud-flats and moving sands. This is all land that has been saved from the sea, and thus has an ambiguous status. Parts of its territory, in both the lower and upper reaches, have often been deemed to be wild and inhospitable. Strangers were not welcomed. Even at the beginning of the twenty-first century, walking alone by the shores of the estuary, it is possible to feel great fear—fear of the solitude, fear of being abandoned, fear of what is alien represented by the river itself. It may be a fear of the primaeval Thames.

There are the Whalebone Marshes and the Halstow Marshes, Dagnam Saltings and the Grain and Allhallows Marshes, lying low and flat across the horizon. There are salt-marshes and brackish fresh-water marshes, the latter used for grazing. Some of these grazing marshes, however, are now being turned to cereals. There are no trees, because no deeply rooting plant can grow in marshland. It is hard to imagine a more desolate landscape. Yet, with its constantly changing light, it has its own beauty. It is the home of sea-lavender and golden samphire, and of the flowing salt-marsh grasses; its creeks and pools are fringed with sea-aster. And there are the endless birds, the ducks and heron and geese and curlews, the sandpipers and plovers and redshanks, that love the loneliness of the marshes.

The communities of the marshes have always been smaller, and more isolated, than those upon firmer ground. Of the Hundred of Hoo, the area of territory between the Thames and the river Medway, it has been said that "it is the last place God made—and never finished." A clergyman of the neighbourhood once wrote that "it was understood to be an out-of-the-way, wild sort of place in which, unless obliged to do so, people did not live." And it is wild—or, rather, it has traces of wildness about it. This is not the wildness of nature, but the wildness of desolation. It is not a human place. You can walk along the river wall of the Hundred of Hoo for miles, between the river and the grass, without encountering anyone at all. It was notorious as the place for smugglers. The hamlet of Allhallows was, according to the eighteenth-century antiquarian, Edward Hasted, in "a most unfrequented and dreary situation." In the nineteenth century few people visited the Isle of Grain or the Isle of Sheppey. The inhabitants of Grain— the Pannells and the Willsons and the Frys—considered themselves to be a race apart. The population of St. Mary's Hoo increased by four people over the entire course of the nineteenth century. The peninsula of East Tilbury, and the remote Canvey Island, were once entirely estranged from the ordinary current of life. The inhabitants of the estuary were known as "Stackies" or "Stiffies." The towns that persisted, such as Gravesend and Greenhithe, Grays and Erith, managed to survive because they were built upon the few patches of firm ground in the vicinity. There is chalk beneath Greenhithe, and gravel beneath Erith.

There are other names here which seem like some form of atavistic remembrance, some token of an ancient and now forgotten past. The names of the villages, Fobbing and Corringham, Mucking and Thurrock, have survived for a thousand years. From the entry of the Medway Canal to Shorne a stretch of water was known as "the Priveys"; from Shorne to Higham the name of the river was "Down the hole." From Gravesend to Tilbury the water was called "the Blockhouse" or "the Jerkhouse," the derivations of which are uncertain. But the meanings of some names are clear enough. The wide reach of the river from Gravesend and Tilbury seawards is known as "the Hope." The submerged forest near West Thurrock, dating from the primaeval past, was known as "the Roots." In a place where there were once few signs of change, old names linger. Havengore comes from the Anglo-Saxon root of "gore," meaning a triangular tract of land. The name of Maplin derives from the twigs, known as "mapples," from which brooms were once made. Holy Haven has become, over the centuries, Hole Haven.

It has always been an area of sickness. It has been estimated that, in the seventeenth and eighteenth centuries, almost half of the population suffered from malaria or what was then known as the "ague." Thus William Lambarde, in *The Perambulation of Kent* (1576), noted that "Hooh is taken from 'Hoh' in Old English which means Sorrowe or Sicknesse, a suitable name for this unwholesome Hundred." In his *Tour Through the Whole Island of Great Britain* (1724–6) Defoe noted that in the marshes it was not uncommon for the men to have had "from five to six, to fourteen or fifteen wives," but this was the consequence of mortality rather than profligacy. The men of the marshes had grown up in that unhealthy locality and were "season'd to the place" but the women, from the "uplands," were not so fortunate. "When they came out of their native air into the marshes among the fogs and damps, then they presently changed their complexion, got an ague or two, and seldom held it above half a year." The two rows of thirteen little tombstones in Cooling Churchyard, the inspiration for the gloomy scene at the beginning of *Great Expectations*, are no doubt the tokens of infantine malaria. The inhabitants of this feverish territory were described in the eighteenth century as of a "dingy yellow colour," and it was reported that "it is not unusual to see a poor man, his wife, and whole family of five or six children hovering over their fire in the hovel, shaking with an ague all at the same time." The children were given opium to keep them from harm, so that they became "wasted" and "wizened like monkeys," while the adults indulged excessively in what were called "spirituous liquors."

There were many who came to the estuary for the sport of shooting wildfowl, but they "often return with an Essex ague on their backs, which they find a heavier load than the fowls they have shot." In the nineteenth century the common question among local people was "Have you had your ague this spring?" A parliamentary committee, established in 1864, established that the cause of the infection was the ubiquitous anopheles mosquito that bred in the stagnant waters of the marshlands. The parasite it carried has now been identified as *Plasmodium vivax*. This may be no more comprehensible than the earlier descriptions of "spirituous miasma" emanating from the vaporous marshland.

By some form of melancholy parallel the estuarial river was also the home of the plague ships and the quarantine ships. In the seventeenth century those suffering from the plague or yellow fever were placed on vessels anchored off Dead Man's Island, just north of Chetney on the North Kent

Marshes. The island received its name, of course, from the bodies that were buried there; in *The Thames Transformed* (1976) Jeffery Harrison and Peter Grant reported that "to this day one has only to wade across Shepherd's Creek to Dead Man's to be able to find human bones with no effort, a surprising number showing signs of osteomyelitis, a chronic bone infection." A plague hospital was to be established upon the shore, at Chetney Hill, but construction work was abandoned when the land was found to be unstable. This has been one of the dark places of the earth. But where there are cares, there are also cures. In the eighteenth and nineteenth centuries doctors frequented the marshes to collect specimens from the abundant beds of leeches in the neighbourhood.

For many centuries the area between Barking and Gravesend was deserted except for some odd cottages, churches, farms and riverside inns for travellers along the Thames. There were trackways through the marshes, and pasture land. It was a good place to rear the beasts of the field; the marshes were known to be "kind to cattle," and the dearest meat was known as "marsh mutton." Now the north side of the estuary is lined with oil refineries, gas plants and sewage treatment plants; there are cement works and petrochemical works. Here is industrial architecture on a giant scale, like Nineveh or Babylon emerging on the banks of the river. And this, too, is now part of its history. The Thames estuary was the cradle of the electric power station, when at the end of the nineteenth century Sebastian de Ferranti built the first long-distance transmission station at Deptford. There will come a time when these installations, if they are allowed to survive, will be defined by their ancientness like the earthworks of the region.

There are communities on either shore; there have always been settlers, but now they come in larger waves as part of the new "Thames corridor" spreading out towards Europe. There are developments in place for towns such as Thurrock and Gravesend. The region of the lower river has been taken up in the general regeneration of the Thames. Yet there are still areas of dereliction; ancient jetties, quays and harbours have been left to decay. There are the hulks of scuppered or lost ships. It is still a place of slimy stones emerging from the mud, of old landing stages and ancient roofless buildings slowly merging with the water and the sand. And the marshlands still exude the same ancient air of desolation.

But then there is the sea. The Thames, now wide and exultant, has been conceived as rushing into its embrace. The mark of their meeting is the

An Alternative Topography,
from Source to Sea

❦

KEMBLE: Once known as Kemele or Camele, meaning boundary. The derivation, however, might be from the ancient British god Camulos. The river
collects itself here, so to speak, from a number of little streamlets or rivulets
that meander through the fields. Harrison says that the stripling river "first
of all receiueth the Kemble water called the Coue." The early inhabitants of
the area were the British Dobunni, whose territory was later occupied by the
Romans. A Roman burial site was discovered here. It is mentioned in the
charters of the Anglo-Saxon kings, the earliest dating to AD 682. Two
Saxon cemeteries have also been found here. There used to be a grove or
wood close to the church, which was described by a nineteenth-century antiquary as "the scene of the peculiar sacrificial rites of that race"; no particular evidence has been provided for this claim. The church itself was struck
by lightning in 1834. The yew-tree in the churchyard is the oldest living organism in the village, which is well known for the ubiquity of the water-
crowfoot or *Ranunculus aquatilis*. The first ducks of the Thames are to be
seen here. The Thames used to be known to the locals as "the brook," which

in many respects it resembles. It is diminutive, with an agreeable tinkling
sound. Before the advent of modern life the village organised an annual festival known as Jackimans Club; there was also a wake, during which the effigy of an ox was paraded around the village. The neighbourhood is not
heavily populated and few, if any, people are to be seen along the banks of
the river. The bridge that leads from Kemble to the neighbouring village of
Ewen has the distinction of being the first bridge, topographically, on the
Thames. The inn at Kemble was kept by one "Damper" Adams, a maker of
wooden ploughs. His ale was so notoriously bad that a gang of men stole the
casks and poured the beer into the river. The names of the villages in this region of the Upper Thames have a peculiar charm, leading one American essayist to remark that "an atmosphere of legendary melody spreads over the
land." The oldest legends here, however, were of battlefields and border
territory. It was once a very bloody place. Camulos himself was a warrior
deity, often linked with Mars. Where there is trade there is power, and where
there is power there is strife. The whole region has been striated with conflict throughout its human history, and the fields and meadows of the Upper
Thames have often been cited as the location of battles between the various
British tribes, between Saxons and Britons, between Romans and Britons.

EWEN: The name can be derived from Aewilme, meaning spring or source, yet
   another confusion in the confusing provenance of the Thames. As a source
   of springs it was deemed to be a holy place. On eighteenth-century maps it

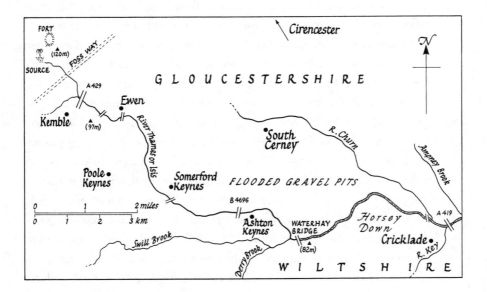

is spelled as Yeoing, and was pronounced by the locals as Yeowin. The river here is cleared twice each year, for the unimpeded passage of the water in its infantine state. The area was known for the number of its centenarians, and was thus pronounced to be especially healthful. The inhabitants were known for their appetites as well as their great age. One inhabitant, Cornelius Uzzle, devoured 12 pounds of bacon—6 pounds raw and 6 pounds parboiled—at the Wild Duck Inn. The Wild Duck exists still, and is renowned for its excellent food. The entire area, downriver from Kemble and Ewen, has been very fruitful for archaeologists; there have been sites here from the Palaeolithic, Mesolithic and Neolithic periods as well as their later counterparts. The Upper Thames can in fact make the claim of being the most ancient, and most continuously inhabited, territory of the British Isles. It can be said with some certainty that all the towns and villages of the Upper Thames are based upon British or Saxon originals; they are by fords, or by trackways, or sit defensively upon frontier lands.

Somerford Keynes: Pronounced Canes. The presence of a ford here, in the summer months, is plain enough. The other part of the name comes from Sir Ralph de Keynes, who held all the land in the vicinity during the reign of King John. There is a Saxon "megalithic" doorway in the church, the relic of the earliest building on the site. There is also a Viking carving of two playful dragons. It is conjectured that the Saxon church was built by St. Aldhelm, who was a landowner here long before the arrival of Ralph de Keynes. The Upper Thames was a relatively heavily populated area in the early centuries of the Christian era. There were once five mills in the locality, indicating that the river once ran faster through these sleeping fields. In fact the village is still sometimes affected by floods. There are small hamlets in the immediate neighbourhood, inspiring William Morris's line concerning "the little stream whose hamlets scarce have names." It is, or was, a place of intensive agricultural labour. As one rustic put it, at the beginning of the twentieth century when rural dialects were still preserved, "pleny o' 'ard graft an' nat much bezide at Zummerverd."

Ashton Keynes: The name derives from the Anglo-Saxon words *esc* meaning ash and *tun* meaning place. It might thus have been designated as the settlement by the ash-trees. Neolithic axe-heads have been uncovered in the vicinity. William Cobbett, in *Rural Rides* (1830), described it as a "very curious place," principally because it is made up of a number of parallel streets criss-crossed by the rivulets of the Thames. There are twenty bridges in the village, each one leading to a little house. The river is united in the centre of the village, and then runs under several arches before disappearing within a line of beeches. The first fish of the river are to be seen here. It was once of importance as a market town, and there are traces of a monastery. There are extant four crosses along the highways, dating from the fourteenth century; they have been described as preaching crosses, but their true purpose is unexplained. The biography of the village, by Madge Patterson and Ernie Ward, is suggestively entitled *Ashton Keynes: A Village with No History*.

POOLE KEYNES: The name is of unknown origin. But this may be the oldest settlement on the Upper Thames, the remains of Paleolithic habitation having been found here. That would give it a date some 1,750,000 years ago. The church, of fourteenth-century foundation, is therefore a recent development. The neighbourhood has so long a history of human settlement that its momentum has slowed in recent years.

CRICKLADE: The first town upon the river, some 10 miles from the source at Thames Head. The name may refer to a river-crossing beside a hill, in this case Horsey Down to the west, while others derive it from the two British words *cricw* and *ladh* meaning stony or rocky country. Or could it be a reflection of *Cerrig-let*, meaning the stony place where the Churn finds an outlet into the Thames? There were some antiquarians who believed it to be a corruption of *Greek-lade*, or assembly of learned scholars and monks. It was reported in monkish chronicles that in 1180 BC Brutus, the Trojan survivor, came here with a group of his countrymen and established a university among the early Britons. Samuel Ireland and others also believed it to be the site of the first university in England, but one founded by Panda of Mercia in AD 650 and thus predating Oxford downriver. A Saxon *burh* or enclosure has been found here. We have Drayton, therefore, hailing the town as:

> Greeklade whose great name yet vaunts that learned tongue,
> Where to Great Britain first the sacred muses sung.

The more these origins are examined, the more ambiguous and uncertain they become. One of the town's two churches is dedicated to St. Sampson, an ancient Celtic saint. At the southern base of the tower, on the roof of the church, is a sculpture of a dragon and a knight; in the old tradition of the place a dragon did infest this region, until being despatched by Sir Guy of Warwick. There is a fractured stone effigy of an unknown man in the church, said to be the image of one who fell from the tower and was killed; it was not fashioned by hand, but grew on the spot where the man died. St. Augustine held a synod in the vicinity. There was once a community of Nonconformists here, too, and until the end of the nineteenth century baptisms were conducted at a rustic bridge called Hatchetts on the outskirts of the town. The Roman avenue called Ermin Street or the Irmin Way passed through it, before traversing the river, and King Alfred built a wall around the town. The Danes under Cnut eventually sacked it, but a wooden castle was built here in the twelfth century. It once possessed a Mint, and "Cricklade coins" have been unearthed in several vicinities. In recompense for their protection of his mother, Maud, Henry II granted the townspeople a charter allowing them to trade in any part of the kingdom. As an old anonymous verse put it:

> Light men laugh and hurry past,
> Sentry of the Roman Way;
> Shall you live to laugh the last,
> Wise old Cricklade? You, or they?

Wisdom may take many forms. The town was well known in the eighteenth and early nineteenth centuries for the venality of its inhabitants in general elections. Cobbett remarks that "a more rascally looking place I never set eyes upon. The labourers seem miserably poor. Their dwellings are little better than pig beds, and their looks indicate that their food is not nearly equal to that of a pig. In my whole life I never saw wretchedness equal to this." The inhabitants of Cricklade also had an unusual manner of conducting funerals, whereby the coffin was placed at the front of the post-chaise. The town has now shrugged off its dubious reputation but it still exudes quietness and retirement from the world. By the end of the nineteenth century, according to Charles Dickens junior, "it has not been the scene of any remarkable events." Its early history was more adventurous. What other small town can boast the legends of Brutus and of Augustine, of Alfred and of Cnut? And a dragon? In the North Meadow here there is a splendid flowering of the rare Thames plant, the snake's-head fritillary.

CASTLE EATON: Sometimes known as Eton Meysi or Ettonne, it is the site of a
castle, as its name suggests, to the north-west of Eaton, meaning farm or
river settlement; *ey* is the island, and *tun* is the dwelling or settlement. There
was a castle here described by Leland as "*Eiton* Castelle, wher great Ruines
of a Building in *Wyleshire* . . . Eiton the Lord *Zouches* Castelle." Nothing of
it remains. The church is of Norman foundation, with a stone turret for the
sanctus bell, and the bank is covered with flowers. Roger North, author of
The Lives of the Norths (1890), declaimed of this stretch of the river that "we
came nearer to perfection of life there than I was ever sensible of otherwise." An Iron Age round house has been found here. And the bell rings
out: "Holy! Holy! Holy!"

KEMPSFORD: Originally known as Kynemeresforde, meaning Cynemaer's ford
or perhaps ford of the great marsh. A defensive post was established by the
Saxons at this crossing of the river. At the second hour of the night on 16
January 800, as the *Anglo-Saxon Chronicle* reports, "here the moon grew
dark . . . Ealdorman Ethelmund rode from the Hwicce across at Kempsford;
then Ealdorman Weohstan met him with the Wilsoeti or Wiltshire men; and
there was a big battle, and both ealdormen were killed there and the Wiltshire men took the victory." Between Castle Eaton and Kempsford there are
still meadows known as "the Battlefield." This peaceful land was once much
given to slaughter. Henry, Earl of Lancaster is said to have stabbed his in-
amorata and thrown her body into the Thames at this place; her ghost is

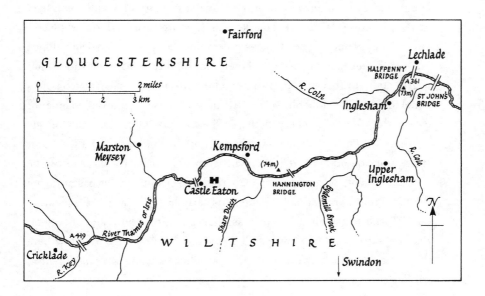

reported to walk the avenue of yew-trees that leads from the churchyard to the river. Henry's grandson was drowned by the bank of the Thames here. The boy's father, in his grief, left Kempsford for ever. As he left, his horse cast off one of its iron shoes; the villagers kept it, and nailed it beneath the latch on the north door of the church. A horseshoe is still there. W. H. Hutton described Kempsford "as almost the most beautiful village on the Thames." There may be an association with Chaucer. John of Gaunt is supposed to have erected the church here in honour of Blanche, his departed wife. Chaucer was one of Gaunt's affinity, and wrote *The Book of the Duchess* as a memorial to Blanche. He also wrote some lines that have a strong association with the Thames itself:

> A gardyn saw I, ful of blosmy bowes,
> Upon a river, in a grene mede,
> Ther as that swetnesse evermore y-now is,
> With floures whyte, blewe, yelowe, and rede;
> And colde welle-stremes, no-thing dede,
> That swommen ful of smale fisshes lighte,
> With finnes rede and scales sylver-brighte.

Kempsford still marks the boundary between Gloucestershire and Wiltshire.

INGLESHAM: Inga's meadowland or, alternatively, the river meadow of Ingen; or it may derive from the Saxon *inga*, a holy well into which pins were thrown for good fortune; or from King Ine, the "law-giver" and seventh-century monarch of Wessex. The hamlet is remarkable for its tiny church of St. John the Baptist, a Saxon foundation based, curiously, upon a Byzantine model. There is a Saxon preaching cross in the churchyard. It is best known, however, for its ancient bas-relief of the Virgin and Child in the south aisle. There is a plaque upon the wall, stating that "this church was repaired in 1888–9 through the energy and with the help of William Morris who loved it." It was at Inglesham that Shelley and his companions gave up their attempt to sail to the source of the Thames. This abortive journey also inspired Thomas Love Peacock's *Crotchet Castle*.

LECHLADE: The wharf or crossing by the Lech or Leach, the small river that here joins the Thames. The river was known as *lech*, the British word for stone, because of its cold or petrifying nature. It is the site where four counties meet. Leland described it in the seventeenth century as "a praty old toune." It has all the marks of antiquity. On his return from Inglesham Shelley lingered in the churchyard here and wrote "Stanzas in a Summer Evening Churchyard":

> The winds are still, or the dry church-tower grass
> Knows not their gentle motions as they pass.

The grass is not as dry as the poet imagined. The churchyard was considered to be so wet from the influence of the river that to be interred there was the next best thing to being buried at sea. The spire of the church of St. Lawrence, once dedicated to St. Mary, can be seen by the Thames traveller for miles and provides one of the most enduring compositions along the river. From some perspectives it looks as if it is rising out of the water. Of this Shelley wrote, in the same poem:

> Clothing in hues of heaven thy dim and distant spire,
> Around whose lessening and invisible height
> Gather among the stars the clouds of night.

The prospect of the spire is the origin of the ancient saying, "as sure as God's in Gloucestershire." It was not always so placid. Lechlade marked the true beginning of Thames commerce. From here the especial commodity was cheese, especially sage cheese, sent down the river to Oxford and to London. The stone that created the dome of St. Paul's was also loaded here. One Lechlade bargemaster recorded in 1793 that he carried down to London "iron, copper, tin . . . cannon, cheese, nails, all iron goods and bomb shells." He took back in return timber, groceries, coal and gunpowder. It has two bridges, St. John's Bridge and Halfpenny Bridge; the former has the distinction of being (perhaps) the oldest bridge across the Thames, while St. John's Lock is the first lock. The statue of Old Father Thames, once beside the source of the Thames at Thames Head, has been placed here. The hospice of St. John's Priory, of the thirteenth century, provides the site for the present Trout Inn. The round huts of the Dobunni have been found in the vicinity, as well as a sixth-century Anglo-Saxon cemetery with some five hundred burials.

BUSCOT: Or the cottage of Bugsweard. It is named Boroardescote in the *Domesday Book*. It is famous principally for having a church with no aisle.

There is here a sign for "Cheese Wharf," now disused, and the area was once well known for its brandy distilled from beetroot. The beverage was not popular. From the seventeenth century onwards very little changed, at least until the beginning of the twentieth century. The industrial revolution did not approach this region, and in visual terms it remained unaltered. Hilaire Belloc, in *The Historic Thames* (1914), claimed that "you might put a man of the fifteenth century onto the water below St. John's Lock, and, until he came to Buscot Lock, he would hardly know that he had passed into a time other than his own."

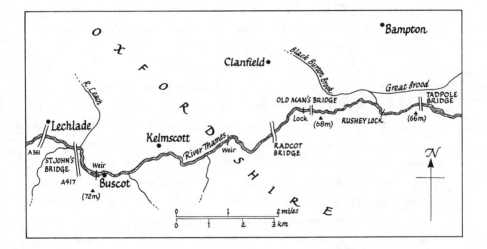

KELMSCOT: Or the cottage of Caenhelm. Now sacred to the memory of William Morris, whose manor house—spelled as Kelmscott—lies just a few yards from the river. Morris explained to a friend, in a letter of 1871, that "I have been looking about for a house for the wife and kids, and whither do you guess my eye is turned now? Kelmscott, a little village about two miles above Radcott bridge—a heaven on earth." Rossetti was less enamoured of the area, describing it as "the doziest clump of old grey beehives." The fact that Morris spelled the place with two *t*s suggests that he was not aware of its true provenance.

EATON HASTINGS: This denotes a farm by the river in the possession of the Hastings family. It is called Etona in the *Domesday Book*, but there are local antiquaries who believe that its name was taken from a big bend in the river known as "Hell's Turn."

BAMPTON: From the Anglo-Saxon *bam* meaning bean tree, and *tun* meaning dwelling. This may mean a settlement around a great tree, or around a wooden building. It was also known as Bampton-in-the-Bush, suggesting the former. The church was once well known for having three rectors, and three separate vicarages in the church close. The Bampton morris dancers are the oldest troupes in the country; there are three in existence, bound together by familial ties, and by report they are continuing an indigenous tradition of dancing that has lasted six hundred years. There are many photographs of the Bampton morris dancers from many different eras, with fiddle, bladder, bells and drum. A newspaper account of them in 1877 noted that they "busily tripped the light fantastic toe to the sound of fiddle and tambourine." The longevity of the pursuit is another indication of the conservatism of the river region.

RADCOT: The site of a reed cottage or a red cottage; reed seems to be more likely. Radcot Bridge may be the oldest bridge on the river. Since a Saxon charter declares the presence of a bridge here in AD 958, Radcot may bear the palm. Like many bridges upon the Upper Thames it was the site of various skirmishes and alarms during the Civil War. This was the shipping point for cheese and Burford stone. In the eighteenth century Samuel Ireland remarked upon the decayed state of the tributary. In his *Magna Britannia* (1720) Thomas Cox reports that there was a great causeway from the bridge that led directly to Friar Bacon's study in Oxford, but it has long since vanished. The reasons for its existence are in any case obscure. The

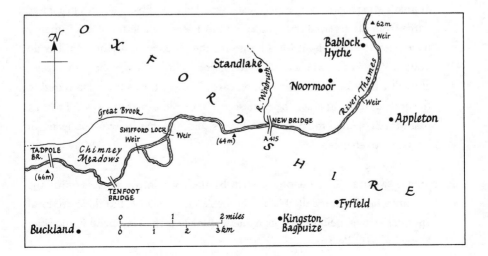

Thames here was once very deep and was said to abound with fish. Yet in its infancy the river here changes all the time; sometimes it is swift, and sometimes slow; its colour varies from blue to grey in a moment; it meanders, and it rushes forward; in one stretch it seems deep, and in another very shallow.

SHIFFORD: A sheep ford. Reached from Radcot by way of Old Man's Bridge, Tadpole Bridge and Ten Foot Bridge, it is now no more than a name. Yet it was here that Alfred called a parliament. "There sate at Siford," according to the transcript of a contemporaneous Anglo-Saxon poem in the first volume of *Reliquiae Antiquae* (1841), "many thanes, many bishops, and many learned men, proud earls and awful knights. There was Earl Alfric, very learned in the law, and Alfred, England's herdsman—England's darling." The site is now a large bare field, with a farm and a ruined church that is meant to harbour "Alfred's stone." The wind here can be very strong.

BABLOCK HYTHE: A landing place on Babba's stream. Camden spells it Bablac. It used to be well known from Matthew Arnold's invocation, in *The Scholar Gipsy*, of "crossing the stripling Thames at Bablock-hithe." But tastes in poetry change. There is still a ferry here, however, run by the manager of the local inn. It was once principally a horse-ferry, for the beasts of the field. Nathaniel Hawthorne came here in 1860, and found an old woman working the ferry. He particularly noticed the circular fireplace in the middle of her cottage, which must have been established on the pattern of the ancient British huts that have been found in the vicinity. *Pace* Arnold the Thames is no stripling here, but relatively deep and broad. Just to the west of Bablock Hythe are three prehistoric standing stones known as the "Devil's Quoits"; they may be the remains of an ancient monument or, as some local antiquarians believe, the token of a battle between the Saxons and the Britons. A coin thrown into Bablock Hythe is supposed to be returned sevenfold, but this may be a legend of the ferrymen.

EYNSHAM: Homestead of Aegen. Leland wrote it as Eignes-ham. A Saxon *witenagemot* met here under the guidance of Ethelred the Unready in 1008. No doubt it was convened at the Benedictine abbey, of which only a few stones now remain. There was once a custom that the inhabitants of Eynsham could cut down as much timber from the manor-lands as they could carry, with their own hands, into the precincts of the abbey. Outside the village is a toll-bridge across the Thames, one of two upon the river. It is Swinford

Bridge, named after the ford for swine that once crossed this stretch of water. John Wesley had to swim across on his horse when the ferry here was inundated.

GODSTOW: The place of God. All that remains is a precinct wall and the ruins of a small chapel. There was once a nunnery here. The amour of Henry II, Fair Rosamund, spent the last years of her life in retreat in this place. It was said that she was eventually poisoned by Henry's wife, Eleanor of Aquitaine. Her coffin was one of those later used to build a path across adjacent fields, when once an ancient hazel-tree:

> . . . lightly throws its humble shade
> Where Rosamonda's form is laid.

The Thames gypsies, on the other hand, used to believe that at the time of her death she was turned into a holy briar which bled if you plucked a twig. The Trout Inn, once the hospice of the nunnery, has peacocks. There is a deep and irradiant blue in the depths of the water before Godstow Bridge.

BINSEY: The island of Byni, once surrounded by a skein of streams and rivulets; or, according to some, derived from *bene ea*, "island of prayer." Long considered to be a holy place, its sacred well became the treacle well in Alice's adventures. Curiously enough the villagers used to refer to the mud-holes, left after the winter rains, as "treacle mines." The village was also the home of Miss Prickett, the governess of Alice Liddell and the model for the Red Queen. So Binsey is indeed a holy place. The first incumbent of Binsey Church for whom records exist, was Nicholas Breakspear; he became Adrian IV, the only English Pope. The poplars were celebrated in a poem by Gerard Manley Hopkins.

OSNEY: Island of Osa, or perhaps Oz. This was once an area of many streams, creating small islands of settlement. It was the site of Ouseney Abbey, of which the church contained twenty-four altars. Rewley Abbey occupied the northern part of Osney Island. That, too, has disappeared. The episcopal chair of Ouseney was transferred to the conventual church of St. Frideswide, the local saint, which then in turn became the cathedral church of Christ Church, Oxford. The famous bell of Ouseney Abbey, Great Tom, is now rung in Tom Tower at Christ Church.

OXFORD: The ford where oxen may cross. The old city seal represents an ox crossing a ford. Yet the name may derive from Ouseford or Ouseney ford, the ford at or near Ouseney itself. Ouse, or Ouze, was almost a generic name for rivers. The neighbourhood is now more famous for its university. According to Geoffrey of Monmouth, Oxford was built in 1009 BC by Memphric, king of the Britons, and is thus one of the most ancient cities in the world. The ev-

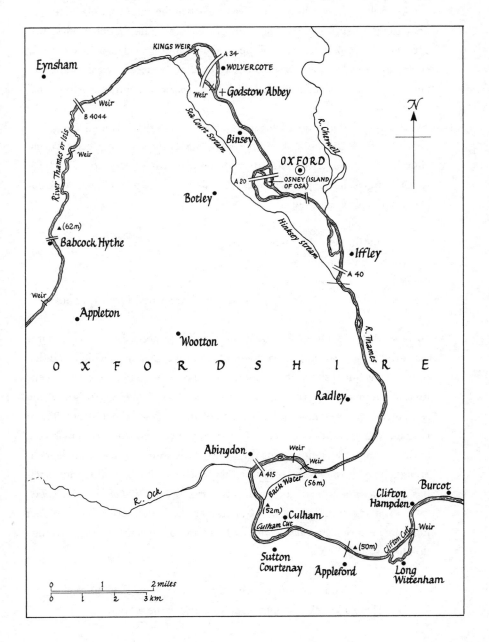

idence for his claim has unfortunately been lost, but under the name of *Caer-Memphric* or *Caer Pen Halgoit* it was mentioned by many writers as "the glory of cities, the seat of princes and muses" until its destruction by Plautius in the reign of Claudius. It was "much affected" by the Saxons, and then burned by the Danes. Alfred set his halls "*infra muros Oxoniae,*" so the defensive walls must have been of very ancient date. Alfred is said to have established the university itself. Others believe that it was created at the end of the eleventh century, for sixty students, by Theobald of Etampes. The first chancellor was appointed in 1214. The city, built upon a plateau of gravel, is almost entirely encircled by water. John Wycliff described it as "watered by rills and fountains . . . it has been rightly called the house of God and the gate of heaven."

IFFLEY: Plovers' wood or glade; or it may derive from the Saxon *giftilege*, "the field of gifts." On a hill above the river stands the most perfect Norman church in the country. The thirteenth-century mill burned down in 1908. Keith Douglas, fighting in Normandy in 1940, wrote a poem in which he envisages his spirit returning

> another evening, when this boat
> travels with you alone towards Iffley.

He died in that year. The village is still much treasured for its quietness.

ABINGDON: Aebba's hill, or a settlement owned by Aebba. Leland says that it was originally known as Seukesham, of unknown meaning, which Camden translates as Shovesham. But there was an abbess Aebba in the seventh century, to whom the kings of Kent granted much land. This is the origin of the settlement, which stands on the junction of the Ock and the Thames. There is an alternative story of Aben, a Christian prince who survived a massacre at Stonehenge by Hengist, but this seems little more than a pious legend. Hengist may, however, be connected with nearby Hinksey. Abingdon itself has a worthy monastic history and, according to *The Old Booke of Abbendon*, "was in ancient times a famous city, goodly to behold, full of riches." In fact it became too rich. In *Piers Plowman* Langland berates the abbot of Abingdon for his high living:

> And than shal the Abbot of Abyngdone, and al his issue forever
> Have a knock of a kynge, and incurable the wounde.

The monks diverted the course of the Thames, so that it would flow past the walls of their foundation. It is also recorded that the master of every barge containing herring was obliged to give 100 of them to the cook of the monastery. In St. Helen's Church there is a memorial tablet to one W. Lee who "had in his lifetime issue from his loins two hundred but three."

CLIFTON HAMPDEN: A cliff settlement, later given the Hampden family name. At this point the river runs over a stretch of hard sandstone, out of which the "cliff" of the name is made. The change of material has forced the river to swerve westward. The stone church of St. Michael and All Saints stands upon this outcrop of rock. There is a memorial in this church to Sergeant William Dyke, who fired the first shot at the battle of Waterloo—accidentally. The neo-Gothic bridge is the unmistakable work of Sir George Gilbert Scott. Jerome K. Jerome patronised the public house here, the Barley Mow, which he described as "the quaintest most old world inn up the river." It survives in chastened state.

DORCHESTER: One of the river's holy places, nestling beside the famous Sinodun Hills, and the centre of the ministry of St. Birinus. In Celtic *dwr* means "water." So we have *caer dauri* or *caer doren*, "the city on the water." Leland therefore calls it Hydropolis. This stretch of the river was deep and swift. There was once a Roman garrison here. There are also traces of an amphitheatre. What was once a great city has now become a small village, with the bare ruined fragments of its Saxon cathedral as an indication of its previous status as the greatest see in England. There still stands the abbey church, in which the relics of St. Birinus are to be found. In the church also is a monument to a lady who "sunk and died a Martyr to Excessive Sensibility." It is said that no viper can live in the parish of Dorchester.

BURCOT: Bryda's cottage, or Bride's Cottage. Perhaps a dowry? Charles Dickens junior reported it to be "of no importance."

LONG WITTENHAM and LITTLE WITTENHAM: The settlement or meadows of Witta by the bend in the river. Originally a single Wittenham, which eventually diverged into two. They are 1 mile apart by road but—because of the bend in the river—3½ miles apart by water. Antiquities have been found here in abundance, including the skeleton of an Anglo-Saxon. An altar to Jupiter Optimus Maximus was found at Little Wittenham. At Long Wittenham the same burial place had been used continually through the Iron Age, Roman, Saxon and Christian eras. Here the Thame meets the Thames.

BENSON: The farm of Baensa, or settlement of Benesa's people. Previously known as Bensington. Offa's palace was close to the church here. It was the site of a battle between Wessex and Mercia. Nothing much has since happened, although it was said to have been a refuge for St. Frideswide during one of that saint's unhappy flights.

WALLINGFORD: Ford owned by the tribe of Wealh or the Walingas (unlike Shillingford, close by, which was under the control of the Scillingas). *Wealh* is the Anglo-Saxon word for foreigner, or slave, or Briton—hence "welsh." It seems likely, then, that the ford was once protected or defended by a group of indigenous Britons, most likely the Berkshire tribe of the Atrebates. It may then be the chief city known in the *Itinerary* of Antoninus as Calleva, and may claim a history as old as that of London. Others more prosaically derive the name from "walled ford." The town was once enclosed by Saxon earth-works, which can still be seen; the river lay on the fourth side, and the streets were laid out in a military grid pattern in the Roman manner. A Norman castle was built here on the foundations of an old Roman fortification. But this great castle was, even by Leland's time, "sore in ruines, and for the most part defaced." It was eventually destroyed during the Civil War. The bridge has seventeen arches. There were once fourteen churches, but the town was severely depopulated by the Black Death in the fourteenth century. In the twentieth century it was the home of Agatha Christie.

STREATLEY and GORING: "Twinned" towns on either bank of the river, not a unique phenomenon along the Thames. The names refer, in turn, to a grove or clearing by the road and the place of Gara's people (Goring was once known as Garinges). The "street" of Streatley may be the Ridgeway that passes along the chalk downs, crosses the Icknield Way, and then drops down here to create a ford across the river, or may refer to the Icknield Way itself, the oldest road in Britain, extending from Norfolk to Buckinghamshire. They are both tracks of great antiquity, therefore, and their meeting at Streatley and Goring is a matter of some significance. Certainly there has been a settlement here, as they said in the middle ages, beyond the memory of man. Here the river cuts through the chalk, north to south, to create the "Goring gap." It inspired a famous verse:

> I'd rather much sit here and
> laze
> Than scale the hill at
> Streatley.

The climb is by no means arduous, however, and the views of the river are rewarding. The Thames now turns fatefully eastward, adopts the Kennet at Reading, and flows on towards the sea. Each town had its own church and its own mill. Oscar Wilde stayed here in 1893, and one of the characters in *An Ideal Husband* is named Lord Goring.

WHITCHURCH and PANGBOURNE: Another pairing: the place of the white church, and a stream belonging to the sons of Paega. A son of the Thames, Kenneth Grahame, used to live at Pangbourne.

MAPLEDURHAM: A settlement by the maple trees. Mapulder is the British name for the maple. The mill here is mentioned in the *Domesday Book*; it is still in operation, and is thus the oldest working mill upon the river. Mapledurham House, of Tudor construction, is still owned by members of the original family. It has been the fictional home of Soames Forsyte and Mr. Toad.

READING: Settlement of Reada's tribe, Reada being a local Saxon leader who led his people up the Thames and invaded this territory. Other derivations trace it from *rhea* meaning river and from *redin* meaning fern; Leland said that fern was "growing hereabouts in great plenty." There was once a great castle, and an even greater abbey, here. The earliest known English song, "Sumer is icumen in," was written in its cloisters. In the nineteenth century the town was well known, and somewhat scorned, as the principal manufactory of biscuits. From the ruins of the abbey you can see the prison where Oscar Wilde was incarcerated. The town is now a thriving centre of technology, and has little regard for its past.

SONNING: Settlement of Sunna's people, another tribal division of the Saxons by the river. But there is a previous history of Palaeolithic and Mesolithic settlers. There is a ritual enclosure here dating from 2000 BC. There is also a piece of nineteenth-century doggerel by James Sadler:

> Is there a spot more lovely than the rest,
> By art improved, by nature truly blest?
> > A noble river at its base is running,
> It is a little village known as Sonning.

SHIPLAKE: The stretch of water where sheep are washed. Tennyson married in the church, and Eric Blair (aka George Orwell) lived here as a boy. Just beyond the village, by the weir, the river Loddon joins the Thames. The confluence provides the setting for *Leucojum aestivum*: the Loddon lily or summer snowflake. It is also the habitat for the less attractive Loddon pondweed.

WARGRAVE: The grove by the weirs, where the Loddon decants into the Thames. There was a village recorded here from the eleventh century. The church was burned down by suffragettes in 1914, on the grounds that the vicar refused to remove the verb "obey" from the marriage service. Madame Tussaud is buried in the churchyard. She lies near Thomas Day, once well known for his didactic novel *Sandford and Merton*. He died after being thrown from a horse, while trying to prove that animals can best be tamed by kindness. The river at this point is the site of the annual Wargrave and Shiplake Regatta which includes more than 600 competitors, and 350 races, within the space of two days. The boatsmen compete with traditional skiffs, which have been on the river since the nineteenth century.

HENLEY: The meaning is contested between "high wood" or "clearing" or "the old place." If it is the last then the British term—*hen-le* (on the same principle as *hen-dre* meaning old town and *hen-gwrt* meaning old court) would suggest that it is very old indeed. In the ancient records of the corporation it is also named Hanleganz and Hannebury. At the time of the *Domesday Book* there were three manors and one church in the area. Once largely populated by bargemen, by the eighteenth century it had become a popular resort. It is in large part a Georgian town, and the bridge (1786) is very fine. The site of the famous regatta, the course of water here was chosen for the first university boat races between Oxford and Cambridge. The Cambridge colour was then pink. In the first ever boat race of June 1829 the two boats collided, and the race was started again. Oxford won. The Red Lion inn here inspired the following lines from Thomas Shenstone, who scratched them upon one of its windows:

> Whoe'er has travelled life's dull round,
>   Where'er his stages may have been,
> May sigh to think he still has found
> The warmest welcome at an inn.

Along the bank can be found the River and Rowing Museum. The famous boating firm of Hobbs & Sons is close by.

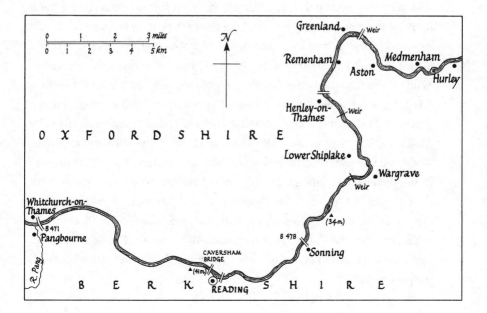

MEDMENHAM: Variously explicated as the middle ham or homestead, a middle-sized settlement or the land remaining after the draining of a pool. The manor house or "abbey" once housed a small community of Cistercian monks, but it became more celebrated as the home of the Hell Fire Club whose motto was *Fay ce que voudra,* or "Do what you will." Its leading member, Sir Francis Dashwood, decorated the existing house with fanciful arches in the Gothic style. Their misdeeds were somewhat exaggerated, but it has been reported that the devil once appeared among them in the shape of a baboon. By the end of the eighteenth century it had been colonised by poor families who showed around curious visitors. It was restored in 1898, and is now used by the Royal Air Force.

HURLEY: A curve in the river. Once known as Esgareston or the town of Esgar, it is an ancient place. The first church was built, during the mission of St. Birinus, in approximately AD 635. During that saint's mission churches sprang up on both banks of the Thames beside the sites where he preached and baptised; thus the churches at Windsor and Eton, Hurley and Medmenham, Whitchurch and Pangbourne, Goring and Streatley, and so on. This little-known saint can truly be said to have changed the topography of the Thames. The sister of Edward the Confessor, Editha, was buried somewhere beneath the flagstones of Hurley Church. The *Domesday Book* records the presence of twenty-five villagers and ten slaves. The inn, the Olde Bell, is said to be the oldest public house in the country; it was originally the guest house of the monastery. The wall of the eleventh-century monastery can still be seen in the courtyard, or "paradise," of a house by the river. There is a plaque here: "The priory of St. Mary, Hurley, founded in the reign of William the Conqueror by Geoffrey de Mandeville and his wife Lecelina, AD 1086. A cell to Westminster Abbey." A cell means here an extension, not a gaol. In 1391 the prior complained to Richard II that "they are troubled by Thames floods, their houses laid in ruins, and the deaths of their occupants." There are two twelfth-century barns. Early in his reign Henry VIII granted to the Benedictines "the great wood called Hurley Wood" in exchange for their garden in London "called Covent Garden." It was a good bargain for the sovereign. On the ruins of the monastery was built Ladye Place, in the cellars of which was plotted the deposition of James II. The house was demolished in 1837, and three bodies in Benedictine habits were found beneath the pavement.

BISHAM: Bissel's ham or homestead, or perhaps hamlet on the river Biss. It is sometimes difficult to disentangle place names from family names, when they were for centuries indistinguishable. Did the territory get its name from the people, or the people from the territory? Most noticeable for the presence of Bisham Abbey, a Tudor manor house built on the remnants of a twelfth-century abbey. Henry VIII granted the original house to Anne of Cleves, after he had ungraciously abandoned her, but she eventually passed it to Sir Philip Hoby. It was he who restored the present house. The princess Elizabeth was "entertained," or imprisoned, here for three years, during the reign of her sister, but the building is most celebrated for the "Bisham ghost." Lady Hoby murdered her son, for the sin of blotting his copy-books, by the simple expedient of shutting him up in a room in the house. Some say that she whipped him to death. Of course her spirit eternally regrets the deed, and forever washes its hands in a self-supporting basin. Curiously enough, copy-books were found under the floorboards during a later restoration. Bisham Abbey is now a national sports centre.

MARLOW: Low and marshy ground, or perhaps the residue of a lake or mere. Camden derives it from "the chalk commonly called marle," however, which he believed to be plentiful in the region. The Roman Catholic church of St. Peter's here harbours the mummified hand of St. James, rescued from

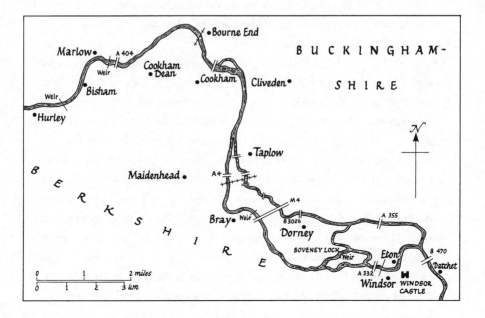

Reading Abbey. The fingers are curled into a kind of claw. In the vestry of All Saints hangs a portrait of the Spotted Boy, a young black boy with an unfortunate disfigurement of large white spots; he and the showman who exhibited him are both buried in the same grave within the churchyard. The builder of the suspension bridge here, William Tierney Clark, erected the famous bridge that links Buda with Pest. The town is perhaps most famous for the residence of Percy Bysshe Shelley and Mary Shelley in West Street; a new book about them, published by the Marlow Society, is entitled *The Monsters of Marlow*. Mary Shelley wrote much of *Frankenstein* here and, down the road, Thomas Love Peacock wrote *Nightmare Abbey*. There must be something in the air. The young T. S. Eliot also resided here. Did Marlow inspire part of *The Waste Land*? There was once a famous question, "Who ate the puppy pie under Marlow Bridge?," designed to throw the local bargees and boatmen into a fit of vituperative bad temper. The landlord of the inn at Medmenham had received information that certain bargemen were about to raid his kitchen. Having only moments before drowned a litter of puppies, he cooked them and baked them in a pie that he placed in the larder. The larder was robbed, the pie taken and consumed, according to legend, beneath Marlow Bridge. The provocative question is rarely asked now, on the very good grounds that it would not be understood. There may not in any case be much laughter. James Thorne, in his *Rambles by Rivers* (1847), said of Marlow that "the countrymen hereabouts are not of a mirthful character, and their liveliness is of a very laborious character."

COOKHAM: Perhaps from *cwch-ium*, the Celtic for boat-place; or perhaps from *cocc-ham*, or home on the hill. Could it really mean cook's home? In *Domesday* it is spelled as Cocheham. Lower, in his *Patronymica Britannica* (1860), believes that *coke* is the old spelling for cook from the Latin *coquus*. Skeat also believes that the Saxon *coc* or *cook* in Cookham is derived from the Latin. Curiously enough the cook of Eleanor of Aquitaine is buried in the local church, as well as the "master spicer" of Henry VI. What's in a name? Cookham is one of the most famous places upon the river largely because of the residence, and the paintings, of Stanley Spencer. But it has other claims to attention. There are two megaliths here, known as the Cookham Stone and the Tarry Stone. The latter, however, may be a meteorite. On the Cookham floodplain were found a cluster of Bronze Age burial mounds. It seems likely that the earliest inhabitants here had travelled upstream from their first settlements in Kent. Roman and Saxon skeletons have been found in abundance.

There is a field of Cookham known as Noah's Ark, and this name is believed to derive from the story that the first and wholly legendary king of the Anglo-Saxons, Sceaf, was the son of Noah and was born in the Ark. So the Bible came to Cookham before the paintings of Stanley Spencer confirmed the association. The Saxon *witenamagot* met here during the reign of Ethelred the Unready, very likely by the Tarry Stone. There was an abbey in Cookham by AD 716. It is a place of ancient association and ancient settlement in which the layers of the past are impacted just beneath the surface. The historic and the prehistoric are rarely found in such close connection. The river-bed, especially along the course of the old ferry, has yielded relics of every period. When the modern owners of a cottage wished to install a damp course, the builders found several layers of previous floors—reverting, in the end, to a floor of beaten chalk that could not be dated. A house may always have been there, ever since the arrival of humankind in Cookham.

CLIVEDEN: A steep valley in the cliffs. It is now the spectacular setting for a mansion with an eminent if somewhat chequered history. The first house was built in 1666 by George Villiers, second Duke of Buckingham. It burned down in 1795, the fatal result of a maid-servant reading by candlelight in bed. The succeeding house also burned down in 1849. The present house was constructed in 1851 by Sir Charles Barry, and was described at the time as resembling three or four large packing-cases. It has housed among others the Duke of Westminster, William Waldorf Astor, the National Trust and Stanford University of California. It is now advertised as a luxury hotel. The gardens, however, are open to the public. Charles Kingsley wrote that it harboured "the most beautiful landscape that I have ever seen or care to see in the vale of the Thames from Taplow or from Cliveden." The Cliveden woods or "hanging woods" are a remnant of the primaeval forests that once covered the region. The cliff itself rises 140 feet (42 m), and offers harmonies of oak and beech, ash and chestnut, in profusion. They are rivalled only by the Quarry Woods, opposite Marlow, where the beech and oak and ash and evergreen riot. The woods by the Thames are indeed magical places, redolent with intimations of ancientness. The Quarry Woods are the paradigm of the Wild Wood in *The Wind in the Willows*. Green lichen spreads here in autumn. It is here that the Mole experiences "the Terror of the Wild Wood": "The whole wood seemed running now, running hard, hunting, chasing, closing in round something or—somebody?" It is the cold touch of the primaeval world.

MAIDENHEAD: It was believed by Camden that the town was named after the head of a maiden saint once venerated here as a sacred relic. The head was popularly believed to have once adorned the neck of one of the eleven thousand virgins martyred with St. Ursula at Cologne. Skeat and Ekwall both believed that the word derives from *maegden hyth* or "landing place for maidens"—in other words, an easy place to land. It has also been deemed to be taken from a hythe by a meadow, a *magne* or large hythe, a mid-hythe between Windsor and Reading, or a *mai dun* hythe, meaning a hythe by a great hill. The great hill in question is in fact the burial mound of the Saxon chieftain Taeppa (who gave his name to Taplow on the opposite bank) whose funereal effects are now to be found in the British Museum. In any case, at the time of *Domesday*, the place was called Elenstone or Ellington. The railway bridge is that depicted by Turner in *Rain, Steam, and Speed*. It was designed by Isambard Kingdom Brunel and, at the time, people believed it was impossible that the bridge would stand up; there are two elliptical spans of brick arching, each one of 128 feet, with no support except their own structure. They are still the widest and flattest brick arches in the world. It is also known as the "echo" bridge, to the delight of those who use the tow-path.

BRAY: A moist or muddy place, or perhaps the brow of a hill. It was best known for its vicar, who changed his religious affiliation so often, between the reigns of Henry VIII and Elizabeth I, that he became a by-word for the clerical turncoat. A famous ballad was written on the subject, of which the chorus goes:

> And this is law I will maintain
>> Until my dying day, sir,
> That whatsoever King shall reign,
>> I'll be Vicar of Bray, sir.

DORNEY: Or *Dornei* in *Domesday*, the island or dry ground frequented by bumble-bees. Presumably once an eyot where honey was harvested. In the gardens of the Tudor mansion, Dorney Court, was grown the first pineapple in England. There is a painting at Ham House of the Dorney gardener, on bended knee, presenting the imposing fruit to Charles II. The king is pointing to it in a relaxed manner.

BOVENEY: Above the island, or perhaps above island. The little church of St. Mary Boveney, from the twelfth century, stands alone by the river. It is unused, but is still illuminated by candles. The appeal for its restoration is conducted under the auspices of the "Friends of Friendless Churches." Just downstream from Boveney Weir lies "Athens," the place where the schoolboys from Eton used to plunge naked into the river; hence the Grecian name. The bank here has always been known as a bathing place. Karl Philipp Moritz, in 1782, recorded that "the bank here was rather steep, so they had built a flight of steps down into the water for the benefit of bathers who could not swim. A pair of red-cheeked young apprentices strolled down from the town, had their clothes off in a wink, and dived in."

ETON and WINDSOR: Towns united by the river, as well as by their history. Windsor originally Wyndelshora—or, in Leland, Windelsore—seems naturally enough to mean a winding shore, or it might conceivably allude to that part of the river-bank that has a windlass and some, therefore, have said that it is an abbreviation of "wind us over." Others believe that it is a corruption of "wynd is sore," referring to the gusty weather. Eton is derived from eyot-tun, or settlement on the island, and *not* tun by the eau. The castle, and the school, are too well known to detain a determined Thames traveller. The castle itself is of some interest geographically. It is built upon a knoll of chalk that rises precipitately from the thick clay. That is why William the Conqueror decided to site his castle here. It seems to be artificial, and may thus be prehistoric. William may have intuited, or been informed of, some ancient source of power. The castle was effectively rebuilt by Edward III from 1360 to 1374, using for that purpose what was essentially slave labour. Hundreds of men from the surrounding countryside were "impressed" and obliged to work on the castle against their wills. The Saxon palace was located in Old Windsor, 2 miles downstream. In Thames Field, now the site of the Eton Rowing Course, have been found prehistoric barrows, Anglo-Saxon graves, and medieval structures.

DATCHET: Etymology very uncertain, but believed to be Celtic or British in origin. It seems to incorporate *cet* meaning wood, except for the fact that there were no woods in the vicinity. There is a riverine town in France called Dacetia, which is deemed to mean "best place" in Gaulish. In *Domesday* Datchet is known as Daceta. It was described as "a low and wat'ry place," and in the 1800s was denounced as "Black Datchet." It is perhaps most famous for the scene of Falstaff's disgrace in *The Merry Wives of Windsor*, when he was flung into "the muddy ditch at Datchet mead" by the river. The

Thames shore here was said, in the same play, to be "shelvy and shallow." It remains so.

RUNNYMEDE: Of uncertain meaning, possibly a running mead. Or place for horse races; it was indeed a race-course at the end of the eighteenth century. Or a rune-mead or place of runes, a site for magical divination. Or it derives from the Saxon *runieg* (regular meeting) and *mede* (mead or meadow) and was thus a field of council, or it comes from *rhine,* meaning river or ditch. It is all beyond conjecture. We live in a landscape for which we have lost the original meanings. Best known for the famous encounter between King John and his barons. There is an island in the middle of the river, now known as Magna Carta Island, which declares that this was the place of agreement. There is even a great stone upon which the precious document was supposed to rest.

STAINES: Or stones. What stones? Could it refer to standing stones, now de-molished, or to a milestone or Roman milliarium? A group of "negen stanes" or nine stones is mentioned in a twelfth-century charter of Chertsey Abbey, and it is believed that these stones marked the boundaries of the

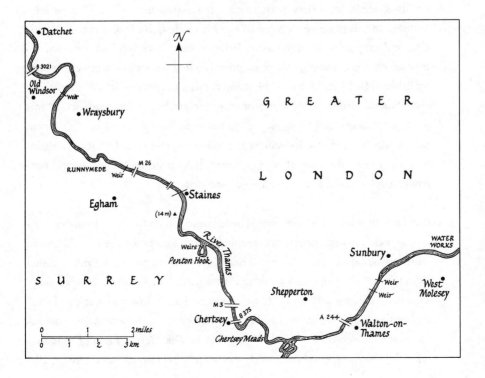

abbey lands. Were they originally part of a megalithic monument? The site is now a roundabout beside Staines Bridge. Curiously enough, London Stone is sited here, to mark what was once the limit of London's authority over the river. Staines is an ancient place, with the traces of Mesolithic settlement. A Roman town was also constructed here, called Ad Pontes, meaning By the Bridges. The *Itinerary* of Antoninus suggests that there was a bridge here before the coming of the Romans, however, which would make Staines a very ancient crossing place indeed. There is also evidence of a Roman bridge, and a Saxon bridge, and a Norman bridge, across the Thames, and even a theory that the settlement was called Stones because of the number of broken bridges.

PENTON HOOK: A curious curve in the river, which means that the traveller must walk for half a mile in order to cover a hundred yards in distance. There must be something of impenetrable hardness that deters the river from taking the shortest course. There is now a cut through it.

CHERTSEY: Cearta's *ey,* or island. The *Ceroti insula* or island of Cerotus is mentioned in Bede. From the seventh century it was the home of the celebrated Benedictine abbey of St. Peter. It was savaged by the Danes in the ninth century, and rebuilt by King Edgar in 964. It became a great town, as large in extent as Windsor, and its position acted as a fulcrum for the development of the Thames Valley. Henry VIII made a more permanent impression than the Danes, however, and the abbey was razed at the time of the Reformation. Abraham Cowley came to Chertsey to avoid the noise and business of London; much to Samuel Johnson's delight, however, he suffered a number of illnesses and misadventures, succumbing to an early death while gathering hay in the fields. For Johnson it was a lesson against solitude. At Chertsey are found the last of the Thames water-meadows.

SHEPPERTON: The home of the shepherds; Scepertone in *Domesday*. Part of the bank is known as War Close in which, according to William Harrison, "have been dug up Spurs, Swords etc. with great numbers of Men's bones; and at a little distance, to the west, part of a Roman Camp is still visible." A site of ancient battles, therefore, probably between the Romans and the Catuvellauni. Most famous as the home of film and television studios, where there have no doubt been re-enactments of just such battles. There is a ferry service between the Shepperton shore and Weybridge. A foot ferry across the same stretch of water is mentioned in the *Domesday Book*. Here also is the "Desborough Cut," a short waterway laid across an island, while the Thames itself continues its sinuous and meandering course. There is some confusion concerning the state of the river at this point. It seems, in the course of recorded history to have altered its course, signified by the fact that the old parishes own areas of land on both sides of the river. The river, in other words, has moved.

SUNBURY: In ancient records known as Sunnabyri, Sunneberie, Suneberie. If we take it as the conflation of Saxon *sunna* and *byri*, we have the sun town or perhaps a town with a southern aspect. Others believe that it is named after the burgh of a chieftain Sunna.

HAMPTON: The farmstead by the bend in the river. In *Domesday* it is known as Hamntone. Here is to be found Garrick Temple, a folly conceived by the actor, David Garrick, to contain a statue of William Shakespeare. The statue by Roubilliac, modelled on Garrick himself, has for some reason been placed in the British Museum. Capability Brown designed the temple. Samuel Johnson said of Hampton, "Ah, David, it is the leaving of such places that makes a death-bed terrible." Just downstream is Tagg's Island, a hotel and pleasure resort designed by the early twentieth-century impresario, Fred Karno. The area is perhaps best known for the propinquity of Hampton Court Palace.

KINGSTON: There can be little doubt about the essential derivation of this place-name. It may be the stone of kings or the manor of kings, but the royal association is clear. It was here that many of the Saxon kings were crowned. In 838 Egbert summoned a meeting of nobles and ecclesiastics at "*Kyningestun, famosa illa locus.*" The King's Stone, now in front of the guildhall, was originally sited near the church door and is generally regarded as the throne upon which the Saxon kings of Wessex were inaugurated. In a charter of Edred, in AD 946, Kingston is expressly mentioned as the place of coronation. Speed calculates that nine sovereigns were in fact crowned here. The *Domesday Book* records the presence of three salmon fisheries. The present emblem of Royal Kingston consists of three salmon on a blue background. The first wooden bridge connecting Kingston and Hampton Wick was erected in 1219. The water was once deemed very clear and pure.

TEDDINGTON: The settlement of the people of Todda or Totty. In old records it is known as Todington or Totyngton. Some people believe the name to be a corruption of Tide-end Town, on the presumption that the tidal river does indeed come to an end here. The first lock on the river is situated at this point. The first lock-keeper was given a blunderbuss, with bayonet attached, to deter irate fishermen and boatmen. Noël Coward was born here, Thomas Traherne was rector here, and R. D. Blackmore, author of *Lorna Doone*, lived here.

EEL PIE ISLAND: It should really be known as Twickenham Ait. But eel pies, naturally, were once sold here. In the summer seasons of the nineteenth century, large crowds came to partake of the eels; members of benefit societies and trade unions mingled with respectable citizens and decent artisans for a memorable "outing." In the 1960s the hotel became the venue for acts such as the Rolling Stones and the Who, David Bowie and Rod Stewart. The island is now the insular home of a somewhat eccentric community.

TWICKENHAM: Presumably meaning the settlement or enclosure of Twica or, perhaps, land by a river fork. Known previously as Twitnam, Twittanham, Twicenham. The first written reference, in a charter of AD 704, describes it as Tuican hom and Tuiccanham. There was a ferry between here and Richmond by the fifteenth century. It is perhaps most famous by association. Its residents have included Sir Francis Bacon, Godfrey Kneller, Mary Wortley Montague, Alexander Pope, Henry Fielding, John Donne, Horace Walpole, J. W. M. Turner, Alfred Tennyson, Alexander Herzen, the Duke of Orleans and the exiled King Manoel of Portugal. It was memorialised by Pope in a puzzling couplet:

Which fairer scenes enrich,
Grots, statues, urns, and Johnston's dog and bitch.

The dog and bitch were two statues flanking the lawn of Orleans House, then owned by Mr. Secretary Johnston. In the church there is a monument to Pope, with the epitaph written by the poet himself, "for one who would not be buried in Westminster Abbey"; bitter to the last. Daniel Defoe described the neighbourhood as "so full of beautiful buildings, charming gardens, and rich habitations of gentlemen of quality, that nothing in the world

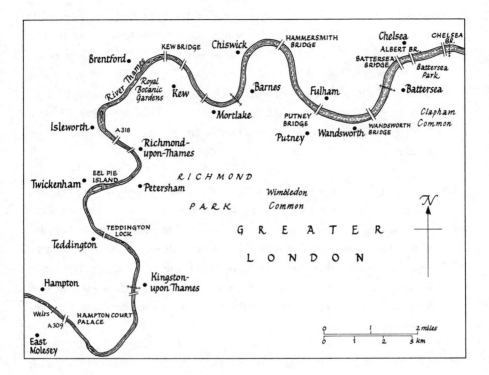

can imitate it." But then a Frenchman said once to Pope: "All this is very fine, but take away the river and it is good for nothing." This is perhaps accurate. The river is everything here. In the nineteenth century the neighbourhood was described by Dickens in *Little Dorrit* as "lovely and placid." Now well known for its rugby stadium.

PETERSHAM: The ham or settlement of Peohtre. The church is also of St. Peter. A nineteenth-century resident of the village recorded a conversation with an old inhabitant: "I remember the time when the people as lived here was people. Now there's nobody here worth a damn."

RICHMOND: The name has no local derivation, since it was first named by Henry VII after his Yorkshire earldom. An area much painted and much described. Thus in Walter Scott's *Heart of Midlothian* (1818) we read that the Thames, "here turreted with villas and there garlanded with forests, moved on slowly and majestically, like the mighty monarch of the scene, to which all of its other beauties were but accessories, and bore on his bosom an hundred barks and skiffs, whose white sails and gaily fluttering pennons gave life to the whole." The riverscape from Richmond Hill has been a favourite of painters for three centuries. In 1902 it became the first view to be protected by an Act of Parliament. Some lines on the view, written by James Thomson, had even been written on a board and nailed to a nearby tree so that nobody could be in any doubt about the "enchanting vale" and the "smiling meads." To quote from Defoe, "the whole country here shines with a lustre not to be described . . . at a distance they are all nature, near hand all art; but both in the extreamest beauty." It is no exaggeration to state that this was the area that initiated and nourished the English art of the landscaped garden, and thus changed the topography of the European world. Karl Philipp Moritz, in his travels, exclaimed of Richmond that "in its way it was the purest revelation of Nature that I have ever seen in my life." This was nature mediated through the picturesque, and is a token of the almost hysterical approbation that Richmond once received.

SHEEN: The name probably derives from the Old English *sceon*, meaning shelters, perhaps a reference to shelters for the beasts of the field. An alternative suggestion derives the name from the Old English *sceone*, meaning beautiful. From that root comes "shine," perhaps to be interpreted by Defoe's description of "the beauty with which the banks of the Thames shine on either side of the river." The castle of the Plantagenets, Shene Palace, once stood in the area now occupied by Richmond Green.

ISLEWORTH: The village known to the compilers of the *Domesday Book* as Ghistelworde. Its name is also found as Yhistleworth, Istelworth, Ysselsworth and Thistleworth. The etymologists have run riot. The most likely derivation, however, is from Celtic *uisc* for water and the Saxon *worth* for village. The confluence of Celtic and Saxon names is rare but it is indeed a village by the water, lying beside the river Crane as well as the Thames. It once had a reputation for remoteness, and at the beginning of the twentieth century it was described as "an ancient and almost forgotten village" with a "somewhat squalid waterside picturesqueness." It is no longer squalid but the dwellings by the waterside are still picturesque—not least among them the famous inn, the London Apprentice. The church beside it is a strange hybrid, a modern building fastened to a fourteenth-century tower. The eyots, or islands, in front of the town were once used to harvest osiers. There was a royal palace in Isleworth, owned by Richard, Earl of Cornwall, brother to Henry III and nominal King of Rome.

BRENTFORD: There was indeed a ford across the river Brent here, and also one across the Thames. There is a legend of "Two Kings of Brentford," but their identity is now unknown. Brentford itself once had a reputation for dirt and squalor. John Gay, in his epistle to the Earl of Burlington (1712), described it as

> Brentford, tedious town,
> For dirty streets and white-legged chickens known.

Thomson continued the abuse in his *Castle of Indolence* (1748) with "Brentford town, a town of mud." George II admired the place because, in its dirty and ill-paved state, it reminded him of his native country. "I like to ride dro' Brentford," his majesty is claimed to have remarked, "it ish so like Hanoversh!" It used to be said of a man with a very red face that "he is like the Red Lion of Brentford," alluding to the sign of the principal inn here. In the eighteenth century it became a great brewing town and in 1805 it joined the Grand Junction Canal, adding to the general noise, dirt and squalor. It is now much improved.

KEW: Known variously as Kayhough, Kayhoo, Keyhowe, Keye, Kayo and Kewe. The name would seem to be a reference to a key or quay by the riverside, or it may mean a place upon a promontory. Erasmus Darwin celebrated the gardens in his couplet:

> So sits enthroned, in vegetable pride,
> Imperial Kew, by Thames's glittering side.

The vegetable pride is still very much in evidence. The Botanic Gardens are most famous for the palm house and the pagoda.

CHISWICK: The meaning may be cheese farm, as in Keswick. Hogarth and Whistler were both buried in the local churchyard. Chiswick House is close by. It was for a period in use as a lunatic asylum. Now it is open to the public. Once known for its nursery gardens and its market gardens, the neighbourhood was called "the great garden of London." Chiswick was also celebrated for its brewing industries, of which there are records from the thirteenth century. Now best known for the Chiswick roundabout.

MORTLAKE: In *Domesday* it becomes Mortelage. The name does not mean lake of the dead. Leland and others believed that it conveyed the Latin *mortuus lacus*, or the dead channel of a river that has changed its course. Yet that hardly seems appropriate to this stretch of the Thames. It may mean the stream owned by Morta, with *lacu* as stream. Or it may be related to the Old English *mort*, the name for a young salmon. The great Elizabethan magus, John Dee, lived in a house by the river. It was here that the angel Uriel appeared to him, and gave him a translucent stone by means of which he might summon the spirits. The first English tapestry factory was established here in 1619. There was also a famous pottery manufactory.

PUTNEY: One of the twin towns beside the Thames, Putney on the Surrey shore and Fulham on the Middlesex shore. The churches that stand on opposite sides of the bridge, All Saints and St. Mary's, were said to have been built by two giant sisters; they possessed only one hammer, and would throw it to each other across the water with the words "Put it nigh!" or "Heave it full home!"; hence Putnigh and Fulhome. This is of course mere conjecture. Putney is in *Domesday* called Putelei, but in subsequent accounts it is spelled Puttenheth or Pottenheth. It may mean the landing place of Putta. The neighbourhood was famous in the seventeenth and eighteenth centuries for its fishery. Fishing has once again become a popular sport here. There used to be a ferry, but a bridge replaced that service in the early eighteenth century. A London MP declared that "the erection of a bridge over the river Thames at Putney will not only injure the great and important city which I have the honour to represent, not only destroy its correspondence and commerce, but actually annihilate it altogether." It used to be the custom for travellers to proceed by water to Putney, and from there take a coach. It is still well known for its rowing clubs, and has in fact become the centre for Thames rowing. Once a village, famous as the birthplace of Thomas Cromwell and Edward Gibbon, it spread along the banks until in the nineteenth century it was known for "a succession of factories and small cottage houses, which serve to shelter labourers and artisans" as well as "unwholesome looking swamps" which divide the space with "yards and quays and wagon sheds." It became known as the manufactory of gin, starch, candles, beer and vitriol.

FULHAM: Fullenhanne or Fullenholme, the place of fowls or the place of birds; or, perhaps, the enclosure of a fuller. Others suggest that the name means "foul home" or muddy settlement. Once known for its market gardens, and for being the site of the first gas-works in Britain. It was the home of the Bishop of London until 1973. Samuel Richardson and Rudyard Kipling also lived here. Once considered more genteel than Putney, but the respective status of the two towns has now been reversed. "Fulham dice" was the phrase for false dice.

BATTERSEA: The name is a puzzle, with etymologists invoking St. Patrick, St. Peter or batter pudding as its origin. It was written Patrice-cey in *Domesday*, and then became Batrichsey. Batter pudding is too obvious a derivation. It may, however, mean Badric's or Batta's island. The town was once well known for its asparagus, and is now most famous for its dogs' home. There is an anonymous poem on the subject:

> To me, Oh, far dearer,
> And brighter, and clearer,
> The Thames as it ripples at fair Battersea.

The river is also more tempestuous here; the waves at Battersea Bridge are known for their roughness.

CHELSEA: It is mentioned in the *Domesday Book* as Chelched, but then amended into Cercehede. In the eighth century, when a synod was called here by Offa, it had become Ceolshythe. It was also known as Cealchythe, which might mean a landing place for chalk or lime, or a landing place on gravel. There has been a church on the site of Chelsea Old Church since the eighth century. The house of Thomas More was situated here, and a memorial to his family is to be found in the church itself. This stretch of the Thames was known ironically as "the Cocknies' Sea." The local young men of the early nineteenth century were known as "kiddies" who "wore their hair in close curls on the side of their heads, done upon leaden rollers; hats turned or looped up on the sides; and to their breeches eight, and sometimes ten, small buttons were seen at their knees, with a profusion of strings, after the famed 'Sixteen-string Jack.'" So Chelsea has always been a centre of fashion.

LAMBETH: Loam-hithe or muddy bank; or perhaps Lamhytha, the landing place for lambs. In *Domesday* called Lanchei. Best known for its palace, home of the Archbishop of Canterbury. In the church here is located the Tradescant Museum of Garden History. The home of various magicians and astrologers, perhaps attracted by the Hebrew connotations of the name as the home of the lamb. Beth-el was in Hebrew the name for a sacred place. But it was always a somewhat rough neighbourhood. Blake moved here in the eighteenth century, among various louche and radical neighbours. It was believed that the swampy air on the south side of the river encouraged enervation and vice, Lambeth being known as one of the "great sinks and common receptacles of all the vice and immorality of London." It became well known for its potteries and for the prevalence of what were known as "stink industries." It also became a haven for boat-builders and boat-repairers. In the nineteenth century it was considered to be a "hideous aspect of the foreshore, overladen with dank tenements, rotten wharves and dirty boat houses." There is a remarkable series of early photographs, showing the whole picturesque and dilapidated riverine settlement that was cleared away for the Albert Embankment and its adjacent roads.

WESTMINSTER: The Saxons called it Thornege, meaning the Isle of Thorns. The island may have been formed by an arm of the river, called the Long Ditch, but it was more likely to have been surrounded by low marshy ground from which the higher ground emerged. It was once the site of a temple to Apollo. The present abbey in the west began to rise in the eleventh century, but there had been a monastery here from the early seventh century. Sebert, king of East Saxons, erected the abbey church and named it West Mynstre in distinction to the East Minster, or St. Paul's, which previously had been founded by his uncle Ethelbert. The remains of Sebert are still within the abbey. The Duke of Wellington insisted that the present Par-

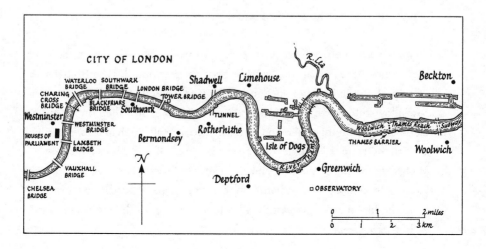

liament face directly upon the river, so that the building could never be surrounded by irate crowds.

CITY and CENTRAL LONDON: The river is the origin of London. One possible derivation of the city's name is the Celtic *llyn-dun*, or the hill fort by the pool. That would of course suggest that the Celts built a settlement here before the Romans. It was the first place upstream from the estuary where a bluff of hard ground was protected by two hills. There are some who claim that the Thames *is* London—that it is the epitome, the liquid essence, the spirit, of London. When the *Illustrated London News* was first published, the title page of that paper showed the Thames; the river was the presiding deity. The poet John Masefield described it as "the great street paved with water," the central highway and principal avenue of the city. It is as closely linked to the city as the blood is to the body, and it can be claimed with some confidence that no other capital in the world has been so dependent upon its river. It was not simply its market and its port and its highway. The Thames gave London the dignity and the grandeur, the aesthetic possibilities, which it would not otherwise possess. That is why most of the city's great architectural monuments are placed along the river. Yet it is curious that Londoners themselves rarely attend to the Thames. They pass over it hurriedly; they try not to walk beside it, and they rarely venture upon it. It does not lead anywhere. It cannot be used as transport to the cinema or the theatre or the public house. And so it is neglected. It is not deemed to be interesting. In most of London, even in its riverine portions, the Thames can scarcely be seen. It is just glimpsed between buildings. And, for its own part, the river is content to remain aloof. It is not intimate or insinuating. It still seems primaeval, dark, and altogether obscure.

SOUTHWARK: Or the south work. A defensive wall was built beside the bank here. Some believe that the "work" was a fortress built by the Romans. At the top of Battle Bridge Lane, going down to Tooley Street, there is a narrow alley still known as "English Grounds." It was so called on a London map of 1848. On that old map there was also a small hatched area described as "Irish Grounds." Could this be a memorial of the nineteenth-century pitched fights between Irish and English labourers? There is no point in looking for a more ancient battle on this site; the name of the bridge comes from the fact that it was part of a hostel belonging to the monks of Battle Abbey in Sussex.

WAPPING: The settlement of Waeppa's people. This early tribe or band inhabited the ground now supporting the Hawksmoor church of St. George's in the East. Once known as Wapping on the Wose, or Wapping in the mud. Samuel Johnson urged Boswell to "explore Wapping" in order thoroughly to understand the London world. It still acts as an example. Once a place of fat fields and pastures, it became a riverside neighbourhood in the seventeenth and eighteenth centuries, described as a "continual street, with alleys of small tenements or cottages, built by sailors' victuallers." It was a place of pubs and brothels, in other words. It became an adjunct to the London Docks in the nineteenth century, then a slum and wasteland in the twentieth; now in the twenty-first century an arena for luxury apartments, estate agents and the headquarters of Times International.

BERMONDSEY: The eye or island of Beormund. The word *eye* is now reserved for the London Eye by the Thames, but it was originally used for a number of small islands upon the marshland or floodplain of the Thames. Bermondsey itself began existence as a causeway across the marsh, leading to a mid-Saxon minster. In the fourteenth century a Cluniac abbey arose in the same place, and became the centre of the commercial as well as the spiritual life of the area. By the eighteenth century, like many settlements beside the river, Bermondsey attracted the more noxious trades such as tanning and glue manufacture. Its various and disagreeable smells became famous. They were not necessarily unwelcomed, however; the smell of tanning was believed to be efficacious against the plague. There are still streets named Tanner Street, Morocco Street and Leathermarket Street. The phrase "mad as a hatter" originates here from the ailments that afflicted the hatters of Bermondsey, when they breathed in the fumes of a highly toxic mercury solution in the course of their work. It also has the honour (if such it is) of containing Jacob's Island immortalised as Bill Sikes's lair in *Oliver Twist* with "every repulsive lineament of poverty, every loathsome indication of filth, rot and garbage." Sikes's house was in Eckett Street, long since demolished.

SHADWELL: It does not mean "well of shadows," or "shady wells." The name derives from Ceadeles's well, Ceadeles being a pre-Christian water deity. Shad Thames by Bermondsey is supposed to be a corruption of the Street of St. John at the Thames, the Knights of St. John owning mills in the neighbourhood, but there may be a connection with Ceadeles.

LIMEHOUSE: The place of lime oasts or lime kilns. There have been lime-workers here from the fourteenth century to the disappearance of the last kilns in 1935. There was a porcelain factory in Limehouse in the eighteenth century and the area was also known for its ship-building. In the nineteenth century it was known as Chinatown, and acquired a reputation for its opium dens and what were known as "dopers." It never was as dangerous or as heinous as its reputation suggested, although writers as diverse as Oscar Wilde and Sax Rohmer introduced a great deal of romantic intrigue within the neighbourhood. It is no wonder that most Londoners shunned the area. It is now filled with expensive riverside apartments.

ROTHERHITHE: Or Redriff; Redriff Road survives. The name is popularly sup-posed to refer to a red reef, and it is said that just below the entrance to Mill-wall Dock there is a patch of light red gravel which runs across the river bottom. But it may derive from *redhra*, the Saxon for sailor, and *hythe* for haven. In that case it has been connected with sailors and shipping for more than a thousand years. Alternatively it may mean a landing place for cattle. From here the Pilgrim Fathers set sail for Plymouth and the New World. In the eighteenth century it was a village inhabited by seafaring men and tradesmen in the various nautical businesses. Lemuel Gulliver lived here. In the nineteenth century it became the home for various docks, many with a Baltic or Scandinavian connection. Grain and timber were the principal car-goes, although "Sicily sulphur"—sulphur from Palermo—was also an im-portant commodity. The remains of a manor house, built by Edward III, can be seen beside the river-bank just west of the church. Galleywall Road here, once spelled Galley Wall, was popularly believed to mark the edge of the great ditch that Canute built to allow his galleys to circumvent the Thames.

DEPTFORD: Deep ford. There was once a Roman bridge here, but it decayed. Deptford Bridge is now on the site. A Saxon settlement has been found. It may have been known as Meretun, meaning the dwelling place in the marsh, and in AD 871 Ethelred defeated the Danes at this place. It is perhaps most famous as the location of Christopher Marlowe's death. Peter the Great lived for several months at Sayes Court, owned by John Evelyn. His favourite pas-time was to be driven in a wheelbarrow, drunk, through Evelyn's neat hedges. There is still a Czar Street, but the house has long since disappeared. He was especially interested in the Royal Naval Dockyard, established by Henry VII in 1513. Raleigh, Frobisher and Drake all sailed from here.

GREENWICH: From the Saxon *Grenewic* or *Grenevic*, the green port, *wic* referring to a place where dry soil meets the river. Or perhaps the name means the village on the green, or even a dairy farm. It has attracted settlers from the Mesolithic period forwards. There was a royal palace here from the time of Edward I, which in the fifteenth century was known as L'Pleazaunce or Placentia. Both Henry VIII and Elizabeth I were born here. Hawksmoor built the church of St. Alphege, named after the Archbishop of Canterbury, Ealpheg, who on the site was beaten to death with ox-bones by the invading Danes in 1012. The setting for the Royal Observatory, and the Royal Hospital which is now the home of the University of Greenwich. It is considered by some to represent the most beautiful view upon the river. Defoe believed that the water of the Thames at this point "is very sweet and fresh, especially at the tide of ebb." This may no longer be true. Greenwich gin is still manufactured here. Just to the east of the town is Horseshoe Breach, a breach in the river-bank that has never been reclaimed, and Dead Dog Bay. Greenwich has become a World Heritage Site.

THE ISLE OF DOGS: It is a peninsula, rather than an island. Once known as Stebunheath [Stepney] Marsh. The origin of the name is unclear. Was it a place where dead dogs were washed on the foreshore? Were the dog-kennels of Edward III situated here? In the eleventh century it was a woody marsh, upon which the Bishop of London kept five hundred hogs. So perhaps it was once the Isle of Hogs? It might also be a corruption of Isle of Ducks, or even Isle of Dykes. There is the story that a waterman murdered a man here, whose dog then swam back and forth across the river until he was noticed and followed. The corpse was discovered and, when the dog began to snarl at the waterman, so was the murderer. Hence the Isle of the Dog. There is yet another legend of a lost hunting party, whose phantom dogs wailed in the night. There was once a primaeval forest here, the remains of which have been uncovered 8 feet (2.4 m) beneath the surface of the water; in the nineteenth century it was described as "a mass of decayed trees, leaves and branches, accompanying huge trunks, rotted through, yet perfect in every fibre; the bark was uninjured, and the whole evidently torn up by the roots." The West India Docks were built in the early nineteenth century. Until the 1980s it was inhabited by a tightly knit and of course peninsular community. A stone chapel dedicated to St. Mary was found here. Now the home of "Docklands" marked by the huge erection of Canary Wharf.

WOOLWICH: Wool farm; or a settlement where wool was traded. The river here was once considered treacherous, with unpredictable deeps and shallows. Harrison described the river at this point as of a "vast bigness." It is indeed over a mile in width and, on the flood, the water is salt. The whole riverine area was once known as Bugsby's Marshes. Now Woolwich Reach is preceded by Bugsby's Reach, containing Bugsby's Hole. The Hole was a place of execution in the eighteenth century, but now is essentially a small beach where rusty and dilapidated boats are to be found. No one knows the identity of Bugsby. Some say that he was a pirate, others that he was a market gardener or a devil. Woolwich was once the home of the military Arsenal. It is now the site of the Thames Barrier.

ERITH: Place where gravel was shipped; or perhaps a landing place of gravel. Seven or eight Saxon skeletons were found on the top of a hill beside the river. Once known as Lesnes or Lessness. The ruins of Lessness Abbey are still to be seen. The area was always low, flat and marshy with a reputation for being unhealthy.

GREENHITHE: Or Gretenrcse, meaning green landing place. Once the site of very productive chalk pits.

DAGENHAM: Daecca's ham or settlement. Nearby Barking is named after Berica's people. The home of the once famous Dagenham Breach when, in 1707, 5,000 acres (2,023 ha) of marshland were submerged by the river. The inundated area was not drained and embanked until 1721. The home of the

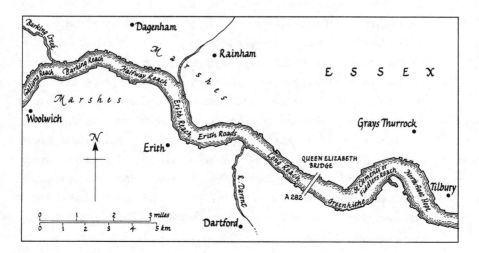

Ford Motor Company. A large lake to the north of the factory marks the remains of the breach.

GRAYS THURROCK: The manor of Thurrock belonged to Richard de Grays. Thurrock may derive from Thoar's Oak. Or it may come from the Saxon term *thorrocke*, describing the bottom part of a boat where the bilge water collects. It may simply mean a dung-heap in a field. The latter seems the most likely. This is where the Black Shelf Sand begins. This area of the river is known as St. Clement's Reach, because the church of St. Clement in West Thurrock was built for the Canterbury pilgrims and fishermen who congregated along this stretch. The church was once in an isolated and desolate spot, surrounded by marshland, but it is now dominated by modern factories and refineries. The river at this place is also known as Fiddlers' Reach, as a result of the legend that three fiddlers were drowned here and that their musical improvisations still cause the water to be restless and choppy; alternatively it is believed that seamen once used to call an irregular swell of the water "fiddling." An early nineteenth-century guide described Grays Thurrock as consisting "principally of one irregular street situated on a small creek navigable for vessels of small burden." It is now a sizeable town. The area is still occupied by waste-tips and waste-heaps, thus reverting to the meaning of its old name. The Queen Elizabeth the Second Bridge, a cable-stayed bridge, leads the M25 across the Thames Estuary.

TILBURY: The fort or burgh of Tilla. West Tilbury was the site chosen for the Camp Royal in 1588, where Elizabeth I delivered her celebrated speech to her army preparing for Spanish invaders. Now the site of Tilbury Fort, built in the 1670s as a defence against Dutch incursions along the river. Perhaps the fort of Tilla was situated on the same spot. There was once a Mint here, and the name appears on a coin from the reign of Edward the Confessor. Defoe reported "the whole shore being low, and spread with marshes and unhealthy ground."

GRAVESEND: It does not mean "end of the grave" where, according to once popular legend, the Great Plague finally stopped. In the *Domesday Book* it is known as Gravesham, or the town of the Grave, otherwise Graff, the earl or chief magistrate of the neighbourhood. The point of entry to the Port of London, where coastal pilots secede their place to river pilots. In the

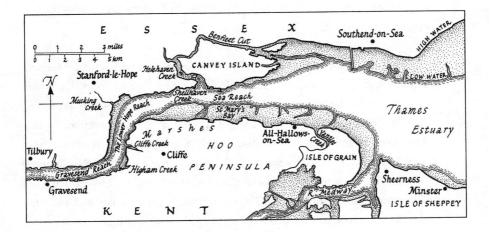

fourteenth century the watermen here were granted the exclusive right to transport passengers to London. This was once the place of arrivals and departures, where explorers and colonists, transported prisoners and emigrants, were vouchsafed their last glimpse of the land they were leaving. It was at Gravesend Reach that David Copperfield bade farewell to Mr. Peggotty, and where the Micawbers disappeared from sight. A nineteenth-century account of the Thames describes the place as associated with "meetings and partings, with great changes of fortune, with the keenest moments in the drama of life." The river, from Gravesend and Tilbury to the sea, is known as "the Hope." So a haunted place, one which Conrad described as having once been "one of the dark places of the earth." The town pier of 1834 survives still. The town marks the beginning of the Saxon Shore that winds its way to Hastings.

CLIFFE: Called Clive or Cloveshoo or Cliffe-at-Hoo. Also once known as Bishops' Cliffe, since all the Saxon bishops in the province of Canterbury held an annual synod "in the place which is called Clofeshoch." It is believed that this represents the first parliamentary system to be inaugurated in England. There was once a thriving port here; from its position upon the cliff, it was a significant location. In 1797 it was reported that "Cliffe seems daily growing into further ruin and poverty, the number of inhabitants lessening yearly and several of the houses, for want of them lying in ruins." By the nineteenth century it was described as "a lonely, primitive place." No doubt the ague destroyed the people. So by degrees human settlement disappeared.

ISLE OF SHEPPEY: From the Saxon *sceapige*, in consequence of the great quantity of sheep bred upon it. Known to Ptolemy as Toliapis. Here, at Minster-upon-Sea, is one of the oldest churches in Britain; it was founded by Queen Sexburga in AD 670. There was originally a temple to Apollo on the same site. For many centuries it was a battleground between the Danes and Saxons. In 832 it was overrun "by the heathen men." It has not been the same since.

CANVEY ISLAND: The island of Cana's people. Some 4,000 (1,620 ha) acres of land, once flat marshland. It may be the Convennos or Counos of Ptolemy and other ancient writers. There are extensive signs of Romano-British occupation. In the second century it was the home of salt-makers, whose settlement was destroyed in some natural disaster when the island was submerged. It has always been at the mercy of the sea. At a later date it was an island of shepherds. Then it became the home for a large community of Dutch, who in the early seventeenth century used their skills at reclaiming land in exchange for rights of settlement. A place, in William Harrison's words, "which some call marshes onlie, and liken them to an ipocras bag, some to a vice, scrue, or wide sleeve, because they are verie small at the east end and large at the west." In the early nineteenth century it was reported that "only people who cared little whether they lived or died would undertake the farm work on the island." But the ague disappeared in the middle of the nineteenth century, largely because of improved drainage and the reduced population of mosquitoes. At the beginning of the twentieth century it was described as "the loneliest place in the Home Counties" but a large urban community was developed in subsequent years. It also became a holiday resort for Londoners. The great flood of 1953 killed eighty-three residents.

Bibliography

Adams, Anna (ed.), *Thames: An Anthology of River Poems* (London, 1999)

Adams, F. D., *The Birth and Development of the Geological Sciences* (London, 1938)

Addison, William, *Thames Estuary* (London, 1954)

Adkins, R. and Jackson, R., *Neolithic Stone and Flint Axes from the River Thames* (London, 1978)

Anderson, Jo, *Anchor and Hope* (London, 1980)

Anderson, J. R. L., *The Upper Thames* (London, 1970)

Anon., *Chronicles of London Bridge* (London, 1839)

Anon., *The Royal River* (London, 1885)

Armstrong, Walter, *The Thames*, two volumes (London, 1886)

Arnold, Ralph, *The Hundred of Hoo* (London, 1947)

Astbury, A. K., *Estuary* (London, 1980)

Atterbury, Paul (ed.), *Nicholson's Guide to the Thames* (London, 1969)

Bachelard, Gaston, *L'Eau et les Rêves* (Paris, 1964)

Ball, E. and Ball, P. W., *Cruising on the Thames* (Newton Abbot, 1970)

Barclay, Alistair and Harding, Jan (eds.), *Pathways and Ceremonies* (Oxford, 1999)

Barclay, Alistair, Lambrick, George, Moore, John and Robinson, Mark, *Lines in the Landscape* (Oxford, 2003)

Barham, Tony, *Witchcraft in the Thames Valley* (Bourne End, 1973)

Bates, Brian, *The Real Middle Earth* (London, 2002)

Bates, L. M., *The Spirit of London's River* (Old Woking, 1980)

——, *Thames Cavalcade* (Lavenham, Suffolk, 1991)

Batey, Mavis, Buttery, Henrietta, Lambert, David and Wilkie, Kim, *Arcadian Thames* (London, 1994)

Belloc, Hilaire, *The Historic Thames* (London, 1914)

Benson, Don and Miles, David, *The Upper Thames Valley* (Oxford, 1974)

Besant, Walter, *The Thames* (London, 1903)

Blair, John, *The Anglo-Saxon Age* (Oxford, 1984)

Bolland, R. R., *Victorians on the Thames* (Tunbridge Wells, 1974)

Bootle, Robin and Bootle, Valerie, *The Story of Cookham* (Cookham, 1990)

Bradley, Richard, *An Archaeology of Natural Places* (London, 2000)

——, *The Passage of Arms* (Cambridge, 1990)

Bridgland, D. R., *The Quaternary of the Thames* (London, 1994)

Brittain, Robert, *Rivers, Man and Myths* (New York, 1958)

Broodbank, Sir Joseph, *History of the Port of London*, two volumes (London, 1921)

Brown, N. W., and Reed, Graham, *London's Waterfront* (London, 2003)

Bunge, J. H. O., *Tideless Thames in Future London* (London, 1944)

Burke, Thomas, *Limehouse Nights* (London, 1917)

——, *The Song Book of Quong Lee* (London, 1920)

Burstall, Patricia, *The Golden Age of the Thames* (London, 1981)

Burton, W. (ed.), *A Commentary upon Antoninus* (London, 1661)

Butzer, K. W., *Early Hydraulic Civilisation in Egypt* (Chicago, 1976)

Byrne, L. S. R. and Churchill, E. L., *The Eton Book of the River* (Eton, 1952)

Cairns, A. J., *The Book of Marlow* (Marlow, 1976)

Carroll, Lewis, *Alice's Adventures in Wonderland* (London, 1865)

——, *Through the Looking-Glass* (London, 1871)

Céline, Louis-Ferdinand, *Guignol's Band* (New York, 1944)

Chandler, J. (ed.), *John Leland's Itinerary* (Stroud, 1993)

Chaplin, P. H., *The Thames from Source to Tideway* (Weybridge, 1982)

Christianson, C. P., *The Riverside Gardens* (London, 2005)

Church, A. J., *Isis and Thamesis* (London, 1886)

Clews, Brian and Trodd, Paul, *Thames Valley and the Chilterns* (London, 1987)

Cobbett, William, *Rural Rides* (London, 1830)

Collis, J. S., *The Moving Waters* (London, 1956)

Combe, William, *An History of the River Thames* (London, 1794–96)

Conrad, Joseph, *The Mirror of the Sea* (London, 1906)

——, *Some Reminiscences* (London, 1912)

——, *Youth and Two Other Stories* (London, 1902)

Cook, John, *Old Father Thames and Sleeping Beauty* (Bristol, 1966)

Cope, Julian, *The Modern Antiquarian* (London, 1998)

Cornish, C. J., *The Naturalist on the Thames* (London, 1902)

Cove-Smith, Christopher, *The River Thames Book* (Huntingdon, 1996)

Cracknell, B. E., *Canvey Island* (Leicester, 1959)

——, *Portrait of London River* (London, 1968)

Croad, Stephen, *Liquid History* (London, 2003)

Cunliffe, Barry and Miles, David (eds.), *Aspects of the Iron Age in Central Southern Britain* (Oxford, 1984)

Cuss, H. W. J., *The Valley of the Upper Thames* (London, 1998)

Daniell, A. E., *London's Riverside Churches* (London, 1897)

Darby, Stephen, *Chapters in the History of Cookham* (London, 1909)

Darvill, Timothy, *Prehistoric Britain* (London, 1987)

Davies, G. H., *A Walk Along the Thames Path* (London, 1989)

Defoe, Daniel, *A Tour Thro' the Whole Island of Great Britain* (London, 1724)

Dickens, Charles, junior, *A Dictionary of the Thames* (London, 1887)

Dix, Frank L., *Royal River Highway* (London, 1985)

Drayton, Michael, *Polyolbion. Or a Chorographicall Description of Tracts, Rivers, Mountaines, Forests* (London, 1612)

Eade, Brian, *Along the Thames* (Stroud, 1997)

———, *Forgotten Thames* (Stroud, 2002)

Ebel, Suzanne and Impey, Doreen, *London's Riverside* (London, 1975)

Edmonds, Mark, *Ancestral Geographies of the Neolithic* (London, 1999)

Egan, Pierce, *The Pilgrims of the Thames* (London, 1838)

Ellmers, Christopher, *City and River* (London, 1989)

Ellmers, Christopher and Ellmers, Werner, *London's Lost Riverscape* (London, 1988)

———, *London's Riverscape Lost and Found* (London, 2000)

Emanuel, W. V., *River Thames* (London, 1940)

Emmons, Ron, *Walks along the Thames Path* (London, 2001)

Fearnside, W. G., *Thames and Medway* (London, 1830)

Fidler, Kathleen, *The Thames in Story* (London, 1971)

Foreman, S., Hiller, J. and Petts, D., *Gathering the People, Settling the Land* (Oxford, 2002)

Fowler, Peter, *Wessex* (London, 1967)

Freethy, Ron, *The Natural History of Rivers* (Lavenham, 1986)

Gaze, W. C., *On and Along the Thames* (London, 1913)

Getty, Adele, *Goddess* (London, 1990)

Gibbard, P. L., *Pleistocene History of the Lower Thames Valley* (Cambridge, 1994)

———, *Pleistocene History of the Middle Thames Valley* (London, 1985)

Gibbings, Robert, *Sweet Thames Run Softly* (London, 1940)

Goldsack, Paul, *River Thames* (Chalfont St. Peter, 2003)

Goodsall, R. H., *The Widening Thames* (London, 1965)

Gordon, R. M., *The Thames Torso Murders of Victorian London* (London, 2002)

Grahame, Kenneth, *Dream Days* (London, 1898)

———, *The Golden Age* (London, 1895)

———, *Pagan Papers* (London, 1900)

———, *The Wind in the Willows* (London, 1908)

Grieve, Hilda, *The Great Tide* (Chelmsford, 1959)

Hadland, Tony, *Thames Valley Papists* (Oxford, 1992)

Hall, Mr. and Mrs. S. C., *The Book of the Thames* (London, 1859)

Harper, C. G., *Thames Valley Villages*, two volumes (London, 1910)

Harrison, Ian, *The Thames from Source to Sea* (London, 2004)

Harrison, Jeffery and Grant, Peter, *The Thames Transformed* (London, 1976)

Harrison, William, *An Historicall Description of the Islande of Britayne* (London, 1587)

Hastings, Macdonald, *A Glimpse of Arcadia* (London, 1960)

Hatts, Leigh, *The Thames Path* (Milnthorpe, 1998)

Hawksmoor, Nicholas, *A Short Historical Account of London Bridge* (London, 1736)

Hayward, Graham, *Stanford's River Thames Companion* (London, 1988)

Hefferman, Hilary, *South Thames* (Chalford, 1996)

Herbert, A. P., *The Thames* (London, 1966)

——, *The Water Gipsies* (London, 1930)

Herendeen, W. H., *From Landscape to Literature* (Pittsburgh, 1986)

Higgins, Walter, *Father Thames* (London, 1923)

Hill, David, *Turner on the Thames* (London, 1993)

Hobbs, A. E., *Trout of the Thames* (London, 1947)

Hodgson, F. C., *Thames-Side in the Past* (London, 1913)

Holgate, Robin, *Neolithic Settlement of the Thames Basin* (London, 1988)

Horn, Roni, *Another Water* (Zurich, 2000)

Hornak, Angelo, *London and the Thames* (London, 1999)

Household, Humphrey, *The Thames and Severn Canal* (Newton Abbot, 1969)

Howard, Philip, *London's River* (London, 1975)

Hutton, W. H., *By Thames and Cotswold* (London, 1908)

Ireland, Samuel, *Picturesque Views on the River Thames* (London, 1792)

Irwin, John and Herbert, Jocelyn (eds.), *Sweete Themmes* (London, 1951)

James, Henry, *English Hours* (London, 1905)

James, Simon, *The Atlantic Celts* (London, 1999)

Jefferies, Richard, *After London* (London, 1885)

——, *The Modern Thames* (London, 1885)

——, *The Open Air* (London, 1893)

Jenkins, Alan, *The Book of the Thames* (London, 1983)

Jerome, Jerome K., *My Life and Times* (London, 1926)

——, *Three Men in a Boat* (London, 1908)

Jerrold, Blanchard, *London: A Pilgrimage* (London, 1872)

Jones, David, *Anathemata* (London, 1952)

Jones, S. R., *Thames Triumphant* (London, 1943)

King, Thomson, *Water: Miracle of Nature* (London, 1953)

Krausse, A. S., *A Pictorial History of the Thames* (London, 1889)

Kuenen, P. H., *Realms of Water* (London, 1955)

Lawrence, Tom, *Exploring the Thames Valley* (Newbury, 1990)

Leapman, Michael, *London's River* (London, 1991)

Leopold, L. B. and Davis, K. S., *Water* (New York, 1966)

Leslie, G. D., *Our River* (London, 1881)

Letts, Vanessa, *River Thames* (Melton Constable, 2001)

Leyland, John, *Thames Illustrated* (London, 1901)

Linney, A. J., *Lure and Lore of London's River* (London, 1932)

Long, Roger, *Reputedly Haunted Inns of the Chilterns and Thames Valley* (Arundel, 1993)

Mackay, Charles, *The Thames and Its Tributaries*, two volumes (London, 1840)

Mare, Eric de, *London's Riverside* (London, 1958)

——, *Time on the Thames* (London, 1952)

Martin, Frank, *Rogues' River* (Hornchurch, 1983)

Martin, Graham, *Historic Churches of the Thames Valley* (London, 1973)

Matless, David, *Landscape and Englishness* (London, 1998)

Maxwell, Donald, *A Pilgrimage of the Thames* (London, 1932)

Maxwell, G. S., *The Authors' Thames* (London, 1924)

McCarthy, J., *The Grey River* (London, 1889)

McFetrich, David, *Spanning the River* (London, 2006)

Merrifield, Ralph, *The Archaeology of Ritual and Magic* (London, 1987)

Middleton, Tom, *The Book of Maidenhead* (Buckingham, 1975)

Mitchell, Anne, *Ghosts Along the Thames* (Bourne End, 1972)

Mitton, G. E., *The Thames* (London, 1906)

Morgan, G. H., *Forgotten Thameside* (Letchworth, 1966)

Morisawa, Marie, *Streams* (New York, 1968)

Moritz, K. P., *Journeys of a German in England* (London, 1965)

Morley, F. V., *River Thames* (London, 1926)

Morris, John, *The Age of Arthur* (London, 1993)

Noel-Hume, Ivor, *Treasure in the Thames* (London, 1956)

O'Donnell, Elliott, *Great Thames Mysteries* (London, 1928)

Ormsby, Hilda, *London on the Thames* (London, 1928)

Osmond, Laurie, *The Thames Flows Down* (London, 1957)

Pask, A. T., *The Eyes of the Thames* (London, 1889)

Peacock, T. L., *The Genius of the Thames* (London, 1812)

Peel, J. H. B., *Portrait of the Thames* (London, 1967)

Pennell, Joseph and Robins, Elizabeth, *The Stream of Pleasure* (London, 1891)

Perkins, Angela, *The Book of Sonning* (Chesham, 1977)

——, *Twenty Five Thames Years* (London, 1987)

Perrott, David (ed.), *The Ordnance Survey Guide to the River Thames* (London, 1984)

Phillips, Geoffrey, *Thames Crossings* (London, 1981)

Pilkington, Roger, *Thames Waters* (London, 1956)

Pople, Kenneth, *Stanley Spencer* (London, 1991)

Prichard, Mari and Carpenter, Humphrey, *A Thames Companion* (London, 1975)

Pryor, Francis, *Britain BC* (London, 2003)

Pudney, John, *Crossing London's River* (London, 1972)

Raleigh, Walter, *The History of the World* (London, 1614)

Read, Susan (ed.), *The Thames of Henry Taunt* (Gloucester, 1989)

Reed, Nicholas, *Monet and the Thames* (London, 1998)

Rice, H. S., *Ghosts of the Chilterns and the Thames Valley* (Burnham, 1983)

Robertson, E. A., *Thames Portrait* (London, 1937)

Robertson, H. R., *Life on the Upper Thames* (London, 1875)

Rogers, Daniel, *The Thames* (Austin, 1994)

Rohmer, Sax, *The Book of Fu-Manchu* (New York, 1930)

Rolt, L. T. C., *The Thames from Mouth to Source* (London, 1951)

Ross, Anne, *Pagan Celtic Britain* (London, 1967)

Rothenstein, John and Turner, Vincent, *London's River* (London, 1951)

Ryan, E. K. W., *The Thames from the Towpath* (London, 1938)

Salter, J. H. and Salter, J. A., *Salters' Guide to the Thames* (Oxford, n.d.)

Savill, Mervyn, *Tide of London* (London, 1951)

Schama, Simon, *Landscape and Memory* (London, 1995)

Schneer, Jonathan, *The Thames* (London, 2005)

Sharp, David, *The Thames Path* (London, 1996)

Shrapnel, Norman, *A View of the Thames* (London, 1977)

Simper, Robert, *Thames Tideway* (London, 1997)

Sinclair, Iain, *Downriver* (London, 1991)

Smith, Denis, *Civil Engineering Heritage* (London, 2001)

Smyth, A. P., *King Alfred the Great* (Oxford, 1995)

Squire, John, *Solo and Duet* (London, 1943)

Stead, I. M., *Celtic Dragons from the River Thames* (London, 1984)

Stout, Adam, *Where Two Rivers Meet* (Reading, 1994)

Stow, John, *The Survey of London* (London, 1912)

Tempest, Paul, *Downstream to Greenwich* (Greenwich, 1975)

Thacker, F. S., *The Stripling Thames* (London, 1909)

———, *The Thames Highway*, two volumes (London, 1914 and Kew, 1920)

Thames Journal: Journal of the River Thames Society

Thomas, Charles, *Celtic Britain* (London, 1986)

Thomas, Christopher (ed.), *London's Archaeological Secrets* (London, 2003)

Thompson, A. G., *Scrap Book of London River* (London, 1937)

Thomson, T. R., *A Short History of Cricklade* (Minety, 1946)

Thorne, James, *Rambles by Rivers* (London, 1847)

Thurman, Christopher, *London's River* (London, 2003)

Tilley, Christopher, *A Phenomenology of Landscape* (Oxford, 1994)

Tomlinson, H. M., *London River* (London, 1925)

Tuan, Yi-Fu, *The Hydrologic Cycle and the Wisdom of God* (Toronto, 1968)

Turner, James, *The Politics of Landscape* (Cambridge, Ma, 1979)

Vincent, J. E., *The Story of the Thames* (London, 1909)

Wack, H. W., *In Thamesland* (London, 1906)

Watson, Bruce, Brigham, Trevor and Dyson, Tony, *London Bridge* (London, 2001)

Waugh, Priscilla, *Searching the Thames* (London, 1999)

Webster, G., *The Roman Invasion of Britain* (London, 1980)

Weightman, Gavin, *London River* (London, 1990)

Wheeler, Alwyne, *The Tidal Thames* (London, 1979)

Williams, Alfred, *Folk Songs of the Upper Thames* (London, 1923)

——, *Round About Middle Thames* (Stroud, 1982)

——, *Round About the Upper Thames* (London, 1922)

Williams, J. and Brown, N., *An Archaeological Research Framework for the Greater Thames Estuary* (Chelmsford, 1999)

Wilson, D. G., *The Making of the Middle Thames* (Bourne End, 1977)

——, *The Victorian Thames* (Stroud, 1993)

Winbolt, S. E., *Britain BC* (London, 1943)

Wittfogel, K. A., *Oriental Despotism* (New Haven, 1957)

Wood, Michael, *In Search of the Dark Ages* (London, 1981)

Wright, Laura, *Sources of London English* (Oxford, 1996)

Wright, Patrick, *The River* (London, 1999)

Wykes, Alan, *An Eye on the Thames* (London, 1966)

Wyman, John, *Lower Palaeolithic Archaeology in Britain* (London, 1968)

Index

Italicized page numbers refer to text illustrations.

Author's Acknowledgements

I would like to thank my publishers for the initiation of this project. I must also thank my two researchers, Thomas Wright and Murrough O'Brien, for their indefatigable work. But my particular thanks must go to my two colleagues, Nicholas Robertson and Iain Johnston, who accompanied me on the pedestrian pilgrimage from source to sea and who also helped the conception and completion of this work.

Illustration Credits

The line drawings on the part titles are from *The Book of the Thames from Its Rise to Its Fall* by Mr. and Mrs. S. C. Hall (London, Virtue and Company, 1859)

SECTION ONE

The source of the Thames at Trewsbury Mead (Collections/Chris Cole)

Mammoth tooth found in the Thames (Museum of London/Bridgeman Art Library)

Prehistoric dagger and scabbard, *c.*550–450 BC, found in the Thames, probably at Mortlake (Museum of London/Bridgeman)

Bronze head of the Emperor Hadrian found in the Thames near London Bridge. Hadrian visited London in AD 122 and this bust probably commemorates his visit (Museum of London)

Medieval pilgrim badges of saints. The badges signified that a traveller had completed a journey to a pilgrimage site or shrine. Many such badges have been found in the Thames (Museum of London/Heritage Images)

Ducking a Scold, 1812, by Thomas Rowlandson (Harris Museum and Art Gallery, Preston, Lancashire/Bridgeman)

Angler on a riverbank, woodcut illustration to the *Roxburgh Ballads*, volume 7 (Mary Evans Picture Library)

From *The Oarsman's and Angler's Map of the River Thames from its Source to London Bridge* (London, 1893). The detail shows the stretch from Chertsey to Richmond.

Radcot Bridge, the oldest bridge on the Thames (www.old-england.com)

Harleyford eel nets made from willow (www.old-england.com)

A weir-keeper and fisherman called Harper, Oxfordshire, 1900, photographed by Henry Taunt (English Heritage/Heritage Images)

Mapledurham mill. The mill is still working and producing stone-ground flour (www.old-england.com)

A traveller waits to be ferried across the Thames, woodcut illustration to the *Roxburgh Ballads*, volume 5 (Mary Evans Picture Library)

Cliveden ferry, Cliveden, 1885, photographed by Henry Taunt (English Heritage, National Monuments Record/Heritage Images)

SECTION TWO

Map of Chertsey Abbey, Surrey, fifteenth century, drawn to settle a dispute over pasture (The National Archives/Heritage Images)

Dorchester Abbey, Near Wallingford, Autumn Evening by Newton Bennett (Victoria and Albert Museum, London/Bridgeman)

The Tower of London, fifteenth-century manuscript illumination by French school, Ms Fr 2644 fol.154v (Bibliothèque Nationale, Paris/Bridgeman)

Lambeth Palace, seat of the Archbishop of Canterbury, engraved by Johannes Kip after Leonard Knyff (Private Collection/Bridgeman)

Windsor Castle from the River Meadow on the Thames, c.1827–30 by William Daniell (Private Collection/Bridgeman)

Westminster from Lambeth, with the Ceremonial Barge of the Ironmongers' Company, c.1745, by Samuel Scott (Yale Center for British Art, Paul Mellon Collection/Bridgeman)

Old London Bridge, c.1630 by Claude de Jongh. The view is framed by the turrets of the Tower of London on the left and the ancient tower of the Church of St. Mary Overy on the right (Private Collection/Bridgeman)

The Opening of New London Bridge, 1st August 1831 by English school. The bridge was opened by King William IV and Queen Adelaide during a river pageant (Science Museum, London/Bridgeman)

View of the Greenwich Railway Viaduct at Deptford, 1836, by G. F. Bragg (Guildhall Library, City of London/Bridgeman)

The Millennium Footbridge (Marc Atkins/Panoptika.net)

Doggett's Coat and Badge Rowing Race, c.1820. From plate 13 of *Fashion and Folly*. The race is one of the world's oldest rowing races, held annually along the Thames from London Bridge to Chelsea (Museum of London/Heritage Images)

Henley Regatta, c.1900. First held in 1839, the regatta has been held annually ever since, with the exception of the two World Wars (www.old-england.com)

Pleasure boats on the Thames below Whitchurch Lock, Pangbourne, 1907 (Mary Evans Picture Library)

The lock at Goring-on-Thames (www.old-england.com)

The Londoner's Leisure—the Thames. 1926 poster by Gregory Brown produced by the Southern Railway to advertise their day trips along the Thames (Science and Society Picture Library)

SECTION THREE

Howland Great Wet Dock, Rotherhithe, 1717. Engraved by Johannes Kip after J. Badslade (City of London Libraries and Guildhall Art Gallery/Heritage Images)

Perry's Dock at Blackwall, 1806, by Thomas Rowlandson. The dock was built in 1789 and was later incorporated into the East India Docks (Guildhall Library, City of London/Bridgeman)

A View of the East India Docks, 1808, by William Daniell (Guildhall Library, City of London/Bridgeman)

Wapping, Elevated View of the Dock, 1803 by Thomas and William Daniell (Guildhall Library, City of London/Bridgeman)

Inside the Docks engraving by Gustave Doré from *London: A Pilgrimage* by Gustave Doré and Blanchard Jerrold (1872)

Procession of the Cod Company from St. Giles's to Billingsgate, 1810, by Thomas Rowlandson. Fishwives with baskets on their heads, and with the market behind them (British Museum/Bridgeman)

The Thames Tunnel built by Sir Marc Isambard Brunel. The print shows transverse and cross sections of the tunnel and the tunneling shield used to excavate the tunnel (Science and Society Picture Library)

Faraday Giving his Card to Father Thames from *Punch*, 21 July 1855 (The Royal Institution, London/Bridgeman)

The Fleet Sewer, c.1840 by English school (Guildhall Library, City of London/Bridgeman)

The Thames Embankment, 1867, plate from the *Illustrated London News*, volume 67/1. One of several plans for the Thames Embankment, drawn up by Sir Joseph Bazalgette (Science Museum Library/Science and Society)

A Smock Mill on the Thames by Peter de Wint. The name of this type of mill is said to derive from its likeness in shape to the linen smocks worn by British countrymen (Agnew's London/Bridgeman)

A View of Goding's New Lion Ale Brewery, Fowler's Iron Works and Walker's Shot Manufactory, Lambeth by Francis Calcraft Turner (Guildhall Library, City of London/Bridgeman)

Unloading barrels at London docks, near Tower Bridge, c.1930s (NMPFT *Daily Herald* Archive/Science and Society)

Lots Road Power Station at night, 26 November 1931, photographed by George Woodbine. The power station opened in 1905 and supplied electricity to the London Underground until 2002 (NMPFT *Daily Herald* Archive/Science and Society)

The Thames Barrier, Woolwich (Marc Atkins/Panoptika.net)

Canary Wharf, London Docklands (Marc Atkins/Panoptika.net)

SECTION FOUR

Kew Gardens: The Pagoda and Bridge, 1762, by Richard Wilson (Yale Center for British Art, Paul Mellon Collection/Bridgeman)

Westminster Bridge, with the Lord Mayor's Procession on the Thames, 1747, by Canaletto (Yale Center for British Art, Paul Mellon Collection/Bridgeman)

Abingdon, Oxfordshire, c.1805, by Joseph Mallord William Turner (Agnew's, London/ Bridgeman)

Rain, Steam and Speed—the Great Western Railway, painted before 1844, by Joseph Mallord William Turner (National Gallery, London/Bridgeman)

Willows Beside a Stream, 1805, by Joseph Mallord William Turner (Tate, London, 2007)

Water Willow, 1871, by Dante Charles Gabriel Rossetti. The painting is a portrait of Jane Morris, wife of William Morris and shows Kelmscott Manor in the background (Delaware Art Museum, Wilmington, Samuel and Mary R. Bancroft Memorial/ Bridgeman)

Grey and Silver: The Thames by James Abbott McNeill Whistler (Hunterian Art Gallery, University of Glasgow/Bridgeman)

The Little Pool, etching by James Abbott McNeill Whistler (Leeds Museums and Galleries/Bridgeman)

"Ode on a Distant Prospect of Eton College," from *The Poems of Thomas Gray*, published in 1797–98 and illustrated by William Blake (Yale Center for British Art, Paul Mellon Collection/Bridgeman)

Baptism, 1952, by Stanley Spencer (Private Collection/Bridgeman/Estate of Stanley Spencer/DACS, 2007)

The River: David Copperfield and Mr. Peggotty rescue Martha from the river, illustration by Phiz from *David Copperfield* by Charles Dickens

The Bird of Prey: the opening scene from *Our Mutual Friend* by Charles Dickens, illustration by Marcus Stone

Tom and the Dragonflies, illustration by Warwick Goble from *The Water Babies* by Charles Kingsley (Mary Evans Picture Library)

Alice and the Pool of Tears, illustration by John Tenniel from *Alice in Wonderland* by Lewis Carroll (Mary Evans Picture Library)

Illustration for *Three Men in a Boat* by Jerome K. Jerome by Randolph Caldecott in *The Graphic* (Mary Evans Picture Library)

Ratty and Mole, illustration by Arthur Rackham from *The Wind in the Willows* by Kenneth Grahame (Mary Evans Picture Library)

Barrage Balloons Outside a British Port by Eric Ravilious (Leeds Museums and Galleries/Bridgeman)

Hadleigh Castle: the mouth of the Thames—morning after a stormy night, 1829, by John Constable (Yale Center for British Art, Paul Mellon Collection/Bridgeman)

ON THE JACKET

Thames ferryman, woodcut illustration to *The Bagford Ballads*, 1680 (Mary Evans Picture Library)

A Most Certain, Strange and True Discovery of a Witch, 1643 engraving, by English school (The Bridgeman Art Library)

ON THE CASE

FRONT

A View of the Fireworks and Illuminations at his grace the Duke of Richmond's at Whitehall and on the River Thames, on Monday 15th May 1749, colored engraving, by English school (The Bridgeman Art Library)
Photograph of the London Eye (Silvia Otte/Getty Images)

SPINE:

A bridge near Lechlade, Glouchestershire. From *Picturesque Views on the River Thames,* 1799, by Samuel Ireland (Science and Society Picture Library)
View of London and the Thames, by Giovanni Antonio Canaletto (National Gallery, Prague, Czech Republic; Bridgeman-Giraudon/Art Resource, NY)

BACK:

View of London Bridge, *c.* 1632, oil on panel, by Claude de Jongh (Yale Center for British Art, Paul Mellon Fund/The Bridgeman Art Library
England: Richmond Hill on the Prince Regent's Birthday by Joseph Mallord William Turner. Exhibited 1819. Oil on canvas, 180.0 x 334.6 cm. (Clore Collection, Tate Gallery, London/Art Resource, NY)

ALBION
The Origins of the English Imagination

In *Albion*, Ackroyd ranges across literature and painting, philosophy and science, architecture and music, from Anglo-Saxon times to the twentieth century. Considering what is most English about artists as diverse as Chaucer, William Hogarth, Benjamin Britten, and Virginia Woolf, he identifies contradictory elements: pragmatism and whimsy, blood and gore, a passion for the past, a delight in eccentricity, and much more.

History/978-0-385-49773-2

THE CLERKENWELL TALES

This novel ingeniously draws on Chaucer's *The Canterbury Tales* to re-create London's fourteenth-century religious and political intrigues. Sister Clarice, a nun, is predicting the death of King Richard II and the demise of the Church. Her visions are dismissed as madness, until she accurately foretells a series of terrorist explosions. What is the role of the apocalyptic Predestined Men? And the clandestine Dominus? And what powers, ultimately, will prevail?

Fiction/Literature/978-1-4000-7595-9

THE LIFE OF THOMAS MORE

Thomas More (1478–1535) was a renowned statesman; the author of a political fantasy that gave a name to a literary genre and a worldview (*Utopia*); and, most famously, a Catholic martyr and saint. Born into the professional classes, Thomas More applied his formidable intellect and well-placed connections to become the most powerful man in England, second only to the king. As much a work of history as a biography, *The Life of Thomas More* gives a portrait of the everyday, religious, and intellectual life of the early sixteenth century. In Ackroyd's hands, this renowned "man for all seasons" emerges in the fullness of his complex humanity.

Biography/History/978-0-385-49693-3

THE FALL OF TROY

Obermann, an acclaimed German scholar, fervently believes that his discovery of the ancient ruins of Troy will prove that the heroes of the *Iliad*, a work he has cherished all his life, actually existed. But Sophia, Obermann's young Greek wife, has her suspicions about his motivations—suspicions that only increase when she finds a cache of artifacts that her husband has hidden, and when a more skeptical archaeologist dies from a mysterious fever. With exquisite detail, Ackroyd again demonstrates his ability to evoke time and place, creating a brilliantly told story of heroes and scoundrels, and the temptation to shape the truth to fit a passionately held belief.

Fiction/978-0-307-38649-6

LONDON
The Biography

Here are two thousand years of London's history and folklore, its chroniclers and criminals and plain citizens, its food and drink and countless pleasures. Blackfriar's and Charing Cross, Paddington and Bedlam. Westminster Abbey and St. Martin in the Fields. Cockneys and vagrants. Immigrants, peasants, and punks. The Plague, the Great Fire, the Blitz. Through a unique thematic tour of the physical city and its inimitable soul, London comes alive.

History/978-0-385-49771-8

THE PLATO PAPERS

At the turn of the thirty-eighth century, London's greatest orator, Plato, lectures on the obscured and confusing era that began in A.D. 1500. Basing his work on an incomplete archaeological record, he pieces scraps of evidence together into a semicoherent whole. By the close of his lecture series, however, Plato is drawn closer to the subject of his academic fascination than he ever could have anticipated.

Fiction/Literature/978-0-385-49769-5

SHAKESPEARE
The Biography

With characteristic narrative panache, Ackroyd immerses us in sixteenth-century Stratford and the rural landscape that would appear in Shakespeare's plays. He takes us through Shakespeare's London neighborhood and the fertile, competitive theater world where he worked as actor and writer. In joining these intimate details with profound intuitions about the playwright and his work, Ackroyd has produced an altogether engaging masterpiece.

Biography/Literature/978-1-4000-7598-0

THE LAMBS OF LONDON

Charles and Mary Lamb, who will in time achieve lasting fame as the authors of *Tales from Shakespeare* for children, are still living at home, caring for their dotty and maddening parents. Reading Shakespeare is the siblings' favorite reprieve, and they are delighted when an ambitious young bookseller comes into their lives claiming to possess a "lost" Shakesperian play. Soon all of London is greatly anticipating the opening night of a star-studded production of the play, not knowing that they have all been duped by a charlatan and a fraud.

Fiction/978-1-4000-7958-2

ANCHOR BOOKS
Available at your local bookstore, or visit
www.randomhouse.com